OUT TO WORK

A History of Wage-Earning Women
in the United States

20th Anniversary Edition

ALICE KESSLER-HARRIS

OXFORD
UNIVERSITY PRESS

D0028883

OXFORD
UNIVERSITY PRESS

Oxford   New York
Auckland   Bangkok   Buenos Aires
Cape Town   Chennai   Dar es Salaam   Delhi   Hong Kong   Istanbul
Karachi   Kolkata   Kuala Lumpur   Madrid   Melbourne   Mexico City   Mumbai
Nairobi   São Paulo   Shanghai   Taipei   Tokyo   Toronto

Copyright © 2003 by Alice Kessler-Harris

Published by Oxford University Press, Inc.
198 Madison Avenue, New York, New York 10016
www.oup.com

First edition published by Oxford University Press, New York, 1982
First issued as an Oxford University Press paperback, 1983

Oxford is a registered trademark of Oxford University Press

Library of Congress Cataloging-in-Publication Data
Kessler-Harris, Alice.
Out to work.
ISBN-13 978 0-19-515709-3 (pbk.)

Bibliography: p.
Includes index.
1. Women—Employment—United States—History.
2. Working class women—United States—History.
I. Title.
HD6095.K449   331.4'0973   81-11237
AACR2

Printed in the United States of America

For my father, with love.
A pám e müvemet neked szentelem.

Preface

As a candidate for the presidency in 1980, Ronald Reagan explained to reporters why his wife Nancy had abandoned her career. "She didn't feel she could manage both career and home," said Reagan, "and she chose the one she felt was the most important." The working-class husbands interviewed by Lillian Rubin for her book *Worlds of Pain* would have applauded the choice. "I think our biggest problem is her working," said one. "She started working and she started getting too independent." And another: "I don't want her to work, and I don't want her to go to school. What for? She doesn't have to. She's got plenty to keep her busy right here."

Almost all American women have been wives at some point in their lives. As such, they have had a particular place in American culture, holding together the fabric of American life. Some of the longest and most vicious battles in our past have been fought over issues that touched on the home and family: equal rights for women, access to birth control information, legal abortion. Suffrage for women was once considered an accomplishment that would divide husband from wife; the vote belonged to the family, not to individuals. A woman's ability to work for wages was, and perhaps still is, such an issue. What would be the effect of her own wages on woman's independence—on her desire to marry?—asked traditionalists. How would wage work alter her ability to fit comfortably into the home if she married? How would it alter her sense of herself, her willingness to play carefully designated roles? Would it result, as Karl Marx warned in the midst of the British industrial revolution, "in a new form of family and new relations between the sexes?"

For generations, Americans avoided these questions by closing off options to women—by restricting, constraining, manipulating, and discouraging women from taking paths that challenged the psychic and social underpinnings of the prevailing family structure. Male and female children were socialized to particular expectations of the family and household. All else seemed outrageous, and it was treated as such. Women's place was in the home. When they strode bravely into the work force, they landed in its lowest places, without coercion, with their full consent and understanding and even encouragement. This was part of no grand conspiracy, no human design. To most people it seemed totally natural. Women's assigned role fit neatly into a set of societal expectations of the home.

But those expectations were never static, nor did they apply equally across class lines or within different racial and ethnic groups. Poverty frequently led black women and immigrant women to reject stay-at-home lives in traditional nuclear families: instead they sometimes constructed unconventional families that enabled them to seek wage work or sought the kinds of jobs that provided the greatest flexibility in arranging their time. And wealth could provide women with access to education that encouraged a search for rewarding work. Women who rejected accepted life styles challenged narrow sex-role definitions, laying claim to a broader concept of womanliness. As Sojourner Truth, ex-slave, abolitionist, and suffragist, eloquently proclaimed when she displayed the muscles she had developed from plowing, planting, and harvesting: "Ain't I a woman?"

Over time, the home and the economy of which it is a part have changed in ways that have urged many other women to seek lives outside the confines of the home. The result has been a steady reshaping of woman's social roles, but always, until the present, within a framework informed by her ability to effectively take care of the changing home.

The constraints of the home typically placed women in a disadvantaged place in the labor force that in turn seemed to reinforce the patriarchal family structure. But as the requirements of keeping a home have changed, so too has the framework of women's lives. Whereas once only poor and working-class families required two incomes to operate a household, in contemporary America the need for two incomes cuts across class lines. Wives in all income groups are now earning wages. And the attitudes, expectations, and training of young girls are altering to reflect this new reality. New psychic sets threaten to undermine women's commitment to the home. Could the predictions of Marx and Engels that women's entry into wage labor would eliminate "the last remnants of male domination in the proletarian home" at last be coming true? What are the historical roots of this dilemma? And where does its resolution lie?

This book explores the transformation of women's work into wage labor in the United States. It examines the historical integration of women into the labor force and its consequences for women's self-perceptions and for their positions as workers. It attempts to illuminate the relationship between wage-earning and family roles: the tensions between them as well as their mutually reinforcing aspects. It looks at women's labor force position in general and at the same time attempts to explain particular class, ethnic, and racial patterns over time. Understanding these processes requires us to explore how the form of wage work simultaneously sustained the patriarchal family and set in motion the tensions that seem now to be breaking it down. It requires a new look at labor force patterns from the perspective of the women who worked for wages, as well as those who did not. It involves tracing a consistent and coherent ideology of womanhood through the twists and turns of changing perceptions, labor force needs, and family structure until the ideology breaks down in the present as a result of its own contradictions.

In the interest of clarity, I have eliminated many familiar and dramatic instances of the struggle the book explains, but does not chronicle. I am painfully aware of these absences. Such battles as the great uprising of young garment workers in New York in 1909–10 and the 1912 strike of immigrant textile workers in Lawrence, Massachusetts, appear only fleetingly. Yet the brave women who tried to protect their tents from armed deputies who had evicted them from company houses in Tennessee in 1929, and the women office workers who risked their jobs when they joined organizations like Nine to Five in the 1970s have earned their places in history. And the list could go on endlessly. I hope others will continue to reconstruct and describe those great and heroic struggles in which women did more than their share.

The diversity of women's experience as wage workers is complex, and I have been able to suggest only some of the outlines. Far more detailed discussion and research would be needed merely to expose its deep roots. Since I have focused on the dynamics of a female wage labor force, I have paid less attention than I would have wished to the central roles of women who are peripheral to this historical development. Slave women, agricultural workers of all kinds, most professional women, housewives in their roles as agents of social reproduction: these are among the important groups that hover on the edges of the narrative, and whose roles in maintaining the wage labor of others will, I hope, be clear. In sacrificing attention to separate categories of women, I have been sensitive to the limits imposed on women's gender identification by racial and ethnic boundaries. Gender, as it intersects both these cultural roots and issues of class, constitutes the moving force of this history.

The narrative begins in the colonial period, in which traditional notions of the family were transferred from England, and wage-earning for women fitted into a tightly patterned economy. It moves from there to the early industrialization process, which drew on women for certain kinds of tasks and at the same time posed serious questions about their relationship to home and family. In the second section, the narrative confronts women's emerging attempts to juggle both roles. Who shall work, and at what? What of the relationships between women whose lives are bound by wage labor and those for whom it is inconceivable? These chapters explore early ideological barriers to wage work—how in a rapidly industrializing economy, ideas about women as well as women's own ideas regulated their behavior and their relationship to wage work. The section concludes with the institutionalization of women's work force roles in what we have come to know as protective labor legislation. Finally, in the 1920s, as consumerism became the economic by-word and an insistent technology created new incentives, ideas about wage labor for women began to change. Reinforced by a changing family and a new individualism, new pressures to leave the home emerged. Different for different women, and continuing unevenly in the 1930s and 1940s, these pressures expanded in the 1950s. The discordance between ideas about women's real work being at home and economic pressures that insisted on wage labor created an impossible bind: women could effectively fulfill family obligations only by leaving the home. The tension exploded in the women's movement of the late 1960s and early 1970s to produce the contemporary debate over the proper role of women.

This debate is informed by a different set of choices than those that have preceded it. It is rooted in the recognition that women's work force participation is no longer cyclical—dependent either on the vagaries of economic depression and prosperity or on such life-cycle determinants as marriage, widowhood, and child-rearing. Rather, the long-term tendency of women to enter the work force derives from the changing household itself, and from the new expectations of personal relationships and self-fulfillment that accompany modern life. For the first time women have crossed the half-way point: more women work for wages than occupy so-called traditional roles. It is now the norm, not the exception, for women, even married women with small children, to work for wages.

For most women, what may have begun as a matter of supplementing family income has become integral to family life styles, demanding compromises in household responsibility and perhaps in the location and structure of the household itself. And for many women, wage work that may have begun as an adjunct to family survival or a temporary stop-gap between school and children quickly takes its own direction, impetus, and interest. As the notion of more or less permanent wage work for women spreads, it raises twin demands for changes in the family and changes at work. These undermine the reciprocally confirming system of values that has for so long affirmed women's special place.

Challenges to an old value system have been partially responsible for producing a vigorous New Right in the eighties. In the name of the family and traditional roles, women are asked to give up personal ambition and devote themselves once again to children and the happiness of their mates. Such demands for a return to the past fly in the face of changing economic reality; to defend them, the self-styled champions of women assume strident moralistic and ideological tones. But, as this book demonstrates, the past embodied a carefully worked-out set of compromises that balanced the needs of the home with those of industry. If its premises are correct, the economic and technological pulls that are now shifting that balance will offer powerful resistance to reconstructing traditional forms of behavior. Wishful thinking cannot change the economic and social conditions that have pulled women into the labor market and altered their perceptions of self. To return to the past may be beyond the will and the capacity of women. For we have created a new woman, an individual whose dynamic ability now has to become part of any equation for America's future. This book traces her struggle to come into being.

In the nine years during which this book has been part of my life, I have incurred more debts than can be readily acknowledged. I therefore make this attempt at thanks humbly, fully aware that it names only a small number of those on whom I have relied.

A writer's most precious commodity is time. This book would have been even longer in the making had I not been generously supported by grants from the National Endowment for the Humanities and the Louis M. Rabinowitz Foundation. The Radcliffe Institute (now known as the Mary Ingraham Bunting Institute) provided a fellowship that enabled me to complete an early draft of the manuscript, and the Centre for the Study of Social History at the University of Warwick offered me a year-long visiting appointment that provided the distance

My deepest appreciation goes to my daughter Ilona who, though never consulted about whether she wanted to share her growing years with her mother's book, did so lovingly, and to Bert, critic, companion, colleague, and friend, in all the best senses of those words.

New York   Alice Kessler-Harris
August 1981

Contents

I

Forming the Female Wage
Labor Force: Colonial America
to the Civil War

1

Limits of Independence in the Colonial Economy

In the early settlements of seventeenth-century America, only one group of women—domestic servants—could properly be called wage earners. By the end of the colonial period, the stage had been set for women to take their places in the nineteenth-century movement of people into the wage labor force. Women's transition from paid and unpaid family-centered roles to wage labor of all kinds began early in the American past. Separated from the European soil, and facing dramatically different conditions in the organization and availability of land and labor, the colonists might have reconsidered the roles of women. They had plenty of land, and in the early years they were desperately short of workers. But the colonists chose to create conditions of women's work that resembled those of Europe more closely than they departed from them. European traditions and expectations regulated women's access to apprenticeship and thus to the most lucrative skills. And in this new world, patterns of land distribution quickly confirmed old assumptions about women's place. Together, women's relationship to the land and to saleable skills permanently influenced their economic possibilities.

For free, white, male immigrants to the colonies, land provided the major source of economic independence, if not of future wealth. Even those who came to the New World with a craft relied on their land to meet important family needs. For male indentured servants, land was sometimes offered as an incentive to serve out their terms. But most white women, like black males and females and unlike most white men, did not hold land, nor did they have access to the skills that

could have freed them from economic dependence. Lacking these resources, women routinely, though not always, became dependent.

From a community's viewpoint, marriage was the natural and desirable role for white women, and their economic subordination assured
the colonists that most women would follow this path. The typical
portrait of the colonial woman depicts a strong, sturdy goodwife, producing household necessities and plying her crafts and her plow beside
a yeoman husband. Numerous offspring affirmed the value of homespun mothering. Hard physical labor reaped a visible reward, as it
transformed the fruits of the earth into life-sustaining products. This
idyllic portrait is not wholly false. There was satisfaction to be gained
from family labor.

As long as household production and the near-certainty of marriage
for women made a virtue out of domestic skill, few protested. But by
the early eighteenth century in some colonies, a surplus of unwed and
widowed women swelled the totals of those in need of support. Simultaneously, advancing technology decreased requirements for women's
labor in the home. Women were chastised for idleness and driven to
seek useful employment. What choices did they have? They could do
women's traditional tasks: various branches of spinning, weaving, and
sewing. They could undertake household service in other people's
families and work in the fields. And fortunately for some, an emerging
economy provided flexibility that allowed individual women to exercise initiative outside traditional patterns. Heroic women offer for us
models of possibility that are tributes to the accomplishments of cour-
ageous individuals. But these models do not represent the direction of
women's participation in the economy as a whole—a direction confirmed and articulated in the years around the Revolution, when a
disintegrating mercantile economy allowed emerging manufacturers
to benefit from long-standing social custom.

The family was the centerpiece of the economic system. In Puritan
New England, it was a keystone of social order. The Massachusetts Bay
Colony self-consciously encouraged families to be "little cells of
righteousness where the mother and father disciplined not only their
children but also their servants and any boarders they might take in."[1]
Unmarried men and women normally placed themselves in family
homes in order to be guided by the parents. Family members were
encouraged to supervise one another in order to guard the morals of
the community as a whole. In the Plymouth colony, according to one
historian, the family functioned as a business, a school, a training
institution, a church, and often as a welfare institution. "Family and
community," John Demos concludes, ". . . formed part of the same

moral equation. The one supported the other and they became in a sense indistinguishable."[2] Although in the middle and southern colonies, distance between farms and the absence of Puritan orthodoxy reduced the family's supervisory role, a shortage of women until at least the end of the seventeenth century meant that for a woman to be single and to live alone would have been highly unusual.

Compulsory labor in this closed circle was a necessity, and social and community sanction supported it. In Puritan New England, religious injunction offered a convenient device for mobilizing workers. A prosperous community was evidence of divine favor and gave townspeople a special moral incentive to weed out those who would not pull their own weight. The southern colonies, lacking effective ideological coercion, resorted first to compulsion and then to economic incentives. Early Virginians created a paramilitary structure to coerce the first generation of colonials into regular work habits. When this failed, land grants and higher wages became the rewards of those who worked hardest to produce profits for the entrepreneurial company.[3]

Coming out of an England where gangs of vagabonds roamed the streets and beggars threatened ordinary folk, while the authorities tried desperately to share jobs among those with skills, colonial leaders had no compunctions about forced labor. In the old country, wage ceilings were common, vagabonds were beaten, and beggars not infrequently burned through the ear, whipped until bloody, or put to death. Colonists reserved such harsh treatment for slaves and sometimes for servants. But neither would they condone idleness among the free. The Massachusetts Bay Company made this clear in 1629 when it instructed Governor John Endicott to make sure that "Noe idle drone bee permitted to live amongst us."[4] Action followed instruction. Almost all of the colonies tried to prevent idleness by training young children to useful occupations. The children of the poor seem to have been particularly vulnerable to forced service. Almost all the colonies had a regulation something like that of Boston, which ordered the poor "to dispose of their severall children . . . abroad for servants, to serve by indentures . . . according to their ages and capacities, which if they refuse or neglect to do the Magistrates and Selectmen will take their said children from them, and place them with such masters as they shall provide according as the law directs."[5] Girls were no exception to these regulations, and like boys, were bound out to be servants from the age of eight up.

A narrow line separated the goal of helping individuals avoid poverty from that of coercing them into serving the needs of the growing economy. Virginia, for example, decreed as early as 1646 that "to avoid sloth and idleness wherewith young children are easily corrupted as also for relief of such parents whose poverty extends not to give them breeding," children should be bound to be tradesmen or husbandmen, "to be brought up in some good and lawful calling." But the statute went on to accuse many parents "through fond indulgences or perverse obstinacy" of refusing to part with their children. Therefore, it ordered county commissioners to choose from each county two children, "male or female," of poor parents and send them "to be employed in the public flax houses." Other seventeenth-century statutes confirmed this direction. One, of 1672, empowered county courts to place out all children "whose parents are not able to bring them up apprentices to tradesmen, the males till one and twenty years of age, and the females to other necessary employments till 18 years of age. . . ." Massachusetts had similar laws. The General Court asserted that since the education of all children was of "singular behoof and benefit to any commonwealth," masters must teach children a skill or a trade in return for the use of their services for a period of years.[6]

But these regulations do not seem to have worked very well, for the colonial record is sprinkled with attempts to solve the twin problems of idleness and poverty. Women were not exempt from either moral persuasion or compulsion. Salem sent Margarett Page, a "lazy, luytering person," to jail in 1643, "where she may be sett to work for her liveinge." Massachusetts and Connecticut resorted to corporal punishment. Connecticut specified that an idle person be "openly whipt on his or her naked body, not exceeding the number of fifteen stripes." Virginia settled for a more general regulation in 1672. Complaining that "the number of vagabonds idle and dissolut persons" had increased, it encouraged "the justices of peace in every county [to] put the laws of England against vagrant, idle and dissolut persons in strict execution. . . ." Almost all the colonies permitted towns to bring "idle and unprofitable" persons before the local courts, to be disposed of "as the court saw fit"; sometimes this meant expulsion from the town, which was often done to widows with small children. More commonly, as in Connecticut, for example, selectmen were instructed to "diligently inspect into the affairs of poor or idle persons and if likely to be reduced to want," to dispose of them to service.[7]

There was no question that both men and women should work, and in crucial respects the same expectations held for both. If they did different tasks, husbands, wives, sons, daughters, and male and female servants all helped to sustain the household. A hierarchical world ascribed roles to everyone, and neither a God-given nor a natural order made exceptions for women. People worked according to their places in the world, each in a defined role, but the lines were loosely drawn. Historian Alice Clark's apt comment on seventeenth-century England could as well apply to the American colonies. "The idea is seldom encountered," she observed, "that a man supports his wife; husband and wife were then mutually dependent and together supported the children."[8] The trustees of the Georgia plantations would have agreed. To attract emigrants to America they advertised the generous availability of work for wives and children. Eighteenth-century Massachusetts wives who refused to serve their households by laboring obediently as well as frugally gave their husbands grounds for divorce.[9]

In the division of responsibility, women got the bulk of internal domestic chores. Normally they took care of the house—including the preparation of food, cloth, candles and soap—and supervised farm animals and kitchen garden, while husbands did the plowing, planting, and harvesting. Yet interaction never stopped. Husbands helped at the spinning and weaving when farm work was done. In the southern colonies, wives hoed and female servants worked in the fields. Male apprentices often found themselves doing household chores. Female servants spent as much time in the workshop as in the household. Mothers taught young children their letters, while fathers tended to take over the educational process as offspring grew older. Wives routinely developed competency in their husband's businesses; they could and did inherit them when death demanded it.

Women's assigned work was equally a calling with men's. As carpenters and masons were respected, so was the goodwife. The Puritans acknowledged women as partners in a joint enterprise and recognized domestic work as essential to survival. So self-evident was its value in homes where the materials for clothing, food, and other necessities were grown and prepared that girls were bound out to learn these tasks as they would be to any other trade. Discipline being as important as the tasks to be learned, even the wealthy and respected bound their daughters out to teach them obedience and thrift—things a fond and overindulgent parent might overlook. Such notables as Rhode Island's Roger Williams and Massachusetts justice Samuel Sewall, who presided over some of the witch trials of the late seventeenth century, committed their daughters to domestic service.[10]

It would be a mistake, however, not to acknowledge that domestic work fell low on any hierarchical scale. Despite the self-evident importance of work done at home, the role of the wife was distinctly secondary to that of the husband. Yet white married women, whatever the disadvantages attached to their sex, had a clearly defined status. In everything having to do with the household, with the tasks surrounding it, and with the maintenance of the people who lived there, they enjoyed respect and some autonomy.[11]

The position of servants and slaves was a good deal less comfortable. Because it required no capital investment and no training that was difficult of access, unmarried and poor women typically chose domestic service. Some came as indentured servants or redemptioners—from one-half to two-thirds of all white immigrants entered the colonies this way. In order to repay the cost of passages, women, like men, agreed to serve a master for a period usually ranging from four to seven years. In addition to those whose parents might board them out as children, untold numbers of women hired themselves out for a year or more at a time to pay debts or to put a roof over their heads. As part of their household chores, female servants often learned how to spin and weave. Yet unlike some men, they could not readily acquire the additional skills that would raise them into artisan status, and so remained servants until marriage or luck released them.

The wage for all servants was normally the cost of survival—room and board for the years of service, plus whatever it took to bring a servant over, and a little extra to start her off in life. Lucky servants might get a small additional wage: perhaps three pounds a year, or a suit of clothing on completion of their service. Cash was rare, and servants frequently received their pay in tobacco, corn, or other produce. The amount varied from colony to colony. North Carolina, New Jersey, and Maryland all allotted women goods, clothing, and wages equal to those of men servants.

Yet male servants were more valuable. Before the Revolution masters typically paid 40 to 50 percent more for a male than the fifteen pounds it cost to purchase the work of a female. And the material incentive many colonies granted a master who transported a male servant was double what he could get for transporting a female. North Carolina, for example, agreed in 1666 to give an additional hundred acres of land to the master who would bring a male servant, and only fifty to the one who brought a female servant. The desperate shortage of women in the early years in all the colonies seems to have been offset by the need for men who could help to defend them, leading South Carolina to offer incentives for male servants and none for females. With respect to blacks, whom masters wished to enslave and therefore could not arm, the price for women was higher than that for men.[12] A graphic illustration of the relative value of women's work appears in the court trial of two mid-eighteenth-century criminals. In 1738, Jane Campbell and James Keating were each convicted of larceny and fined eighteen pounds for the offense. Since neither could pay, they were sentenced to work off the debt. It took Keating one year of service to do so, to Campbell's two.[13]

The law that regulated fair treatment for all indentured servants subjected a woman who transgressed to special penalties that reflected a master's vested interest in her labor. Since her labor had been purchased for a period of years, the female was barred from doing anything that threatened to impair or interrupt her service. She could not marry without permission. If she had a child by a man who would not, or could not, buy out her remaining term, she served as much as two years extra to compensate for her reduced services and to punish the sin. Pregnancy occurred frequently among servants. About one of every five women servants in seventeenth-century Maryland seems to have been pregnant before her service ended, and the figure does not seem to have declined in the next century.[14] Ann Hardie of Ann Arundel, Maryland, was sentenced in 1747 to serve a total of a year and a half extra for having a bastard child; the child's father was required to serve six months as punishment and an additional nine months for the child's maintenance. As late as 1780, a Frederick County court imposed seven years on Fanny Drearden for having a "base born child."[15] These harsh sentences were not mitigated even if the young woman could prove what was often the case, that her own master had fathered the child.

Those who bound themselves out to service had no control over their time. A master could sell the services of a servant with time remaining in her indenture to anyone who resided within the colony. Some contemporary advertisements reveal the degradation that resulted from such sales. The *American Weekly* advertised in 1731 "A likely young Dutch servant woman's time for three years to be disposed of, she is a very good seamstress at Extraordinary or plain work, and pretty handy at house work"; the following appeared in the *New York Gazette* in February 1749: "To be sold: A young wench about 29 years old that drinks no strong drink, and gets no children, a very good drudge."[16]

Women servants had few avenues of escape from harsh conditions. They could run away—as many men did—but the possibilities for safe survival and inconspicuous existence in frontier conditions must have been far less for a woman alone than for the single male. Advertisements for male runaway servants far exceeded the occasional demands for the return of women, who made up nearly one-third of all bound servants in that period. Yet these figures tell us little about women's dissatisfaction. They may have preferred to take out their grievances within the family, a possibility confirmed by the number of masters and mistresses who complained bitterly of the trouble they had with servants. Hints of distress emerge from the servants themselves. Elizabeth Sprigg wrote to her father of her life in Maryland in 1756 that she toiled "almost day and night," that she had "scarce anything but Indian corn and salt to eat," and that she was "almost naked no shoes nor stockings to wear."[17]

For servants, as opposed to slaves, the law provided certain boundaries which masters could not transgress. Amounts of food and clothing were specified; freedom dues were written into contracts and enforced by colonial courts; corporal punishments were banned. No such legal structure protected the slave. Most early colonists treated slaves like indentured servants, freeing them after several years of labor. But within twenty years after the first shipload of black people was sold at Jamestown in 1619, colonies recognized that nothing prevented them from binding persons of color for a lifetime and that their children were, therefore, also bound for their lifetimes. Black women instantly became more valuable than white women. Because the children of black women contributed to the wealth of the master, black women were rewarded, not punished, for reproduction.[18] In contrast to indentured servants, a female slave cost more than a male.

The absence of a legal contract enabled masters to use black slave women at will, lending female slaves to sexual abuse. And none of the informal protections that applied to white women applied to black women. White owners who might hesitate to assign white women to plant, plow, and dig the fields exploited black women shamelessly in these jobs. Before 1660, Virginia and Maryland explicitly acknowledged the use of black women in their fields by taxing them in just the same way they taxed male field hands. Yet all the hard work required to keep a household going also devolved on the shoulders of slave women. They laundered, cooked, nursed, and cleaned in the big house and also had those obligations for other slaves and their own families. The tasks slave women faced in struggling to maintain a family existence provide an extreme example of the difficulties faced by people without independent means of sustenance.

Even free women could find opportunities for independence only rarely. The colonies' first female lawyer, Margaret Brent, was among the lucky. She arrived in Maryland in 1638, at a time when women could own land there. By purchase and by other means she acquired large tracts of land, on the basis of which she built a fortune. One can name a few women—Mary Tranton, Winifred Seaborne, Frances White—otherwise unknown, who acquired parcels of land that they built into comfortable competencies in the early years of settlement. In those years, women could own land in other colonies besides Maryland. Pennsylvania offered seventy-five acres to women who came in at their own expense. If they brought servants and children, their grants were so much larger. Salem briefly offered "maids lotts" to women without husbands. Before 1699, South Carolina agreed to give pieces of land to men or women servants who completed their indentures. Virginia undertook to import children over twelve who would serve as apprentices, after which the colony agreed to settle them on "the public land with best conditions where they shall have houses with stock of corn and cattle to begin with and afterwards the moiety of all increase and profit whatsoever."[19]

There was no question that women could be successful farmers. Too many examples of women who developed their own land, improved on land inherited from fathers and husbands, or managed the family estate in the absence of distant husbands refute any attempt at another conclusion. These women range from Margaret Hardenbrook Philipse, a New Amsterdam widow who converted her land into a commercial fortune, to Eliza Lucas Pinckney, who developed the first indigo crop.[20]

But self-evident success was not enough: or perhaps it was too much. Independent land ownership offered women subsistence outside marriage or domestic service, and colonies soon began to recognize that giving land to women undermined their dependent role. As early as 1634, Maryland began to reconsider its generous policy. A bill introduced into the House of Delegates that year threatened to remove land from spinsters. "Unless she marry within seven years after land shall fall to hir," wrote an opponent summarizing its provisions, "she must either dispose away of hir land, or else she shall forfeite it to the nexte of kinne, and if she have but one Mannor, whereas she canne not alienate it, it is gonne, unlesse she get a husband." Fortunately for women like Margaret Brent the bill was vetoed by Lord Baltimore, the proprietor. Massachusetts' Governor Endicott refused land to Deborah Holmes, "being a maid"; he wanted to avoid "all presedents and evill events of graunting lotts unto single maidens not disposed of." Holmes got a bushel of Indian corn instead. Georgia, settled a hundred years later, not only refused to grant women land, but denied them even the right to inherit it. This harsh policy, justified by the belief that estates required men who could defend them, was modified when fathers discovered that they could not bequeath land even to daughters who were their only children.[21]

Custom tended to be kinder than law. Women could normally inherit land from their fathers, although an occasional colony like Virginia allowed women only temporary control pending the arrival of male offspring. Dutch New York, an exception, forbade primogeniture, encouraging parents to divide land equally among all children. Elsewhere, fathers tended to favor sons over daughters and older sons over younger ones.[22]

Married women were little better off than "maids." In most colonies, the head right—land granted to a settler on arrival—was conveyed through women to their husbands. Everywhere, property laws stipulated that upon marriage, a woman's property went to her husband to use as his own. Women whose husbands simply disappeared were in an unfortunate quandary. Maryland required a special act of the colonial assembly before Susannah Tracy, whose husband had deserted her and her child, could sell a tract of land in 1709. But a Virginia woman of 1752 was not so lucky. When the Virginia House of Burgesses passed a similar bill to enable her to sell off a piece of land, the Board of Trade in England disallowed it, fearing that it would create a bad precedent.[23]

Most commonly, women acquired title to land by outliving their husbands. A widow's dower normally entitled her to one-third of a husband's real and household property for the duration of her widowhood. In Massachusetts, many wills bequeathed real property to children, instructing them merely to allow their mother a room to use and some personal possessions. This pattern did not prevail in Maryland, where husbands tended to leave land to their widows for life, and personal property without restriction. A widow who managed to inherit all of a deceased husband's property for the duration of her lifetime could retain it even if she remarried by exercising a little care. Special agreements protected her own inheritance from her new husband. Yet after her death, real property reverted to male heirs.[24]

Against this harsh land policy, we have record of occasional rebellion. In 1715 Magdalena Zeh led a group of women who drove out the local sheriff "when he challenged their right to live as squatters along the Schoharie River" in New York. One historian describes how, "armed with brooms, rakes and hoes, they dragged the unfortunate man through barnyards, rode him on a rail, and finally dumped him on a bridge on the road back to Albany."[25]

Though land holding, trading, and selling were primarily male activities, women could and did participate when necessary, usually as surrogates for husbands and fathers, sometimes as their beneficiaries. Such occasional exceptions grew fewer, however, as colonial policy discouraged women not only from land ownership, but even from representing their husbands in legal matters. Necessity, not right, governed the ability of some women to continue to hold land. A small plot could keep a woman with dependent children off the public dole. In a self-sufficient agrarian economy, long-term land deprivation imposed a heavy burden. It deprived women of economic independence, control of a household, and political influence. Without these advantages, colonial women as a group remained at the mercy of fathers and husbands or government authorities.

As law deprived women of land, so social custom influenced the skills they would learn. In the mercantile system that governed the colonies at their outset, work was strictly regulated. From the British perspective, the colonies were a giant labor organization designed to supply essential raw materials to the mother country and to purchase finished products from it at a comfortable profit to its entrepreneurs. The closed world that mercantilism described promised a harmonious commonwealth in which all would work together and in their place for the general economic welfare. Prosperity demanded a hard-working and skilled labor force. To provide necessary training, the colonies continued an apprenticeship system similar to that of old England. Its base was the Tudor-Stuart statutes of artificers which controlled access to the trades. Until experience modified them, these served as America's guideposts.

The apprenticeship system involved both costs and gains for the artisans trained in it. A young person committed seven years of labor without pay to a master who agreed to provide instruction in a craft. On completion of the requisite training, a journeyman who continued to work for a master could not be dismissed, was normally fed and lodged in the master's family and was cared for if ill. While in the Old World craft guilds had been strong enough to regulate access to the trade to all but those they certified, in America a chronic labor shortage and geographical dispersion deprived guilds of such power. Yet they could drive prices up and restrict the number who learned a particular skill. To control guilds and to prevent artisans from taking advantage of the labor shortage, courts tried to regulate wage rates and assessed severe fines against those who colluded to raise them. They pegged wages both to the scarcity of skill and to an idea of how a particular kind of laborer was expected to live. Luckily for the skilled, labor shortage rendered these wage ceilings ineffective despite numerous instances of punishment for violations. An apprenticeship system that limited access to training turned the possession of a skill into valuable property. It offered the possibility of geographical mobility to those who could, with tools on their backs, travel from town to town, settling where opportunity presented itself.

This path was normally closed to women. An enlightened father might teach his daughter his own lucrative occupation, and an enterprising wife would certainly learn all she could about her husband's craft. The chronic shortage of skilled labor and a family system of production encouraged sharing such knowledge with women. These factors account for the occasional female blacksmiths, silversmiths, gunsmiths, shoemakers, tanners, and printers who, toward the end of the colonial period, seem to have served regular apprenticeships. But most women learned their crafts at a father's knee or a husband's bench. There being as yet little fear of competition from women, small incentive existed to drive women who "stole" a trade out of it.

Training in household skills, even when young girls were contracted out as servants and called apprentices, afforded none of the protection of the traditional apprenticeship. No attempt was made to limit access to household skills. For the most part, knowledge of sewing, weaving, spinning, preserving, soap-making, gardening, and the like was spread as widely as possible, boys as well as girls being encouraged to learn how to spin and weave. These occupations could be quite lucrative. Yet they were taught with household subsistence, not income, in mind. A typical contract binding out a young girl might specify that she "be taught housewifery" and "to read the English Tongue." More enterprising parents tried to make these skills marketable by contracting to have their daughters taught to "make mantos [women's cloaks or loose dresses], Pettycoats, . . . sew and make plaine work," in addition to the other household arts. This seems to have become more common as the colonies matured.

The consequences of differing expectations of men and women emerge in some colonial policies. By the mid-1650s, when colonies began to insist on some form of literacy, girls fell far behind. Legislation that required masters to teach boys to read and write demanded only reading for girls. Where girls were taught to write, boys might be asked to cipher. And already by the early 1700s, a note of doubt crept into the idea of education for girls. Massachusetts common schools admitted them only when they found it financially necessary to fill spaces left by boys absent in the summer and harvest seasons. Qualifying clauses accompanied lower standards of learning expected of girls. For example a 1771 Massachusetts law required boys to learn how to read, write and cipher, while it asked of girls only that they learn to read and write "if they shall be capable."[26]

Women were not entirely without resources. A little capital permitted them to open and operate small shops selling items ranging from pastries and dry goods to hardware and liquor. Women customarily operated taverns and boarding houses. In at least one instance, an innkeeper, deprived of the services of a wife he had recently buried, found that his license was canceled because without a wife he was not "so capable of keeping a publicke house, there being alsoe another ordinary in the towne." By 1714 Boston, with a population of 34,000, had thirty-four licensed inns, of which twelve were run by women. Of its forty-one retailers of alcoholic beverages, seventeen were female.[27] Some became prosperous. Yet even these were not free of complaint. One group of New York businesswomen complained in 1733 that they were neglected in the favors bestowed by the governor: "We the widows of this city," they announced,

> have had a meeting, and as our case is something Deplorable, we beg you will give it a Place in your Weekly Journal, that we may be relieved, it is as follows: We are Housekeepers, Pay our Taxes, carry on Trade and most of us are she Merchants, and as we in some measure contribute to the Support of Government, we ought to be entitled to some of the Sweets of it; but we find ourselves entirely neglected, while the Husbands that live in our Neighborhood are daily invited to Dine at [the English Governor's] Court; we have the vanity to think we can be full as Entertaining, and make as brave a Defence in Case of an Invasion and perhaps not turn Taile so soon as some of them.[28]

And there were always exceptional women who despised or circumvented social usage to become lawyers, like Margaret Brent, or entrepreneurs, like Martha Smith, who almost single-handedly built the whaling industry. Although their prescribed roles restricted them, even married women in America could conduct businesses and supervise estates in far greater measure than would have been possible in England. It seems to have been easier to assume unconventional roles in the southern colonies than in those dominated by Puritan influence. Southern agriculture, based on cash crops grown by slaves and servants on large tracts of land, required extensive management often undertaken by women. Responsibility for the household and farm led women into experiments with crops and management. Virginia and Maryland offer us examples such as Elizabeth Yates and Mary Trantis. Eliza Lucas Pinckney, who experimented with indigo, grew up in South Carolina.

In contrast, the Puritans seemed to attach particular importance to regulating female behavior. The Massachusetts Bay Colony expelled Anne Hutchinson in 1637 for preaching to men and refusing to stop even when ordered to do so. After her departure the colony hounded at least twenty other women for the crime of self-expression. Dorothy Talbye was among them. Unable to carry out the magistrates' injunction to carry herself "more dutifully to her husband," she became insane, murdered her child, and was hanged in 1638. The same year, the magistrates sentenced a Mistress Oliver to be whipped and to stand for half an hour with a cleft stick in her tongue. Her crime, like Hutchinson's, was that of defying the magistrates and then reproaching them for daring to punish her.[29] In 1640, Mistress Ann Hibbens was

excommunicated from the church for complaining that carpenter John
Davis and his brother joiners produced work of poor quality and high
cost. At her trial, the magistrates insisted that her "want of wifelike
subjection to her husband" confirmed their suspicions that her protests
were really attacks against Godly authority. Yet her habit of protesting
apparently did not cease, for sixteen years later, two years after her
well-respected husband died, she was executed as a witch.[30]

Women could and did succeed at a host of occupations but, as in
their attempts to acquire land, they did so by struggling against colonial
policy and not as a result of it. All the colonies encouraged women
to stick to the complex tasks of home and management. In the words
of John Winthrop as he sentenced Anne Hutchinson to banishment, if
she "had attended her household affairs, and such things as belong to
women, and not gone out of her way and calling to meddle in such
things as are proper for men, she had kept her wits, and might have
improved them usefully and honorably in the place that God had set
her."[31]

As the number of unmarried women multiplied toward the end of the
seventeenth century, issues of training women for home roles began to
give way to the problem of what to do with women who had no homes.
Although marriage remained women's expected calling, a growing
surplus of females eliminated that possibility for some. Unmarried
women exceeded eligible men in northeastern towns by the end of the
seventeenth century. By 1765, Massachusetts, where the loss of men
due to war and migration was particularly heavy, had a ratio of 90.3
adult white males to every 100 adult females.[32]

The restraints imposed on women had long since crippled their
capacity to survive alone in economic comfort. Discouraged from farming the land alone and from learning lucrative skills, women entered
such paid employments as opened up to them. But these employments
were restricted. Lacking property, a craft, or some small capital, women
without husbands often faced starvation unless the town would support
them. They joined the ranks of the poor who became a problem to
towns by the end of the seventeenth century. Town ordinances that
badgered and coerced young men into apprenticeships to alleviate a
continuing shortage of skilled labor could not be applied to women,
especially if they had children.

Women had earlier been accused of idleness and singled out for
failing to make an adequate contribution to economic development.
Along with girls and boys, the Massachusetts General Court in 1656
ordered "women . . . to spin according to their skill and abilitie."[33]
By 1675, the continuing shortage of yarn encouraged towns to provide

the capital to set up woolen mills and to pay "spinners, weavers and other workers." The need for yarn and the desire to remove people from the public relief rolls seem to have been closely connected. The Virginia statutes reveal how consciously people made the connection. In 1668 the House of Burgesses empowered counties to build houses for "educating and instructing poor children in the knowledge of spinning, weaving, and other useful occupations and trades, and . . . to take poor children from indigent parents to place them to work in those houses." This act was necessary, as the burgesses pointed out, "for the better converting wool, flax hemp, and other commodities into manufactures, and for the increase of artificers in the country."[34]

But these methods made no dent in the problem of poverty, and by the early part of the eighteenth century, communities in New England where the numbers of poor were greatest began to defend themselves more vigorously against the rising costs of relief. Town overseers who earlier had treated unemployment as a problem of virtue as well as economics turned to solutions that would relieve the taxpayers' burden. Rhode Island, Massachusetts, and Connecticut allowed women with children and without husbands to settle in their towns only after they had been "warned out." "Warning out" did not always mean forcibly ordering women away. Rather it served as a device to indicate that such individuals could not lay claim to relief from public charities. Yet in practice their positions on the outskirts of economic society allowed women little possibility of attaining economic independence. So New England witnessed the cruel anomaly of the widow forced to move from town to town in search of a place where she and her brood could find some means of sustenance.[35]

The apparent solution lay in putting women to work to generate new revenues. In Boston, which had higher proportions of poor citizens than any other large town of the period, widows had become so numerous by the 1730s that the town collected some £900 to build a workhouse. The widows for whom it was designed refused to go there, objecting to the indignity, to the rigidity of its rules, and to being cut off from friends and community. So the town fathers abandoned it, suggesting instead a manufactory—the first attempt in the colonies to organize female labor under one roof.[36] The Society for Encouraging Industry and Employeing the Poor, under whose auspices the manufactory opened in 1750, declared that it wanted both to manufacture woolen cloth and to employ "our own women and children who are now in great measure idle."[37] Private subscriptions failed to support this endeavor, so the town itself donated £130 and passed a tax on luxuries in order to insure its continuing support. But Boston's poor women resisted this attempt at providing for their maintenance no less than they had objected to the workhouse. The regular workday offered no time for maternal duties, and spinning, although still popular in rural areas, was a skill they had long since abandoned.

The idea that women should be encouraged to work in manufactories survived despite women's initial resistance. Searching for labor in the late eighteenth century, manufacturers took advantage of the notion that setting women to work would relieve town poverty to seek special dispensations for their enterprises. As some Beverly, Massachusetts, entrepreneurs promised in their 1789 petition for a factory permit, they would employ "otherwise useless, if not burdensome, women and children."[38] Colonies eagerly took advantage of these offers. New Hampshire empowered the Overseers of the Poor to bind out all poor or idle to factory owners in the late eighteenth century. And Georgia offered bounties to women who became proficient at reeling silk—an incentive that matched that colony's reluctance to allow women to control land.[39] Although towns continued to rely on poor women and children to staff these establishments, women only reluctantly gave up their independence.

Those who had a choice preferred the relative autonomy of taking in work to be done at home to the rigid schedules involved in working outside it. The process of spinning and weaving cloth to specifications at home, known as given-out work or putting-out work, expanded in the latter half of the eighteenth century as the pressure for increased production mounted. This was a by-product of British mercantile laws which, by inhibiting the development of factories of any size, encouraged the perpetuation of home manufacture. This, of course, was not women's task alone. Shoes, pewter, and iron products came from the shops of male artisans. But women carried the burden of making cloth, clothing, hats, and food. Colonial laws and regulations compensated for the absence of English goods by offering bonuses to women who performed these tasks. Advertisements pleaded for "every good spinner that can apply, however remote from the factory" and offered "ready money" for "any parcel either great or small, of hemp, flax or woolen yarn."

The pressures of mercantilism and colonial resistance to British restrictions mounted in the last half of the eighteenth century. Finally the unpopular Stamp Acts of 1764 led the colonists to retaliate with a series of "nonimportation" agreements that made buying domestic goods a patriotic act. In Lynn, Massachusetts, shoemakers multiplied their production perhaps ten times over between 1760 and 1768. The demand for homespun rose, encouraging merchants to speed production by a variety of methods. Drawing on a feverish public feeling about industry, managers offered public approval to those who would spin for the manufactory. They "returned their thanks to all these industrious women who are now employed in spinning for the factory. The skill and deligence [sic] of many entitles them to the public acknowledgement. We hope that, as you have begun, so you will go on and never be weary in well doing."[40] Public spinning bees invited ladies to take up their looms on the Boston Common. Women were regaled with ditties that urged them to

> Throw aside your high topknots of pride
> Wear none but your own country linen
> Of economy boast, let your pride be the most
> To show cloaths of your own make and spinning.[41]

Home manufactures mounted dramatically as merchants offered higher prices for spun yarn. New York's governor reported, for example, that "every house swarms with children, who are set to work as soon as they are able to Spin and Card; and as every family is furnished with a loom, the Itinerant weavers who travel about the country, put the finishing hand to the work."[42]

Women who had spun and knitted largely for family use now found themselves capable of commanding steady, if small, incomes from their goods. But the pressure that encouraged women to work at home soon had a contrary effect. The movement toward political independence that led women to develop their household skills also fostered the creation of technology to increase the quantity of manufactured goods. In the resulting competition between household manufactures and factory-made goods, the household quickly lost ground.

2

From Household Manufactures to Wage Work

The American Revolution and the period that followed it offered both ideological and economic lessons to those who cared to listen. Alongside grand expostulations about individual liberty and freedom from tyranny lay challenges posed by more developed industrial nations. Britain and France threatened to flood the new nation with goods that would stifle American economic initiative and create permanent dependence. A way had to be found to create an economic foundation sturdy enough to protect citizens from both the armed might and the insidious trading pressures of other nations. To do this, Federalists such as Alexander Hamilton felt that the United States had to develop a balanced economy.

In a society still almost totally agrarian, still rooted in the conviction that land was the basis of an independent republic, such views meant convincing an unwilling populace that nonagricultural production was desirable and necessary. No one wanted to threaten the society's agrarian base, or to deprive the land of the labor that would both extend America's borders and coax from it maximal yields. And no one wanted to reproduce the poverty and degradation of English industrialism. But there were many who, with Hamilton and his ally, manufacturing promoter Tench Coxe, believed the new nation could avoid the evils of industrialization and yet derive the benefits of national self-sufficiency. Industrial growth, they believed, would complement and support a rich agricultural production and an independent national economy.

Advocates of self-sufficiency continued to argue from the mercantile notions of community well-being that had governed colonial society.

Since, in their view, each part of a society sustained the welfare of all, the work of each individual should be seen as part of the whole. For all its positive values, an agrarian nation might lose its political independence if it could not survive in the economic marketplace. In the vision of the first generation of Federalists, a beneficent system of manufactures meant encouraging individual entrepreneurs to invest capital in ways that would help the nation toward self-sufficiency as well as reward them with substantial profits. At the same time manufacturers would make more effective use of potential workers—some of whom were no longer needed on the land. The image that literary historian Leo Marx has called the "machine in the garden" tempted even those who, like Jefferson, were committed to a permanent yeomanry. It offered the possibility of self-sufficiency in manufactures alongside the continuing benefits of cultivating the land. Yet, by encouraging individual incentive and initiative, it carried the seeds of transition from a mercantile conception of the general welfare to laissez-faire individualism. Notions of community well-being and a balanced economy soon ran into newborn pressures to seek profits in a competitive marketplace.

The work of women was critical in this transition. As long as the war for independence lasted, patriotic women of all classes responded to appeals to contribute their labor. For the most part, they worked at home. Women spun and wove and knitted, replacing some of the finished goods cut off by the war. But peace brought new problems. Industrial expansion would need an efficient labor force—trained and willing to use new machinery under supervision. Could a largely agrarian population unused to laboring for masters be persuaded not merely to sell their labor, but to sell it in confined quarters and under conditions that could remove them from their agrarian roots? Luckily patriotism enlisted economic and demographic pressures in the campaign. The poverty of urban women, together with the growing numbers of young rural women no longer needed in their parents' households, offered a starting point. Benjamin Rush, an early advocate of manufactures, predicted in 1775 that women and children would make up two-thirds of the manufacturing labor force.[1] Their potential as workers in new factories became the lynchpin on which the balance between agriculture and industry would be maintained.

In the postrevolutionary period, these women as well as some men entered the wage labor force under the protective umbrella of community; that is, a general concern for their condition of work and wages was part of the bargain. But as manufactures expanded in the 1810s and 1820s, protection diminished for men and women. To replace it, men were offered the opportunity for economic advancement.

Women, however, benefited from no such trade-off. Their movement into the wage labor force, encouraged by pleas to patriotism and by injunctions to render useful service, offered them no path to competitive success. Consequently, the transition by which women passed into the work force differed dramatically from that undergone by men.

They entered the wage labor force without expectations of upward mobility, justifying their participation in terms of patriotic duty, of family commitment, or sheer survival. Confusing messages produced confusing role perceptions. Home and family were to remain the centerpieces of their lives. Yet America's lack of an adequate supply of workers and ongoing need for cheap labor required that women become the first industrial proletariat. Their accomplishments, unlike those of men, were measured concretely in terms of wages gained, years served, and items made. A better job was one that paid more; but at the same time, a good woman was one who traded work for marriage. Women knew they were essential workers, yet wage work was not to be essential in their lives.

This paradox best captures the changing position of wage-earning women in the period from the 1770s to about 1830. It is rooted in the shift from a mercantile to a laissez-faire economy which transformed the nature of work for all but had particular significance for women. For all of its restrictions on unimpeded economic development, mercantilism carried with it a sense of balance, a notion of progress that included community well-being, and social restraints that minimally forced individuals to justify outrageously self-serving acts in terms of the welfare of the whole. Loosening these constraints produced a tangle in which women found themselves caught.

Mills for fulling woolen cloth, grinding grain, sawing lumber, and carding cotton flax sprang up as early as the eighteenth century as towns grew prosperous enough to build them. These first mills and manufactories grew out of the communities in which they developed. When Samuel Slater's Pawtucket spinning mill opened in 1790—the first to incorporate spinning machinery under a factory roof—it sparked a surge of similar establishments in the surrounding countryside. They too were simply part of the communities on which they were reciprocally dependent. As in the earlier mills, labor came from the community; mill owners took what was available. So, for example, early advertisements reveal little gender discrimination, and perhaps even an emphasis on male children. "Wanted Immediately," advertised a New York cotton and linen manufactory, "A number of APPRENTICES, either girls or boys, twelve years old and upwards; they will be found in everything during their apprenticeship, and taught the different branches belonging to the cotton business." At least one mill in Ulster County, New York, employed boys exclusively to weave flax and hemp.[2]

The sex of mill hands was less important than having a regular work force. Hiring local farmers left the mill vulnerable to inconvenient and costly delays during plowing and harvest times. Incipient manufacturers quickly discovered the advantages of employing children and women, preferably those who had no direct ties to the land and whose labor could be purchased at minimal cost. Widows, potentially the most dependent labor population, proved particularly desirable, especially if they had children of working age. A Baltimore cotton mill announced in 1808 that "work will be given out to women at their homes, and widows will have preference in all cases where work is given out. . . ."[3] Widowhood often carried with it poverty, landlessness, and the need to survive economically without male support. These attributes of a stable work force attracted manufacturers who all the while asserted their charity in employing the needy.

Early appeals to support manufactures, and even to protect them with tariffs, drew heavily on the traditional notion of a mutually dependent society in which industry would enable women and children to pull their own weight. Hamilton was prominent among those who articulated prevailing mercantile sentiment. Far from undermining agriculture, he argued, industry could produce for the husbandman "a new source of profit and support from the increased industry of his wife and daughters. . . ."[4] The argument was ably popularized by Mathew Carey, Philadelphia entrepreneur and philanthropist, in a series of lectures and essays published in 1820 and 1821. Farmers, he observed, were no longer self-sufficient. They were as dependent on manufactured goods as city dwellers were on the products of the soil. And the two should therefore work together. Wives and children of farmers were told that if they could "gather up fragments of time, which would otherwise have been inevitably lost. . . . [i]t is probable that the profits of their labor were nearly equal, perhaps superior to the profits of farming."[5] Together, the farmer on the land and women in the factory would move forward; and so would the nation. At least, that was the theory.

The promoters of manufactures, North and South, sustained these arguments and calmed the fears of agrarian defenders by claiming that they would take advantage of the large number of idle women who had plagued colonial towns. Like the Beverly entrepreneurs who had sought a factory permit in 1789. Hamilton argued that the great advantage of establishing manufactures was "the employment of persons who would otherwise be idle." Tench Coxe added a capstone in 1812

when he congratulated the country on the increase of women wage
earners. "Female aid in manufactures," he said, "prevents the diversion
of men and boys from agriculture."[6] Rhode Island cotton manufacturers took full advantage of the opportunity. Pleading for tariff
protection in 1815, they argued that they employed 26,000 people,
part time, at spinning in their homes and claimed that "the benefits
resulting from this vast amount of labor are much more extensively
diffused than if the whole were done by people constantly engaged in
the business, a considerable portion being performed by those who
are partially occupied in other pursuits, particularly the weaving which
is almost wholly executed at the farm-houses throughout the country. . . ." Whether it employed women in their own homes or in
central shops mattered less than industry's ability to hire those who
would otherwise remain "idle."[7]

But the logical corollary did not emerge until 1821 when Mathew
Carey articulated it. If factory labor was merely the use of those who
would otherwise be idle, then "it was cheap and of little account."[8]
Factory owners could perceive themselves, and were sometimes perceived, as benefiting the community by giving people jobs. Perceptions
of workers as otherwise idle quickly reduced them to vulnerable positions where they could be treated as of little account. The mercantile
equation that offered to make women equal partners with men in
the development of industry in fact set the stage for their shared
degradation.

The transition was rooted in two of the deepest fears of the Calvinist
tradition: idleness and dependence. Twin sins that marked the non-
productive member of society, they had become more prevalent since
the late colonial period. Demographic changes were partly responsible.
As American independence opened western lands and the tired soil
of the Northeast prompted single men to move west, the relative
proportions of women in town and urban areas began to increase.[9]
Poverty became more visible as it spread from Boston, where it had
long been a problem, to other port cities like New York, Philadelphia,
and Baltimore. Women unable to earn their livings moved to almshouses. Continuing the colonial tradition of asking dependent people
to earn their keep, towns handed out sewing to women in almshouses
as well as to poor women at home. The minimal prices they paid became the price for all women. "Given-out" work—the task of the
thrifty and industrious in the revolutionary period—became in its
aftermath the job of the poor and dependent.

As a relatively cheap and reliable labor force made up of women
began to emerge, the new manufactures they produced contributed to
changes in female labor at home. A generation earlier, the home had

relied almost entirely on its own efforts to feed, clothe, and shelter the family. By 1800 it had begun to turn to manufactories for some of its essentials. In an uneven pattern, beginning in the settled northeastern areas about 1790 and extending west and south over the next fifty years, manufactured products—yard goods, candles, brooms—began to replace those formerly made in the household. The greatest change occurred in centralized textile production. Before the Revolution only the affluent had purchased yard goods, usually finely woven fabrics imported from Britain and Europe. But slowly, the processes of manufacturing woolen, linen, and cotton cloth became cheap enough so that many more women preferred to buy rather than make fabric.[10]

By the early nineteenth century, the process speeded up to the point where a decline in household manufactures produced some concern that domestic textile skills would be lost. Arthur Scholfield, an early entrepreneur, illustrates the incentive women had to buy manufactured goods. In 1801 he advertised his willingness to "card" wool at twelve and a half cents per pound. This laborious process involved first removing all the dung, burrs, briers, and sticks that clung to sheep, then picking the finer bits of trash, grooming the remainder, and pulling it into a thick rough thread that could be wrapped into rolls. Such work, surely, any woman with means would be glad to throw off. Six months later, by means of a new invention, he could reduce his price to nine cents a pound; and not long after that he added weaving to his business.[11]

In every family this meant a new distribution of female energy. Women at home gladly took advantage of the new machinery to reduce their labor. Other women performed the tasks of making textile goods in the spinning mill instead of at home. Still others continued to work at home, producing to specification goods that could be easily bartered for necessary items. Women could now rely on carders and fullers for tasks formerly performed at home, and some used the services of the enterprising people who offered to dye wool, to press cloth, to weave spun yarn, to distribute yarn for spinning, and so on. Any piece of the process, at the housewife's discretion, could be farmed out. Some women spun yarn at home and traded it for woven goods. Others traded raw wool and cotton for the spun yarn which they would then weave. Slowly, textile manufacturing became centralized, until the whole process from raw material to finished fabric took place under one roof. This final consolidation was the achievement of the mills that opened at Waltham, Massachusetts, in 1814.

If no smooth progression marked the decline of household manufactures, the general trend is clear. After Slater established his spinning mill, more and more women began to trade their raw flax and wool for spun yarn. By 1810 a third of the fabric in the United States was produced outside the home. New technology and economic pressures postponed the eventual end of household manufactures. The spinning jenny, invented in 1807 and conveniently small enough for home use, encouraged many women, especially in frontier areas, to continue to spin their own yarn. From 1807 to 1812, when the embargo and the Napoleonic wars cut off access to European manufactures, incentives to household production multiplied. And again in 1819 a brief depression and a shortage of cash accompanied by an upsurge of patriotism in 1819–21 encouraged many to make their own material and clothing. During these years, rural counties offered prizes to the household that produced the greatest quantity of goods. The Philadelphia weekly *Niles' Register* goaded its readers into greater production by such stories as that of the Virginia farmer whose father's household depended entirely on European goods, and yet whose two daughters "last summer and fall, besides going two quarters to school, spun one hundred and sixty pounds of wool, not a thread drawn by any one but themselves."[12] But the homespun fabrics that enjoyed popularity in this period quickly gave way to English brocades, finely woven wools, and prettily printed calicoes. After 1824, the proportion of homemade goods tumbled dramatically.

By 1830 the trend was well established. Until then, per capita household manufactures of finished goods continued to increase in the frontier areas. Thereafter, nationwide figures reflect a decline graphically illustrated by New York State. In 1825 that state's homemakers produced 8.95 yards of finished textile goods per person or a total of 16.5 million yards. In 1835 they produced only 4.03 yards per person for a total of 8.8 million yards. By 1855 the state's households averaged only a quarter of a yard of fabric per person.[13] Household spinning and weaving had become dying arts.

The aggregate effect of these changes on the farm wife was startling. A woman who in 1790 could expect to produce all her own yarn and weave her own cloth found by 1830 that it was hardly worth her while to sit at the loom. Rolla Tryon, historian of household manufactures, estimates that between 1815 and 1830 the price of manufacturing brown shirting dropped from forty-two cents to seven and a half cents a yard. The 4 yards of fabric an average home weaver could make in a day could not compete with a power loom that produced 90–160 yards in the same time.[14] As the cost of manufactured goods declined and their quality improved, household production declined even further. Women began to spend more time sewing and less producing cloth, even for their own households. This trend was not confined to textiles. Falling prices for an ever-increasing variety of manufactured goods drove out such skills as candle-, soap-, cloth-, and bread-making, formerly resident in every household. Except in areas still untouched by new canals or the emerging railroad system, household manufactures, unable to compete with a commercial economy, all but disappeared.

The process raised questions about the relative value of household labor itself. The Philadelphia *Banner of the Constitution*, a voice of manufacturers, stated the case most bluntly in 1831:

> The improvements in machinery have superseded all household manufactures so entirely that labor devoted to them, so far as useful production is concerned, is as much thrown away as if it were employed turning so many grindstones. . . . Take away the employment of females in the different branches of manufactures chiefly in cotton and wool, and there is absolutely no market, no demand, for the great mass of female labor existing in the community. It is an inert, unproductive, untried power—an unknown capability.[15]

The net result was not necessarily to reduce the farm wife's labor but to minimize the need for extra female help. As the rural household carried less of the burden of production, the need for female labor in it diminished. The household contribution of daughters sank from vital to marginal significance.[16] Although no one would argue a one-to-one relationship between the function of the household and its composition, by the early nineteenth century the birth rate had begun to decline and households to shrink visibly in size. Towns like Andover, Massachusetts, experienced "an absolute decline in population."[17] By 1850 the average white native-born woman would bear only five children—half as many as her great-grandmother. Declining family size and fewer household chores enabled poorer households to release daughters from family work. To make up for lower productivity in the home, young women went off to work in factories for a while before returning home. Ancillary members of the household became scarcer. Unmarried women could find places in towns, perhaps teaching school. The hired woman, formerly essential, slowly disappeared. Household size continued to contract throughout the first half of the nineteenth century, as the work done there gravitated toward commercial enterprise.

But if the farm family utilized female labor somewhat less, it began to need cash that much more. The steady transition from a self-sufficient bartering subsistence to a market economy forced farm families that had managed to survive by virtue of their simple existence to earn money in order to pay for household goods and to borrow money in order to improve their yield. As farms became increasingly dependent on income from their flax, wool, and grain products in order to meet the costs of manufactured goods, the temptation to invest in machinery that would increase production led to debt, and to the urgent need for cash. All the more reason, then, for debt-ridden fathers to encourage their children, especially their unmarried daughters (for whom custom in any event restricted work in the fields), to seek paid employment elsewhere. And reason enough for wives to seek given-out work to supplement family income.

In most areas of New England, the transition occurred slowly. The close interaction between household work and work removed to a central location obscured the steady trend. Women previously employed at home gradually began to seek paid employment. At first they brought work home. The boot and shoe industry is a case in point. During most of the eighteenth century women sewed uppers as time permitted in their own families' shops. Toward the end of the century, their daughters found themselves doing the same for merchants who distributed the cut leather to them in their homes. Instead of working part time, they worked full time, encouraging the transition from custom work to domestic labor in the shoe industry. As shoe manufacturing became concentrated in central locations, women were at first required to pick up and return the goods, then finally, in the 1840s, to leave their homes in order to sew in factories under supervision.[18] By the 1850s most women employed in the boot and shoe industry worked in factories.

The ability of this industry to utilize household labor contributed to its rapid growth. According to one historian, by the 1830s it was the largest single employer of women in Massachusetts. But women engaged in other industries made the same transition from handicraft worker to home worker and thence to the factory. Braiding and plaiting straw bonnets, initially a fireside task performed at whim to produce extra cash, became an industry in the late eighteenth century when store owners gave out straw to women who sewed it to specification in their homes. By the late 1820s, small factories in places like Medway, West Upton, and Framingham, Massachusetts, had brought women workers together to produce more than half a million dollars' worth of hats, some of which relied on straw first sewn by women who were still at home.[19]

The effect of the process was insidious. Whereas for men it was at least possible to enter factories as skilled workers exercising their craft, no such possibilities existed for women. From the beginning the transition from household manufactures for personal use, to domestic production for a merchant, and then to factory production was predicated on breaking down the labor process into ever smaller parts. In sharp contrast to the independent woman who sewed or knitted at her own pace and then sold what her craft had produced, women who spun for a market or bound shoes for a factory had little control over what they were doing and worked instead to specifications determined by a selling agent or "factor." Where their labor at home had been highly skilled and self-regulated, the condition of employment outside it required leaving their skills behind and obeying another's clock. Thus, women quickly and very early confronted a de-skilling process that would occur later for men. The result was to leave them wholly at the mercy of labor market forces—dependent on others for jobs and wages.

Encouraged by a labor supply that was developing on its own and that they were simultaneously helping to develop, merchant capitalists invested in paper mills and textile and glass factories. These had attractive potential. In Pennsylvania expenses for setting up a textile mill could be covered within a year. The Boston manufacturing company that founded the Lowell Mills paid a 20 percent dividend within three years and maintained that rate until 1825. The return on capital hovered around 10 percent annually for Chicopee mills in the early 1830s. From industry's rudimentary beginnings in 1790, Rhode Island boasted 33 textile factories in 1812 and Massachusetts, 20. Pennsylvania, slower to start than New England, could nevertheless count 106 cotton mills by 1840.[20] Although agriculture was still by far the major occupation for the population as a whole, among the 4 percent of Americans who worked in manufacturing jobs the number of women far exceeded that of men. By 1840, 37 percent of America's workers earned their livings outside agriculture. Less than 10 percent of these were in manufacturing. But women constituted half of the total and sometimes as many as 90 percent of those employed in shoe factories, textile mills, and millinery shops.

The entire process, from the diminution of family production to the simultaneous expansion of domestic labor and development of the factory system, dramatically altered public perception of women's potential value and, as a result, women's own perceptions of themselves. Fears of idle and dependent womanhood gave way to enthusiastic proposals for using women in new industries.[21] Called upon to enter the wage labor force out of a sense of responsibility to family and community, women only belatedly discovered that no reciprocal responsibility protected them. They would be left to fend for themselves.

As workers, women may have had little choice but to seek jobs. As community members, they participated in a lively contemporary debate about what wage-earning would mean for them. The debate was complicated by a general wariness about the social effects of the new mills and factories.

In the first two decades of the nineteenth century, wage work drew a sharp line between affluent women, who could afford to practice household arts without pay until marriage, and women, married or single, who needed to support themselves or help their families in the period of young adulthood before they set up their own families. Those who needed an income could soften the division between themselves and the better off if they worked at relatively genteel jobs such as teaching and writing, or if they worked at home.

For married women and those with young children to support, given-out (or "putting-out") work had long provided a way of producing income. Although the rewards were limited, the work could be done part-time or part-year, and set aside when children or household duties intervened. Competition for such work increased as the demand for farm income rose, and in the early 1800s self-supporting women complained that their wages were reduced by the willingness of "farmer's wives" to undertake home work for less than prevailing rates in the cities. As rates fell, women who relied on given-out work as their sole support may never have had the option of putting it aside. But the relative gentility associated with working at home obscured for a time the penury that resulted. By the 1830s, the poverty of "sewing women" had become a national scandal.

The degradation of the poorest wage-earning women sharpened distinctions between those who earned wages and those who did not. By the 1830s, engaging in even such skilled crafts as dressmaking and millinery work became a source of tension. Thus Rachel Stearns, a schoolteacher, complained to her sister in 1810 that it was "quite too degrading to go to Uncle F's and sew."[22] Families that a generation earlier might have sent their daughters to other households for training in domestic chores now had difficulty hiring help, for young women undertook paid domestic labor less and less willingly. In the mid-1830s it was necessary for the Lynn *Record* to defend shoe-binding, one of the oldest putting-out industries. "Ladies," declared the *Record*, "do not feel themselves degraded by this any more than by any other kind of needlework.[23]

If all wage work carried a certain onus, work in a factory carried with it the skepticism of the community as well. In contrast to merchants, who praised centralization of production, single women and widows who considered working in industry came from families and communities that often resisted new forms of production. Whether she was the daughter of a declining artisan, of an unskilled laborer, or of a local farmer, the new factory recruit would have heard ambivalence expressed about the factory. Artisans feared loss of their own influence as they observed mill owners and merchants unite to buttress their economic self-interest. They condemned displays of new wealth that emphasized class differences and accompanied emerging political control over small communities. Some artisans allied themselves with farmers who went to court over control of water power and contested land usage.

Artisans were more ambivalent about the effect of mills on their own lives. Some identified with the values of mill owners, adopting patterns of steady, disciplined work. Others nursed what one historian has called an "oppositional tradition." They fiercely defended the skills and the relative autonomy that unskilled labor in textile mills threatened to displace. And they feared the imposed discipline and loss of self-regulated decision-making power implicit in factory work. Lack of craft skills did not prevent unskilled workers, such as those imported to work in Slater's Pawtucket mills, from sharing the antagonism of the skilled. Two-thirds of these workers were children, and most of the rest were young women. Yet, like artisans, they resisted regular work and joined in early strikes. Their grudging ambivalence and their fears of the new mill produced some explicit hostility which manifested itself in extensive absenteeism, high turnover rates, strikes, and sometimes arson.[24]

Given the prevailing distrust of mills among much of the urban and rural population, the first generation of female factory workers must have had a difficult set of decisions to make. Yet limited options and high factory wages reduced the social onus attached, eroding their resistance and that of their families. An unknown novelist, writing in 1814, captures the conflict. Mary, heroine of *The Factory Girl*, has just told her grandmother and guardian that she has got a job in a factory. Grandma is heartbroken: "It will indeed, be a sad day to me when you go into the factory," she says, "for I shall be thinking all the time, what your poor father would say, were he alive, to have you get your bread in such a manner; not but that he would love you the better for being industrious, and so dutiful to your grandmother— for I know it is not to get fine clothes for yourself, but comforts for me, that makes you so desirous to go out to work; but I don't think he would consent. Oh no, I am sure he would not consent to your being with people who were not good and serious."[25]

Such scruples reflect the doubts of many contemporaries—doubts that did not appear to recede markedly even as the need for wages reduced family resistance in practice. A series of letters from her New Hampshire family to Sabrina Bennett debated the merits of factory work. Bennett, the daughter of a Gilmanton, New Hampshire, farmer, worked in Haverhill, Massachusetts, as a skilled dressmaker from September, 1836, to 1851 when she married. In the interim she corresponded with a wide network of family and friends—among them several young women whose comments about factory work reveal what must have been a general conflict. "I suppose your mother would think it far beneath your dignity to be a factory girl," writes Aunt Melinda Edwards to Sabrina in 1839. "I do not know what my employment will be this summer," comments Persis Edwards. "Mother is not willing I should go to the factory." And from Mary Killvye, "Mother says she cannot consent to my ever returning again."[26] Time does not seem to have diminished the negative feelings of the parental generation. Ann Appleton moved from her home in Haverhill to Manchester, New Hampshire, in 1847, when she was just twenty years old. Before she acquired the mill job she was to hold for four years, she wrote home that the aunt with whom she lived "did not want [me] to go to the factory without there is nothing else for me to do, but there is plenty for me at present."[27]

Women about to enter the mills required reassurance. "Their [sic] are very many young ladies at work in the factories that have given up millinery, dress-making and school-keeping for to work in the mill . . . ," wrote Melinda Edwards to Sabrina Bennett in 1839.[28] To some the mill appeared as a last resort, as Sabrina's aunt makes clear to her brother Richard Bennett. She would have been glad, she writes, if her daughter Ann "could have gone to Haverhill and learnt the trade, but she thinks she must try the mill a spell first for the want of clothes that is fit to wear."[29] Ann included a note in the same envelope in which she tried to cover up her embarrassment. "I think it would be best for me to work in the mill a year and then I shall be better prepared to learn a trade." But the clearest statement of the trade-offs involved in factory work came from a New England operative writing in the pages of the *Lowell Offering*, a weekly paper subsidized by mill owners and produced by workers, in response to a criticism leveled by the transcendentalist philosopher Orestes Brownson. "Strange it would be," she wrote, "if . . . one of the most lucrative female employments should be rejected because it is toilsome, or because some people are prejudiced against it. Yankee girls have too much independence for that."[30]

To some extent these doubts about factory work were mitigated by the introduction of the boarding-house system, initiated at Waltham, Massachusetts, by Francis Cabot Lowell. For their work force, Slater and others had relied on family labor drawn from the communities in which mills were located. These so-called family mills faced persistent problems of high turnover and labor shortage. In contrast,

Lowell and the Boston Manufacturing Company he organized with members of his family decided to draw on the young unmarried daughters of New England farmers. But Lowell recognized the need to assuage community opposition to factories in general and to acknowledge the moral imperative that assigned women to the home. To counteract prejudice, Lowell argued that the young single daughters of farm families could fulfill their family responsibilities by engaging in hard work away from home. And to sustain notions of women's roles he and his associates established carefully supervised boarding houses for women who would spend a few years at wage work before marriage. They offered salaries sufficiently high to save for a trousseau, to help pay off a mortgage, or to send a brother through college. At the same time, parents were assured that their daughters would experience hard work and discipline in a healthy semirural environment. A few years of labor in the mills would make them into better wives and mothers.

Lowell died in 1817, after setting up an experimental version of what came to be known as the Waltham system. His partners, reorganized as the Boston Associates, offered a fitting memorial. They founded a new town on the banks of the Merrimack River, to be called Lowell, and in it built the Merrimack Valley Manufacturing Corporation complex—the grandest cotton mill yet seen. This mill, which began producing cotton textiles in 1823, made the Waltham system famous. Like the others that copied the pattern later, the mills at Lowell attracted a reliable labor force easily disciplined in industrial routines and cheaper than male workers. In return they offered a training ground in morality.

The mills may never have lived up to Lowell's high standards. From the beginning, young women complained of overcrowded sleeping rooms and rigid supervision. They were vulnerable to arbitrary wage cuts and, beginning in the 1830s, to increasing attempts to speed up the rate of production. Yet perhaps half of all New England mills functioned on the Lowell model by the 1840s. Their influence far exceeded their direct impact on the women who worked there, for they introduced and sustained the possibility of well-paid, respectable work for women.

A collective sigh of relief must have escaped from numerous New England and mid-Atlantic young women at the prospect of being able to earn a living. At least in the early years the hardships suffered by mill girls could be balanced against the meaningful economic opportunities available. Compared to the other options facing women who needed to earn wages, the new jobs in mills and manufactories surely seemed a real boon. In return for industry, women could anticipate some measure of economic independence, and a good deal more geographical mobility than had earlier been the case. Unlike domestic service, the workday, however long, had a beginning and an end. Unlike home work in industries such as hat-making and shoe-binding, mill work offered relatively high wages, the possibilities of close companionship with other young women, perhaps even an adventure away from parental supervision. And unlike dame-school teaching, the work was regular; it paid better wages and was probably less demanding. In the initial years, at least, the idea of going to a factory was exciting. It offered women without family, money, or capital options and choices that seemed to preserve their dignity and did not shut them off from future marriages. Harriet Hanson Robinson, who worked at Lowell in the 1830s, referred to mill work as "the first field that had ever been open to her outside of her own restricted home." Yet again, she recalled the women who came to Lowell depressed and hopeless, "but the first money they earned! When they felt the jingle of silver in their pocket, there for the first time, their heads became erect and they walked as if on air."[31]

The joy of relative independence, recurrent in the literature, is difficult to discount. In *The Factory Girl*, Mary, old enough at last to seek work in the local mill, proclaims, "Oh how happy I shall be when I see my dear grandmother sitting at her teatable enjoying her favourite repast, which I have earned for her."[32] A series of letters written in 1847 and 1848 from Ann Appleton to her sister Sarah recalls her own experience of the same phenomenon. Appleton, who became a highly skilled and well-paid harness knitter at Lowell, writes of her first pay: "He paid me—four dollars for two weeks work. What do you think of that! By and by when I get to knit real fast then I shall pay my board and after all that shall have twice as much as though I were binding shoes. I guess you catch me to do that little thing again, not I! You cannot think how funny it seems to have some money." Three months later she wrote, "Since I have wrote you another pay day has come around. I earned 14 dollars and a half, 9 and a half dollars beside my board. . . . I like it as well as ever and Sarah, don't I feel independent of everyone! The thoughts that I am living on no one is a happy one indeed to me [sic]."[33] One effusive novelist spoke of Lowell, in hyperbole, as an "asylum left to shelter the lone wanderer and heart-stricken orphan."[34]

As important as the feeling of having cash in one's pocket was the sense of choice that many women experienced for the first time. The Bennett family letters reveal the extent of both geographical and job mobility. Lucy Davis of Nashua, New Hampshire, indicated that she had given up mill work and now debated whether to go to

Boston to work at her trade. "If I thought I could make more, I would go . . . I like the place and people hear verry much but wish to work whare I can make the most [sic]."[35] Friends contemplated joining Sabrina in Haverhill—"Sabrina do write the particulars as it respects my returning"[36]—or requested aid in searching for jobs: "I will tell you what we want," wrote one young aunt; "Mary and I want to come to Haverhill and spend the summer if you think we can get a good chance and good wages. If Mary comes she will want to do housework or nursing . . . I should like to sew—I will go out by the day or go into some family as seamstress or go into a milliners shop just which way you think I can do best."[37]

Family ties and friendship networks encouraged limited geographical mobility, and women used them to help each other. "If you should have any idea of working in a factory I will do the best I can to get you a place with us." "Now Sabrina, if you will get either of us a place and send word we will be [on]."[38] "The rest of us moved here to Nashville thinking they (the girls and Charles) would probably work in the Mill. . . ."[39] "Tell me how you employed [sic] don't delay, if you work at your trade I should be glad to work with you."[40] Such correspondence reveals by the 1830s a social culture that permitted wage work for women of a certain class and encouraged young women to prepare themselves, in a limited number of trades, to earn their livings as best they could while they remained single. Moving away from the family of origin seemed to be a normal event. And boarding-house living was clearly not without its compensations. Ann Appleton gloried in it. "I tell you Sarah it is good to be a boarder. I leave my work at seven o'clock then I come home and do what I please. I done't even have my bed to make. Quite a lady to be sure."[41]

Ann, who was better paid than most of her fellow workers, may have been fortunate. For even in 1847, when living conditions were beginning to deteriorate, she had her own front room in a relatively small house of seventeen boarders. Others were less lucky. Complaints of high charges, overcrowding, and poor food abounded, especially after corporations tried to cut their expenses in the 1840s. It was not uncommon for young women to share beds, to use trunks both for storage and as tables, and to lack common amenities such as wash stands.[42] These were small complaints next to the advantages of earning a decent wage. When that advantage was threatened, women began to reconsider their position.

In the meantime, they, like men, faced the necessary adjustment required by factory work. For women as for men, the transition to wage labor involved learning to pay attention to orders and to clocks; it meant postponing gratification and learning to handle cash wages. Women's secondary position in their families may have smoothed the transition initially. Obedience to supervisors, to the factors or middle men who enforced home-work specifications, and to foremen merely replaced obedience to fathers and husbands. Culturally ingrained habits of thrift, attention to morality, and self-sacrifice all conspired to make women particularly good recruits to wage labor. Yet women who were expected to become good wives needed as well to develop the self-regulation and initiative to organize and execute domestic affairs. A continuation of factory routines threatened to undermine these qualities. Women who were supposed to be self-regulating in their future homes were fined for lateness, for reading, for talking in factories. To reconcile this tension between the conditions of wage work and women's future roles a series of regulatory devices developed. They derived from a consensus about women's primary commitment to the home. And they centered on the understanding that conditions of work ought not to inhibit future home roles.

Some of these devices were self-imposed. Women stayed in the factory an average of less than five years. They alternated factory jobs with other available employment such as hat-making, dressmaking, and teaching. They interspersed extended holidays—sometimes as much as several months at a time—with stints of fifteen to eighteen months in the mills.[43] Yet mostly, the devices that influenced women's behavior towards their jobs were imposed by employers in a coherent system that was not questioned by workers—male or female. Jobs, for example, were distributed according to sex. Men supervised, did the heavy work, and were the skilled mechanics. Women spun, wove, carded, dressed, and did everything else. Women could move up the economic ladder only within those occupations defined as theirs. Normally, increased earnings came from increased productivity through experience at the same job. So women achieved peak earning capacity quickly and maintained a plateau until they left the mills. If men moved up they did so by achieving supervisory positions. The division was not always so rigid; improved machinery and regional preferences often led to a redistribution of male and female jobs. Yet, by and large, men and women did different work.

These differences reflected the society's understanding about the nature of work for men and women as well as the relative scarcity of, and keen competition for, skilled male laborers. In addition, manufacturers who wished to compete with relatively inexpensive European products had a special incentive to hold women's wages down. Nevertheless, to attract women to work in factories required levels of pay substantially higher than those offered elsewhere, and at the beginning, women felt themselves well paid for their labor.

Some comparisons are revealing. Starting wages in the least skilled men's jobs paid more than those earned by highly skilled and experienced women. Lowell women made about $1.90 per week plus board, which amounted to another dollar per week, while the men in the plants averaged 80 cents per day. At Chicopee in 1832, women and girls averaged $2.75 per week out of which they paid about one-third for board and room. The women who worked in the South Hadley, Massachusetts, paper mills in 1832 earned about 33 cents a day, compared to 85 cents for men. But the women got board in addition. A woman could thus earn between $1.80 and $2.00 a week clear of expenses in a boarding-house mill. Family-type mills paid somewhat less, but both exceeded the pay of every other women's job.

By contrast, Philadelphia seamstresses and tailoresses who worked at home in 1821 made about $58 per year, out of which they paid for thread, heat, light, and all living expenses. On this sum they could not survive without help. Carey reported that $12\frac{1}{2}$ cents was not an unusually low sum to offer a woman for making a shirt. By diligent labor she might make one in fourteen hours of steady work. Hats and shoes paid too little to earn a living. A shoe binder in this period could earn from 72 cents to $2.00 a week—but the work was seasonal. Hatmakers—also seasonally employed—might make from $1.50 to $1.75 a week, less their board. The boarding-house mills had the additional advantage of paying cash wages. Family mills almost always paid in credit at the company store, and small shops sometimes held back pay for weeks at a time.[44]

Relatively high pay carried with it possibilities for independence that undermined women's subordinate and secondary position in society. To ensure that such independence did not threaten women's traditional roles, mill owners resorted to paternalistic regulations which, like the devices of low pay and job distribution, circumscribed women's ability to exercise their new freedom. The boarding houses in which the young single daughters of farm families lived exacted high standards of behavior from their residents. No one could be out after ten P.M. Church attendance was required. Young women had to keep only the best company. The mill women themselves, at least in the early years, determined to preserve their own respectability. They defended their new opportunity in the language of dignity and morality. A fictional factory worker described her future coworkers as "much better than you suppose" and including "some very good girls." Harriet Hanson Robinson echoed the defense: "many good women came there to work because then women could not make a living anywhere but in the factory."[45] And Ann Appleton, who in little more than a year would pay fifty cents more a month for her board in order to live with a pious family, carefully wrote to sister Sarah that "the girls in the shop . . . are real good girls."[46] In a manner reminiscent of the early Puritans, they supervised one another, ostracizing those suspected of immorality.[47]

For young women the regulations provided justification for their presence as wage workers and simultaneously rationalized the hard work they were doing. Paternalistic rules that circumscribed women's behavior served employers in several ways. Insistence on specified times for sleeping, eating, and waking, regular church attendance, and strict morality contributed to a well-disciplined work force. They served to maintain the separation between men and women, confirming women's attachments to their homes. The same regulations buttressed the family order on which a largely agrarian society rested and limited public opposition to industrialization by reducing fears about creating a permanent proletariat. They thus sustained a vision of an agrarian utopia whose manufacturing population was merely temporary. America's young female workers who joined reading circles and paraded in white dresses on Sundays would never, it seemed, repeat the experience of England's degraded proletariat. So, for example, Mathew Carey sketches eight or ten young girls employed in a woolen mill: "they appeared perfectly happy, singing church music most melodiously."[48] Preserving this myth was critical to maintaining the idea of a working population grounded in the family and in the land. Only in such a context could hard work and extended hours be interpreted as healthy. Harriet Hanson Robinson recalled the fourteen hours a day she spent in the mills: "I remember the old life well. How good it was, and how many good women came there to work. . . ."[49] In the context of temporary work, even twelve and fourteen hours a day could be justified if the object was to further family interests.

The balance between high pay and stringent self- and superimposed regulation seemed to hold for a while. It took some time before the young women who entered the early mill towns recognized the tension inherent in their position. As long as high wages and a benevolent paternalism provided a comfortable haven, their social dignity remained intact. Women could maintain their "feminine" behavior and praise mill life as preparation for future homemaking. But employers found it difficult to maintain these critical preconditions. By the mid-1830s, they were being pushed to repay debts for machinery and to reduce prices in order to compete with newer mills. To meet these costs mill owners began to exert pressure on workers to speed up production and to accept lower real wages. Workdays lengthened.

Rules became more rigid. Living conditions worsened as employers tightened discipline to exact more work. These pressures led female workers in the Waltham-style mills to question their own relationship to factory work. Faced with reduced wages and work conditions that threatened to undermine their dignity, the proud Yankee mill girls began to protest.

To enforce their stringent regulations, employers resorted to heavy punishments that tell us something of the dissatisfactions of those employed in the mills. As early as 1826 and 1827, offenses such as misconduct, captiousness, refusal to obey orders, and insubordination to the overseer brought instant dismissal. In their heyday in the 1830s most mills required a year's commitment of each employee. Supervisors held back a portion of the wages and withheld certificates of good character from those who left before they had fulfilled their obligation. Fines, blacklists, dishonorable discharges, or revocation of two or more weeks' pay punished those accused of poor work, tardiness, or troublemaking. A person who left a mill without notice, had not demonstrated "good character," or had worked less than a year might be subject to one or more penalties. Failure to obtain an honorable discharge meant that other mill doors were closed to her.[50]

Problems of recruitment and rapid turnover resulted. High wages notwithstanding, mill owners and supervisors of family- as well as Waltham-style mills complained repeatedly of the difficulty of getting an adequate labor supply. They offered bonuses of a dollar or more a head to agents who scoured the countryside for workers. Additional bonuses went to workers who agreed to stay longer than a year. In periods of rampant discontent, such as during the strikes (then called turnouts) of 1834 and 1836, mills were forced to operate at reduced capacity for want of sufficient labor.[51]

Turnover rates in the mills tell us something about the conflicts of the women working in them. Historian Thomas Dublin estimates that the typical female worker in the Hamilton Company mills, located in Lowell, worked for about three and a half years in three separate, year-long stints. In between she took long vacations at home, or other jobs teaching or sewing. Men, in contrast, tended to work for an average of four and a half years without a break. For the mid-1830s, Dublin's computations reveal an extraordinarily high turnover rate. In one five-week period, 25.7 percent of the workers listed on the payrolls of the company entered or left employment. Among the women, 26.4 percent changed, as compared to 20.8 percent of the men.[52] These figures reflect the options open to women as well as their ability to return to their homes for lengthy periods.

But the early mill strikes provide the best gauge of how operatives felt about themselves. Pawtucket's female weavers voted to abandon their looms in 1824, after a reduction in piece rates. In 1828, just two years after mills in Dover, New Hampshire, had started operation, employees walked out in protest against low wages and long hours. Three years later, Paterson, New Jersey, mill women and children walked out to protest a change in the lunch hour. And discontent surfaced in Lowell when 800 women left their jobs in February of 1834 and 1,500 left in October of 1836 to protest a rise in board rates without an increase in wages.[53]

Nor were strikes peculiar to the textile industry. From the mid-1820s to the mid-1830s workers exhibited an extraordinarily high level of discontent. Seamstresses and tailoresses organized themselves first in New York City about 1825. In 1831, the United Tailoresses' Society submitted a bill of prices to an employers' association and then struck to reinforce its demands. In 1833, Philadelphia seamstresses organized to present lists of prices. They got their way without a strike and in the process managed to form the first federation of women workers in America: the Female Improvement Society of the City and County of Philadelphia.[54] Shoe binders in Philadelphia and Lynn attempted to unite as early as 1828 and achieved some success by 1833. When the Lynn shoe binders struck for higher wages in 1834, they threatened to quit altogether. "It is well known," they argued, "that in factories young ladies receive a high price for their services and unless our females receive nearly an equal amount, they may be induced to seek employment in the factory, the printing office, or some other place where they may receive just compensation for their services."[55] New York's umbrella sewers and book binders had temporary organizations in the 1830s.

Protests occurred for widely different reasons, and each represents a different set of issues. But in a period when labor organization was barely legal, certain common elements stand out. The strikes reflect a high level of community among women. In Lowell, where women lived and worked together, this might have been expected. But Paterson's women and children lived in their own families, and many of the Philadelphia women who collected dues to support strikes could hardly have had personal or work contact. While some groups, like the Lynn shoe binders, had precedent and encouragement from male workers who had previously organized, others, like the New York seamstresses, apparently acted alone. Elements of female solidarity were strong everywhere. Several factors account for this. Men who took jobs for wages tended to be seeking upward mobility. Competition among them for promotion and success undermined loyalty to each other. Women, by contrast, had little access to mobility, except by perfecting their own skills. Helping other women did not visibly reduce their own chances for higher pay, and wage work itself did not assume the same proportion in their lives. The existence of homogeneous and highly sex-segregated labor force seems to have encouraged women to strike.

Protests among women in this early period reflect the degree to which wages offered the possibility of economic independence. Women wage earners fought fiercely against the erosion of a privilege that had not come without conflict. At Lowell, insofar as the wage represented the possibility of returning home, taking extended vacations, or saving a little money, it symbolized and preserved women's sense of independence. "What," asked one operative in 1843, "are we coming to? I can hardly clear my way having saved from four weeks steady work, but *three hundred and ninety-one cents!*"[56] In the Paterson strike, the entire community joined to protest a blatant violation of community norms represented by the lunch-hour shift. Those who worked in putting-out industries were more vulnerable than those in factories. Yet even there, women managed by combination and pressure to sustain some sense of self-worth by resisting price reductions and occasionally, as in Philadelphia in 1833, even by winning increases.

Metaphors of liberty, which occur repeatedly in the language of women in strike situations in this period, reflect the consciousness of this generation of wage-earning women. Willing to hire themselves out for wage work, they nevertheless insisted that they be treated as part of the community of people from which they came. Who among the Dover girls, chanted striking workers in 1828, could "ever bear, the shocking fate of slaves to share?" And in 1834 and 1836 Lowell strikers waxed equally indignant: "As our fathers resisted unto blood the lordly avarice of the British ministry, so we, their daughters, never will wear the yoke which has been prepared for us," declared a resolution of the Factory Girls Association in 1836. And 1,500 strikers marched through the streets singing a now-familiar refrain:

> Oh isn't it a pity that such a pretty girl as I
> Should be sent to the factory to pine away and die.
> Oh! I cannot be a slave
> I will not be a slave
> For I'm so fond of liberty
> That I can not be a slave.[57]

Such sentiments made mill women particularly responsive to the appeal of abolitionists in the 1830s. Residents of Lowell formed one of Massachusetts' first female antislavery societies in 1833. And towns such as Salem, New Haverhill, Lyon, and Fall River—with high concentrations of wage-earning women—all had female antislavery activities in 1834.

Even as the real possibilities of financial independence through mill work were vanishing, appeals to pride continued. The *Voice of Industry*, purchased by the Lowell Female Labor Reform Association in 1845, and leader of the struggle for a shorter workday, published a poem by John Greenleaf Whittier in 1846. Not remarkable for its lyricism, the poem nevertheless captures a sense of women's self-worth as it contrasted with the perceived sin of the slave owner.

> She sings by her wheel, at the low cottage door,
> Which the long evening shadow is stretching before,
> With a music as sweet as a music which seems,
> Breathed softly and faint in the ear of our dreams. . . . .
>
> Who comes in his pride to that low cottage door;
> The haughty and rich to the humble and poor?
> Tis the great Southern planter; the master who waves
> His whip of dominion o'er hundreds of slaves.
>
> Nay, Ellen—for shame! Let those Yankee fools spin
> Who would pass for our slaves with a change of their skin;
> Let them toil as they will, at the loom or the wheel,
> Too stupid for shame, and too vulgar to feel!
>
> But thou art too lovely and precious a gem,
> To be bound to their burdens and sullied by them;
> For shame! Ellen, shame! cast thy bondage aside,
> And away to the South, as my blessing and pride. . . .
>
> Oh, come to my home, where my servants shall all
> Depart at thy bidding and come at thy call;
> They shall heed thee as mistress with trembling and awe,
> And each wish of thy heart shall be felt as a law.
>
> Oh, could ye have seen her—the pride of our girls,
> Arise and cast back the dark wealth of her curls;
> With a scorn in her eye which the gazer could feel,
> And a glance like the sunshine that flashes on steel!
>
> Go back, haughty Southron! thy treasures of gold
> Are dim with the blood of the hearts thou has sold;
> Thy house may be lovely, but round it I hear
> The crack of the whip and the footsteps of fear. . . .
>
> Full low at thy bidding thy negroes may kneel,
> With the iron of bondage on spirits and heel;
> Yet know that the Yankee Girl sooner would be
> In FETTERS with THEM, than in freedom with THEE![58]

In retrospect, women's protests assume an ambiguous cast. Although the first generation of wage-earning women expected wage labor to sustain their liberty, longer hours and lower wages increasingly restricted freedom in return for a livelihood. In struggling against what they felt to be a palpable injustice, women were affirming the notion of independence they understood as the core of republican ideology. But they got little support from the press or from public bodies. For the notion of liberty for women violated nineteenth-century sensibilities about female roles. As one mill worker, writing in the *Lowell Offering* in 1845, put it sarcastically: "Independence of means, unless married or inherited, is not consonant with female delicacy!"[59]

Those who responded publicly to women strikers attacked their femininity, revealing both the pattern of behavior they expected of all women and their fear that women would leave their sphere. Onlookers ridiculed Dover's marching women. A recruiting agent for the Lowell mills described striking women as "amazonian" and hoped that they would simply leave town. The Philadelphia *National Gazette* mocked female strikers: "By and by the Governor may have to call out the militia to prevent a gynocracy." The Boston *Transcript* called a rather mild statement by Mrs. Lavinia Wright, a leader of organized tailoresses, "a clamorous and unfeminine declaration of personal rights which it is obvious a wise providence never destined her to exercise."[60] The harsh words flung at women who transcended their roles could only have grown out of a sense of betrayal. To the editors who upheld public morality, women had challenged public order by moving toward independence. To female workers who wanted independence, the demand seemed no more than the just reward of hard work. In the 1830s, public consciousness was just beginning to absorb the degree to which wage work would encourage women to adopt behavior patterns and values that challenged those of women who did not work for wages.

Dawning perceptions of the impact of wage work on notions of womanhood illuminate the complicated transition that occurred between the American revolution and the Jacksonian counterrevolution. There had never been a question as to whether women would participate in the wage labor force. And even debate as to how they participated was governed more by issues of physical strength and available labor supply than by those of propriety. Communities that feared idleness and dependency had welcomed expanding industrial opportunities and gladly encouraged women and children to undertake wage work. It was left to the market to regulate wages for mill hands and prices for home workers, and to social custom and technology to determine the conditions of work and its speed. But the Boston

Transcript's outburst at Lavinia Wright signaled an emerging debate about women's own relationship to their work—a debate that forced into public consciousness notions of where women were to work, how they were to conduct themselves at work, and ultimately about whether wage work was compatible with home roles.

For a brief period in the 1820s and 1830s, the Waltham-style mills offered women a vision of economic independence. In opening up the possibility of decent and well-paid wage work, they made plausible, even to large numbers who did not work in them, life outside the confines of a restrictive home environment. They satisfied some of the needs of those operatives who, as one exclaimed in 1843, "do not believe in matrimony."[61] But the 1837 depression ushered in a period that threatened to reduce even the most privileged female wage earners to the ranks of the oppressed. Thereafter, a woman who had "no one to depend upon" found making a living more difficult. "It is peculiarly her prerogative," said one operative, "to want, suffer and toil for a pittance which will just keep soul and body together." The symbolic significance of the battle between the need for women's labor and social injunctions not to violate "female delicacy" penetrated far beyond the Lowell mills. If wage work perpetuated poverty instead of relieving the home, what was its role in women's lives? Was it destined merely to ensure industrious habits? And what was to be its function in the continuing development of industry?

3

Industrial Wage Earners and the Domestic Ideology

"The rest of us have moved here to Nashville," Jemima Sandborn wrote to her brother Richard Bennett in 1843, "thinking they (the girls and Charles) would probably work in the Mill but we have had bad luck getting them in—only Jane has got in yet."[1] The halcyon days when women seemed to be able to determine their own destinies were gone forever.

The depression of 1837–39, the first major downturn of the industrializing nation, was the turning point. It threw as many as one-third of New York City's working population out of work. Thousands of New England factory operatives returned to their homes until the panic subsided. In the meantime, savings were withdrawn, pauperism grew dramatically, a sense of insecurity about possibilities for work spread. Women could no longer rely on the assurance of readily available jobs, and all workers faced the necessity of accepting reduced wages.

The depression marked the development of a market economy characterized by increasing dependence on wage labor and attempts to organize work in central locations. It revealed the difficulty women would have in sustaining a partnership between wage work and the home, where they could not rely on paid work. It illuminated a wage labor force no longer in such short supply that it could command extraordinary conditions of work. It pointed to transitions in women's work that made it increasingly difficult for workers to preserve the dignity that mediated between home and wage work.

Despite continuing increases in the numbers earning wages after the depression, and spot shortages notwithstanding, industry's dependence on women had peaked. Employers continued to recruit women actively, offering agents as much as three or four dollars for each new worker they brought into the mills, and in some geographical areas mills suffered from the absence of particular skills. Yet women complained of the difficulty of finding places at all. This was a harbinger of change.

Because it inhibited economic options, the depression lent credence to the fears of a degraded proletariat which had informed the debate over industrialization. It revealed the nation's rapid movement toward a market economy and, by constricting possibilities for female independence, encouraged the development of a new ideology that, as we shall see, helped to alter the behavior patterns of women at home as well as in the marketplace. For though the laws of the market—impersonal, unsympathetic, and geared to consumption—were said to be the province of men, they demanded new kinds of household conformity.

Urbanization and expansion of transportation encouraged the development of new systems for distributing goods, centralizing jobs, and providing incentives to efficient production. The new factories accounted for huge productivity increases, allowing employers to lower prices as they reaped larger profits. They thus discouraged home production except at very low wages. We have already seen how women who remained at home had sometimes taken up given-out work when they found fewer opportunities to supplement family income by stretching their own labor to meet family needs. Now, well-off women, usually native-born, gradually abandoned the practice of contributing to the economic survival of the household by utilizing their "spare time" for wage work, and by engaging either in full-time work before marriage or part-time work during it. The wives of respectable mechanics, like those of more affluent citizens, continued to do housework for their families, while daughters of poorer parents may have undertaken paid work until marriage and ceased thereafter. Necessity might subsequently require some contribute to family sustenance, but probably less than 5 percent of the total of married women worked outside their own homes for wages, and by 1860 no more than 15 percent of all women could be found in the wage labor force at any one time.

Those who continued to work for wages were poorer women—free blacks and immigrants, widows, and those who migrated to cities in search of jobs—women who still sought to replace the work they had formerly done for their own households with paid work. The declining profitability of women's work at home encouraged more women to seek jobs in factories, expanding the labor supply in urban areas and contributing to a general reduction in factory wages. And beginning in the mid-1840s, an increasing stream of immigrants contributed to the supply of labor. Forty-five thousand immigrants entered the United States in 1835, 84,000 in 1840, 369,000 in 1850: altogether a total of 4,200,000 in the twenty-year period between 1840 and 1860. This figure was six times more than America had seen in the preceding twenty years. About 40 percent of the newcomers were Irish refugees from the great famines of 1846 and 1847. Slightly less than half of the Irish were women—many of them young and single, without families to support them. With neither capital nor industrial skills, immigrants headed for the cities hoping to find work.

In 1840 there were still only a dozen towns with populations of over 25,000 people. By 1850, 36 percent of New England's population lived in cities of over 10,000. By 1860, the number of cities with populations of over 25,000 had tripled, and 37 percent of the nation's individuals lived in them.[2] In these towns, women rarely had a plot of land to grow vegetables and keep chickens, so contributing to the family income meant taking in boarders, laundry, or sewing. For the poorest families there was little question of keeping wives or daughters out of the labor force. In the North, male immigrants and native- and foreign-born women competed with each other for jobs that grew ever more scarce.

Racial prejudices excluded black women from competing in the same labor markets as whites. By 1860, about half a million free Negroes lived in urban areas. Whether they lived in northern cities like Boston, Philadelphia, New York, or Cincinnati, or in the South, they tended to occupy the fringes of economic life. Excluded by their sex from skilled jobs, and harassed because of their race by even the newest immigrants, free black women normally found themselves confined to the most onerous jobs. They tended to work as washerwomen and cooks, and sometimes as seamstresses and dressmakers.

Counting all these, relatively small numbers of women actually worked for wages outside their homes in 1840. Somewhere around 2.25 percent of all females over ten years old worked in industry. At least 6 percent worked as domestics, and perhaps 1 percent as teachers or writers. Another sprinkling worked as book binders and printers. About 10 percent of all women took jobs outside their homes in 1840. Among these, most were young women who expected to spend an average of three to five years making a living before dropping out of the work force to raise a family. In 1840 single women constituted the great bulk of women wage earners. About 70 percent of those who worked hired themselves out as servants. Another 25 percent worked in manufacturing, and the remainder had a variety of jobs including teaching, nursing, typesetting, and binding books.[3]

But these figures hide important distinctions. Next to the tiny number of married women who went out to work, the number who took in work was, by contrast, large. Most married women still lived in small towns and rural areas and spent most of their time caring for household and children. For all the relative decrease in putting-out work in urban areas, untold numbers of rural women supplemented family income by selling the surplus products of their household labors and doing various kinds of putting-out work. Some continued to operate the domestic factories of their forebears, producing butter and cheese for market as well as for home use. Others competed directly with the rapidly increasing numbers of women who, living in cities, supported themselves and their families on income derived solely from the garments they sewed or the boots they bound at home. Estimates vary as to how many women relied on putting-out work as their sole support. We know of 18,000 women who braided hats in Massachusetts, and of 15,000 who bound shoes at home. Mathew Carey estimated that by 1831 the nation's four largest cities had between twelve and thirteen thousand women who worked at home. And the New York *Daily Tribune* counted the number of seamstresses who worked at home in New York City in 1845 at more than 10,000.[4]

Whether they worked inside or outside their homes, female wage earners fulfilled the hopes of the most ardent Hamiltonian. They constituted the essential core of industrial development. Although their relative proportion in manufactures declined between 1840 and 1860, women continued to be the source of cheap labor in small-goods production. In 1840, about half of the total number of workers in manufacturing, including those who worked at home, were female. So were nearly one quarter of those who worked in factories. The totals varied by region. About 65 percent of New England's industrial labor was female. But only 10 percent of southern factory workers were free white women. Some mills depended almost entirely on female workers: 85 to 90 percent of the operatives in New England textile mills were women. Shoe and hat manufacturers, in the process of centralizing their production into factories, drew on women for all the unskilled phases of their operations. Nearly all of the nation's men's clothing was made by women who sewed at home for contractors. Although the proportion of female printers was dropping, women formed the core of the book-binding trades. Areas like domestic service that had always relied heavily on women became increasingly dependent on them as men found new opportunities in industry.

Women's rewards did not reflect their importance in the industrialization process, as the hardy, who set out to demonstrate independence, quickly discovered. Louisa May Alcott began a novel in 1861 that described the rough road awaiting women. Calling it *Success* when she first started it, Alcott finally published the book twelve years later under the title *Work: A Story of Experience*. In the period of gestation, Alcott had struggled to make a living for herself, her aged parents, and her sisters. The experiences of her fictional heroine reflect her own trials. In *Work*, Christie Devon sets out to become independent through her own efforts. She runs the gamut of options offered to women, including various kinds of domestic service and sewing. Unable to make a steady living, she considers prostitution. But the horrors of an outcast life haunt her and she is driven finally to the tempting solution of suicide: "Why wear out my life struggling for the bread I have no heart to eat?" she asks despairingly.[5] Rescued at the last minute by one who had "strayed," Christie determines to seek ways of providing economic independence and dignity for women. To do so she decides to create new models of cooperative and humane work.

That was Alcott's fantasy. It remained only a distant dream for most wage-earning women. Faced with industry's new need to compete successfully in a national marketplace, they found little protection for their conditions of work in community values. In fact, the opposite happened. As women from middling to affluent families became entirely removed from a direct connection with wage work, a widening gulf stretched between them and those in the poorest jobs. This distance left wage-earning women particularly vulnerable. Its wellspring, and the core of divisions among women, was the domestic code or ideology, which held that the home required woman's moral and spiritual presence far more than her wage labor.

The domestic code reflected earlier conceptions of women as the purer sex. In its nineteenth-century incarnation the ideology was rooted in a response to competitive society and the need to preserve the home as a sanctuary. The growth of industry and urbanization had increased the number of men who worked in impersonal factories outside the immediate surroundings of home and community. Simultaneously, the old Puritan ethic which stressed morality, hard work, and the common welfare was supplemented by the ethic of laissez-faire economics, which emphasized individualism, success, and competition. The concurrent redefinition of home and family required more constricted women's roles. Men who worked hard to achieve success in the wider world would need wives who were emotionally supportive and who could manage the household competently.

For the prosperous and growing urban middle class, womanhood came to serve as the repository of the higher moral and ethical values lost in the cold business community. Among less affluent families there emerged "the concept of the home as a sanctuary or retreat, beyond the pale of the outside world, where the husband might soothe his harassed spirit and breathe fresh life into his benumbed faculties." Simultaneously, the woman became a lady. Meek and passive, modest and silent, upper- and middle-class women were expected to submit to the wills of their husbands and fathers. Piety, purity, and submissiveness became the ideal. The art of homemaking was now professionalized, with some educators arguing that women must be trained for it.[6]

At the family's center lay new notions of mothering. Because men were removed from contact with children during their lengthy and exhausting day, women assumed greater responsibility for training and supervising children. In what historian Bernard Wishy calls the reappraisal of family life that took place after 1830, motherhood rose to new heights, and children became the focus of womanly activity. Mothers were asked to give up wealth, frivolity, and fashion in order to prepare themselves for a great calling. "The mother was the obvious source of everything that would save or damn the child—the historical and spiritual destiny of America lay in her hands."[7]

In its most extreme form, the developing ideology described the female as functioning only within her special sphere. "The home was the bulwark against social disorder, "notes one historian," and woman was the creator of the home . . . she occupied a desperately necessary place as symbol and center of the one institution that prevented society from flying apart." Social order, then, "required a family structure that involved the subordination of women."[8] A popular nineteenth-century schoolbook argued, "When a woman quits her own department . . . she departs from that sphere which is assigned to her in the order of society, because she neglects her duty and leaves her own department vacant. . . ."[9] Though many strong female voices objected to the constraints on women, they received little support from the majority of middle-class women, who were persuaded that they were functioning usefully. In return for an ideology that glorified their roles and perhaps offered some power within the family, women were denied a broad range of social and economic options. Whereas for men, especially white men, the industrialization process included such potential benefits as economic mobility, freedom from some social restrictions, and occupational choice, women continued to be bound by the household and its ideological and economic constraints.

The domestic code contributed to stability by encouraging, even coercing, the male head of household to work harder in order to support his family and provide for his wife. For his wife to be earning income meant that the husband had failed. This both exacerbated her sense of dependence and helped to isolate men in an endless search for upward mobility and financial success. The idea that women should be able to stay at home—the better to mother their children— justified hard work, long hours, and economic exploitation for male workers. A New York *Post* writer in 1829 accurately summed up a prevailing attitude when he asserted that the only way to make husbands sober and industrious was to keep women dependent by means of insufficient wages.[10] This was not a hard prescription to fill, for the rise of the domestic ideology coincided with the de-skilling of women's work, which increased competition for jobs as it removed them from household to factory.

The conjunction of ideological and economic circumstances that laid the financial burden of family support at the feet of men at precisely the point when the factory system removed from women any possibility of profitable household labor had severe consequences for women. If their work in the home was to be glorified and idealized, then wage work would be judged by whether it enhanced or, mini- mally, did not detract from home roles. Idealizing the family forced women to articulate reasons for working and to formalize a sense of jobs as instruments for family survival. Self-realization, ambition, inde- pendence were nowhere to be found in the new creed. In contrast to the young women who packed their bags to go to Lowell in the 1820s with a sense of adventure as well as of their important contribution to family life, the married and unmarried women of the next genera- tion could justify wage work only by visible poverty.

Many of those who worked for a living, as well as those who spoke for workers and presumably to them, expressed an understanding, albeit ambivalent, of the domestic code. For example, in 1834 *The Man*, a paper that normally spoke for the interests of skilled workers, reprinted an article on European customs that condemned outdoor work for women. It concluded by praising American women for their "domesticity of character and occupation"—attributes the paper described as their "greatest merit."[11] The Lowell Female Labor Re- form Association's *Voice of Industry* attacked idle "ladies." Yet the paper revealed a fine concern for salvaging the domesticity of working- class women. Thus, one article reprinted from the *Farmers' and Mechanics' Ledger* urged the wealthy to acquire "habits of useful industry," while another reproduced the sermon of a prominent Boston minister which told the *Voice of Industry*'s female wage-earning readers that theirs was

> the nobler task of moulding the infant mind; it is for you to give their character to succeeding ages; it is yours to control the stormy passions of man, to inspire him with those sentiments which subdue his ferocity, and make his heart gentle and soft; it is yours to open to him the truest and purest source of happiness, and prompt him to the love of virtue and religion. A WIFE, A MOTHER! How sacred and venerable these names! What nobler objects can the most aspiring ambition propose to itself than to fulfill the duties which these relations imply![12]

As if they recognized the contradiction between these words and the lives of most of their readers, the editors of the *Voice of Industry* later modified their stance. Woman's moral sphere, while still separate, could be extended to incorporate "all the departments of society" where her "quiet influence" would do "its holy and benign work, on all that shall come within its range. . . ."[13]

The fiction published in the pages of the *Voice of Industry* confirms the degree to which models of self-sacrifice, patience, and virtue were offered to wage-earning women with little sense of contradiction. Side by side with tales of long-suffering young wives, sweetly forgiving drunken and philandering husbands—thereby reclaiming them to happiness—were articles praising the militancy of mill women. One issue recounted the story of Ally Ray, a shoemaker's daughter who by luck, ability, and earnest desire, left her working-class roots behind and made herself worthy to be the bride of a fine young man. Others included articles extolling the dignity of labor.[14]

What little evidence we have from wage-earning women reveals that women did not cease to work but that their wage work was overlain with ambiguity. Charlotte Woodward tells us that she sewed gloves secretly in her bedroom "because all society was built on the theory that men, not women, earned money, and that men alone supported the family."[15] An anonymous writer in the *Lowell Offering* recalled her first visit from the factory back to the village where she was raised. "We were prepared for a cool reception . . . nor were we in the least disappointed. They at first stood aloof from us with a look of mingled envy and contempt."[16]

And Ann Appleton, who would surely have denied that she had any prejudice against being a factory girl, breathed a nearly audible sigh of relief at avoiding the worst torments of factory life. Describing her new job as a harness knitter where she could work in an anteroom of the factory complex, she wrote to her sister that her family thought it "so much prettier for me than working in a shop or factory either. They are full as much pleased as myself. Tell Aunt Hanna and grandmother I should admire to have them come in and see me to work, for the place is as pretty as any parlor."[17] And proud as she was of earning money to support herself and to spare, she still cared sufficiently about gentility to pay an extra half-dollar a month in order to live in a place which she described as "more genteel." She defended this expense on the grounds that "I want to be as much so as I can conveniently."[18] Such perceptions existed alongside, and in tension with, struggles for better working conditions.

As these ideas about "proper roles" or domesticity for women became institutionalized in the first half of the nineteenth century, they had serious consequences for those who could not meet their rigid prescriptions. By defining the role at home as the measure of respectability, the domestic code indirectly sharpened class differences. In this period of early industrialization, more women than ever before aspired to display the attributes of the "lady"—elegant dress, servants, and the absence of an economic contribution to household maintenance. These requirements excluded from respectability most women who had to work in the paid labor force and created for them a set of perhaps unattainable aspirations centered on the family.

Together with changed working conditions, these new ideas about women's role eroded still further the promise of independence that had originally accompanied their wage labor. For immigrant women entering the United States eager and willing to work, and for free black women of the North and South, the domestic code had little immediate meaning. They sought jobs to contribute to family income. Yet the ideas embodied in the code had an enormous impact on their lives. The ideology that exalted home roles condemned the lives of those forced to undertake wage work. Sympathetic perceptions of women wage earners sacrificing for the sake of their families gave way to charges of selfishness and family neglect. So the small minority of women who continued to work for wages after their teenage years found themselves entirely without sympathetic support—almost an outcast group. Further, without the mobility incentives and training in skills offered to men, women found neither focus for their job aspirations nor protection from exploitation. For them, questions about how work could complement present and future family roles had less meaning than the fear that excessive work would doom them to lives without time for self-improvement or preparation for marriage.

Virginia Penny, author of an 1861 compilation of jobs available to women, demonstrated one consequence of the domestic ideology—

the way it restricted job possibilities. The 533 jobs she found effectively documented what Alcott set out to illustrate, and what every woman who needed to earn a living already knew. Jobs for women offered painfully little of anything but the barest sustenance. The list reveals how narrow were the options for training and preparation in a job market that largely excluded women. And it reminded women with aspirations to gentility that they could hardly expect to preserve their womanliness and earn a living as well. Even the incentive to make up such a list indicated, as Penny put it in her introduction, "the want of pursuits . . . by which women can earn a respectable livelihood."[19] Penny provides moving support for Alcott's attempts to find solutions for women's survival that did not involve engaging in a competitive battle for jobs. She demonstrates the extent to which even the protagonists of women's right to work accepted notions of femininity when she says there is a "general difference in character and habits of those engaged in various occupations and their comparative morality and intelligence."[20]

Women who wished to work discovered the economic impact of their limited choices. A study of one working-class community in New York City—the Five Points district—in 1855 reveals that from one-quarter to nearly one-third of married immigrant women there continued to earn money throughout their active years. The overwhelming majority of these women, and those of other immigrant groups, converted their skills into income for the family by sewing at home or taking in laundry. Others braided hats, made buttons, or rolled cigars. Such jobs were typical of those taken by wives in poor urban families who worked to make ends meet.

Unmarried relatives could enter domestic service—numerically by far the most important women's job and one that had also begun to change with the market economy. In the colonies, white servants had participated with the family in all household activities. Their duties tended to be general, and they normally worked alongside the housewife. By the mid-nineteenth century, servants and farm help, in the North at least, were no longer as widespread as they had been, and the character of demands on them began to change. A comfortable, but by no means affluent, northern home before the Civil War might have maintained an all-purpose servant, as well as a laundress who came weekly and a dressmaker who appeared seasonally for several weeks at a time. The more affluent might also have a cook, a hired hand for the vegetable garden, a scullery maid, and perhaps even a lady's maid. In the South, where slavery prevailed, the number of household servants was greater. But the vast majority of households relied on a single "maid of all work." Far from being a companion in the household endeavor, the servant suffered from notions of unacceptable wage work which threw up barriers between her and her mistress. Her lot visibly deteriorated as she shouldered the work of an entire household.

The sheer drudgery involved led many women to avoid domestic jobs if they could. For an average wage of $1.00 to $1.25 per week plus board (nearly $1.00 less than an ordinary factory worker but about the same as a schoolteacher), the servant worked up to sixteen hours a day with one afternoon a week off. In New York City, where wages averaged higher than elsewhere in the East, the typical Irish servant earned $6.00 a month in the mid-1840s, while cooks and lady's maids got more. To attract women to these jobs was more or less difficult, depending on economic conditions. Urban Irish, German, and black women seem to have sought such work out before the Civil War as a better-paid alternative to sewing at home. One study of mid-century Buffalo suggests that "virtually every Irish girl during adolescence spent several years as a live-in domestic." These girls began leaving home at eleven, and by the age of fourteen, 60 percent of Irish females no longer lived with their parents. German girls went into service with equal frequency, but stayed for shorter periods of time. In New York City, 25 percent of all Irish immigrant women worked as domestic servants in 1855. This figure was the highest of any immigrant group, but not as high as that for free black women— 50 percent of whom worked as domestics.

Complaints about the lack of sufficient domestic servants were endemic throughout the nineteenth century. In 1826 the New York Society for the Encouragement of Faithful Domestic Service went so far as to offer prizes for servants who stayed at their jobs. For one year's service the recipient got a Bible. For two years, she got a three-dollar cash bonus and so on up to a total of ten dollars. Yet even severe labor shortages did not end discrimination against black and Irish women who competed against each other for meager rewards.[21]

Even in this period of narrowing options, the Jacksonian spirit of egalitarianism in a competitive framework had some benefits for women. Public schools that had been closed to females in the early 1800s opened their doors to poor girls as well as boys in the 1830s. For working-class girls the schools that multiplied in the 1830s and 1840s served a dual function: they trained them to work both at home and for wages. Factory owners recognized schools as aids in training and disciplining future workers. The evidence indicates that many entrepreneurs promoted schools and cooperated fully in requiring their youthful employees, male and female, to attend them for a limited number of weeks yearly. The largest cotton mill in

Lawrence, Massachusetts, donated land for eleven schools, and the school committee, dominated by corporation executives, instructed teachers to "assiduously teach their pupils to avoid idleness, truancy, falsehood, deceit, thievery, obscenity, profanity and every other wicked and disgraceful practice."[22] Charles Storrow, the company's president, requested aid of Horace Mann in setting up a state normal school, the better to train teachers of young minds. But discipline, respect for authority, adherence to routine, and the rudiments of reading, writing, and arithmetic were essential to women's future whether at home, in the work force, or in teaching.

The benefits of education did not always extend to greater job opportunity for women. For white male workers, schools offered the promise of opportunity to get ahead. Skilled men, organized in working men's associations, recognized education as an important asset, and many working-class communities offered willing support. But the amount of education thought essential for boys was limited to reading, writing, and arithmetical skills. Most children left school before they had completed the fourth grade. Girls whose parents had no pressing need of income often stayed on. They were not, after all, expected to go out into the world to make their livings, and as long as the major function of schooling was seen as socialization, not vocational preparation, it posed no threat. Of course, colleges, and even the lyceums that offered community lectures, remained adamantly closed to females until the 1860s when the pressure of feminism opened them.

Yet the same moral code that denied the legitimacy of wage work provided justification for opening up educational institutions on the grounds that educated women made better mothers. And it also offered a rationale for women to become teachers, missionaries, and writers. Women had, of course, always taught children within the family and in small dame schools. That job remained compatible with subsequent marriage and promised to enhance a woman's moral sensibilities. For a salary of little more than a dollar a week plus board—less than a skilled factory operative earned—she could work an annual term of twelve to sixteen weeks and face idleness for the rest of the year. If she took in sewing or eked out her salary with occasional piecework, she might survive quite nicely.

The teacher's plight became less desperate as the century wore on. In the early part of the nineteenth century, schools hired women only for summer terms, when girls were most likely to be in attendance. By the 1830s and 1840s, however, the spread of compulsory public education and lengthening school terms encouraged more and more towns to employ women year-round to fill their expanding classrooms.

Although women's wages rose to between $1.50 and $2.00 per week plus board, they remained an average of one-third less than those of male teachers and so offered school boards a substantial incentive to hire women. Single women managed reasonably well on these pittances. Former mill girl Lucy Larcom wrote to her old friend Harriet Hanson Robinson in 1857, "I find no way of getting out of teaching, though I don't prefer to spend my life so. It is exceedingly pleasant here, however, considering that it is a school, and I know of no more suitable situation for an elderly maiden like myself. I have a nice room neatly furnished, which I occupy alone with my books, the best company I could ask for; I wish you could drop in and see me; you would *almost* wish yourself an old maid, I fancy."[23]

Limited as career possibilities were, even a taste of education led some women to seek more—to reject the family option entirely and to select a profession instead. But the rationale that worked for teaching failed them here. Obstacles confronted them at every turn. Midwifery, the time-honored way for women to help each other as well as to earn their keep, had by the 1820s been taken over by medical schools, and entry was now barred to women. As one Boston physician rationalized in 1828, "A female could scarce pass through the course of education requisite to prepare her as she ought to be prepared, for the practice of midwifery without destroying those moral qualities of character which are essential to the office."[24] The few women who, like Elizabeth Blackwell, struggled for admission to medical schools knowingly gave up marriage as an option. Most genteel women would not have considered nursing an acceptable job. Before the Civil War it was a haphazard occupation requiring little formal training, and its status declined as medical schools and physicians tightened their hold over available knowledge. Though the New York *Daily Tribune* argued in 1845 that nursing was "most unjustly regarded in the light of menial service," for it was a profession that "no menial, no servile nature [could] fitly occupy," daughters of middle-income parents did not choose it, and even after the war it was largely the choice of children of immigrants.[25] Law was a closed profession. "There has been," said the *Tribune* flatly, "no female lawyer and probably will be none." Virginia Penny discouraged women from entering the field, arguing that "the noisy scenes witnessed in a courtroom are scarcely compatible with the reserve, quietude and gentleness that characterize a woman of refinement."[26]

What then remained? A woman without means and eager to retain a claim to respectability could become a governess or a companion. If she felt the call she could become a missionary. Evangelical churches had been known to arrange marriages so women could venture into foreign lands or minister to American Indians. She might try to earn her living by writing—an acceptable if somewhat risky option. In the 1830s and 1840s, women wrote sentimental fiction for the new ladies' magazines, propounding a message of love and duty that influenced American culture for generations to come. Among the best-known names, Lydia Huntley Sigourney, Sarah Josepha Hale, Fanny Fern, Louisa May Alcott managed to keep whole families together on their incomes and to enjoy unsullied reputations as well. Though Nathaniel Hawthorne derided them as "scribbling women," they generated new careers as popular fiction writers and contributors to women's magazines. The costs were sometimes high. Talented women like Emily Dickinson hid their work for fear of running afoul of propriety. Sarah Payson Willis Parton used a pseudonym—Fanny Fern—all her life. Sarah Hale, as editor of *Godey's Lady's Book*, preached the virtues of domesticity, though her own life illustrated its disadvantages. And Alcott lived a life of such exemplary virtue, supporting an entire extended family on the proceeds of her writing, that she could be forgiven for creating an occasional rebellious female protagonist.[27]

Women for whom none of these options worked could turn to prostitution. In 1859 William Sanger published a report of his research into the lives of 2,000 female prostitutes who had been incarcerated in New York's Blackwell's Island prison. The results tell us something of the kinds of women who resorted to prostitution in this period. Nearly a quarter were married women whose husbands had either deserted or mistreated them. About the same percentage had worked at some branch of the sewing trades, and almost half said they had been servants before engaging in prostitution. These figures reflect the limited employment options open to women, and they tell us something about the precarious nature of such employment. Slightly more than a quarter of those interviewed claimed they had been destitute when they became prostitutes. Another quarter suggested they had chosen the work freely. One suspects that most women drifted in and out of prostitution as economic conditions changed. Recent research into the occupational structure of Nashville, Tennessee, before the Civil War confirms this suspicion. Slave women there did work reserved for white women in northern cities. Consequently large proportions of Nashville's white women were classified as "sporting women" by census takers. Their lives cannot have been easy. A quarter of New York's population of prostitutes died annually, Sanger suggests; a young prostitute could expect to live only about four years after she entered the life.[28]

. . .

As relatively grim options discouraged all but the neediest from seeking wage work, so behavior patterns that seemed appropriate to home and family exposed women to exploitation in the work place. The belief that women belonged at home permitted employers to pay wages that were merely supplemental. Except for the early days in the New England mills, average wages never exceeded the cost of mere survival. Nor was it desirable from the perspective of employers that they should. But since survival was measured in terms of what a woman might expect to contribute to a household with other wage workers, those who were truly independent or who supported families were badly off. In 1836 the *National Laborer* estimated women's wages nationwide and in "every branch of business" at no more than $37\frac{1}{2}$ cents a day; in 1845 the New York *Tribune* calculated $2.00 a week as the wage for nondomestic labor. Since the cost of weekly board before the Civil War averaged from $1.50 to $1.75 a week, this meant that a fully employed year-round worker might have 50 cents a week for clothing, medicine, church, leisure, and savings. Even a short period of unemployment would wipe out any surplus. Average wages seem to have remained stable until the Civil War. By then the cost of weekly board in urban areas began to rise to $1.50 and $2.00 a week.[29]

Even the wages of mill operatives, which ran about $3.50 a week without board in 1855, had dropped substantially in real terms since their peak in the mid-1830s. Though women were earning as much or more in dollars, the cost of board far outstripped their wages.[30] None of this reckoning, of course, calculates the real costs of a paternalistic system. Except in the boarding mills, which employed less than half the total of cotton-mill workers, wages were often partly paid in credit at the company store; piece rates, characteristic of nearly all mill jobs, were manipulated to exact greater productivity without a comparable increase in take-home pay. Then, too, there were the distinctions between male and female wages. Until the late nineteenth century women's wages customarily ranged from one-third to half those of men. In the mills, the most highly skilled women could not earn as much as the lowest-paid man until the 1850s, when the use of men in low-paid women's jobs created some overlap. Distinctions in job categories make it difficult to compare male and female wages, but Vera Shlakman's study of Chicopee weavers gives us one instance where the two worked side by side at the same task, and women earned less than three-quarters of what the men received. Distinctions were even more dramatic in paper mills, where men earned $3.00 for every $2.00 earned by women.[31]

The jumble of statistics—inaccurate, confused, and selective as they are—reveals at least that from 1820, when one can first speak of industrial labor for women in a recognizable sense, to the onset of the Civil War, material conditions of women working for wages declined substantially. A relative decrease in job opportunities in home work and factory work compared to the numbers of women looking for jobs, coupled with increased urbanization, had created a competitive labor supply and reduced women's wages to the point where few could survive on their earnings alone.

The changed position of the stereotypical New England farmer's daughter reflects some of the problems of declining conditions. With roots in the soil and a family willing, if not comfortably able, to sustain her, she was not normally faced with destitution. But she did face a loss of independence. After 1837, at about the time that real wages in the mills began to decline, employers increased pressure to produce more by lengthening the working day and multiplying the number of looms to be tended or spindles to be watched. Harriet Hanson Robinson could recall the early 1830s as a period when cotton-mill operatives who tended one or two looms had time to spare. By the 1850s, technological improvement enabled workers to supervise four to six looms, under intense pressure. Women in the mills who might have worked a reasonably paced eleven or twelve hours daily in 1834 toiled through a rapid and insistent thirteen-and-a-half hour day by 1850. And though public pressure and workers' petitions reduced these hours to eleven by the mid-1850s, cuts in price and machine speedup eliminated whatever gain workers might have had.

Deteriorating conditions challenged the compromise that had enabled women to enter the mills in the first place. For if the mills, as some argued, stifled opportunity and intellectual growth and broke down health and spirit, then they no longer served to prepare women for family work. Instead they threatened to produce a factory population that replicated the dreaded English degradation. Others, however, still perceived the mills as places to earn money quickly and in relative abundance so as to allow them to return to their families or to set up their own households. Even rapidly declining wages still outstripped those available elsewhere. And hard work and long hours seemed a reasonable trade-off.

The conflict broke into the open around mid-1845 when the *Voice of Industry* became the instrument of the Lowell Female Labor Reform Association, formed by mill workers to fight for the ten-hour day. Petitions and testimony before the Massachusetts Industrial Commission illustrate the tension. Those who favored a legal maximum of ten hours of work daily argued that America's factories demanded more hours of labor than anywhere else in the world: "A woman in a factory in New England worked one hour and some minutes longer, every day in the year than a woman in a British factory."[32] An average of twelve hours a day year round, ranging to thirteen and a half in the spring, was common. Advocates of a ten-hour day rested their case on a telling point: American women, like their British counterparts, were becoming physically degenerate. Long hours and the "bad effect of close and heated air . . . must in time affect the physical condition of the people of New England. To say nothing of the intellectual degeneracy which must necessarily result from the want of mental recreation and cultivation."[33] Sarah Bagley, editor of the *Voice of Industry* and a leader of the Female Labor Reform Association, caught the ultimate contradiction. The degradation of labor, she argued, challenged the basis of republican institutions. "At one time," she wrote, "they tell us that our 'free institutions' are based upon the *virtue* and *intelligence* of the American people, and the influence of the mother, form and mould the man—and the next breath, that the way to make the mothers of the next generation virtuous is to enclose them within the brick walls of a cotton mill from twelve and a half to thirteen and a half hours per day. How is it about the intelligence? Do not overlook that part in the premises lest you come to wrong conclusions."[34]

But the opposing argument was equally powerful. To many women more hours of work meant higher wages. Since most women assumed their work lives to be temporary, their object was to work as much as possible in the few years at their disposal. Clementine Averill, a mill girl, stated this position succinctly when she responded to criticism of long hours in 1846. "We never work more than twelve and a half hours a day; the majority would not be willing to work less, if their earnings were less, as they only intend working a few years, and they wish to make all they can while here, for they have only one object in view."[35] The *Voice of Industry* emphatically disagreed.

The ten-hours campaign bore yet an additional burden. On its back women laid the argument for the dignity of labor itself. What mill women meant by dignity was the possibility of elevating themselves, exercising some sense of creative intelligence over their work. And this was precisely what the ten-hour day promised to do. As one mill poet wrote:

> Those laws which elevate mankind
> Command us to enlarge our minds,
> To cultivate our mental powers,
> And thus endow these minds of ours.

TIME, for this is all we claim,
Time we struggle to obtain,
Then in the name of freedom rise,
Nor rest, till we obtain the prize.[36]

Sarah Bagley said it more directly. "The great and leading object of the 10 hour movement," she editorialized for the Female Labor Reform Association, "is to give the laborer more time to attend to his or her mental, moral and physical wants—to cultivate and bring out the hidden treasures of the inner being—to subdue the low, the animal nature, and elevate, ennoble and perfect the good, the true and the God-like which dwells in all the children of the common Parent."[37]

If ten hours could not be achieved, even an extra ten minutes would help. When, in April of 1847, Lowell mills increased the periods allowed for breakfasts and dinners from thirty-five to forty-five minutes each, the *Voice of Industry* inveighed against women who returned early from their rest and stood waiting for the gates to open. "Why are they not in their rooms storing their minds with useful practical knowledge which shall fit them high [sic] and noble stations in the moral and intellectual world? . . . Awake and resolve from this time forth to *live*, not merely to gain a bare subsistence, but to live for nobler, worthier objects."[38]

In support of their requests for shorter hours, factory operatives composed tracts, and thousands of operatives signed petitions which they deposited on the desks of Massachusetts legislators. These petitions, often passionately phrased, demanded a legislated limit on the number of hours men and women could work in the mills. "We the undersigned, peaceable, industrious and hardworking men and women of Lowell," went the petition signed by 2,000 mostly female operatives, "confined in unhealthy apartments, exposed to the poisonous contagion of air, vegetable, animal and mineral properties, debarred from proper Physical Exercise, Mental discipline, and Mastication cruelly limited, and thereby hastening us on through pain, disease and privation, down to a premature grave, pray the legislature to institute a ten-hour working day in all the factories of the state."[39]

Mill women understood implicitly that the contradiction between endless hours of labor and the ability to fulfill effectively the wife/mother role could prove fatal to their last remaining aspiration for independence. If they wished to work at all, they needed to preserve conditions compatible with dignity. Already their roles were under severe attack. A public meeting in Philadelphia urged that a "wholesome law should be passed, which will prevent the taking of females as apprentices in factories, as the future welfare of our country depends much upon the virtue and intelligence of the female character."[40] The

Voice of Industry was clearly defensive. It quoted an editorial from the *Lowell Offering*: "Whence originated the idea that it was derogatory to a lady's dignity, or a blot upon female character to labor? And who was the first to say sneeringly, 'Oh she works for a Living.' Surely such ideas and expressions ought not to grow upon republican soil."[41]

Paradoxically, it was out of the desire to preserve what was best about the conditions under which women labored—dignity, human concerns, and intellectual life—that mill women isolated themselves from the incoming Irish toward the end of the decade. Commenting on the Chicopee mills in 1852, one Massachusetts paper observed that "foreign girls have been employed in such numbers that what American girls are employed there experience considerable difficulty in finding society among their workmates congenial to their tastes and feelings."[42] Already squeezed by falling wages and demands for increased productivity, they saw immigrant Irish men and women as threats to their dignity and status. Mill women campaigned actively for abolition and feelingly compared their own condition with that of the southern slave. Yet they refused to see the incoming Irish as potential allies. "If they have *black* slaves, have we not white ones?" asked one operative, while another condemned slavery in all its forms:

> Behold it on the Southern plaine!
> Go View it o'er the Eastern main!
> From Russia's serfs oppressed most vile
> To the servile sons of Erin's isle.[43]

Distinctions among workers formalized what was rapidly becoming a segmented work force. A labor market that had enabled mill women to move easily from job to job in the 1820s and 1830s now constricted, creating sharp distinctions among jobs and who would hold them. Boarding houses, formerly bastions of morality, began to house men and women, Irish and native-born. Living and working conditions that no longer met the requirements of Yankee girls undermined the homogeneity and solidarity of mill women. In effect, the restrictive ideas held by Yankee girls about jobs for women made the deteriorating conditions of wage work harder to bear and created divisions within the work force that made unity all but impossible. These divisions reinforced and recapitulated those between women in and out of the work force. For the Irish this meant assignment to jobs at the bottom of the economic scale.

Those who gravitated toward the mill towns filled jobs vacated by New England women and faced barriers to upward mobility. The mills hired Irish males as well as females in the least skilled jobs at the lowest feasible wages. From 15 to 20 percent of textile operatives were males, and for the first time they worked alongside women tending power looms. The introduction in the 1850s of the spinning mule—a machine that required physical strength and replaced the widely used jenny—encouraged the hiring of more males.

By the mid-1850s, an overwhelmingly native-born mill population had been replaced. In 1840, only 2 percent of the cotton workers at one Chicopee mill were Irish. Sixty percent were Irish by 1858. In 1852, half of all factory operatives in New England mills were already foreign-born.[44] Given an alternative labor supply, mill owners' pretensions to morality swiftly disappeared. Some operatives, refusing to acknowledge the economics behind this transition, continued to believe as late as 1849 that corporation owners would raise wages so as to attract once more "the sort of girl who had made the industry what it was."[45] Skeptics felt that the mills had lost the respect of the community because standards of morality and the old spirit of mutual surveillance had declined. Caroline Ware, historian of the textile industry, assesses the position of the employers: "Necessity had forced them to gain and hold the respect of the community in order to attract the requisite workers and they were only too eager to be relieved of that necessity by the advent of a class of labor which had no standing in the community and no prejudice against mill-work."[46] Native-born women simply stopped applying for jobs.

To the extent that the boarding house had helped to maintain illusions of gentility and a supportive atmosphere, it too disintegrated. Some mills continued to build houses for employees, and others, particularly in the new mill towns in the South, enforced rules about church attendance or contributed uplifting books to libraries. Adjusting their brand of morality to suit the circumstances, Graniteville, South Carolina, mill owners in 1855 described themselves as "pioneers in developing the real character of the poor people of South Carolina. Graniteville is truly the home of the poor widow and helpless children, or for a family brought to ruin by a drunken, worthless father. Here they meet with protection, are educated free of charge, and brought up to habits of industry under the care of intelligent men."[47] For the most part, however, rigid control gave way to less severe discipline, unenforced rules, and houses wholly owned and operated by townspeople or corporations without any pretense of morality.[48]

The changes in the social groups from which labor was drawn stigmatized the entire community of workers. Without the moral justification of preparing for family service, factory jobs tumbled to the ranks of other jobs. An 1847 novel indicates the end of the favorable climate of opinion. In A. I. Cummings's *Factory Girl*, two dashing young men spy mill operatives Calliste and Louisa in church and the following conversation ensues:

> "Who were those two young ladies that I pointed out to you at church today? . . ."
>
> "O, they were only factory girls." . . .
>
> "*Factory Girls* did you say? Had you said birds of paradise, or angels, you would have so much astonished me. . . . By the way are you acquainted with them, Alfred?"
>
> "Acquainted with *factory girls*? What do you ask me such a question for? Do you suppose that I would disgrace my character by associating with that class? Not I, unless it were for a little fun or a——— conquest."[49]

These comments reflect the harsh poverty into which some workers had already sunk as well as prejudices against factory workers in general. Some clues point to how close even those fully employed were to destitution. In January 1860 the Pemberton mill, a large cotton textile manufacturing establishment on the Merrimack River near Lawrence, Massachusetts, collapsed, killing 88 people and injuring a large number of the remaining 600 employees. The records of the relief committee formed by the New England Society for the Promotion of Manufactures to take care of the physical suffering graphically depict the thin line between pauperism and poverty that existed for employees. Fully employed people were reported as having left their families destitute "with nothing to eat." One woman, self-supporting, was described as "entirely destitute." Another was said to owe "for her board and her boarding mistress is unwilling to keep her as she is out of work."[50] Many were given provisions; some could not look for work because their only clothes had been lost in the collapse.[51]

Seamstresses who had begun complaining in the 1820s and 1830s that they could no longer earn enough to sustain life at the low prices they were paid had to work even harder for their pittance by the 1840s. In 1845, the New York *Daily Tribune* estimated that there were probably about twice as many women seeking work as seamstresses "as would find employment at fair wages." These 10,000 women, the *Tribune* concluded, constituted an oversupply of workers who could not possibly earn enough to keep themselves alive. "One and a half to two dollars per week," it declared, "is represented as the average recompense of good work-women engaged at plain sewing, and there are very many who cannot, by faith and diligence, earn more than a dollar a week."[52] The sewing machine, introduced in the 1850s, far from lightening the seamstresses' load increased pressure to produce

more. The machine encouraged centralization into small shops where
work could be routinized and efficiently distributed. Seamstresses faced
continual unemployment: cycles of harsh overwork followed by idleness. Their problems, which had seemed unique in the 1830s, now
emerged as the pattern of existence for all wage-earning women. And
a literature of sentimental poetry developed to expose their martyrdom.
The following poem from Edward Zane Carroll Judson's *Mysteries
and Miseries of New York*, published in 1849, is typical:

> Wan and Weary—sick and cheerless,
>   By a feeble taper's light,
> Sat and sang the never-tearless,
>   At the dreary dead of night;
>   The burden of her lay
>   Was work, work away
>   Thro' the night and day
>   Was work, work away.
>
> We are many in the city
>   Who the weary needle ply;
> None to aid and few to pity
>   Tho' we sicken down and die;
>   But tis work, work away
>   By night and by day
>   Oh, 'tis work, work away
>   We've no time to pray.
>
> Work we ever—pay is scanty
>   Scarce enough to gain us bread;
> Starving in the midst of plenty,
>   Better far we all were dead!
>   For 'tis work, work away
>   By night and by day
>   Oh, 'tis work, work away
>   We've no time to play.
>
> Hearts are breaking—souls are sinking
>   'Neath the heavy load they bear,
> Yet live *Christians* never thinking
>   What our many sorrows are,
>   While we work, work away
>   By night and by day,
>   While we work, work away
>   With scarce time to pray![53]

Though Harriet Hanson Robinson remembered no physical abuse
in the mills, it was frequently reported and drew some comment as

early as the 1830s. *The Man,* a labor paper, published a poem in 1834 that described an overseer's cruel torture of a sick operative:

> And with his thong he beat her
> And cursed her as she wept.[54]

And a Pennsylvania labor paper recorded the testimony of an operative who declared she had "seen poor innocent females not only 'docked' of a half day's wages for going to work a few minutes after set time, but beat over the shoulder by a rope with knots on the end, until their backs were black and blue; and if they left on that account they would be docked a week's wages."[55] Herman Melville caught the symbolic aspect of this abuse in his short story "Tartarus of Maids," published in *Harper's Magazine* in 1855. The virginal women he describes, clothed in white and innocent of all wrongdoing, are being martyred to the cause of capitalist enterprise.

Mill work took its toll. For every Robinson and Larcom and Appleton who extolled its virtues, there were those who succumbed to its pressure. Sabrina Bennett's Aunt Melinda Edwards complained of her work in a Nashua, New Hampshire, mill: "I was so sick of it at first, I wished a factory had never been thought of. . . ."[56] She adjusted, however: "The longer I stay the better I like [sic] and I think if nothing unforeseen calls me away I shall stay here until fall." Others were not so fortunate. Lucy Davis wrote that the work was "much harder than I expected and quite new to me. After I had been there a number of days I was obliged to stay out sick but I did not mean to give it up so tried again but was obliged to give it up altogether. I have now been out about one week and am some better than when I left but not very well."[57]

As low wages and rigorous working schedules replaced the old paternalism as a means of regulating the labor force, attempts to supervise the spiritual and moral well-being of employees disappeared. For the general sense of responsibility for community welfare that characterized the early-nineteenth-century factory, the mid-century corporation substituted the competitive market, tempered by charity. When the Pemberton mill collapsed, for example, the relief committee construed its role very narrowly—a reflection of the employers' views of responsibility toward workers. It instantly "determined . . . not . . . to make compensation for losses, for where would be the end of such an undertaking, but . . . simply . . . to relieve persons and families suffering through destitution or personal injuries caused by this particular event."[58] The committee thus divided the families of the dead into three groups. To families entirely dependent on the lost member, they gave $200 to $500. To those partially dependent, they gave $100 to $200. And to those not at all dependent on the deceased member, they gave $50 to $100. Those who had lost small children on whom they might have depended for a lifetime of support were compensated least.

Another effect of the domestic code was to encourage male workers to discriminate against women. Because men required women's services at home and measured their own comfort in part by how effectively they kept their wives and daughters out of the work force, they had an incentive to keep all wives and daughters at home. And many men viewed the exploitative conditions under which women worked as impediments to improving their own working conditions. The resulting resistance to women earning wages left little room for supporting their struggle against rapidly deteriorating conditions.

Part of the problem was that men's jobs were changing. As women had found their household spinning and weaving skills transferred to factories in the 1820s and 1830s, so, by the 1840s, the factory system had spread its tentacles to the inner reaches of male crafts. This gradual de-skilling process found women competing against male immigrants for some jobs, and men struggling to keep women out of occupations once exclusively theirs. While men and women normally did not compete for the same jobs, employers often substituted one for the other in response to changing technology and labor market conditions. New England textile factories, whose workers were 90 percent female in 1828, were only 69 percent female in 1848, and that proportion was to decline even further, nationwide.[59] The ratio of Massachusetts teachers who were male had dropped from about 50 percent in 1840 to 14 percent in 1865, with the shift to women accelerating during the Civil War.[60] Women's lower pay and higher turnover rates would contribute to feminizing the profession permanently. Carpet-weaving plants, revolutionized by the invention of the Bigelow loom, began to replace male workers with women in the 1840s. With these looms, one commentator noted, "A young woman easily does the work which by the hand process, required the hard labor of three men." A disgruntled factory laborer captured the prevailing dilemma in 1846 when he wrote to the *Harbinger*, a publication of the utopian Brook Farm, that the power loom cast a pall over the prospects of his fellow male laborers. "If we are allowed to work them at all, we shall have to work at very low wages, probably at the same rate as girls."[61]

The continuing process of stereotyping jobs by sex enabled employers to play men and women off against each other, reducing wages for both. By 1865, the labor press was complaining of "a persistent effort on the part of capitalists and employers to introduce females into its various departments of labor heretofore filled by the opposite sex." Male workers feared that the price of labor would fall "to the female standard, which is generally less than one half the sum paid to men."[62] This argument was by no means new. Repeatedly in the 1830s and with growing stridency thereafter, organized men insisted that wages paid to them would be higher if women were barred from the work force. In 1836, a National Trades Union committee urged in a report that female labor be excluded from factories. After explaining that the natural responsibility and moral sensibility of women best suited them to domesticity, the report argued that female labor produced "ruinous competition . . . to male labor" whose final end would be that "the workman is discharged or reduced to a corresponding rate of wages with the female operative." The report continued:

> One thing . . . must be apparent to every reflecting female, that all her exertions are scarce sufficient to keep her alive; that the price of her labor each year is reduced, and that she in a measure stands in the way of the male when attempting to raise his prices or equalize his labor, and that her efforts to sustain herself and family are actually the same as tying a stone around the neck of her natural protector, Man, and destroying him with the weight she has brought to his assistance. This is the true and natural consequence of female labor when carried beyond the family.[63]

The solution rested, according to the *National Laborer*, in paying every man his just dues. If "every man engaged in useful labor was properly remunerated," declared the paper, "the female portion of their families would not need to leave their homes and domestic duties to earn their own subsistence. . . ."[64] Perhaps inevitably, skilled men often chose to defend their jobs and to rationalize women's labor at home by invoking their need for domestic comfort. They thus became party to the domestic code, partners in reducing women's wages and ultimately perhaps in reducing their own. Recognizing that conventional ideas about women's place locked wage-earning women into poorly paid jobs, skilled male workers nevertheless failed to respond by attacking notions of domesticity and urging fair wages for all workers. Instead they reacted defensively, citing the economic role women actually played in the nineteenth-century labor market as a reason for shutting them out of wage work altogether.

From the perspective of skilled male workers, pressure to keep women out of certain jobs was the only way of saving their own. As John Andrews and W. D. P. Bliss, historians of women's trade union activities, put it: "Where women were just beginning to enter the various trades in competition with men, they met the open opposition of men, but where women were once established as permanent factors in any given trade, the men encouraged them to organize to prevent the lowering of wage standards."[65] So, for example, a woman who applied for an office position in 1849 was refused after her potential co-workers protested, arguing that "women were physically, mentally, and emotionally unsuited for the work. . . ."[66] Waitresses tried out in a fancy club were dismissed as unsatisfactory. The National Typographical Union protested women's employment in 1854, for although some women compositors earned four or five times as much as factory operatives, they made only half of what men made. Journeymen printers walked out on strike in one shop when women were hired as typesetters. And the members of some locals signed agreements never to work with or instruct a woman.[67]

But the response to women's labor was by no means consistent. As early as the 1830s Baltimore's journeyman tailors, New York's book binders, and Massachusetts' cordwainers all encouraged their female counterparts to unite for better working conditions. The National Trades Union officially supported the striking Lowell operatives who walked out in October of 1836, requesting its members to send contributions.[68] The carpenters gave generous donations to New York's sewing women, who formed the Working Women's Protective Union in 1863. Newspapers like *The Man* and *The Workingman's Advocate* repeatedly called attention to the poor conditions of seamstresses and women in other jobs. It seems that workingmen who were not in labor unions, who were often immigrants by the 1850s, and for whom the financial contributions of wives and daughters were self-evidently necessary supported the struggles of women to improve their own conditions. The workingmen's parties and the labor reform associations of the 1840s and 1850s drew on the same consciousness of the unity of all labor that illuminated the Female Labor Reform Association. As the Association's president noted in 1846 in reporting that the male and female associations had met together, "men can do nothing without us, and we cannot do much without them."[69] In defense of the Association's purpose, "to raise the standard of influence and moral worth" for all workers, communities of workers supported women. They cheered Nashua, New Hampshire, mill workers who refused to work by candlelight in 1846. They followed women who smashed down a Pittsburgh mill gate after employers locked them out for demanding a ten-hour day.[70]

By the time the Civil War erupted, one could distinguish several segments within the female working population. Roughly half of all women would never undertake wage work at all. Of the remaining half, about two-thirds stopped working at marriage and one-third was somehow or other engaged in an endless effort to earn income. They began as servants or in factories and, married or not, continued to eke out minimal incomes supporting children and sometimes husbands off and on throughout their lives. Increasingly, these women tended to be immigrants, urban dwellers, and women classed as "degraded" before they took their first jobs. The figures can be viewed another way. The 1860 census estimated that 15 percent of all women were then engaged in paid labor. To this figure must be added those who took in boarders, worked with husbands at home or on farms, those temporarily out of the work force as a result of childbirth or family sickness, and those who simply would not admit to a census taker that they engaged in any form of paid labor. These additions would perhaps double the total number of women in the labor market. Such women accounted for about 90 percent of all domestic servants and, still, 60 percent of the textile factory operatives. They were half of the manufacturing labor force.

From the remaining 70 percent they were divided by boundaries of prosperity, charity, and self-interest. Republican virtue, once vested in the notion that women's economic contribution inside and outside the family would enhance the freedom of the nation, had utterly reversed itself. Women who had been told in 1820 that their economic independence would sustain the family discovered by 1840 that they could sustain the republic only by raising virtuous children.

Theoretically, at least, notions about the proper place of women ought to have acknowledged the tension between the need for labor and the need to maintain the household. Instead, the domestic code, combined with the chores of nineteenth-century housekeeping, succeeded fairly well in confining all but the poorest married women to their homes. The moral imperative helped to maintain social order by sustaining stable families. It kept most married women out of the labor force, assigning them to paid work at home where necessary. It relegated them to supportive roles in relation to the male work force, elaborated their consumer functions, and encouraged the development of a justifying rationale. Poor rewards and unpleasant working conditions dissuaded even the unmarried from most wage work.

To the observer, entry into the work force appeared to be naturally regulated. When, commanded by economic necessity, young women entered the wage labor force, they were expected to stay as briefly as possible, holding up to themselves an ideal of family as the primary commitment. Marriage appropriately terminated wage work. Notions of independence fought a tough battle against the harsh realities of women workers' lives, as Alcott's novel *Work* aptly demonstrates. Middle-class women saw wage-earning as a social and economic transgression, and working-class men more often than not felt threatened by the competition offered by unskilled women.

So ended even limited community protection for women whose wage labor defined them as without virtue. Necessity still drove women to seek paid work. But notions of virtue isolated them from "good" women, questioned the right of any woman to work, and ensured that work was so unattractive as to provide no temptation for any who could avoid it. As the New York *Daily Tribune* remarked, "It is a general truth that the nature of an employment exerts a very strong influence over the manners and habits and even the appearance of those engaged in it."[71] Wage work became the refuge of immigrants, the desperately poor, and those without male support. These women constituted what Douglas North has called a "non-competing wage group" of sporadically and marginally employed people who exercised a downward pull on wages and working conditions.[72] In place of the proud mill girl, women in this group became what they had never been before: objects of pity and subjects of sympathy. Women had risen to the challenge of wage work out of a proud independence; but those who continued to work did so largely out of desperate necessity.

II

The Idea of Home and Mother at Work: The Civil War to World War I

4

"Why Is It Can a Woman Not Be Virtuous If She Does Mingle with the Toilers?"

Republican virtue, once vested in independent womanhood, now rested at the family hearth. But social prescription ran afoul of everyday reality: circumstances—family and work—made it impossible for many women to rest anywhere. For wage earners the gap between prescription and reality created conflict that transcended the harsh conditions of work. A self-described working woman expressed it best in a letter she wrote in 1874. She applauded men's efforts to help women alleviate their conditions, she wrote, for "the world does not accord any privileges to women. If she was to fight for her interests, they would say how 'rough' and 'coarse' she is. Society would put her finger of scorn on her. Why is it can a woman not be virtuous if she does mingle with the toilers?" And yet this anonymous correspondent ended with a note of hope. "I think that it is among the possible that you find the virtuous," she concluded.[1] What was possible for wage-earning women in this period after the Civil War when they seemed beyond virtue? It turned out to be a fruitful time, for though the domestic code exposed women to particularly vicious forms of exploitation, the harsh conditions of their work led them to protest and to become militant in their own defense.

The Civil War provided the background against which wage-earning women began to reevaluate their condition. The war with its demands for greater productivity encouraged manufacturers to recruit females as well as to increase the intensity of labor. It accelerated the process of incorporation, loosening the last vestiges of mercantile control. Congress legislated stiff tariffs in 1863, and passed a contract labor law in 1864 that permitted employers to recruit workers overseas, underwrite their transportation costs, and bring them to the United States for jobs to which they were committed for a specified length of time. Generous land grants helped to extend a continental railroad network that integrated and made accessible a national marketplace for manufactured products.

These material aids to private industrial expansion paralleled an extension of corporate rights in the name of entrepreneurial liberty. As before the Civil War, the courts denied wage earners the right to negotiate collectively with employers, who were free to reach the best bargain they could with each worker. This notion, which forbade "conspiracies" of workers to raise their wages, did not exempt women —leaving them, as the lowest-skilled workers, in poor bargaining positions. During the war large numbers of women—contemporaries estimated about 300,000—who might otherwise never have sought jobs entered the labor market. Lacking the financial support of men who had been drafted into the army, and without industrial work experience, they were particularly vulnerable. And although the Civil War expanded job opportunities for some women—opening clerical jobs in government to them, legitimizing nursing as a profession, and dramatically increasing the number of female teachers— it did not benefit all. Elizabeth Massey's conclusion that "the war did more in four years to change [women's] economic status than had been accomplished in any preceding generation" probably applies to professional and educated women.[2] For them, new economic opportunities posed new life choices. Visions of life outside woman's restricted sphere became plausible.

The war's effect on less-skilled women was more problematic. The combination of large numbers of women seeking work and the need for rapid production yielded a particularly disorganized labor market. Wage-earning women complained bitterly of economic hardship, seeking remedies from a sympathetic public, from trade unions, and from government. Lacking the incentive of job-related upward mobility, wage-earning women fought to satisfy immediate and pressing needs. For them, bread-and-butter issues such as wages, hours, sanitary conditions, and safety regulations assumed crucial importance. Skilled males, in contrast, saw these issues as part of a larger package that involved the right to control their own jobs, resistance to new hierarchical structures in factories, and some influence over the rate of production. In this period these problems rarely touched the lives of wage-earning women. Consequently, the tactics women emphasized differed from those of their male co-workers.

In the period from the Civil War to the depression of 1873, and even after, women engaged in widespread protest and organized extensively in trade unions and production cooperatives. Such activities suggest that women did not readily understand themselves as functioning in limited spheres. And yet the way in which women attempted to alter their conditions reveals a sophisticated awareness of the degree to which wage-earning set them apart from the conventional middle-class portrait. At the same time, local government, trade unions, and women's groups became concerned that this division would create an insurmountable barrier—forever unfitting women who had worked for a living from creating harmonious families.

The first form of protest in the Civil War period was the petition in which wage-earning women asked male law-makers for protection. Petition campaigns to state legislatures and to Congress date back to the 1830s, when women first became heavily involved in the organized antislavery movement. Factory workers, most of them female, adopted the technique in the 1840s in their campaign to win a ten-hour workday. They had no success. In the 1860s, squeezed between rising wartime living costs and wages that climbed too slowly to keep pace with war-caused inflation, women resorted to petitions again.

Sewing women directed their requests to government agencies. This group of women, by 1860 the largest category working for wages outside domestic service, wanted nothing less than a restructuring of their industry. Before the war's outbreak, and early in the war, women had obtained cut fabric from government agents, usually located in supply houses called arsenals. They completed the garments at home and returned them to the agents for a fixed price. As the war progressed, subcontractors stepped into the picture, gathering goods from arsenals and distributing them to women to whom they paid cut rates, before returning the finished products to the arsenals at the prices that were initially paid to seamstresses. Subcontractors reaped hefty middlemen's profits, while seamstresses, distressed by prices that averaged less than half what they had formerly received, suffered the added indignity of repeated attempts to cheat them.[3] Subcontractors resorted to a variety of forms of chicanery. They refused to pay on time, claimed some defect in the completed work as an excuse for not paying at all, and exacted huge fines for lateness. They promised work to unsuspecting women who successfully completed an unpaid trial, then found fault with the work, taking it without payment. As the price of thread doubled during the war, they insisted that workers purchase their own.

The influx of women into the labor force during the Civil War outpaced the additional work available. The sewing machine, invented in 1845, began to replace hand sewing on cheaper-grade garments, reducing the numbers of workers required. It also attracted unskilled men into dressmaking and sectors of the garment industry formerly reserved for women, leading them to ask, in the words of one seamstress, "Why do men do women's work? It is well known that they do, and are paid double for it. While men will do our work, we will be paid badly."[4] Although the ready-made clothing industry expanded rapidly, women's share of the jobs actually declined.

If anything, conditions got worse immediately after the war. The sewing machine had initially promised to raise wages by increasing productivity, and it did open work to women on outer garments, thought to be too heavy for them to hand-sew. But in the end women did not benefit. The machine provided closer control of workers in the industry and additional opportunities for contractors to cheat them. In addition to expenses for heat and light, sewing women who worked at home now faced the cost of purchasing or renting equipment. An unscrupulous contractor might deduct weekly installments from meager wages, and then, by depriving a woman of work in the final weeks of payment, cause her to default so he could reclaim the machine and "sell" it to the next unsuspecting job applicant. Women who could not afford machines at all found themselves seeking employment in large shops where their work and their speed could be closely supervised. Contractors adjusted piece rates to take account of the operators' new speed, and by lowering the cost of the finished product, increased their markets and pocketed the profits of greater production. "You can see them in those shops," said seamstress Aurora Phelps, "seated in long rows, crowded together in a hot close atmosphere, working at piecework, 30, 40, 60, or 100 girls crowded together, working at 20 and 25 cents a day."[5]

The period of transition in this industry from 1860 to the 1880s proved particularly difficult for those who remembered a better time. Aurora Phelps described the process at a public meeting in 1869. "When I was younger, girls learned full trades, now they do not—one stitches seams, another makes button holes, and another sews on the buttons. Once girls learned to do all these, and then they learned to cut garments and carried on business."[6] The reorganized industry offered prices so low as to cause genuine distress. Sewing women complained of being paid four cents a pair for making drawers in 1869. Able to produce only five pairs in a day of hard work, their gross income, minus heat, light and thread, amounted to twenty cents a day. In a period when the cheapest room available in New York City cost about a dollar a week, that left self-supporting women nothing for food, clothing, or medicines. To survive, women lived at home, shared rooms and beds with others, and nearly starved. From Buffalo, New York, Detroit, Michigan, and Portland, Oregon, came reports describing wages barely sufficient to cover room and board.[7]

To combat the outrages of declining wages and deteriorating conditions, women asked that jobs be given directly to them instead of to contractors. Though there was little hope of legislative action, their petitions had two other purposes: they served as the focal points for meetings in which the idea of organization was aired, and they called public attention to widespread distress. A kind of consciousness-raising seems to have been characteristic of these meetings, in which one woman after another stood up to declare her grievances. The New York *Sun*, for example, described one meeting of some 300 women in November 1863: "Many of those present there related their experience. . . . During the various recitals intense interest was manifested by those present, who frequently broke out with deprecatory exclamations at the treatment some operatives received from their employers."[8] *The Revolution*, organ of Susan B. Anthony's National Woman's Suffrage Association, quoted one experienced tailoress: "I have worked from dawn to sundown, not stopping to get one mouthful of food, for twenty-five cents, I have lived on one cracker a day when I could not find work, travelling from place to place in pursuit of it." At the same meeting a Mrs. Curtis testified that she "made shirts for eight cents apiece, and by working early and late could make three in a day! Even the contractor told her he hoped she did not have to live on what he paid her."[9]

Making the hard facts evident would suffice, some women thought, "to induce good employers to raise their prices."[10] The object of several hundred working women who met in New York in 1863, for example, was said to be not to strike, but to "bring the subject of the miserable pay received by them before the public." As one woman put it, "I do not see how these grinding evils of small pay and unjust treatment from employers can be remedied except by holding up to the public gaze and reflection the names and places of business of those who are living on the tears, pain and toil of the daughters of Free America."[11] An "American Workingwoman" who wrote to *Fincher's Trades' Review* in 1864 asserted her faith in an older sense of community. Employees of every firm, she suggested, should "have a private meeting . . . and frame a petition stating our needs and necessities, and asking for an advance in the price of wages, and I believe that nine of every ten would comply with the request to the best of their ability."[12]

Other women, not so sanguine, proposed abolishing the subcontract system rather than reforming employers. The most cautious, like a group of Cincinnati sewing women who petitioned President Lincoln in 1865, asked that arsenals set aside work to be given directly to sewing women. "We are unable to sustain life for the price offered by contractors who fatten on their contracts," they wrote, requesting "that the Government . . . issue the work required directly to us, we giving ample security for the prompt and faithful execution of the work and returning the same at the time required, and in good order."[13]

To obtain aid from either federal or state governments, petitioners recognized they would have to appear not as public flouters of convention but as unfortunate bodies who lacked the opportunity to be in their own families. Playing what was perhaps a tongue-in-cheek role, they pointed out that husbands were scarce. Fathers and brothers on whom they might have depended had died in the war. Their survivors deserved higher prices. A group of Boston sewing women captured the dilemma in April 1869. Meeting in convention, they petitioned the Massachusetts State Legislature to give them homes. After years of suffering through the declining real wages of the Civil War and struggling to live on diminishing incomes, they asked for relief. The preamble to their request is as illuminating as its substance. It contained protestations of ignorance, insistence on weakness, and tearful appeals for care. But these were followed by a quite comprehensive and well-thought-out proposal for public housing that would free women from economic dependence. The language of humility and submission could not obscure an exciting new idea. They worked constantly, they argued, were deprived of honorable society and religion, and even reduced to "ruinous" avocations in order to make ends meet. They prayed the legislators to "think for us, care for us, and take counsel from your ever kind hearts to do for us better than we know how to ask." And then they presented their request:

We, nevertheless, pray your honorable body to cause to be purchased in the neighborhood of Boston, a tract of good cultivated land; and to lay out the same in suitable lots, some of half an acre, some of an acre, and so on to lots of three and five acres with a good (but the cheapest possible) house on each lot. It is our desire that these lots should be let on lease to poor working women of Boston, to whom the state would be willing to furnish rations, tools, seeds and instructions in gardening, until such time as the women would be able to raise their own food, or otherwise become self-supporting; the payment of rent to commence with the third year only, and the rent to be so graduated and so applied as purchase money, that each woman might, in a reasonable time, pay

off . . . the entire cost to the state of the lot on which she lives, with
all other necessary incidental expenses, and become the sole proprietress
of the lot, in fee simple; . . . to pass on to her female heirs in the event
of her death.[14]

The extraordinary suggestion that the state ought to provide housing
for women and their female heirs in perpetuity demanded strong,
unthreatening justification. It was not their fault, they said, that they
had no husbands. Women far outnumbered men in Massachusetts.
Nor was it strength that led them to ask for "a separate existence."
That was evidence only of "a great distress." Women "collected together in a separate village" would, they claimed, be no danger to the
community. Rather, they would "exercise a moral influence on each
other." And to prove their good intentions, they declared their willingness to withdraw their petition entirely if the legislature would
"give us good and kind husbands and suitable homes, make our
condition something distantly approximating to that of your own
wives. . . ." With more references to their weakness and humility,
the petition closed.

Predictably, the Massachusetts legislature did nothing. Yet these
women brilliantly captured the central tension of their situation: a
restraining ideology rooted in revered familial relationships forbade
effective solutions to the dilemma facing female wage workers. Having
been placed out of bounds through no fault of their own, they had
been denied women's traditional protections and left to fend for
themselves. Even before the Civil War, such women had become a
visible "underclass." Had the war not exacerbated the problem by
reducing the number of potential husbands and creating a class of
poor widows out of otherwise respectable wives, they might have
remained so indefinitely. As it was, the march of economic events revealed their predicament in the starkest light. In exposing women's
poor economic conditions, and removing the possibility of self-blame,
the Civil War gave them license to protest and to unionize. And it
gave well-intentioned men, as well as those who feared competition,
the chance to join them.[15]

Organizing for mutual benefit took many forms. Women created
their own trade unions and protective associations. Sometimes these
developed into producer cooperatives owned and managed by their
workers. Sometimes women searched for allies among male trade
unionists. At least in principle, wage-earning women seemed to espouse
the connection between marriage and withdrawal from the labor
market.

Some established their own cooperative contracting firms to circumvent middlemen and bid for work. In Brooklyn the Sewing Woman's Beneficial Association formed in November 1863 to distribute work and share profits, and Detroit's organized sewing women followed suit the next year. Boston's *Daily Evening Voice,* a labor paper, published a series of short articles in 1865 reporting attempts at cooperation in Baltimore, Chicago, and Buffalo, and encouraging Boston's women to create their own cooperative societies to bid on work to be distributed among members. New York City sewing women discussed the notion for three years, from 1865 to 1868, but the only cooperative of which we have evidence is the Sewing Machine Operators' Union, which seems to have been no more than a paper organization created by Susan B. Anthony.[16] Although most sewing cooperatives in this period had limited success, they did provide precedents for later combinations fostered by the Knights of Labor.

In other fields women had better luck. Augusta Lewis, a typographer by trade, organized a group of her New York City colleagues into Women's Typographical Union No. 1, which set up a cooperative printing establishment in 1868. Supported at first by organized feminists, the cooperative succeeded in maintaining rates and distributing profits for more than a year. It might have survived even longer had not Lewis, eager to unite with male typographers, accepted an invitation to merge her union of women into the male organization, Typographical Union No. 6. There she was quickly disillusioned. While the women respected men's strikes and refused to undercut their prices, the men denied women any job assignments at all. "We have never," Lewis declared after a year's experience, "obtained a situation that we could not have obtained had we never heard of a 'Union.' "[17]

Relatively unskilled collar workers in Troy, New York, reacted vigorously to an attempt by employers to destroy their union, founded in 1864. When employers shut them out for refusing to give up their union in 1869, they created the Laundry Union and Cooperative Collar Company. Led by a young Irish worker named Kate Mullaney, workers aimed to manufacture, launder, and iron men's shirt collars themselves. Mullaney solicited funds from women's groups and sold shares all over the East Coast. The cooperative survived for a year, then fell apart, strangled by the efforts of competing manufacturers to persuade companies outside Troy to boycott it, as well as by the timely invention of a paper collar.[18]

Cooperatives accompanied the development of new trade union structures for women. Early combinations of wage-earning women date back to the 1820s when Dover, New Hampshire, textile workers walked out on strike. Though reappearing frequently before the Civil War, these early combinations, like most men's organizations, were always ephemeral. After the war, perhaps because the activities of the first nationwide labor federation, the National Labor Union, stimulated organization and encouraged workingmen to unite, perhaps because the war had exacerbated economic problems and provided a rationale for women to work unapologetically, combinations of women multiplied. These post–Civil War women's trade unions wanted much more than higher wages for their members. They emphasized work sharing, cooperative production, and social insurance, reflecting an earlier sense of solidarity among female wage earners.

The New York *World* placed the beginning of the agitation in 1863. Before then, it reported, "the work girls . . . made little or no effort to obtain better prices. . . ."[19] After that date, numerous attempts to organize encountered all the difficulties facing unskilled and easily replaceable workers who tried to combine. Yet women achieved impressive success. In the worst-paid industries, where large numbers of unemployed women waited to step into empty shoes, organization to raise prices was nearly impossible. Recognizing that, women appealed to the public to help prevent price reductions and turned their organizations to self-help projects. New York's sewing women formed a Working Women's Union in November 1863. When it abandoned the goal of organizing women for higher wages in favor of "protective" aims—providing legal representation for those unjustly treated by employers—some of their number created yet another organization. *Fincher's Trades' Review*, in reporting the new association, quoted its recording secretary, Ellen Patterson, as saying, "We have organized to improve our social conditions as far as possible, and in no case to allow employers to reduce our wages, and lastly, as soon as we have the numbers and the funds, to have an advance of wages and shorter hours." In cities as diverse as Detroit, Chicago, San Francisco, and Baltimore, other women joined together in a variety of organizations. Some associations charged dues to be used to support groups of workers who "could ask for higher wages and refuse to work until they were paid." Others created sickness and death benefit associations or discussed ways of improving conditions. Umbrella makers, among the most exploited of women, caused a stir when they joined these activities at their inception. The Brooklyn Sewing Women's Beneficial Association created a cooperative industry that paid workers current prices and divided any profits among them. Detroit's sewing women, perhaps the most successful, organized a "protective association" in 1865, established a scale of prices, and secured the agreement of several employers to their rates.[20]

Women's limited successes appear even more impressive: in the context of ambivalent support from skilled male workers who doubted that women needed to earn wages at all. Labor papers such as *Fincher's Trades' Review*, the *Daily Evening Voice*, and the *Workingman's Advocate* acknowledged the need for women to earn wages only reluctantly. *Fincher's* bewailed the misfortunes that permitted "sisters and daughters . . . to leave home, even for congenial employment in workshops and factories. . . ." The article continued: "We shall spare no effort to check this most unnatural invasion of our firesides by which the order of nature is reversed, and women, the loveliest of God's creatures, reduced to the menial conditions of savage life, or to be esteemed as the mere serf of society."[21] Like *Fincher's*, the *Workingman's Advocate*, with an audience of skilled workers whose wives more often than not worked in their own homes, upheld the notion of "two spheres." As one article quite succinctly pointed out in 1870, "Man is and should be head of his own department, in the management of his business for the support of his family. Woman should be head in her own department, in the management of household affairs, and in the care and government of the children."[22] And it was clear that the paper subscribed to the stereotype of the personality traits that accompanied this division of roles. Woman, according to one account, was to be "sympathetic, tender, soft-voiced with faith, hope and charity templed in her soul." Her strength lay "in the very weakness of her slighter nature and more delicate frame, and the charm, subtle and sure, of a feminine manner, is a more potent spell than enchanter wove."[23]

These attitudes toward women's work—more hard-line than those that had prevailed before the war—nevertheless faced the reality of women's economic needs after the war, and of the competition induced by the larger female work force. The labor press recognized the need for women without husbands to seek work, decrying, for example, the refusal of business to employ them.

No one hesitates to give employment to a young man because of the probabilities of his entering the army. It is not so much a fear that business will suffer, as a determination to keep women in the track of domestic duties, that leads to this cruel ignoring of her necessities. To hear some very proper persons discourse upon woman's sphere and influence, one would imagine that all women are blessed with comfortable homes, having nothing to do but cultivate amiability and gladden the hearts of those to whom they are blessed by the tie of relationship.[24]

Organized men worried that employers would try to take advantage of newly available females. *Fincher's* lamented a situation where "manufacturers, contractors, and others seem to outvie each other in the invention of some new scheme by which female can take the place of male labor."[25] In self-protection, some male trade unions, like the journeymen tailors, altered their stringent refusals to work with women, resolving instead that "each and every member will make every effort necessary to induce female operatives of the trade to join this association, inasmuch as thereby the best protection is secured for ourselves as well as for the female operatives."[26]

Women took advantage of these openings to solicit male help in organizing themselves, as well as to join male organizations. And while some, like the female typographers of Women's Typographical Union No. 1, felt betrayed by their union brothers, others were luckier. Troy's collar and laundry workers maintained close ties with their relatives in the male iron molders' union, supporting them when they went out on strike and receiving support in return. Women cigar makers, excluded from the Cigar Makers' Union International in 1864, were admitted in 1867 when they demonstrated their capacity to form their own organizations independent of the skilled males. The Daughters of St. Crispin, female shoe workers who began organizing nationally in 1870, maintained close ties with the Knights of St. Crispin, who supported them in several strikes. When members of the Baltimore Daughters of St. Crispin, founded in 1871, were fired after their membership became known, their brother Knights struck in sympathy, closing down the factory and producing, in the words of the *Working-man's Advocate*, "a clear fight between Capital and Labor."[27]

Those who joined the Daughters of St. Crispin wanted above all to make sure that factory workers retained their fair share of work. As a letter from one of their members declared, they proposed to counteract "the littleness of spirit that endeavored to secure the work of the factories, in order to have it done by women outside for one half the wages now given to the operatives." The society had formed to preserve jobs at decent wages, not, its members insisted, "for higher wages, nor for the exclusion of others from working for their daily bread. . . ." What to them was clearly a case of sheer self-preservation was elevated by the *Workingman's Advocate* into an issue of principle. "Have women the right," asked the paper in reporting the strike, "to form protective associations? Woman has an indisputable right to avail herself of all honest and legitimate means to advance her interests, and protect herself against oppression in whatever form, from whatever source it may come. . . . It is her inalienable right, and in asserting it the American Daughter thus reiterates the Spirit and independence of the Mother and Sire of '76."[28]

These examples illustrate the quality of female membership in trade unions. Its impact limited by gender, a strong and purposeful stream of female unionism nevertheless represented women's particular relations to their jobs and working conditions. Sustained female activity continued through the eighties and early nineties. Figures from the Knights of Labor demonstrate its extent. The Knights, organized in 1869 as a secret society, advocated equal pay for women in 1878, and a year later voted to open their doors to women. The first female delegate, a Philadelphia shoemaker named Mary Stirling, presented herself at the 1881 convention; thereafter women joined the Knights in force. A conservative estimate might put the Knights' national membership at 500,000 at its 1886 peak. Women constituted about 10 percent of this number—a proportion only slightly less than their ranks in the industrial labor force. They organized themselves into some 200 separate assemblies of women who ranged from housewives and washwomen to farmers and factory operatives, and they joined mixed assemblies as well. Women's assemblies could constitute powerful forces. In Cincinnati, for example, a women's unit with over 1,000 members "practically controlled the shoe trade."[29]

But after 1886, when the Knights disintegrated, the proportion of women who were active unionists began to decline. By 1900 only about 2.2 percent of union members were women. The skilled craft-oriented American Federation of Labor had no interest in organizing them and expended little effort in doing so. Its neglect focuses attention by comparison on the fifteen- to twenty-year period from about 1863 to the middle of the 1880s, when organizations of women became acceptable to some male labor leaders and when women enthusiastically adopted a variety of clearly class-conscious activities.

While working women struggled to create organizations that would combine their energies into effective pressure for relief, women of the non-wage-earning classes had a different solution to the problems of female exploitation in the work force. For them the social problem appeared as the inverse of that perceived by wage-earning women: the family, not the job, was central. The issues were simple. Was it possible for women to work at the exploitative jobs available to them and still fulfill family responsibilities? Could the work situation be modified to take these family responsibilities into consideration? Could the social expectations that placed women at a disadvantaged position in the labor market be adjusted so that women could better protect themselves? Either way, the middle class saw wage work for poor women as an issue to be dealt with in terms of responsibilities to the family.

This 1869 lithograph advertising a home washing machine and wringer demonstrates the new freedom that mechanical aids offered to some women. *(Courtesy of the Library of Congress)*

Freedom from the home often meant work outside it. These women—among the first to be employed in offices—were hired by the Treasury Department to print bonds for the Civil War effort. *(Courtesy of the National Archives)*

As women's employment expanded, a series of agencies emerged to protect them from unscrupulous employers. Here lawyers for the Working Women's Protective Union hear a complaint against a sewing machine operator. Wood engraving from *Harper's Weekly*, 1874. *(Courtesy of the Library of Congress)*

Top: In a period when most women did not consider professional careers, Mrs. Juliann Jane Tillman became a preacher in the African Methodist Episcopal Church. This is from an 1844 lithograph by A. Hoffy. *(Courtesy of the Library of Congress)*

Bottom: Other women turned to teaching. The Freedmen's Industrial School in Richmond, Virginia. From a sketch by James Taylor in *Frank Leslie's Illustrated Newspaper*, September 22, 1866. *(Courtesy of the Library of Congress)*

The middle-class assumption that married wage-earning women risked neglecting their families and that single ones flirted with sin created tensions between the two groups. It illuminates a basic conceptual difference that explains why active wage earners put their best efforts into organizing and why middle-class women failed to understand the reason for this. Cooperation, petitions, organization—activity that appeared to wage-earning women and men as matters of necessity—appeared superfluous to a middle class concerned with the morality of wage work itself. Problems that translated into militance for wage-earning women appeared to the beneficent middle class to be soluble by circumscribing women's capacity to take jobs. Since most reformers viewed women's job-holding as a result of ill-luck or paternal improvidence, they hoped to save the family, and by implication the nation, from the apparent threat posed by women who worked outside the home by uplifting individual working women and protecting them from the coarsening impact of labor. For worthy widows and poor married women, they would provide work, to be done at home. For single women, they offered boarding houses, clubs, and discussion groups. Such an approach would preserve feminine sensibilities even among those who earned wages, and encourage women to retreat to the home as soon as possible.

No one recognized the impossibility of preserving womanly virtues in the midst of poverty more than the reformer. To insure that women had sufficient incomes, organized middle-class women sought to provide poor women with vocational possibilities they considered appropriate to their sphere. They therefore proposed to train women in areas like domestic service and sewing as well as to create institutions that would help them to live within their means. The efforts of middle-class women to help female wage workers thus emerged as a strange contradiction: to encourage working "girls" to maintain what respectable people called womanly virtues required reformers to protect women in the marketplace, helping them to create a more secure place without encouraging militant action on their behalf.

This response derived from a long tradition of women's self-help activities. And working as well as nonworking women responded to it initially. But its content was conditioned by the women who held the purse strings, who saw wage earners as poor creatures in need of sympathy and were concerned with preserving family roles more than with the social questions raised by labor market conditions. The difference in emphasis did not prevent working and nonworking women from uniting to provide relief for thousands of wage-earning women. Non-wage earners helped to create protective institutional structures which aimed overtly at helping wage earners cope. But they simultaneously reinforced family roles, undermining the legitimacy of labor market participation and paving the way for women to move back into families. At the same time these new institutions had no such impact on unmarried educated women who chose to work for wages, or those who could afford household help. For these special groups, the newly emerging consciousness of the effects of poverty on the family provided the impetus to carve out new careers. As we shall see later, it paved the way for an emerging group of female doctors, journalists, educators, and social activists.

The New York Working Woman's Protective Union offers the clearest example of discordance between the goals of wage-earning women and those of benevolent reformers. The organization grew out of a meeting of representatives of benevolent societies and working women called apparently on the impetus of New York *Sun* editor Moses Beach to air the grievances of sewing women who could no longer afford "the merest family necessities."[30] The meeting produced such bitter denunciations of the discrepancy between the starvation prices received for sewing and the prices at which goods were sold that, in the end, those present were invited to select delegates to another meeting the following week that would form a society to represent their interests.

The second meeting, chaired by Daniel Walford, president of the Workingmen's Union, excluded all onlookers, including the representatives of reform societies, leaving the business of the meeting to fifty-three wage-earning women. They promptly voted to name the new organization "The Workingwomen's Union" and selected a committee of five to draft a constitution. The first version of this document, presented to a meeting on November 24, opened membership in the Workingwomen's Union to "every working woman of good character, other than those employed in household service." The organization would aim for "wages proportioned to the cost of living, and for such shortening of the hours as is due to health and the requirements of household affairs." This draft vested all legislative power in a Board of Delegates—elected by and representing each shop. It passed unanimously.

But representatives of the benevolent societies were not happy. Claiming an insufficient number of authorized delegates, the meeting's acting chairman, a proprietor of the *National Police Gazette*, suggested that the draft be referred to a committee of "Presidents of the Societies" and "other gentlemen" who had contributed to WWPU funds. This second committee, which included only two union representatives, returned on December 16 with a draft that effectively altered the character of the incipient organization. The committee's report is worth quoting at length:

> The general conclusion to which the committee unanimously arrived was, that the difficulties in the way of organizing and carrying on an association to be managed and controlled among yourselves exclusively, were so great as would seriously impair the usefulness of the Union to those who most needed the fostering care. They believed that your wish was, like theirs, to effect the greatest possible good, and this, they are convinced, will be best accomplished by placing the care and management of the Union in the hands of those who, next to yourselves, will feel the deepest interest in its success, and who, by larger experience in business affairs, are better qualified to direct its operations.
>
> For these reasons, they recommend that the name of your Union be changed to "The Working Women's Protective Union" and that its membership and management, with the assistance of a co-operating Advisory Council, be confined to those by whom the funds for its support are mainly contributed, in accordance with the annexed Preamble and Constitution.

The constitution of the new WWPU granted to every working woman, except household servants, "the benefits of the Association and reserved membership and decision-making power to those who contributed $25 or more." The representative board of delegates had disappeared, reduced to a twelve-member advisory council of working women.[31]

The organization that emerged spread to every major industrial city and remained active until 1894. Although its constitution still offered higher wages and shorter hours as goals, in practice the WWPU focused on providing legal services for women victimized by the "frauds and impositions of unscrupulous employers," an employment bureau, and a commitment to expand women's jobs into additional "departments of labor."[32] Some local protective unions built shelters and boarding houses for women. Over its lifespan, the New York WWPU collected thousands of dollars in unpaid wages of from 50 cents to $300 per person and placed 1,500 to 2,000 women in jobs each year. "We do not give shelter, and we do not give charity," said its superintendent in 1883. "We furnish employment and we furnish advice and protection and open, as far as we can, avenues of labor to women."[33] By preventing women from turning to prostitution, the WWPU aimed to protect "women's purity and honor." Women were encouraged to place themselves under the fostering care of "protective" unions, instead of acting for themselves. The demise of the WWPU in 1894 coincided with the start of more active attempts by benevolent women to intervene in the work process. But even before that happened dozens of other organizations with similar aims helped to undermine the indigenous protests of women wage-earners and to reinforce societal assumptions about their home roles.

One such organization was the Working Girls' Society, which catered to a group economically better off than the one that appealed to the WWPU. Grace Hoadley Dodge founded the first Working Girls' Society in New York City in 1885. Dodge, daughter of an old New York family with a long tradition of humanitarian concern, had originally thought to bring factory girls together for fellowship and discussion in 1881. She described the Society later as a place where working girls could "have a good, useful time in the evening."[34] In fact, it and the clubs it spawned in the ten years of its glory were much more.

The societies seem to epitomize the approach of middle-class women to working-class "girls." Afraid that the "girls" would be led astray and into bad companionship or corrupting ideas, they resolved to provide an alternate family. Grace Dodge called the New York Society a "home to all its members," hiding a contempt for the real homes from which most members came.[35] The Society offered an alternative, she argued, to girls sitting at home "in morbid despondency, feeling forsaken, lonely, sad." Working girls had tired, cross mothers, absent or exacting fathers, fretful and trying younger siblings. In contrast, the Society would provide a place where the lessons of thrift and self-reliance through cooperative endeavor could be absorbed, where girls might learn useful household skills, and where good taste and morality could be discussed and absorbed. A manual of advice to those starting clubs cautioned patience and a slow pace. "Remember that rude, vulgar, irritating, disreputable habits, uncorrected during childhood and youth, will need very patient and continual correction before we can see the manners of the working girl become refined, polite, unselfish and thoughtful for others."[36] Discipline and order were essential. Constructive leisure, intelligent discussion, good companionship formed the outward aspects of club activities. But internally, club officers—middle-class supporters and wage-earning members—carefully checked the morality of new members. They placed applicants on trial, checking their living circumstances before admission. While democratic forms led members to feel that they controlled their club's activities, the reality smacked more of manipulation in the interests of inducing in wage-workers ladylike behavior. Language, dress, and culture were carefully watched and reprimands issued to those who did not comply.

Founders anticipated the highest results. Mary White Ovington, later to help start the National Association for the Advancement of Colored People, put it plainly in 1900. The most useful function of

the club was "character building." Club members learned "to maintain a high standard of honor and purity. They are likely to be severe
on the girl who cheats or is dishonest; if she goes astray she is no
longer one of their members."[37] Dodge herself best expressed the
fundamental assumption of the working girls' societies. "The whole
movement," she argued, "shows the true advancement of women—not
desirous for man's work or place, but remaining where circumstances
have placed them, and only anxious to make the best of these circumstances by developing and enlarging the power God has given them."[38]
Here was the doctrine of submission in a guise that insured against
such radical notions as cooperation and trade unionism. The type of
girl attracted by the clubs, in Dodge's own words, "is eager to cooperate with women of leisure in movements where individualism is
cherished, and clubs are governed by democratic rules."[39]

But members did not always believe in the prevailing power of
individual solutions. Increasingly they chose to discuss trade union
matters and the great socioeconomic issues of the day. Slowly Dodge
lost control over the content of discussions, and in time she withdrew.
Yet the influence of these clubs is not to be underrated. In the twelve-
year period in which they thrived, the clubs attracted thousands of
members. New York City alone had eighteen centers with a total of
9,000 women in weekly attendance.[40] In their prime, they fostered
genteel values, modest dress, and behavior designed to encourage
women to aspire to home roles. In so doing, they inhibited self-directed
organization among some women, substituting home-oriented interests
for job-related activity.

Boston's Women's Educational and Industrial Union encountered
similar resistance until it decided to change direction. Founded in
1877 to explore vocational opportunities for poor young girls and to
locate jobs for them, it initially offered classes in domestic service,
waitressing, sewing, and other women's jobs. A school for domestic
servants and one for waitresses proved to be dismal failures, avoided
by those for whom they were designed. To attract people to its school
for domestic service, for example, the WEIU put itself into an impossible position. It offered an eight-month course which included a
three-month paid apprenticeship out of which the aspiring servant
was expected to earn enough to pay for her remaining tuition and
board. Students sent to the school by well-meaning employers quickly
found themselves able to command good pay and sought new jobs
at the course's end. Others used the program as a springboard for good
jobs and refused to finish the course at all. The women wanted what
the WEIU was not yet prepared to offer—access to higher incomes.
Partly as a result, the WEIU turned its attention from the poorest to

those on the next rung of the economic ladder. A program of classes for department store salespeople proved enormously successful with employers, who released their workers for a few hours once each week for up to ten weeks. In return they got employees with greater discipline, higher motivation, and, presumably, some loyalty to their employer. But only when the WEIU began to focus on college students was its future assured. A program of lectures and pamphlets for college graduates in the 1900s spoke directly to the vocational aspirations of women then being sought in the labor market.

The different world views of working-class and middle-class women, implicit in the successes as well as the failures of societies funded by the middle class to help the poor, emerged explicitly where the middle-class group consisted of radicals with nontraditional perceptions of women's roles. In such instances, which occur from 1868 through the first World War, non-wage-earning women wanted to focus struggle around gender-related issues, while wage earners insisted on the primacy of economics. (The disagreement forecasts the split in the 1970s women's movement between those who held race primary and those who believed political activity should emphasize the disabilities shared by all women.) One dramatic example will illustrate how class issues divided women from each other even when they agreed on the desirability of wage work. In the late 1860s, one wing of the women's rights movement, under the leadership of Susan B. Anthony, tried to win working-class women to the cause of suffrage by demonstrating its understanding of the interests of wage earners. With a small group of active suffragists, Anthony founded the Working Woman's Association in 1868. In contrast to most helping groups whose main interest lay in preserving family life, the object of the WWA was the amelioration of working conditions and elevation of those who worked for a living.

From the beginning, the suffragists, middle-class non-wage-earners for the most part, believed that the ballot was essential to this end. And from the beginning the wage earners in the group expressed their sense that there were other causes besides lack of the vote for the degradation of female wage earners. Augusta Lewis, already a moving force among New York's female typographers, articulated two such causes at the Association's second meeting in 1868. Women's lack of skills and men's need to support families, she argued, accounted for differential pay to men and women. Like her colleagues who had voted to take the word "suffrage" out of the Association's name, she refused to make the struggle for the ballot a priority. Emily Peers, a trained compositor who earned the comfortable salary of twenty dollars a week as a forewoman on a New York weekly newspaper, waxed eloquent. Speaking for what she called "my sisters in toil as well as sex," she declared, "I have but little faith in the ballot as a remedy for what we complain of. . . ." Though she acknowledged that the ballot might achieve some alteration in the law, still "custom, more tyrannical than law, would remain, and once possessed of the ballot, a moral force—a woman's truer weapon, would, I fear, be lost."[41]

Peers's faith in "moral force" even in the face of decades of past experience derives from the traditional stance of skilled workers. In 1868 many skilled women, like skilled men, still believed their place in society entitled them to certain job privileges. For women, the notion of a protected place derived additional support from the analogy of the special sphere of the Victorian lady. Unlike radical women such as Mother Jones, who later opposed the ballot on the grounds that the whole economy required reordering, Peers believed that custom, which shaped class relations, protected individuals from irrational acts by their employers. Legislation might attempt to attack problems, but only an appeal to public sensibility could alter woman's economic place. Hers was a vestigial notion—reminiscent of the sense of social place held by groups of workingmen in the fifties, that led them to believe that workers were bound to their employers in a common pact. But it was belied by the experience of most working women in the post–Civil War years. At the same meeting, several of the women compositors argued with Alexander Troup, president of Typographical Union No. 6, over the union's failure to admit women to its ranks. In the end, the women agreed to set up a cooperative society which would regulate its own prices and run a cooperative print shop. Anthony, in contrast, argued that "the ballot alone would enable women to assert their equality and relieve the trade organizations of the opposition of cheap female labor, and bring it into organized co-operation with male labor."[42]

Differences over the ballot did not trouble the two groups of women during the early organizational struggles of the Working Women's Association. As Peers put it in a conciliatory mode, "waiving what is problematical, there is a broad common ground upon which we can stand, agreeing fully and entirely."[43] The early meetings of the WWA attracted as many as two hundred members at a time and served to bring public attention to their grievances. Within a few months, however, problems emerged. Representing Working Women's Association No. 1 at a variety of labor conferences, Anthony insisted on presenting the ballot as a major issue each time. Laboring men, even where they willingly supported equal pay for women to encourage unionization, frequently balked at the political implications of supporting women's right to vote. Since they shared the general notion that families, represented by male heads, rightly constituted the voting unit, they mistrusted those who, like Anthony, put the ballot first. Women wage earners who felt that their economic interests were aligned with those of laboring men joined them in opposing Anthony's single-minded obsession with the ballot.

An uneasy truce prevailed until Anthony blundered into sacred trade union turf in the winter of 1869. When New York's book printers went out on strike, she urged employers to use the opportunity to provide special training for women who could then act as strike-breakers. Worse, she acquiesced silently when the printer of her own paper, *The Revolution*, used several of these women during the strike. Aghast at Anthony's failure to understand rudimentary principles of labor solidarity, Typographical Union No. 6, joined by Augusta Lewis, urged the National Labor Union, meeting at its fourth annual congress, to refuse to seat Anthony. Neither she nor the Working Women's Association was a bona fide representative of labor, they argued. *The Revolution* took the occasion to editorialize bitterly: "The worst enemies of woman's suffrage will ever be the laboring classes of men."[44]

A hostile reception greeted Anthony on her return to New York from the meeting in Baltimore. Skilled wage earners shouted at her: "This association is useless and a sham, and has never done anything for working women."[45] Confronted with what one member called the Association's "lack of good results," Anthony was forced on the defensive. The Association had done a greater thing, she declared, than helping a few starving women: "It had increased the world's respect for all women workers, and thereby bettered the condition of all."[46] But the wage-earning members were not appeased. They dropped out of the organization, leaving Anthony to use the WWA as a vehicle to spread the suffrage campaign.

To assess the degree to which wage work posed a threat to the possibilities of adequate mothering, newspapers and reformers focused attention on the lives of wage-earning women. They were joined in the 1880s by government agencies. Important investigations of capital and labor appeared in 1883, 1884, 1888, 1900, 1910, 1911, and 1914. They reflected exhaustive concern about the conditions of all wage earners, especially women, examining where they lived, what they ate, how long they worked, their education, church attendance, number of children, recreation, clothing, and so on. These were only the public studies. Private groups jumped into the fray: the Women's Educational and Industrial Union, the Russell Sage Foundation for Social Research, social settlement workers, and later muckraking journalists all sought to discover why women worked for wages and how such work affected their families. The mountain of information peaked in 1910–14 when the 19-volume Senate-commissioned report on Woman and Child Wage Earners emerged. State and local surveys were superseded in 1917 when the federal government created the Women-in-Industry Service. This bureau lasted for the duration of the war, to be replaced by the Women's Bureau of the United States Department of Labor. Thereafter, information about working women would no longer be lacking. These informal and formal investigations had little impact on what women did, but they had an enormous effect on perceptions of women who worked.

Investigations quickly concluded that wage-earning women were overwhelmingly poor and single. Since the number of single women seemed to be growing, the number of female wage earners was expected to grow accordingly. The New York *Times* estimated in 1869 that about a quarter of a million young women in the eastern seaboard states could never look forward to any matrimonial alliance, because they outnumbered men by that much.[47] By 1883, one expert witness testified before the Commission on Capital and Labor of the U.S. Education and Labor Committee that since one-third of all women over twenty-one were not married, marriage was "no longer a career for women, nor a means of support for them."[48] Unmarried women threatened to undermine the family by their personal moral laxity: they might have unchaperoned contacts with men, spend money profligately, dress immodestly, or use profane language, as well as indulge in sexual liasons. And they contributed to a rising tide available for work. They thus depressed wages for all workers to the lowest possible level, depriving men of sufficient incomes to marry and creating an unending problem.

One logical solution to problems of wage-earning among women lay in removing them from the work force entirely. Women with husbands would not seek paid work, it was thought, and men with sufficient incomes would keep their wives at home. But how were women to "get husbands"? Imaginative solutions abounded. Women could migrate to the West, where potential husbands exceeded the supply of women. The editor of Boston's *Daily Evening Voice* proposed in 1865 that the state help women to leave. He knew, he said, "of no more useful object" to which the commonwealth could lend its aid than that of opening "the door of emigration to young women who are wanted for teachers, and for every other appropriate as well as domestic employment in the remote West, but who are leading anxious and useless lives in New England."[49] Women responded to such suggestions with scorn as well as with pleas for sympathy. "They cannot go to the West for want of means. As well talk of their going to the moon," said one.[50] And one petition commented, "But our mothers live here. We know not these distant places. We cannot get work where we are acquainted—how can we be certain to get it where we are not acquainted?"[51]

As anxiety about the family mounted, men were accused of neglecting their responsibilities by refusing to marry. Virginia Penny, author of the cyclopedia of women's work, argued that such men should be punished by a special tax whose proceeds would presumably be given to unmarried women.[52] Some observers blamed women. They were so busy working, argued one, that they neglected to develop the domestic skills that might attract partners.[53]

The vain hope that women would solve the low wage problem of working men by marrying persisted into the twentieth century. The Birmingham *Labor Advocate*, an American Federation of Labor–affiliated newspaper whose editor had repeatedly encouraged employers to refuse jobs to women, reported the following story in 1901. Mr. C. B. Myers, delegate to the Milwaukee Metal Polishers' and Brass Workers' Association convention, had announced that workers in one Chicago factory "successfully adopted a new method of preventing women from working in the shop. They marry the women. Mr. Myers furthermore urged upon the convention that instead of seeking to crowd women out of business, the men employed alongside of them either marry them or find good husbands for them." This, according to the editor, "is the first feasible solution that has ever been offered for one of the great problems of the day."[54]

It was tempting, in a situation of surplus labor, to blame women for their own low wages. The "greedy," it was argued, whose families could comfortably support them, undermined the wages of the "needy" who relied on work for economic sustenance. The thinly veiled condemnation of women who chose to work covered up some hostility toward this seemingly expanding group and reflected a lack of resolution over the propriety of wage work for women at all. In 1865, for example, the *Daily Evening Voice* chastised country women who sent for needlework from Boston. These women, the paper asserted, were "not in indigent circumstances, but . . . [earned] the means of freer expenditures for dress or some other darling object of ambition and pride. Such persons will work at very low rates, starvation prices even to the really poor and needy, little considering, or little regarding, the wrong which they do to their suffering sisters."[55]

Employers eagerly reiterated this argument. It was not their fault, they claimed, that wages were low—but that of women who did not "need" to work. They blamed the increasing numbers of women who would not or could not live at home for the low wages. A crowded labor market pitted women against each other in competition for jobs that were only marginally attractive. How, employers asked, could they pay higher wages or improve conditions when women were, after all, so readily available? Publicist Virginia Penny propounded this argument in two best-selling volumes. Industrial work, she wrote, purportedly reproducing the letter of a New England farmer, did not pay better because "so many women are seeking for such work that there is great competition and they underbid each other." One lock manufacturer, she wrote, admitted to her that he did not pay women better "because they compete with each other so much in the light, easy and clean branches of labor and meet competition in light work from boys."[56] Two major studies concluded that women restricted their job aspirations to a limited number of jobs, and this self-imposed restriction exerted "heavy downward pressure on wages."[57]

Notwithstanding endless government statistics demonstrating financial need, the feeling prevailed that women brought their low pay on themselves and their sisters. Thus, Carroll Wright, the United States Commissioner of Labor, said in 1888 of Buffalo's "working girls": "A large proportion will work for small pay, needing money only for dress or pleasure. This cause contributes with others to make wages low."[58] One Massachusetts official commented acidly in 1895, "Girls working, who are not obliged to do so for support, but in order to decorate themselves beyond their needs and station . . . accept an unjust compensation, and also occupy the place which another should have. I repeat . . . women are to blame for women's low wages."[59] On lesser levels, too, this notion circulated. Bessie and Marie Van Vorst, two investigators who published a volume detailing their adventures as pseudo-wage-earners in 1903, repeatedly alleged that their fellow workers were "not working to save" but "for pleasure." In one disingenuous conversation, they asked a fellow worker if she lived at home. "Yes," was the reply, "I don't have to work. I don't pay no board. My father and my brothers supports [*sic*] me and my mother. But," and her eyes twinkled, "I couldn't have the clothes I do if I didn't work."[60]

This persistent assertion deserves attention, for it buttressed a creeping suspicion that despite claims of widowhood and poverty, most women workers were no more than frivolous. If women who earned money had no justification for seeking jobs, they had little chance to elicit the sympathy of those who could ameliorate their condition. And the attack was to redirect itself against married women, who started entering the labor force in large numbers after 1900. Wage-earning women themselves rarely blamed other wage earners, although one perspicacious interviewer quoted a sewing woman to the effect that better pay was not to be had "as long as there is such competition."[61] But in the strikes and parades of this period there is no evidence that wage earners distinguished between those who worked for their survival and those who did so for "extras."

Adequate income could provide nutritious food and decent clothing. It could pay for a comfortable room and provide a place other than her bedroom where a young woman might entertain new friends. A woman with sufficient means to support herself was less prone, it was thought, to succumb to the temptations of the seducer. Income was important because it was the key, though not the only, variable in keeping women "moral"—or fit for motherhood. And morality constituted the central feature of most investigative reports.

All the reports carefully distinguished work conducive to "morality" from that which was not. "We do not hesitate to assert," wrote Carroll Wright, then director of the Massachusetts' Bureau of Labor Statistics, toward the end of his path-breaking 1884 report on the conditions of wage-earning women in Boston, "that the working girls of Boston are, as a rule, living in a moral atmosphere so far as their homes are concerned, and that they are not corrupted by their employers, and that employers do not seek to corrupt them."[62] Wright's 1888 survey of wage-earning women in large cities, conducted after he had become United States Commissioner of Labor, returned to the issue incessantly. "The moral tendencies of the Philadelphia working women are of a distinctly high order." In Richmond, "in the tobacco factories where the races are mixed, immorality is much more noticeable than elsewhere." In Indianapolis, "the moral tone of the work rooms was respectable." In Cincinnati, on the other hand, "the moral tone was low." In Chicago it was high. In Cleveland, the report asserted, "working girls are less worldly and extravagant than in larger cities, less dependent on excitement, less alert and knowing, and consequently seem slow and dull in comparison; but the slowness is respectable and the dullness good." Volume 15 of the massive nineteen-volume report *Woman and Child Wage Earners*, which began appearing in 1910, posed as its central questions: "Is the trend of modern industry dangerous to the character of woman? . . . Are her moral qualities also affected, and if so, in what manner?"[63]

Tracking down the sources of immorality beyond the temptation to stray created by low income, led investigators to a wide variety of sources. Mixing the sexes was one. "Wherever the sexes work indiscriminately together," argued the Bureau of Labor Statistics, "great laxity obtains."[64] Intermingling threatened the virtue of even the best-intentioned young ladies. "There is such an obvious impropriety," declared Robert McClelland, Secretary of the Interior, "in the mixing of the sexes within the walls of a public office that I am determined to arrest the practice."[65] Factories were even worse. Confined in close and sometimes overheated quarters with men, women were exposed to foul talk and careless behavior. "There is one thing existing in our trade that I would like to have abolished," testified a male representative of Cleveland's Cigar Makers' Union No. 17 in 1885, "and that is . . . women and men working together in one shop. That, we claim, is improper and detrimental to morality under the present system."[66]

Living conditions of wage-earning women provoked equal concern. One report blamed women's "moral condition" on the practice of taking male lodgers into already overcrowded tenement homes. For those who did not live at home there were problems of privacy and supervision to be confronted. Government reports were pleased to call these women "adrift." A woman adrift had no home: she lived in a boarding or lodging house, having neither mother nor close woman relative to enable her "to keep out of the wage earning ranks and in the ranks of the housekeeper and home maker." She had no father who would be, "in the last analysis, her support" and who "would care for her in case of illness and lack of employment."[67] One government report estimated that in seven large cities, some 16 percent of women employed in manufacturing were "adrift." Especially large concentrations could be found in Boston, and very small proportions in southern cities.

Most women adrift lived as boarders in private families, often sharing a room or a bed with another member of the household. About a third lived in boarding or lodging houses where privacy might have been greater but caring relationships probably less. The better-off—teachers, office workers, and subsidized students—lived in organized boarding houses for women, and a few lucky ones whose family wealth or professional status permitted it occupied their own homes. None of these conditions was ideal. Lonely women were said to meet and pick up men in dance halls and parks. Women who lived in boarding houses or who rented rooms from crowded families had nowhere to entertain young men. The result, according to one observer, tended either "in the direction of crushing out social intercourse, especially between the sexes, or of carrying it beyond the limit of prudence."[68]

Investigators paid equal attention to the problem of sexual misbehavior in the work place. They worried about whether women dependent on men for their jobs could resist their sexual advances. Here the department store seemed to be the main culprit. Testifying before the Commission on Industrial Relations in 1914, Benjamin

Gitlow, then an organizer for the struggling Retail Clerks' Union, claimed that "a good many girls in many department stores have got to give in to the demands in that respect of certain members, buyers, managers, and floor walkers who take advantage of girls working under them and need the jobs very badly. . . . We know of cases of girls who have got to submit to buyers if they want to hold their positions."[69] This type of situation reached its nadir when black women worked under the supervision of white men. One glass factory became the scene of such endemic sexual abuse that its managers ultimately replaced all of the young female employees with older women.[70]

Certain kinds of work might tempt women into a life of crime. Investigators, who feared the obvious temptations to steal offered by department store work, were confounded to discover that it provided less incentive to criminality than did domestic service. A United States government study undertaken in 1909–10 reported that 77.52 percent of the offenders in one sample of female criminals were in domestic or personal service—a ratio nearly twice as high as their proportions in the wage labor force in the area studied. The data were confirmed by another sample in which domestic servants made up less than 18 percent of the female wage-earning population and 60 percent of the offenders in prison.[71] The data gave special pause to those concerned with young adolescents. A study of girls between ten and fifteen years old arrested for delinquency revealed that 43.3 percent worked as domestic servants, while less than 25 percent of all girls in that age group were domestics. More than a third of these young women were said to be guilty of "immoral conduct," and they were accused of a greater than average propensity to larceny.[72] These figures challenged the notion that domestic work was "safe" for women and good training for the future. But if domestic work was not safe, then nothing was. A prison matron with twenty-years' experience offered her opinion. "Wherever I've been, we got the low grade women, the women who did the hardest and poorest paid work in the community. In the last place where I was matron there weren't any factories, and there the women all came from the poorest kind of domestic service. Here there's nothing but factories, so they come from them."[73]

The deepest fear was that wage-earning women would slip into the ultimate disgrace of prostitution. Low wages, again, seemed at fault. If women could not earn enough by dint of strenuous effort to support themselves, investigators thought, they would inevitably turn to prostitution. *The Revolution* began to argue this position late in the 1860s. And it emerged explicitly in the repeated testimony of dozens of reformers to congressional committees. "You have to give [women] a respectable means of income or else you are apt to drive them to vice," argued popular writer and suffragist Lillie Devereux Blake in 1883.[74] Reformer Helen Campbell's dramatic tales of young girls driven to sell their bodies by constant wage reductions, and cheating employers captured the public conscience. One was that of poor Rose Haggerty, the sole support of her sisters and brothers, whose employer lowered wages once too often, at last driving Rose to prostitution.[75] Few employers followed the example of New Jersey's Public Service Corporation, which was reported in 1913 to have raised its minimum wage to nine dollars per week for women and girls. The act, said a WEIU newsletter, came on the heels of an investigation determining that on a weekly wage of less than nine dollars "there could be no assurance that a girl or woman could live in moral safety. In making this increased payment the company announced its recognition of a moral obligation to pay not only a living wage but a decent living wage."[76]

Occasional clues point to concern in working-class communities about losing one's virtue under the pressure of joblessness or low pay. One young woman wrote to the New York *Sun*, "If we were paid better it would save many young girls from worse than poverty."[77] This sentiment appeared frequently in the labor press; it was summed up by a poet who wrote of the problems of living on two and a half dollars a week:

> If she sins to escape her bondage,
> Is there room for wonder then?[78]

To avoid "sin," wage-earning women insisted, they needed higher wages. A department store clerk who earned five dollars a week and claimed she was "respectable" described how her co-workers fell into bad habits:

> Some of the girls can't get along on their pay and they go wrong. You have to dress well or you can't keep your place, and there's always somebody ready to be your "friend" and put up for your clothes. Still most of the girls keep straight, though I know lots of folks think they don't, but once a girl goes wrong she goes right down hill, so we fight hard to keep ourselves right.[79]

To wage-earning women, prostitution appeared as a rational choice in a world where few opportunities for a comfortable income offered themselves. Maimie Pinzer, a prostitute, summed up her feelings in a letter to her friend and benefactor, Mrs. Fanny Quincy Howe. "I don't propose to get up at 6:30 to be at work at 8 and work in a close, stuffy room with people I despise, until dark, for $6.00 or $7.00 a week! When I could, just by phoning, spend an afternoon with some congenial person and in the end have more than a week's work could pay me."[80] Such choices, rarely understood by middle-class investigators, were apparently not infrequent among young wage-earning women. Kate Richards O'Hare, socialist and journalist, surveyed prostitutes and concluded that "most fallen women" were not poor slum women, but the "equal or superior in education and accomplishments" of other women. "The ranks of the fallen women are not recruited to any great extent from the lower stratum of the working class, but from the upper and middle class. For the most part, we found the fallen women had not been educated with any idea of ever having to earn their own living."[81] O'Hare captured some of the tensions that wage work would continue to pose for women in an industrial society. Poverty and an overcrowded home life pressed women to seek alternatives to traditional home roles. But jobs did not rescue them from oppression. And struggles to alleviate their work situations contradicted society's notion of a woman's proper role.

This concern with crime and prostitution provides clues to a much more subtle problem. The temptations to which young girls were exposed at work, as well as the less tangible effects of leaving the protected home environment, seemed to threaten all women and thus all of society. Virginia Penny put it this way in 1869: "Some people think women are unfitted for the discharge of home duties by staying in stores and factories a few years."[82] Opportunities to see the glittering world outside a deprived home were said to breed discontent, leading department store clerks for example, into a love of finery and frivolity by exposure to beautiful fabrics and fine objects. More generally, some observers thought that wage work impaired woman's maternal functions. It subjected her, in the words of journalist Flora MacDonald Thompson, "to a false system of education which mentally and morally unfits her for economic office in the family."[83] As the Birmingham *Labor Advocate* commented, "the girl who works downtown every day cannot become much of a housekeeper. Housekeeping makes housekeepers."[84]

Domestic workers, engaged in the quintessentially female occupation, disagreed among themselves as to whether this was so. Some argued that living in fine homes encouraged them to emulate the manners and domestic arrangements of their employers; others believed it discouraged them from ever trying to run a home on the limited incomes of worker husbands. One young worker expressed the opinion that "a domestic girl makes a better wife, because, having managed a home during service, she knows how to take care of her own home and is more thrifty than factory girls." Others disagreed. A store worker felt that even if domestic workers knew how to cook, "a store worker knows the value of money and how to spend it wisely; she is broader minded and more wide-awake, and will be a companion, not merely a housekeeper."[85]

Newly discovered information about the physiological effects of work sustained concerns about women leaving the home. Fatigue, excessive alcoholism, disorganization, and disruption of household activity, all problems that affected male workers as well as females, drew persistent attention when they seemed to interfere with women's household roles. These issues had been raised in the 1820s and 1830s in reference to sewing women, and again over the next decades when it became clear that textile mills were bent on deriving maximal labor from their workers. But in the post-Civil War period, the rapidly increasing number of women in the work force brought the issue of overwork to the force. A favorite argument was effectively put forth by Azel Ames, M.D. Menstrual dysfunction, uterine disorders, and insanity were said to result from overwork, routinized work, and certain body positions imposed by some work situations.[86]

Whatever the particular causes, women suffered if dependent on themselves and if they tried to combine household work with wage work. They were nearly always undernourished. Few had sufficient air, sunshine or exercise. Those who worked at sewing machines developed spinal problems, digestive disorders, and frequently consumption. Saleswomen, forced to stand from ten to twelve hours a day, got varicose veins. Textile workers sickened with brown lung disease. "No girl of 18," concluded one expert, "can without physical injury, sit or stand continuously in the most sanitary store, laundry, or factory 10 hours a day without risking her chance for future usefulness as a woman."[87] Tales abounded of heads scalped by machines, bodies burned by flying cinders, and hands mangled by untended machinery. It was said that subjecting future mothers of the race to these evils would produce, in the jargon of the day, stunted and dwarfed children.[88]

Among female wage-earners, health problems contributed to a mortality rate more than double that of non-wage-earners. Death rates of those who worked exceeded those for all men by one-third. In comparison, those who did not earn wages died at about the same rates as men.[89] Azel Ames calculated somewhat gruesomely that in Massachusetts alone, 72,727 wage-earning women had died young. "In the fullness of health and completeness of life, they would have had an opportunity of laboring for themselves, their families, and the public, in all 3,606,350 years; but the total of their labors amounted only to 1,681,125 years, leaving a loss of 1,925,224 by their premature deaths."[90]

After 1900, reformers who called attention to these problems got the support of the newly developing science of industrial medicine. Dr. Alice Hamilton, who became the first female faculty member of the Harvard Medical School in 1911, began her career by looking into the effect of industrial poisons such as lead on pregnant women. Like the reformers who used her material, she wanted to protect maternal health.

Ultimately, concern over the effects of women's work on family life would diminish in response to changing labor force and family needs. Already by the turn of the century, some women had moved to a new form of argument: the revolutionary notion that women should not only be provided the opportunity to work where necessity insisted, but that women—even wives—might choose to do so. In 1903, the editor of *Fair Play* (earlier called *Cry For Justice*), a privately published weekly paper sympathetic to labor, solicited letters from men and women on the question of whether wives should work. Traditional respondents replied in the negative. "The wife who has her own income is thereby rendered a poorer wife," said one; "feeling independent of her natural protector, she becomes more critical, less lenient to his faults and failings. . . ."[91] But in a manner prescient with meaning for the 1920s and after, some women asserted the complementary nature of the two roles. "A wife feeling that she has her own work, and her own compensation," wrote Catherine Markham, wife of poet Edward Markham, "may live a more complete life. She need not shirk any of the great natural responsibilities of the race, but she should insist upon not sinking herself into a mere convenience for posterity. Once prepared for some work outside the narrow range of housekeeping she will be a finer, saner human being—a deeper seeing, wider reaching mother and wife."[92]

For some women the issue was choice; for others, a rejection of marriage that rested on new conceptions of women's personality. One reader responded, "The young woman of today is a highly specialized individual whose tastes and abilities demand expression through some particular form of work. She is ambitious and independent. She has a growing desire for a career of her own and money which she has herself earned."[93] These arguments soon found nourishment in changing economic realities.

5

Women's Choices in an Expanding Labor Market

If a shared set of ideas regulated the external limits of women's labor force participation, individual household needs influenced the shifting labor market in any particular area or time. A variety of factors pulled and pushed women into the work force, and individual women manipulated and structured their lives in direct response to their own reference groups as well as in dim recognition of a larger social ideology.

Applied to the period up to the Civil War, a phrase like "women in the labor force" conjures up a reasonably homogenous group. Although appropriate nods must be given to incoming Irish, French-Canadian and German immigrants, the phrase reflects a wage-earning population that consisted primarily of young women of Anglo-Saxon descent, largely located in New England. After the Civil War, no mere acknowledgment of diversity will do. Ethnic and racial distinctions are at the heart of the industrial labor force. Before the Civil War, women divided themselves into those who did and those who did not leave their homes to engage in wage labor. After the war, daughters of impoverished southern farmers took their places in the urban labor force, as did black women. And genteel widows, North and South, broke through barriers that had discouraged well-educated and affluent women from seeking jobs. If reference to New England can account for 90 percent of the nation's factory women before the Civil War, now the mining towns of Appalachia, the Cumberland, and the Rockies began to play a role. A neat pattern of urban and industrial expansion from east to west shattered into explosive fragments—showering factories, offices, and opportunities over the map.

Great Lakes cities and southern ports offered dramatically different patterns of development. Each had its own mix of economic opportunities, immigrant peoples, and well-intentioned reformers.

It is tempting and sometimes important to separate the pieces out: to explore the choices made by Italians in one place, or Jews in another. This perspective provides rich data revealing the contours of individual and group choice. Yet it obscures the way the developmental interplay of forces yielded an aggregate labor force. Can we then make any general statements about how different women made hard judgments about their labor force participation?

To create a picture of women's work force patterns we need to examine first elements common to all women, then describe variations among particular communities around the periphery, placing class, race, and ethnicity within a changing tapestry of expanding opportunities and shifting household needs. The general social climate that influenced self-perception and aspiration existed alongside the more personal experiences that influenced labor market choice. To see how individual experiences added up to an identifiable pattern of labor market behavior, we need to keep firmly in mind the common background of ideas that affected even women who could not articulate their constraints. A changing set of economic realities intersected with conventional expectations of women's roles, sometimes mocking cherished beliefs, other times reinforcing them—bending here and twisting there into a pattern that we can begin to recognize.

This perspective enables us to understand divisions among women who earned wages. By taking cognizance of the interaction of Old and New World values in respect to wage-earning and family roles, it permits an understanding of dramatic changes in the attitudes of middle-class women toward work in general. Most important of all, it tells us something about an evolving labor market in which women were chosen, but in which they also chose.

The big shift in the labor force after the 1880s occurred among married women. In 1890, more than 90 percent of women over thirty-five were married, and would live most of their lives with "husbands present." That figure altered only slightly in the years after 1900, but what women did with their lives changed dramatically. Up to 1890, the vast majority of these women remained outside the paid labor force, contributing to the family economy in other ways. After that married women began to take jobs with disconcerting frequency. The pressures pushing them into wage labor accelerated. Since so many women married, even small proportional changes in their activities recast the portrait that describes labor market participation for all workers. Thus locating the pressures on married women and within families provides a way of understanding what happened to the labor force as a whole.

To begin with, women were having half as many children at the end of the nineteenth century as at its start. Aggregate figures reveal both a decline in the birth rate and a startling reduction in the number of small children for whom women cared toward the latter part of the century. Between 1860 and 1910, live births dipped by nearly one-third (to about 62 per 1,000 women). Foreign-born women tended to have more children than the native-born. Yet even within this group, live births fell by about 26 percent between 1891 and 1925. Fertility figures for black women declined as well, although their birth rates remained significantly higher than those for the white population.[1] Lower birth rates reduced the numbers of children who required care as well as the number of years women spent in child-rearing. Between 1860 and 1890 the number of children under five per 1,000 women in the population dropped by nearly a third. Women born before 1786 were likely to be sixty years old if they survived until their last child left home. Those who gave birth at the end of the nineteenth century could expect to spend ten years less than their grandmothers tending children.[2]

Given these figures it is not surprising to discover that the size of the average household shrank dramatically. In 1790, half of the population lived in households of more than five people, and more than a third lived in households of more than seven people. By 1900 less than one-third of the population lived in households of five or more persons, and only 20 percent in households of more than seven people.[3] As child-bearing years shortened by nearly half, and women's life spans lengthened, they could expect increasing years of mature life without children or partners. Some would need to find meaningful survival activity, and some would need to support themselves by finding paid work outside the household.

Technological changes accompanied changes in household composition. Production within the household continued to decline as mechanization accelerated. In rapidly expanding urban areas, bread-baking, canning, and preserving, as well as making men's clothing and undergarments, joined laundry work and candle- and soap-making as tasks that self-respecting householders readily purchased elsewhere. By 1900, the Massachusetts Bureau of Labor Statistics noted that much ordinary household work normally done inside the home could be done more cheaply outside it. The Bureau warned presciently: "How far this tendency of having housework done by outside agencies will be carried, is a disputed question, but that the tendency exists, and that it is in line with the general course of industry cannot be denied by the most conservative homemakers."[4]

But how these changes affected a particular household depended on its location and its level of affluence. Women who lived on farms had stopped weaving in the years after the Civil War but continued to make their family's clothing. To pay for cloth and for other manufactured products, they produced and sold butter, fruit, and vegetables, as well as chickens and eggs. Truck farming enabled poor black and white rural women to contribute to family needs and to purchase in return some of the products of new technology. The trade-off, limited though it was, seemed to work. The U.S. Department of Agriculture reported that though women complained of their husbands' reluctance to invest in any equipment that had no direct use on the land, wives nevertheless sought information and recommendations for items such as wacuum cleaners, washers, wringers, fireless cookers, and cream separators. As these appliances helped to reduce time spent in the home, they freed women's "time and strength, which they might turn into cash returns . . . on poultry, the dairy, or in the kitchen garden."[5] They also helped free daughters to migrate to the city for jobs.

Well-off urban dwellers benefited more immediately and more thoroughly from new household technology. In the mid–nineteenth century, some households could afford to subscribe to the new gas lines. Toward the end of the century, electricity began to replace wood and coal in affluent homes. Gas and electricity offered the potential for changing housewifery. For those who could afford them, clean-burning fuels reduced chopping and carrying, eliminated much household soot and dirt created by wood and coal fireplaces, and produced instant heat and light. Gas and electricity set the stage for refrigeration, eliminating the daily marketing trip. Late in the century, better-off families benefited from running water in the home. This replaced the well and the street pump from which women had drawn water and carried it by hand, sometimes up several flights of stairs. And finally, after the turn of the century, the oil, coal, or gas-fired furnace made hot and cold running water possible for all but the poorest homes. Individual houses with abundant energy and water provided the incentive to develop the small power motor, invented in 1889. This motor made electrically driven machinery, such as the vacuum cleaner, a reasonable alternative to household work processes long performed by hand.

Changes in washing facilities offer an example of how the life of a middle-class woman could change. When one needed to draw water, chop wood to heat it, scrub each item by hand, rinse in clear water, and then clean the ashes after, it was little wonder that those who could afford to often employed laundresses. With both housewife and laundress working, laundry took a full day. The rudimentary washing machines in use before the advent of home electricity required steam heat and huge facilities. So cumbersome were they that Catharine Beecher suggested neighborhood laundries where women could send the family wash. Even in the late nineteenth century, hand-cranked washing machine wringers and boilers were as close as the average household came to mechanical help with the laundry. Sending the family wash out to commercial laundries became a common practice for middle-class urban households between 1870 and 1910. The number of women employed in these establishments multiplied by 50 to 100 percent in each decade of those forty years, far outstripping population growth and providing a laundry worker for every 152 people in the population by 1910.[6] Thereafter the growth of laundries was offset by the development of electrically powered automatic washing machines, made possible by the small power motor, which reduced laundry for the middle class to a task that could ultimately be done in a morning of housecleaning. But even those who benefited from innovation in the years before the first World War discovered that transforming technology did not mean eliminating household work. The wash once done by two women, or sent out of the home altogether, was now done by one alone—usually the wife.[7]

To the changes effected by household technology, the expanding factory system contributed its share. The price of ready-made clothing dropped so that even women of limited means could purchase some of their family's apparel. Processed and canned foods, developed for Civil War armies, became standard household fare by the 1880s. Bread was cheaper to buy than to bake. Some crude figures reveal the rate at which the food industry expanded, as well as the paid jobs it opened up. For every 16,000 people in the population in 1870, only one woman was employed in commercial food production. By 1900, one woman for every 3,813 people earned a livelihood producing food—a proportional increase of 400 percent. And by the end of the first World War, the figure jumped to one woman out of every 1,116 persons—another rise of nearly equivalent dimensions.[8] Factory processes that removed some chores from the home, combined with new conveniences in the home, tended to alter, though not to eliminate, some of the drudgery of household work.

The effect of these changes was mixed. Because technology benefited the more affluent first, its most dramatic impact appeared in the growing middle class. Affluent households relegated some domestic chores to machinery, enabling them to reduce the amount of paid and unpaid household help. A dramatic reduction in the numbers of household servants between 1870 and 1914 reflects this tendency.[9] And yet technology was a double-edged sword. In reducing the need for domestic help, it placed the entire burden of household maintenance on the shoulders of one woman, enhancing her isolation within a private household. At the same time less need for help within the home created a reservoir of underemployed, reasonably well-educated young unmarried women whose mothers no longer required their services at home. If these women stayed out of paid labor, they did so increasingly out of respect for the social customs of their class, rather than because their work was necessary to the smooth operation of the household.

Some of these women began to search for paid work in the 1880s. Not poor or weary, they aspired to jobs out of reach of most women. In any picture of the female work force taken before 1890, these women would have been visible exceptions. Like 75 percent of wage earners, they tended to be single; unlike them, they reflected a variety of age groups and income levels. Typical wage earners supported themselves and contributed to family support as well; but no financial imperative impelled the newcomers to wage work. Their numbers increased as a growing disjuncture between the declining tasks of the affluent household and the domestic code that bade women stay inside it fostered rebellion.

The social values that dictated leisure and an absence of paid work for women in effect enforced idleness upon them. For the wealthy married woman, affluence, servants, and a decline in the birth rate could add up to boredom. Not uncommonly, such women developed neurasthenic symptoms in response. They lay abed daily, depressed and tearful, refusing to cope with household tasks. The remedy, according to a school of physicians headed by Dr. S. Weir Mitchell, was bed rest in a darkened room—a cure that was sometimes worse than the problem.[10]

But rebellion found constructive outlets as well, and in the end, these created new possibilities for remunerative work. Some women turned to education. A steady stream of daughters from well-off families fed the growing numbers of coeducational universities and the new colleges for women that opened in the 1870s and 1880s. These women demanded, and received, challenging educations. Graduation brought its own discontent. What were they now to do? They had, convention held, unfitted themselves for marriage. More than 75 percent of the generation of college women who graduated before 1900 remained single.[11] Having rejected marriage, they pushed to extend their sphere of action. Yet society made no provisions for them. Some moved hesitantly into medical schools, attending either the few medical colleges for women or struggling against the exclusionary policies of the established colleges. A few found access to new careers in anthropology and law. Many moved into settlement work or volunteered their services as social investigators. A few hardy souls earned graduate degrees in economics or politics. Like the men who had traditionally taken advantage of European universities, some fled to Europe, where it was not so difficult for a woman to complete her education.

Women who did not become pioneers in new fields could create options out of more traditional routes. Before the Civil War, women had drawn together in associations that extended the injunction to be virtuous in their homes out into the world. In defense of the slave family, they agitated to abolish slavery. To protect sexual purity, they crusaded against prostitution. After the war, women continued to join together in clubs. Some of these merely provided entertainment; others were reading and discussion groups. But many did more than hold weekly meetings. They engaged women with each other in acts of fellowship, overcoming some of the isolation of middle-class homes. They pulled women into the community and, once they were there, tended to "enlarge women's sphere of interest both for self and for communal improvement." In 1892, hundreds of small groups joined together to create the General Federation of Women's Clubs. By 1920, the Federation had nearly a million members.[12] Its goals now explicitly involved community outreach. Members asked themselves what they could do to improve the social environment. Their responses ran the gamut—from investigating sanitation and corruption to raising money for worthy causes such as building hospitals, schools, or homes for the aged.

Some brave women interpreted their social functions more broadly, reaching across class lines to become involved in the struggles of poor wage-earning women for higher wages and better working conditions. Affluent women who became involved in the trade union movement contributed to the success of working women attempting to organize themselves and revealed the common disabilities—limited vocational options, political powerlessness, and family constraints—that linked the two groups. Those who became reformers and social settlement residents investigated and exposed abuses against children and women in factories, publicizing, in consequence, the conditions on which their own leisure rested.[13]

Expanding options in education and in social activity fused with emerging concerns over urban and industrial conditions to create new jobs for middle-class women. Taking their cue from the appeal to maternal roles, women transferred the injunction to guard morality at home into a force for the country's welfare. This unimpeachable effort to extend womanly virtue by stretching helping hands to disadvantaged members of society had multifaceted consequences for women's labor market roles. At its simplest level, it legitimized women's involvement in community and political life, opening doors to social service and investigative jobs that provided the data for progressive period reformers.

Middle-class progressives relied upon expertise to rescue society from the clutches of the greedy and corrupt. Believing that legislative change would follow upon exposure of contemporary conditions, reformers required a well-trained occupational sector that could apply scientific thought to family, civic, and economic problems. In a rough way, this kind of expertise fell within the province of women, who guarded the nation's morality. In their roles as caretakers, or social housekeepers, women, better than men, could point the way to a more virtuous and rational society. So women who became reporters— like Ida Tarbell, who exposed the corruption of the Standard Oil Company of New Jersey—could be seen as acting within the womanly sphere. And suffragists like Harriot Stanton Blatch, could argue that the ballot, which would help women clean up city government, merely extended their housekeeping functions.

Additional openings for women's special expertise emerged out of the progressive analysis of economic opportunity and political democracy. Families crippled by excessive poverty, unemployment, and brutalizing work conditions, the progressives argued, could not expect to produce contributing members of society. To restore opportunity first required identifying and correcting the social sources of poverty. Women who had been involved in charities had a special role to play in shaping new legislative approaches to children and women in the family. Many of the paid jobs created to meet these social concerns went to women who had already demonstrated proficiency as volunteers in areas where men had scarcely stepped. Jobs as factory inspectors, child labor investigators, visiting nurses, and truant officers; jobs in bureaus of labor statistics and in the personnel offices of large industries now opened to women as part of their social role.

To do good required training. Eager to involve state and local government in ameliorating the worst evils of poverty, and anxious to rationalize services to the disadvantaged, women in self-sustaining organizations agitated for professionalizing the social services. They wanted trained economists to analyze the wage structure under which women worked and sociologists to investigate the conditions of family and work lives. They supported the creation of degree-granting programs in social work so that women might be properly trained to interview clients in need of direction and to develop social resources to aid them.

In a strange twist of fate, women, whose earthly mission was still defined in terms of protecting virtue and preserving morality, now found a justification for entering colleges, graduate programs, medical colleges, and law schools. Between 1890 and the first World War— the height of the progressive period—the number of women who sought professional training mushroomed. Between 1900 and 1910 the number of trained nurses multiplied sevenfold. In 1890, 1,000 women made up the sum total of trained social workers. By 1920, there were nearly 30,000. Together, teaching and nursing accounted for three-quarters of the new professionals, but the numbers in prestigious areas such as law, medicine, and science climbed too. In medicine, where women had never been welcomed, the most respected medical schools began to accept female students in the 1880s and 1890s. In these years, women often constituted more than 10 percent of a medical school class. Paradoxically, women's medical colleges, painstakingly nurtured in a period when women were excluded from most medical education, closed their doors in response to what seemed like victory. Then such coeducational institutions as Boston University and Johns Hopkins set admissions quotas for women, limiting them to around 5 percent of any class. Women had won the battle for admission, but they lost the next round of the war for equality.[14]

World War I, with its expansion of social agencies and shortages of men, enabled women to find paid work in all the professional areas. It finally destroyed residual myths that women lacked the physical stamina or intellectual prowess for the most demanding jobs. Taking advantage of the change, and symbolizing it as well, a group of women's colleges set up a Bureau of Vocational Information in New York in 1915. The Bureau, which survived until 1932, tried to find jobs for professional women and at the same time sponsored a series of lectures and seminars designed to encourage college graduates to seek out careers.[15]

By 1920 a cadre of trained and eager women had carved out a series of professional areas, many of which were loosely construed as nurturing. Most women, even professionals, still found themselves in job categories that were heavily female. Social and welfare work employed some 40,000 people by 1920. Nearly two-thirds of them were women, and that proportion was to rise. Nursing, more than 96 percent female, had become a respected profession. In 1920, 1,700 schools offered nurses's training, and they had already produced more than 144,000 graduates. In other medical fields, like physiotherapy and dental hygiene, women made up one-half or more of the workers. And women were the backbone of all the nonsupervisory aspects of education and library work.[16] As these areas expanded, opportunities for women increased enormously.

If the statistics demonstrated an improvement in the structure of job opportunities, they also indicated that women were losing the capacity for informal influence. The professionalization of such fields as medicine and social work led to tight control by professional associations with vested interests in regulating access to and standards within the professions. Women who entered them after the turn of the century had to abide by these rules. Nonprofessional women who wished to "do good" found themselves bound too—by rules not of their making that limited their capacity to provide.

Midwifery is a case in point. Midwives, the typical birth attendants of the nineteenth century, were pushed aside and derogated by the rising medical profession in mid-century, although midwifery persisted into the twentieth century as an important and valued service among immigrant and poor women who preferred to be attended by other women. When the male-dominated American Medical Association consolidated its control of hospitals and state licensing in the early part of the twentieth century, however, midwifery was virtually abolished. Women won a few scattered places in medical schools but lost control over an essential area of health care.[17]

In social work and teaching this pattern was repeated as administration and control were removed from the hands of largely female practitioners to become the nearly exclusive preserve of male bureaucrats. Librarians—who next to nurses and teachers constituted the most popular profession for women—held influential positions in small libraries and none at all in important research collections. Female teachers remained in classrooms, while males became principals and supervisors. Women were entering the professions—but the professions remained largely gender-divided.

The role of social housekeeper had job-creating implications related to the home as well. To stem what appeared to be an exodus of the "right sort" of women from the household, some women attempted to buttress the position of the home. Organized in the Home Economics Association in Lake Placid, New York, in 1899, their movement emphasized moral purpose. Where Catharine Beecher had in the mid–nineteenth century urged young women to acquire training for housewifery and impressed wives with the need for efficient kitchens in order to preserve their strength, the possibilities of training women in the care of their homes aroused in her successors a crusading zeal.

A housewife engaged in purposeful labor, argued the pioneers of home economics, would be unlikely to seek gratification outside the home. Women should therefore learn to use the time freed by advancing technology to raise their standards. They should be equipped with information and skills appropriate to an emerging consumer society. The middle-class housewife could set an example of domesticity to untutored immigrants. These lessons in "right living" could discourage radical thought, reinforce the incentive to strive for social mobility, and sustain harmony in the work place as wives passed on to their husbands the lessons of thrift and the benefits of individual achievement.

With the righteousness of those who believe they have found the truth, members of the Home Economics Association set about educating America's women. Ellen Richards and Mary Hinman Abel pioneered in research on nutrition and sanitation at home. Lillian Gilbreth and Christine Fredericks adopted "scientific management" techniques developed by the engineer Frederick Winslow Taylor. They urged housewives to analyze their tasks and reduce each to its essentials. Housewives should count their steps, observe their movements, and write down their motions in order to improve their efficiency and eliminate domestic drudgery.[18]

Whether these new approaches had any immediate impact on what most women did at home is questionable. At best, they shifted the allocation of women's time while confirming the importance of women's continuing home roles. Economist Heidi Hartman, who has studied transitions in the household in the period around the turn of the century, argues that capitalist production required supportive roles such as household maintenance and emotional sustenance from women in order to maximize men's working capacity. At the same time, the patriarchal family system determined that families would live in single-unit households, making it difficult for women to share their work. Both capitalist production and patriarchy thus contributed to perpetuating the domestic code.[19] Idealizing home roles, as the Home Economics Association did, reinforced the pattern by providing women with a new sense of importance at home.

But in the process of reinforcing domesticity, the home economics movement, like the "scribbling women" of the nineteenth century, generated a series of new careers for women. Appeals to women's roles as housekeepers sanctioned jobs in nutrition, sanitation, and the household arts. The housewife needed to understand food preparation and service in the context of new scientific discoveries. A knowledge of physiology might help. Colleges began to encourage women to study plant and animal biology as well as the science of home economics.

These new subjects legitimized college education for women, who could now argue that education would turn them into better home-makers. Beset by rising standards and new demands on their administrative skills, present and future homemakers turned to knowledge as if it were a panacea.

Proselytizing in these new areas extended the spheres of middle-class women, bringing them into closer contact with poorer women, whose lives by the turn of the century were only beginning to respond to changes in household technology. Members of social settlements—a new breed of social workers—and newly trained home economists tried to persuade poor slum dwellers of the value of good nutrition, cleanliness, and homemade clothing. Paradoxically, some women, released from the home by their privileged class position, spent their best efforts trying to convince less privileged women to perform housework more productively and child care more efficiently.

Statistical data reflect the steady rise in the number of women from groups not previously employed who began to search for jobs. In 1890 only 35.3 percent of all women who worked were native-born daughters of native-born parents. By 1920 this figure had soared to almost 44 percent, while the proportion of native-born daughters in the population increased only slightly.[20] Among this group were women who sought cleaner and better-paying jobs than those typically offered to women. They represented an advance guard, forecasting a new generation of wage-earning women. Pressing for entry into the job market, they created jobs in new fields and began to show up as college professors and presidents, chemists, photographers, dentists, manufacturers, and supervisors. Less affluent native-born white women entered secretarial and office work, finding places for themselves in this new and expanding sector of the work force.

For poor black and white women, the consequences of expanding household technology and increasing possibilities for purchasing services outside the home were mixed. They benefited little from the kind of technology that eased the lives of the more affluent. Many still suffered the dirt and noise of unpaved streets and lacked sewers, regular garbage collection, and running water. Most poor urban households still used wood and coal stoves into the 1920s. These households continued to require hard physical labor and daily attention to keep them running smoothly. The poorer women who lived in them and sometimes headed them entered the labor market not as a result of the technology that prompted middle-class women toward wage work, but out of increasing need for the income required to purchase consumer goods. To keep families economically viable demanded the financial contribution of daughters as well as sons, and sometimes of wives and mothers too.

What could not be, or was no longer, produced at home had to be earned by paid labor. For some women this meant going out to earn a living—replacing their household production with paid labor by following their work into the marketplace. This was a difficult choice unless there was a replacement in the household, since children required supervision and wage earners depended on prepared meals, laundry, and other household services. In homes without running water, heated by coal or wood stoves, maintaining the household and earning wages proved to be a difficult double burden. A wage earner working ten to twelve hours a day, six days a week, could hardly market, prepare adequate meals, launder, and mend clothes.

Most families assigned an available female—wife, daughter, or sister —the task of organizing the household and of stretching the limited incomes of the wage earners. The job was not easy. It included rearing and disciplining children as well as emotional and physical sustenance of the menfolk. But most of all, it required feeding and clothing a family, sometimes under the most discouraging conditions. Clothes had to be made, then made over again after the cloth had worn through. Shopping could be an endless haggle for stale bread and half-rotten vegetables.

The lower the skill level and income of the family's workers, the harder it was for a housewife to get by. Under the poorest conditions, housewifery became no more than an illusion. From at least the 1830s on, substantial portions of the laboring population of every large city lived in conditions of utter misery. In the 1840s, New York City already had a "cellar" population of poor people who lived in dark and airless basements, and by the 1860s, some twenty thousand people lived in wooden "shanty houses"—no more than pieces of clapboard knocked together—on Manhattan's Upper West Side. Even a brief description reveals how difficult "housekeeping" must have been in such an environment. A city inspector told an industrial commission in 1845 of one-room shacks that contained "the family, chairs, usually dirty and broken, cooking utensils, stove, often a bed, a dog or a cat, and sometimes more or less poultry. On the outside, by the door in many cases, are pigs and goats and additional poultry. There is no sink or drainage, and the slops are thrown upon the ground."[21] Even when the worst of these conditions disappeared by the end of the century, housewives who lived in tenements could rarely afford the technology that eased the lives of more affluent women.

In some working-class families higher incomes did enable women to benefit from a few of the rapidly improving amenities of the nineteenth-century city. Among those who were not very poor, living standards rose, permitting women to wash and clean more thoroughly and to pay more attention to nutrition and child care. But the wives of even respectable workers benefited less than those of middling professional and managerial men. Pittsburgh, around 1900, offered working-class neighborhoods fewer sewers and paved streets, and a less dependable water supply, than it provided middle-class neighborhoods. Workers tended to live close to the mills, so their wives battled against constant grime and soot. Unpaved roads were more difficult to clean than those already paved, so that household refuse and horse droppings accumulated in the streets, producing higher rates of disease and death among the poor than among the better off.[22]

By the turn of the century, from one-third to one-half of the populations of major cities such as Baltimore, Philadelphia, Chicago, and Boston consisted of poor immigrant families. Most of these lived in squalid, crowded housing. Indoor running water scarcely existed. One family might share a single toilet with three of four others. Slums were not new, but never had so large a proportion of the American population lived in such overcrowded conditions and never had ideal housekeeping standards been so high. Housewives suffered directly from the absence of city services. To gather sufficient water for a day's washing, drinking, and cooking, they had to get up early, fill huge tubs, and haul them indoors, sometimes up several flights of stairs. The same water had to be disposed of by hauling (or pouring) it downstairs. Few working-class women benefited from washing machines, indoor toilets, or central heating. Lack of refrigeration meant daily shopping trips.

Even in these conditions, the families of unskilled workers frequently found it impossible to live on the income of a single wage-earner. In Lawrence, Massachusetts, where the average male earned $500 a year in 1875, a small family required over $600 to pay for essentials. It could not survive without two incomes. After 1876, wages there fell in response to economic depression. Prices followed too slowly to compensate. Tenement rents in 1893, when wages dipped below the $300 mark, were often $200 a year. By this time a man had difficulty surviving unless his children as well as his wife worked.[23] Steel mill workers in Homestead, Pennsylvania, had an equally difficult time. An immigrant family in 1907–8 could survive on about $1.65 a day— $11.55 a week—in a community where an unskilled mill worker normally earned less than $10.00 a week.[24] Even in prosperous periods, where one person's income could buy the family's bare necessities, the household relied on the contributions of other members—in order to save for a small plot of land, a home, or a farm in the West.[25]

Families dependent on textile mills for income required three or more wage earners to make ends meet. The particular survival strategy depended on the family's situation. Married women frequently stayed at home and took in boarders, sending their daughters to the mill. But just as often, women left their babies in the care of older siblings and went to the mill themselves. In 1909, more than a third of the women working in one New England mill were married, a figure confirmed by a nationwide government survey published the following year.[26] Despite constant accusations that women worked only to supplement family income, the evidence suggests that even in intact male-headed families, need, not caprice, motivated women's wage work. For example, a silk mill owner commented in 1908 that in the mining-mill towns of western Pennsylvania, female factory help, which was at other times scarce, became plentiful when a coal strike threatened. "Prosperous times," he concluded, "enabled the heads of families . . . to keep their daughters at home."[27] One of the volumes of the lengthy Senate report on the conditions of woman and child wage earners published between 1910 and 1912 summarized the issue. "The so-called normal family—father with wife and children dependent upon him for support—is not found . . . ," it reported for southern cotton mill families, and then repeated the assertion for northern mill towns.[28]

Everywhere the industrial process contributed its own pressures on women to enter the labor market. To the widows produced by war and the women who supported diseased and crippled men, it added an increasing toll of industrial victims. Workers died in mines, in steel factories, and on railroads. They died young of consumption, pneumonia, and industrial diseases. Urban working-class families had few resources to fall back on when disaster struck. High unemployment rates, seasonal work, technological dislocation, and real wages that barely kept pace with rising living costs all encouraged women to seek jobs. The result was a steadily rising number of women, married and unmarried, who felt impelled to contribute to their families' economic sustenance. Among teenage girls, three-quarters or more probably sought paid work by 1890, compared to the half who might have done so before the Civil War. When these girls married, financial pressures did not cease. In 1890 the census counted only 3.3 percent of married women working for wages. By 1920, this figure had nearly tripled to 9 percent.[29]

Women who headed families and were responsible for their own or for others' support found the push into the work force even greater. Mary Van Kleeck, who was then a social researcher for the Russell Sage Foundation, discovered that 30.6 percent of female book binders lived in families headed by a mother. In more than a third of the families, mothers as well as daughters worked for wages. The proportion of women living alone varied from city to city. Everywhere their proportion in the labor force was higher than their proportion in the population as a whole. One government report estimated that in seven large cities, some 16 percent of those employed in manufacturing were "adrift."[30]

Economic trends that altered the structure of households and the life styles of those who lived in them were matched by a variety of individual and group needs that played their own roles in labor force participation. Even women in straitened circumstances had occupational choices, and the kinds of jobs they sought reflected a variety of factors including geography, mobility, and income level. But their own ethnic backgrounds and marital status exercised primary control.

Black women, released to an uncertain freedom by the Civil War, had the least choice. In the immediate post–Civil War period, they seemed tempted to withdraw from the labor force. Economist Claudia Goldin, who has studied their rates of labor force participation, notes a dramatic rise in the decade between 1870 and 1880. Apparently economic circumstances forced married women and their daughters from low-income families to seek paid work. The numbers in which they did so reflect their relative poverty. In 1880, 73.3 percent of black single women and 35.4 percent of black married women in seven southern cities reported paid jobs. Among white women only 23.8 percent of the single and 7.3 percent of the married reported paid employment. Even where family income, husband's employment, and demographic factors are held constant, black women were still far more likely to work than white women. Perhaps, as Goldin comments, the wife "was purchasing a substantial insurance policy against her husband's being unemployed."[31]

In contrast, married immigrant women had among the lowest employment rates counted by census takers. The Southern and Eastern European newcomers who constituted nearly a quarter of the immigration to America in 1870 and a rising proportion thereafter took their children's labor for granted, preferring to keep wives at home. Rosa Cristoforo recalled that young Italian girls started wage work at age seven, continuing until marriage, at which point they undertook household labor, usually within the family of the husband's parents, with whom they lived.[32] Jewish women, nurtured in the Old World to provide economic sustenance to husbands engaged in religious study, assumed financial responsibility in the normal course of events. In these families married women rarely worked outside the home. Instead, they contributed to family income by taking boarders, sewing, or other given-out work. Unlike their brothers, who were expected to study, daughters in Jewish families were routinely pulled out of school and sent out to work to supplement parental income. Incentives to upward mobility as well as the fear of poverty led married women to seek income, but the task of fitting into the work force proved difficult. A few—Germans, Swedes, Poles, Bohemians, and French Canadians among them—arranged for home and child care and worked in factories or as domestics even after they married. Most, however, found ways to supplement family incomes without leaving their homes. They sewed and finished garments, made paper flowers and cigars, or worked with their husbands in small businesses. Ethnic preferences and available opportunity determined married women's roles. The United States Industrial Commission, investigating in 1900, reported that Italians routinely employed their wives and sisters as helpers. "If he is a pants operator, she is usually his helper, or if he is a cloakmaker, she is his handsewer and finisher, and so both labor together to cover the expenses of the family."[33]

Immigrant women played their most important, unsung role by performing household services for unmarried members of their community. These services were expected. Rosa Cristoforo recalled, for example, that when her husband, already in the United States, sent for her to come from Italy, the messengers told her that "those men in the iron mines in Missouri need women to do the cooking and washing. Three men have sent back for their wives, and two for some girls to marry." Rosa made the long trans-Atlantic trip and arrived at her husband's side to be told she was to "cook, make beds, clean shacks, and wash clothes . . . for men."[34] Her situation was less typical than that of the majority of immigrant wives, who took lodgers into their own homes. An observer in Lawrence, Massachusetts, reported in 1913 that while boarding houses were not unusual, most single men lived with families and either cooked their own food or paid the woman to cook the food they provided.[35]

Taking in boarders was a favorite means of earning additional income. Estimates as to how many immigrant families did so range widely. A 1912 Lawrence study suggests that 90 percent of the families where the husband was the sole wage earner took in boarders. The income of a single earner clearly could not sustain a family. Even families with more than one wage earner, where the head worked in the mill, had difficulty. Half of these families rented to boarders.[36] In Homestead, Pennsylvania, the figures were slightly lower. Social researcher Margaret Byington estimated that 40 percent of the families there had at least one paying boarder. In cities like New York, where there were greater opportunities for home work as well as for employment in light industry outside the home, fewer families had lodgers. Italian and Jewish wives performed this service only until their families achieved some economic security. The evidence suggests that recent immigrant families and those whose heads worked at lower-level blue-collar jobs had a higher proportion of lodgers. Even in Buffalo, with its numerous small industries, more than 10 percent of married Italian housewives took in boarders.[37]

Looking at the data another way shows that high ratios of lodgers characterized families headed by the foreign-born. One study of 160 families with boarders in a New England textile town reported that 147 were headed by the foreign-born. And the large number of Slavs who kept lodgers in Homestead was matched by only an occasional native-born family.[38] These contributions to family income often went uncounted, even by the women's own families. A fourteen-year-old girl asked her newspaper's advice about whether she should drop out of school to get a job. "My father who is a frail man," she wrote, "is the only one working to support the whole family." Explaining that she wanted to help her parents, she continued, "My mother is now pregnant, but she still has to take care of the three boarders we have in the house." Like the census takers who never counted caring for boarders as work, this young woman overlooked a substantial portion of the family's income when she overlooked her mother's labor.[39]

How many boarders lived in a family varied of course with income and circumstances. In Homestead, a typical Slavic family—husband, wife, and three children—might have from one to four lodgers in their four-room house. New England textile communities reported an average of 2.4 lodgers in each family in 1909, with Polish families taking in an average of 3.4 boarders each. In half of the Homestead families, income from lodgers added more than 25 percent to the family's income, with the wife typically shopping, cooking, and laundering for all the boarders and her own family.[40]

Unlike her mother, a young daughter chose to work outside the home, if she could. For young women with immigrant parents, wage work was the typical experience. Irish families in Cohoes, New York, sent 80 percent of their fifteen- to nineteen-year-old daughters out to work. Three-quarters of young French-Canadians and more than half of English- and American-born young women in this age group earned wages. These numbers fell off rapidly as women removed themselves from the factory upon marriage and childbirth.[41]

Friends and relatives usually helped to locate the novice's first job by introducing her to a foreman. "You had to know somebody to get into one," reported a mill operative of her experience in Manchester,

New Hampshire.[42] In that small town, French-Canadian families controlled access to entry-level jobs in the major plant and determined how new employees would be placed. The pattern was typical. Seventy-five percent of the Italian women in another study got jobs through friends and relatives.[43]

Young girls who lived at home expected to turn over their earnings to the family. The vast majority seem to have done so, receiving in return an allowance for carfare and lunch. Of Boston female store workers interviewed in 1908–9, 55.6 percent said they contributed all their earnings to their families. Among sixteen- and seventeen-year-olds the figures were much higher than for women as a whole. Around 85 percent of those in this age group who worked in New York's stores, and nearly 90 percent of those who worked in factories, turned all their earnings over to the family exchequer. Eighty-six percent of one group of wage-earning Italian women gave their pay envelopes to their families unopened, and the rest gave a part of their wages.[44] Anzia Yezierska, a Russian-Jewish immigrant who became a well-known writer in the twenties, recounted in fiction the fate of a young girl whose father berated her for refusing to conform. Over her father's objections, Sara Smolinsky ran away from home, worked her way through night school and college, and became a teacher. She returned proudly to her parents, only to hear her father berate her: "She's only good to the world, not to her father. Will she hand me her wages from school as a dutiful daughter should?"[45]

Supporting the family financially had its compensations, especially in the freer environment of the western states. Agnes Smedley, who became a well-known journalist in the 1920s, recalled the privileges given to her sister and to a young aunt who contributed to the family income. Helen and Annie, "because they worked and paid for their board and room," had one of the family's four rooms to themselves. Smedley described Annie, at age fifteen, as a "woman of the world . . . by the standards of our world, a woman who earned her own money was a free woman."[46] Such privileges must have provided young women with an enormous incentive to go out to work.

Occasionally, where they were denied, women rebelled. Eager for the economic freedom promised by a steady job, some became ambitious for themselves, wanting to take seriously the promised opportunity of America. Yezierska, for example, ran away from home in order to be independent, removing herself entirely from the family that demanded her services. In the tightly knit Jewish community from which she came, jobs that would help support families won social approval, but ambition for its own sake was not looked on kindly in girls. Yezierska's father turned his back on her. Other fathers forced their daughters to bend to their wills. Immigrant Ella Wolff recalled how, as a young girl, her father pulled her out of school despite the principal's threats to have him imprisoned. Subsequently he refused to allow her either to stay out late enough to go to night school or to waste expensive electricity by reading into the night.[47]

Personal preferences as to the kind of work women wanted to do often yielded to family circumstances and the availability of work. Yet, where they had choices, immigrant women preferred manufacturing to domestic-service jobs. Nearly three out of ten immigrant women who worked—by far the largest proportion—found unskilled and semiskilled jobs in factories. Ethnic origin and economic position took over from there. Overwhelming proportions of Jews and Italians who settled in large cities worked in the garment industry. Jewish women clustered in factories owned and controlled by fellow Jews— ladies' dress and waist shops after 1900, and underwear manufacture. Italian women gravitated toward men's clothing, where the organization of the industry still permitted substantial home work. They felled seams, finished garments, and made artificial flowers. Polish and Slavic women tended to work in textile mills in New England and in the South or in meat-packing and food-processing plants in the Midwest.[48] The desire for companionship as well as the need to be close to home constricted the labor market for these women, reducing the number of jobs in fact available to them.

Despite the lure of demonstrably higher wages and working conditions acknowledged as healthful, white wage-earning women tended to argue that domestic service was most appropriate for those who had no families. They apparently acted on their feelings. "Yankee girls," according to Virginia Penny, would "not go out in that capacity."[49] Work patterns reveal that Irish women—who more than any other immigrant group came to America unaccompanied by families—took domestic jobs in higher proportions than any other immigrant group. Swedes, Poles, and Germans did so in lesser but still substantial proportions. Other groups avoided domestic work altogether. Italians tended to distrust placing their daughters, unsupervised, in other people's households. Jews thought of it as downward mobility. "Even in our worst poverty in Poland," cries Adele Lindner, another of Yezierska's fictional heroines, "none of our people had ever been servants. Tailors, storekeepers, but never a servant. Should I be the first to go down?" And Rose Cohen's mother despaired when her daughter announced she had just taken a job as a domestic—"Is that what I have come to America for, that my children should become servants?"[50] Not surprisingly, two-thirds of 300 Jewish girls placed by agencies in domestic-service jobs left before the end of a year to find alternative work. Despite this resistance, nearly two out of every ten immigrant women worked at domestic-service jobs by 1920. The proportion of the servant population who were foreign-born far exceeded the proportion of foreign-born workers as a whole.[51]

The class, ethnic, and racial constraints that influenced a woman's work choices were all bounded by sex. The job market denied women of every ethnic and class reference group self-directed ambitions toward upward mobility. Everywhere cultural attitudes emphasized marriage and family as goals. To reject them required conscious rebellion. Women were encouraged to adopt those forms of thought and behavior that would lead to marriage. Some sense of role propriety was part of every girl's socialization. Her behavior received approval when it conformed to expected future roles. And perceptions of future roles helped condition what must have seemed like merely personal or at best cultural preference. As men traded the risks of upward mobility against the need for a secure job, so women brought their own value systems to the job market. These were not independent of family or ethnicity.

In a broad sense, notions of propriety and role served as organizational principles for women's work force participation. They created a reciprocally confirming system in which successful job experiences for women were defined in terms of values appropriate to future home life: gentility, neatness, morality, cleanliness. Male jobs, in contrast, encouraged such values as ambition, competition, aggression, and increased income, all of which would add up to success. Such distinctions confirmed women's place in the home, even while they worked for wages. And they provided support for limiting women's access to jobs even where restrictions demonstrably left them in utter poverty. Although women typically chose jobs that reflected home-based values, these choices, regulated as they were by social and cultural norms, could hardly be said to be free. The value system that categorized male and female jobs simultaneously served the interests of stability and predictability in the job market. When women rebelled and attempted to make their way in "men's fields," they discovered that the barriers in front of them extended down into the deepest cultural roots as well as across the domain of most skilled jobs.

Within their own economic sphere wage-earning women developed hierarchies of desirable occupations that were, of course, class based. Professional jobs headed the list. Nursing and teaching, because they did not require sacrifice of the feminine role, remained the most frequent choices. Some new jobs—department store buying, business management, medicine—were not seen as compatible with marriage,

This 1907 photograph depicts the spinning room of the White Oak Cotton Mills in Greensboro, North Carolina. Note the relatively poor dress of the women here and in the following photograph of home-workers, as compared with that of those leaving the Lynn, Massachusetts, factory. *(Courtesy of the Library of Congress)*

These two women sewing in an Elizabeth Street, New York, attic seem to be mother and daughter. *(Photograph by Jacob Riis. Jacob A. Riis collection, Museum of the City of New York)*

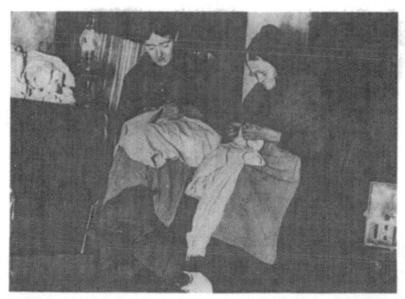

A Lynn, Massachusetts, shoe factory in 1895. Above: An old woman stitching linings belies the notion that all workers were young. Opposite: Workers leave the factory gates; note the hats and the parasols as well as the shirt-waists and skirts then in style. *(Courtesy of the Library of Congress)*

The worst jobs still went to black women. These women, stripping tobacco, worked without backrests or breaks in 1922. *(Courtesy of the National Archives)*

Fully a quarter of women wage-earners had domestic jobs in 1905 when this photograph of maids at the Hotel Astor was taken. *(Photograph by Byron. The Byron Collection, Museum of the City of New York)*

Downstairs, the uniforms disappeared, the faces look older, and the work remained heavy. This scene is from the Hotel Biltmore laundry room about 1912. The irons are gas heated. *(Photograph by Byron. The Byron Collection, Museum of the City of New York)*

New jobs opened up for women with some education. These women are alphabetizing at an indexing firm in 1906. *(Photograph by Byron. The Byron Collection, Museum of the City of New York)*

But work for women remained an activity of questionable moral virtue, as the poster for this 1902 melodrama demonstrates. *(Theatre Collection, Museum of the City of New York)*

and women who held them generally resigned on marriage or chose
not to marry at all. Women with less training tended to choose office
work above department store clerking. And those with few skills were
factory workers, waitresses, and domestic servants, in that order. To
some extent this hierarchy reflected class, ethnic, and racial distinctions
in the work force as a whole as well as the preferences of employers
for "American-born" workers. Yet insofar as it reflected women's own
choices it was based on such values as cleanliness, affirmation of home
roles, and possibilities of remaining "good."

Within each job, informal hierarchies existed, rating work in particular sectors by crude standards of desirability. What made one
job more agreeable than another seems to have had as much to do with
self-imposed restrictions as with the income it produced. Women
talked about taking jobs because they attracted a "nice class of girls."[52]
Conversely, they were warned away from certain occupations. "Factory
girls were immoral," was the advice given by an old neighbor to Mary
Kenney when she went to Chicago to seek work.[53] Factory workers felt
superior to better-paid domestics. A Cohoes, New York, newspaper
reported in 1881 that operatives felt "they take a higher place in the
social scale than is accorded them when they do housework."[54] Adele
Lindner's response to becoming a servant confirms this feeling. "Very
slowly, I buttoned my apron, the badge of the servant. I knew Minnie
and Sadie and all the other girls who worked in shops and factories
would stop associating with me. I had dropped out of their class."[55]

But factories took second place to what were then called mercantile
houses—department stores. The women who worked there, reported
Leonora O'Reilly in 1899, "have a caste feeling about their work and
think that persons working in a mercantile establishment are a little
higher in society than the women who work in a factory."[56] The
feeling of social superiority was reflected in different living styles.
Store workers sacrificed food in order to dress well and to live in
better neighborhoods than factory workers with comparable wages.
Factory workers ate better, giving up the other amenities.[57]

Within jobs, hierarchies reflected a sense of status as often as they
did promotions up the occupational ladder. A woman who did clerical
work in a factory raged against privileges offered to her co-workers
who were located in the main office: "Factory girls are just as good as
the main office girls."[58] Those who made it from factory to office,
according to one observer, "usually became identified with the 'office
girls'" and assumed the prestige of the white collar worker. Mary
Gilson, one of the nation's first personnel managers, recalled how
difficult it was to get even new office workers to mix with their former
factory mates.[59] Certain kinds of jobs in factories commanded greater

Social ranking of women

respect than others although salaries were no higher. Agnes Nestor, later to become a well-known trade union leader, recalls of her years in a glove factory: "like the gloves they made, the kid glove makers felt that they were superior to the rest of us and used to refer haughtily to the rest of us as the 'horsehide girls.' "[60]

Jobs that had a "demoralizing tendency" fell low on the scale. Many women shunned waitresses because they were said to be "more free and easy in manners and speech than other wage earning women."[61] A government investigation of the glass industry reported that taking finished glassware off the leer, a job that required constant stooping and involved the danger of burns, had a "coarsening influence" on the women so employed because it exposed them to "intimate association with a few men." Like the government investigators, other workers ignored the real disadvantages of these jobs, rejecting them not because they were dangerous but because they had the lowest social standing of any in the glass industry.[62]

The desire for gentility overrode poor working conditions and low wages. For example, Boston's Women's Educational and Industrial Union conducted an intensive campaign beginning in 1898 to induce women to leave overcrowded factory jobs for domestic service, with pitiably small success. High wages could not compensate for the social stigma attached. By 1915, still anxious to find out why women would not take up domestic work, the YWCA set up a Commission on Household Employment. Its first report revealed that though factory operatives were aware that domestic workers earned larger net wages and worked in more healthful surroundings, they were persuaded that factory workers had higher social standing as well as more free time. As one worker responded, "A factory girl is out more . . . and has more time to be in the society of others, and so is able to have high social standing if she has good character." Or another: "A girl in a factory is more independent and not thought of as someone's servant." An intriguing answer came from one factory worker who said, "Intelligent people set no stigma on factory workers who are well bred and ladylike. These girls are received in good circles anywhere. Many women of wealth and standing are interested in these girls and even invite them to their homes. But no one has ever invited someone's maid or cook to their home for afternoon tea or any other social affair." Factory work, summed up one factory worker, was far better than domestic service, "but to the girl who is alone or who has bad examples at home, I should say quickly, domestic service."[63]

Like domestic servants, waitresses often earned more than the ordinary factory operative, but social disgrace attended the public character of that job. Among waitresses themselves many disapproved of those who worked in restaurants that served liquor, despite the significantly larger tips available in these places.[64] On the other hand, department store clerks, who put in longer hours, often earned substantially less, and were required to dress better than most factory workers, nonetheless had higher social standing. One mother, separated from her husband, pulled her fifteen-year-old daughter out of an easy factory job with a potential for paying $8.00 per week and sent her to work in a five-and-ten-cent store for $1.25. Rose Schneiderman, later to become a Women's Trade Union League president, reported that when she quit her job as a department store clerk to become a sewing machine operator at twice her former salary, her mother was "far from happy. She thought working in a store much more genteel than working in a factory."[65]

How any individual woman dealt with these issues in her own life reflected the tensions imposed by the constraints of her particular ethnic or racial group and the realities of the job market. Black women, faced with discrimination that confined them to the bottom of the labor market pool, chose laundry and domestic work in preference to agricultural field labor with its taint of slavery. Jewish women, whose culture validated economic contributions to family life, took advantage of vocational training more readily than any other immigrant group. Italian women selected jobs that kept them in close contact with other Italians or where they could continue to supervise (and be supervised by) their families. According to Louise Odencrantz, they sought the clothing trade believing it would teach them how to sew their own clothes after marriage.[66]

Native-born white women most commonly emphasized morality and nice surroundings. Observers noted that "native born girls of Anglo-Saxon stock prefer[red] when possible to choose an occupation socially superior to factory work."[67] For them, one measure of genteel employment was the absence of immigrant or black workmates. Southern white women would not work in laundries or in textile, glass, or tobacco factories alongside black women. San Francisco's white women refused to enter household service when immigration legislation restricted the numbers of Chinese servants available. The job, according to the U.S. Commissioner of Labor, had "so long been the special field of the Chinese that the white girls feel there is something degrading in the work." In the eyes of job-seekers, work took on the character of the people who did it. White women, the commissioner said, would work side by side in occupations that were not defined as predominantly Chinese.[68]

For women from tightly knit ethnic groups, work within the community guaranteed companionship and careful supervision. So ethnic concentration made some jobs acceptable to women who might otherwise have rejected them. The large numbers of Italians in New York City's garment industry (where 52 percent of all working Italian women were employed in 1910), and in candy- and artificial flower-making, seems to have been the result of a desire to remain under the protection of kin, rather than the result of free labor-market choice. Mary Van Kleeck reported in 1910 that one-quarter of all paper-flower workers in large cities were Italian, and their low wages threatened to drive others out of the trade.[69] Jewish women tended to work together in clothing shops where, in New York in 1911, they occupied 60 percent of the jobs in the ladies' garment industry. More than three-quarters of the Polish women who worked for wages in Massachusetts were semiskilled operatives—most of whom labored in textile factories.[70]

Jobs with the highest percentage of "American-born girls" ranked highest. By the early twentieth century, investigators could characterize jobs by the women who held them. Elizabeth Butler made the following comments in her pioneering study of Pittsburgh trades:

> We see English speaking girls holding the positions for which a few months' training and some intelligence are needed, a knowledge of English, or of reading and writing. The Italian girl, hindered by tradition, scarcely figures, but within a limited circle of industries, immigrant Jews hold positions beside girls of native birth. We see much inferior and unpleasant work yielded to Slavic immigrants. . . . The place of the Slav . . . is lowest industrially among the women workers of Pittsburgh.[71]

Since some element in each woman's decision-making process had to do with who her working companions would be, potential employers of women needed to pay attention to their preferences. Mary Gilson reports of her experience in personnel management before the war, "You had to exercise some discretion in the initial placing of the members of certain nationalities. An Irish girl who had been in the United States one month complained bitterly to me about being assigned to a work table with 'thim furriners.' . . . The old feud between Czechs and Germans occasionally flared up, and woe be unto you if you placed a Sicilian girl under a Neapolitan foreman."[72]

This combination of ethnic and cultural influence helped to structure the labor market for employers in ways that seemed "natural." Managers who monitored the "type" of girl hired could lower their wage costs while attracting women who were, from an employer's perspective, the most appropriate workers. Employers' choices are reflected in the comments of observers who could make instant judgments about the nature of a female work force in certain regions and job categories. These comments reflect both the stigma attached to some occupations that "nice" women would not enter for fear of losing reputation and the attempts of employers to structure their labor force in response. The San Jose and Oakland canneries, for example, were said to employ girls of good family and education. But those in San Francisco, which hired "a motley array of people of all races and of both sexes," employed women who were "less intelligent and respectable than those in the canneries throughout the rest of the state." In New Orleans, where cigar and tobacco factories and department stores controlled their labor force by refusing to hire Negroes, female employees were said to be "of a better class than in northern establishments of the same industry." Saleswomen were described as "noticeably refined and educated." In Kentucky, on the other hand, where most workingwomen were "honest, respectable, industrious and polite," the tobacco factories hired women described as "ignorant, coarse and filthy," and the Commissioner of Labor's report commented that "the mixture of races and sexes in this employment, and the character of the work itself, have doubtless had their effect in producing this condition."[73]

Asked why they hired one sex as opposed to another, or certain women as opposed to others, employers sometimes resorted to sex-role stereotypes, but more often fell back on appeals to "natural" roles. Early in the 1870s, as women began moving into a variety of factory jobs, these preferences were already structuring the labor market. Women were described as "inferior in mechanical skill, superior in steadiness," or they were hired because they had qualities like common sense, neatness, and integrity that would cost much more to purchase in men. Honest employers stated their preferences bluntly. A male manager of a large retail shop told journalist Helen Campbell, "We don't want men . . . we wouldn't have them even if they came at the same price. Of course cheapness has something to do with it, and will have, but for my part give me a woman to deal with every time."[74]

Dividing jobs along lines of respectability and adhering to the divisions thus created benefited employers. They could then offer reduced wages to those who sought the privilege of working with native-born girls. Elizabeth Butler's classic study of Baltimore's saleswomen reveals that all thirty-four of that city's largest stores tried to hire some "American" girls in order to maintain their prestige. Some hired only "Americans"; Slavs and blacks were rarely hired; and eight firms refused to hire Jews. Not surprisingly, department stores employed more native-born women than any other major woman-employing industry. These women, along with shoe factory workers, among whom

American-born women were also heavily concentrated, were said to be better educated, to have a higher standard of living, and to possess an assortment of other virtues such as educating their younger brothers and sisters. At the nether end of the scale, the same researcher, investigating household workers, could find not a single native-born "girl" employed in that trade.[75] Divisions by ethnic preference were not unusual. We find evidence for them among Philadelphia seed packers who would employ only American women; among glass manufacturers who gave "old" immigrants the best jobs as opposed to the "new" immigrants, whom they disliked; and among textile manufacturers who reserved the most "aristocratic" jobs for American girls.[76]

These restrictions had the most dramatic effect on black women. In order to maintain the appearance of propriety necessary to attract white women at low wages, southern employers severely restricted occupations in which that region's black women could find work. Carroll Wright, U.S. Commissioner of Labor, pointed to this phenomenon in his Report of 1888, in which he commented on the refusal of employers to hire black people for jobs except in severe shortages of white labor. Most often, as the Missouri Commissioner of Labor Statistics noted in 1900, factories simply would not employ blacks. "It is an exceptional case where you find any colored labor in the factories except as porters. Neither colored female labor nor colored male labor is engaged in the mechanical arts. But a great many of them are employed as domestic help there."[77] Occasionally, in the South, companies which could not obtain white labor decided to operate factories wholly with "colored help." Despite a desperate shortage of white workers, however, most southern plants would not hire blacks, except as one report noted, "for the roughest work about the mill." The U.S. Senate's 1910 investigation of women and child labor in the cotton textile industry reported that of 152 southern mills, only 18 employed any Negro women and children. These constituted little more than 5 percent of the total number of women employed, and were almost exclusively sweepers and scrubbers.[78]

The self-imposed social restrictions on the kinds of jobs women were prepared to take, coupled with employers' eagerness to offer gentility as a partial substitute for wages, resulted in an inevitable crowding of women into a few readily available occupations. They were competing with each other for the same jobs. The "crowding" phenomenon operated on two levels: it denied women in general access to most jobs, and it confined particular women to certain kinds of jobs. Though an extensive number of occupations utilized women, most of the women who worked were employed in relatively few. And though some categories of jobs expanded and others contracted dramatically in the lengthy period from the Civil War to the first World War, the degree of concentration scarcely diminished at all. The 1900 federal census counted five million women working for wages in 294 of a possible 303 occupations. But only 43 of these had more than 5,000 female workers. More specifically, though domestic service accounted for more than 60 percent of all wage-earning women in 1870 and only 25 percent by 1910, crude statistics reveal that women in both years made up from 84 to 86 percent of the workers who fell into this category. Where job shifts did occur, as in some clerical work, or where new jobs were created, such as typewriting, entire categories of jobs normally shifted over or were designated as women's work. Such shifts explain improvements in women's position as a whole. Women benefited not from a hard, slow pull upward, but from new categories of socially acceptable jobs. The overall phenomenon of crowding remained the same. In the entire period, upward of 90 percent of all wage-earning women worked in job areas where women workers were heavily concentrated.[79]

In the end, crowding and competition exacerbated the problems women faced as workers. They sacrificed higher wages for the relative satisfactions of working with compatriots or of doing respected work. Sexual divisions in the job market tended to restrict vocational ambition, bunched together women of like ethnic and racial groups, and limited some jobs to women of particular racial and ethnic backgrounds. Even an expanding pool of jobs could not prevent the resulting cycle of deteriorating work conditions, low wages, and squalid home lives. The result was to raise again the issue of whether home and work roles could ever be compatible, and to destroy, at least temporarily, any possibility that the two could sustain each other.

6

Technology, Efficiency, and Resistance

By the late nineteenth century there was nearly universal agreement on two scores. Women's expanding labor force participation was an unfortunate necessity that threatened to interfere with their more desirable work at home. And nothing that happened at work could be allowed to hinder the capacity of wage-earning women to resume or assume home roles at some future time. We have seen how such ideas channeled women's entrance into the work force, and how, instead of providing them with safe, clean, unpressured jobs, notions of women's place in fact reduced them to the poorest levels. Unskilled, largely unorganized, and crowded into few occupations, women found themselves subject to some of the worst conditions of any wage workers.

The pattern, once established, encouraged employers to hire women because they were said to have characteristics such as docility, attachment to family, little expectation of advancement, and no trade union consciousness. It led employers to assign women to jobs that matched their expectations of women's possibilities and performance. But in the late 1800s and early 1900s, new technology and new forms of industrial organization altered the structure of work, promising new opportunities to women. The struggle to take advantage of these jobs placed women in direct competition with male workers. To protect themselves, male workers, who were rapidly unionizing, drew on the ideology of woman's place to create obstacles for women. These efforts, along with managerial attempts to order the labor market, cemented the existing segmentation in place, defining the boundaries of men's and women's work for more than half a century.

. . .

The rapidity of Gilded Age industrialization created turmoil in male and female jobs. Since only minimal respect remained for custom and ideology—traditionally the barriers inhibiting substitution of white women for more expensive male workers—employers felt free to experiment with the sexual division of labor. As they did so, the contributions of women seemed increasingly threatening to male workers. Worry began early and got worse by the turn of the century. The federal government had provoked hostility when it hired women for some clerical jobs in 1862. Until then there had been no more than a few women scattered in an occasional federal office, employed largely as copyists and low-grade clerks. Under pressure of the war, the Treasury hired some women to cut currency. And in 1862 the Post Office hired eight women among twenty-five new employees to sort mail. The new employees were ridiculed and insulted by male colleagues who "stared, blew smoke in the women's faces, spat tobacco juice, and gave cat-calls or made obnoxious remarks." The women, who earned an average of $300 a year less than men for precisely the same job, were discovered to be as productive as their colleagues, and the department promptly hired more women at the reduced rate. Though some federal officials objected on principle to hiring women, others appreciated the money saved by paying lower salaries.[1] The end of the war brought predictable outcries. The *Workingmen's Advocate* deplored the fact that even the "government of the United States, which squanders millions uselessly every year, has stooped to the hiring of female clerks to do the work of its Departments because they could be got for a smaller sum than males."[2]

But new machinery constituted the most typical reason to substitute women for men. Each time women entered an occupation for which training had become unnecessary, men saw it as an attack. In the pottery industry, skilled jiggermen feared, as they testified in 1900, that female labor operating new machinery would cut their wages in half and drive them out of the trade. It had happened, they said, in Great Britain, where the jobs of Englishmen had already been destroyed.[3] The 1910 government report on the glass industry concluded that not only had certain parts of the work been readjusted so that women could be employed, but "new methods and new machines were devised with this end in view." The resulting reorganization of the work force broke up processes previously performed by skilled men into smaller tasks that "ceased to require skill. Machinery was adapted to women and much of it was and is advertised as being so adapted."[4]

Changes in machinery, of course, had variable results. Sometimes jobs were created for women; but frequently a change had the opposite result. The textile industry witnessed both kinds of changes in the nineteenth century. In 1850, spinning jennies, operated by women in cotton mills, were widely replaced by spinning mules, heavy machines that called for physical strength and lent themselves to a male work force, according to the custom of the day. By the 1890s, when mule spinners, who then earned the relatively high wage of twelve to fourteen dollars a week, began seeking even more pay, several mills took advantage of new ring-spinning machinery to replace these demanding craftsmen with women at from six to eight dollars per week. One mill superintendent described the replacement process in his mill as follows: "A few years ago they were giving us trouble . . . so one Saturday afternoon, after they had gone home, we started right in and smashed up a room full of mules with sledge hammers. When the men came back on Monday morning, they were astonished to find that there was no work for them. That room is now full of ring frames run by girls."[5]

Manufacturers of silk ribbons replaced hand looms operated by skilled male weavers with simpler machinery for which they recruited female operators. But the development of a horizontal warping mill that operated at high speed called for men, and female warpers were forced to give over their jobs. The general tendency of textile mills to speed up the machinery and to require workers to tend more machines led employers to favor males, where they were available, because it was thought they responded better to stress.[6] This tendency offset that of favoring females for simpler machinery. As a result, relative proportions of male and female workers in textiles varied from region to region, heavily influenced by local custom and available labor.

Substituting women for men in the footwear industry was more straightforward. Throughout the early nineteenth century, as this industry made the transition from small craft-centered shops to the factory, women amounted to only a small percentage of the labor force. When the McKay stitcher appeared in 1850, binding and stitching shoes became factory operations, and as the industry as a whole mechanized, women's proportion among shoe operators crept higher and higher. In 1870 they had been only 5 percent of the labor force in the industry. By 1910, they were nearly a quarter.[7]

Just as the transformation of technology encouraged employers to hire women, so changes in managerial styles provided further incentive. In a period of corporate consolidation, when management faced competition in national and even international markets, streamlining production in the factory and organizing effective distribution systems seemed vital. In the factory newly developed techniques such as welfare programs, personnel offices, and scientific management reduced some of the barriers to hiring women. Of these, scientific management reached furthest. Under the guiding hand of Frederick Winslow Taylor, technology was put to the service of more efficient production. The full flower of scientific management involved attempts to determine the way workers spent their time through tight managerial control. Time and motion studies, followed by precise instructions as to the worker's every movement, guaranteed the most effective use of each employee's time. These were to be implemented by managers responsible for gathering together "all of the traditional knowledge which in the past has been possessed by the workingman and then . . . classifying, tabulating and reducing this knowledge to rules, laws, and formulae. . . ."[8] In its most extreme manifestation, the process demanded a rigid depersonalization of the worker. To insure cooperation, Taylor advocated careful selection of obedient workers, close supervision, generous incentives for production above a specified quota, adequate rest periods, and comparatively high wages. All these became possible, Taylor thought, as a result of harmonious cooperation between workers and management. Workers who maximized production, and management, which controlled it, would together benefit from maximum profits.

Despite Taylor's warnings that scientific management could work only if fully practiced, few plants seem to have adopted the system as a whole. What became known as Taylorization more often than not consisted of tighter managerial control, time and motion studies, some efficiency techniques, and an increasing division of labor. Powerful arguments for transforming some male jobs rested in management's desire to gain control over the work place. David Montgomery has successfully documented workers' resistance to this phenomenon and he and Harry Braverman have pointed to the lengths to which management would go to wrest control from skilled workers.[9] Management methods varied from intimidation by exploitation to extensions of regulations and control over personal behavior, specialization of tasks, and ultimately shifts in technology that vested all technical knowledge in the hands of a managerial class.

Among women and the unskilled the thrust toward efficiency had both positive and negative results. Incentive systems and extra bonuses for those who produced above their quotas increased pressure on the factory floor. Those who could not produce lost their jobs. Intense monotony and close supervision of repetitive tasks replaced the physical labor of an earlier period. Women complained of being "pushed to the limit" and of working under conditions that created mental strain.[10] They responded to these, like men, by introducing what was

(Company to war)

called the stint—joining together to restrict their output. "I worked very hard," said one young book binder, "but I tried to keep to a schedule because if one girl turns out too much in a day, they're apt to cut the rates."[11]

But women had, on the surface, less to lose from acquiescing to efficiency techniques. Deprived of training in saleable skills and denied access to supervisory positions, the larger majority of female industrial workers had never had much control over the work process as a whole. For all of its debilitating effect on workers, scientific management offered some benefits to those at the lowest end of the job scale. In return for increasingly mechanized, dehumanized responses, it presented workers with the possibility of a relatively high and rational wage structure, less subject to the whims of individual foremen and to their likes and dislikes among employees By increasing the number of subdivided tasks and encouraging investment in labor-saving machinery, scientific management enhanced the demand for unskilled workers. And concern for fitting the worker to the job provided incentives to hire women, who were thought to accommodate more easily to routine work.

The idea, if not the practice, of scientific management offered women for the first time the systematic prospect of limited upward mobility within their own factories. Since incentives to hard work included the promise of promotion to supervisory jobs, these could not be denied women without reducing their efficiency. Thus, Mary Gilson, personnel manager at the Joseph and Feiss Clothcraft Company, a large men's clothing manufacturer in Cleveland, argued that New England textile mills that would not promote women undermined the principles of good management by depriving them of motivation. "Despite the fact that the majority of wage earners were women," she said,

> no woman had a chance to rise to overseership. When you discussed this with the overseers or with a mill agent you got the usual response that women did not like to work under women. To be sure, they acknowledged that they had never experimented, as we had in Cleveland, where we found that by careful selection and training and by giving the same support to women as to men, women had no more objection to working under women than under men. The prejudice against women entering their bailiwick was deep seated and they had to find excuses for it. The myth of male superiority had to be preserved even at the cost of removing incentive from a large proportion of the operatives.

After the first World War, Gilson used this argument to try to get college women admitted to business schools, including Harvard's prestigious Graduate School of Business. "We were training more and more women for supervisory positions in the Clothcraft Shops," she recalls, "and the evidence that women, if given an opportunity, could 'get ahead' in various other fields of work as well as in our own factory, had tapped a reservoir of ambition."[12] One observer proudly described the possibilities that awaited women in the postwar factory world:

> Before the war there was only the foreman in all the industries where women were employed. Since the war there are both the instructional forewomen and the production forewomen in all the women employing factories. . . . Women are admitted to the classes in foreman training along with the men. . . . Formerly a man set up the machine and a woman operated it. If the machine got out of order she raised two fingers as a sign for the "set-up" man to come. Today the women do this work themselves.[13]

Possibilities of progress for some and even the promise of high wages did not always materialize. Even where they did, they failed to compensate for the "mental strain" created by the new methods. For while efficiency techniques reduced some jobs to dimensions that justified utilizing female workers, they did not make the jobs easier. When the tasks of telephone operators were reduced to a manual of appropriate responses, operators became almost exclusively female. Yet their rapid work pace left them "always nervous, always on edge," with "headaches, backaches, arm and eye strain." Operators sometimes fainted from exhaustion. Pressure produced an extraordinarily high turnover rate—nearly 100 percent over the space of twelve months.[14]

Nor did many employers utilize Taylor's full assortment of relief measures. They failed to balance pressure to produce with shorter days, longer and more frequent rest periods, and occasional days off. Telephone operators worked a nine-hour day on split shifts that extended over a fifteen-hour period. Sales clerks in department stores that began to adopt rational techniques in the 1890s still stood for ten hours a day, got little training, and received persistently low wages.

Like efficiency techniques, new patterns of organization had varying effects. Expanded sales and marketing programs, more complex arrangements for providing and using capital, and an extension of centralized decision-making and bureaucratic control all increased clerical and record-keeping tasks. In the simpler office of 1870, the office clerk tended to be a trusted second lieutenant who handled the books and kept track of inventory. A businessman might have a personal secretary to write letters, keep track of appointments, and serve as confidante. Both employer and employee were likely to be male. New York City boasted only five female shorthand writers in 1870. Nationwide less than one-half of 1 percent of the women who earned

wages worked as clerks, cashiers, typists, or stenographers. By 1900,
2 percent of women workers filled such jobs, and during World War I
the field expanded so rapidly that by 1920 more than 12 percent of all
wage-earning women worked in offices.[15] What had happened?

The developing bureaucracy required people who were fluent in
English, educated enough to respond to a variety of commands efficiently, and without the need for large incomes. Initially reluctant to
hire women, whose distracting influence they feared, employers succumbed to the lure of higher profits—for the jobs offered to women
paid about half of what a comparable man might get. Explaining his
preference for women workers, oue businessman said that young men
wanted to be promoted and to get higher salaries as they courted girls
and then began to raise families. "That kind of a clerk is not a good
investment in certain jobs because for certain jobs you must have
girls, as girls do not have these demands made upon them."[16]

After the first breach of the office walls during the labor shortage
of the Civil War, women moved quickly into most clerical positions.
Their place was assured when the typewriter came into general use
in the 1890s. The machine required nimble fingers—presumably an
attribute of women. Its operators exercised no initiative. They were
expected simply to copy. And the work was clean. Attracted by the
new jobs, large numbers of women not previously employed began
to look for work. These were native-born daughters of native parents,
who had consistently refused jobs next to immigrant women in factories. For them, office work brought only minimal loss of dignity and
offered the chance to earn decent incomes. The best-paid office workers
—those who worked for the federal government, for example—might
earn $900 a year in the 1870s. Though less than male wages for similar
jobs, this compared favorably with other women's jobs. A teacher
could make $500 a year. A stellar "typewriter" could make $7 a week,
and an ordinary office clerk earned $6. A competent cap maker might
earn $7 a week, but seasonal unemployment reduced her wages to
less than $250 for a year's work.

Women's entry into the labor force accompanied a transition in the
structure of offices. Unlike the men they replaced, women did not
work primarily as personal secretaries. Rather, they found themselves
doing tasks that were subdivided to produce maximal efficiency with
minimal training. A year of secretarial training could turn a woman
into a competent typist and stenographer. Lesser amounts were required for file clerks, telephone operators, and receptionists. But her
ability to perform tasks constituted only part of a woman employee's
attraction. Her personality weighed heavily. In 1916, a writer in the

Ladies' Home Journal attributed 50 percent of the stenographer's value to her personality, quoting an employer who declared, "I expect from my stenographer the same service I get from the sun, with this exception: the sun often goes on a strike and it is necessary for me to use artificial light, but I pay my stenographer to work six days out of every seven and I expect her all the while to radiate my office with sunshine and sympathetic interest in the things I am trying to do."[17]

The office worker's job might have made consistent sunshine difficult. Expected to possess all the sympathetic and nurturing characteristics of a good wife, she often performed tasks as routine as those of any factory worker. In the interests of efficiency, managers pooled their labor so that women might be called upon to perform their assigned job for any number of bosses.[18] Even in this early period, managers simplified jobs, reducing tasks to the level of petty detail. One office manager declared women to be more "temperamentally reconciled" to the new jobs than ambitious men. By the 1920s attempts to systematize and control the office led to experiments with scientific management techniques. Creating systems for filing, keeping records, and corresponding became the tasks of an office manager. In a scientifically managed office the clerk or typist could no longer work according to her own methods, but according to methods and at times specified by the manager. Detailed studies were expected to reveal optimal speeds for each task and to break down the work into its simplest components. Though these techniques were never widely adopted, they influenced perceptions of systematic work and affected the tasks of numerous female office clerks.

In the given-out trades the transition first to factory work and then to efficiency techniques produced different results. As long as women made hats, garments, paper flowers, and feathers in the context of a rural family environment, they could trade off their small wages against the advantages of flexible work schedules. Supported by home-grown products, they might get through hard times without work, and they benefited from community sanction against those who cheated or did not pay as promised. These favorable conditions changed as the production of most goods shifted to factories in the 1850s, 1860s and 1870s. During the transition, home work competed with factory products, forcing middlemen to demand a speedup in manufacture at the cost of quality. And centralization of the manufacturing process meant that even the paid work that remained in the home tended to gravitate from rural to urban environments, where community sanctions had less force and women had fewer resources to fall back on. As we have seen, contractors who distributed work from a shop in an impersonal

urban environment succumbed to temptations to cheat and to offer
the lowest possible wages. They ushered in some of the worst abuses
of the sweating system.

In the garment industry, the rapid spread of the sewing machine
after 1860 meant that for a while women, whether they sewed at home
or in a shop, had to bear the increased costs of buying a piece of
equipment. But its long-run effect was to encourage the slow movement
of the work force into factories, where centralized production rationalized the garment-making process.

For a while, garment manufacturers distinguished sharply between
"inside" and "outside" shops. In both, manufacturers distributed cut
garments to contractors who bid against each other. The lowest bid
got the bundle, and the contractor who won it hired his own operators
to make up the pieces. Those who worked "inside" normally supervised the work process under the roof of the manufacturer himself.
Others took the bundles "outside" to their own tenement flats, or to
cheaply rented quarters. Since a contractor's income depended directly
on how cheaply he could get people to finish the garments, he paid
as little as he possibly could, and charged his workers for thread, heat,
light, and power, if he could get away with it. The system encouraged the
use of family labor—which could be employed for endless hours—and of
women. Though immigrant men were sometimes as much as 40 percent
of the machine operators, the core of the labor force consisted of
young, often immigrant women. Whether a woman worked inside or
outside, she was most often paid directly by the contractor to whom
she was responsible. That contractor—perhaps a tailor—in turn got
his bundles from a foreman who coordinated the work of finishing
and pressing completed garments. In inside shops this relationship
left the subcontracting tailor less control than might otherwise seem
possible. Becky Stein, a Philadelphia garment worker, recounted to the
Commission on Industrial Relations in 1916 her sense of grievance at
foremen who could compel a tailor to discharge a finisher against his
will by threatening, "If you won't discharge her, you can't get no
work."[19]

The sewing machine, agitation from reformers who feared the spread
of disease from tenement-made goods, and a desire for closer supervision of the work process all encouraged manufacturers to bring
their contractors inside, and by the early 1900s some branches of the
industry began to eliminate the contractor altogether. As among telephone operators later, the increasing similarity of work and close
association of workers stimulated unionization. Female sewing machine operators employed in the shirtwaist industry led the series of
strikes that breathed life into the moribund International Ladies'

Garment Workers' Union between 1909 and 1911. Shirtwaist manufacture—the newest branch of the garment industry—was organized in fairly large inside shops with relatively decent working conditions. The young female labor force sought freedom from the erratic decisions and often harassing behavior of foremen and supervisors. To get it, they fought for and finally won union recognition.

Not surprisingly, manufacturers, interested in rationalizing their industry, used the young union to institute some efficiency techniques that the union agreed would benefit workers as well as manufacturers. Their agreements are embodied in the Protocols of Peace—a series of compacts negotiated from 1910 to 1917 between local unions and manufacturers' associations representing various branches of the women's garment industry. The protocols normally included provisions for minimum wages, maximum hours, sanitary conditions, and arbitration mechanisms. But some went further. In New York's dress and waist industry, for example, the protocol guaranteed union cooperation in raising worker efficiency and holding manufacturers' costs down in return for guaranteed prices, mutually negotiated and agreed upon by the two parties in advance. The Board of Protocol Standards created under this industry's 1913 agreement set up union/employer time and motion study teams that would recommend appropriate wages and standard procedures and accounting methods. Since efficiency systems were then anathema to organized trade unionists, who were largely skilled, white males, the ILGWU leadership acted cautiously. But, for its semiskilled female membership, notions of efficiency and negotiated prices had tangible benefits. The union acquired a voice in the labor process. Women experienced relatively less harassment by lecherous foremen and received designated and attainable tasks at prescribed prices. The ILGWU's rationale earned the support of Sidney Hillman, president of the newly- formed Amalgamated Clothing Workers' Union, which organized workers in the men's clothing industry. The Amalgamated, 40 percent of whose members were female in 1920, cooperated with employers who tried to increase efficiency on the grounds that it subjected employees to less irrational behavior.[20]

As it encouraged employers to turn to female labor for some jobs, the movement to increase worker productivity and to rationalize the work process produced an upsurge of resistance on the part of both men and women.[21] But whereas men involved in the de-skilling process could and did unionize to defend their status, women discovered that their attempts to do so ran counter to assumptions about their social roles.

When the Knights of Labor flourished in the 1880s, women took advantage of its open membership policy to organize in large numbers. But the American Federation of Labor, founded in 1886, represented relatively privileged workers, willing to sacrifice the larger issue of working-class solidarity for the immediate gain of higher wages. In the creation of what economist Selig Perlman called "a joint partnership of organized labor and organized capital," the Federation cooperated extensively with corporation-dominated government agencies, sought to exclude immigrants, and supported an imperialist foreign policy.[22] Its mechanisms for dealing with the huge numbers of women entering the labor force are an integral part of the puzzle surrounding the interaction of ideological and economic forces in regulating labor market participation.

In the period from 1897 to 1920, the AFL underwent dramatic expansion. It consolidated and confirmed its leadership over a number of independent unions, including the dying Knights of Labor. Membership increased from about 265,000 in 1897 to more than four million by 1920, and included four-fifths of all organized workers. In the same period, the proportion of women working in the industrial labor force climbed by about 20 percent. Rapid and heady expansion offered a golden opportunity for organizers. That they did not take advantage of it is one of the most important facts in the history of labor organizing in America.

Figures for union membership are notoriously unreliable, and estimates fluctuate widely. But something like 3.3 percent of the women who were engaged in industrial occupations in 1900 were organized into trade unions. As low as that figure was, it began to decrease around 1902 and 1903, reaching a low of 1.5 percent in 1910. Then, a surge of organization among garment workers raised it. A reasonable estimate might place 6.6 percent of wage-earning women in trade unions by 1920—nearly half of them in the clothing trades and another 25 percent in printing. The rest belonged to a variety of unions, including meat packers, electrical workers, railway clerks, textile workers, boot and shoe workers, and hotel employees. In a decade that saw little change in the relative proportion of female and male workers, the proportion of women who were trade union members quadrupled, increasing at more than twice the rate for trade union members in general. Even so, the relative numbers of wage-earning women who were trade union members remained tiny. One in every five men in the industrial work force belonged to a union, compared to one in every fifteen women. Although more than 20 percent of the labor force was female, less than 8 percent of organized workers were women.

The dearth of women in unions had historic roots. These are readily located in the personality and behavioral patterns that derived from traditional family expectations. The young, unskilled workers who looked to marriage to escape the shop or factory were not ideal candidates for unionization. At the turn of the century, 87 percent of female workers were unmarried and nearly half were under twenty-five. Wage-earning women often came from groups without a union tradition: about half were immigrants or daughters of immigrants who shared rural backgrounds. In the cities, the figure sometimes rose to 90 percent.[23] Like immigrant and black men, women formed a large reservoir of unskilled workers. Because they offered employers the advantage of low pay and exploitative working conditions, employers had a special incentive to resist unionization among women. As John Andrews, writing in the 1911 Report on the Condition of Woman and Child Wage Earners, put it: "The moment she organizes a union and seeks by organization to secure better wages she diminishes or destroys what is to the employer her chief value."[24] Women who wished to unionize had to fight on two fronts: against the weight of tradition and expectation, and against employers.

There was yet a third battle front—the trade union itself—and it might have been the most important of all. Instead of recognizing women as workers and encouraging them to join in organizational struggles, male unionists insisted on women's primary function in the home and remained stubbornly ambivalent about their efforts. They understood that employers had an important economic incentive for hiring women, and so their rhetoric, reflecting fears of being undercut, affirmed a commitment to unionize women wage earners and to extract equal pay for them. Yet in practice trade unionists remained locked into patriarchal attitudes that valued women's contributions to the home. Women's duties as mothers and wives, most felt, echoing the arguments of the preceding generation, were so valuable that women ought not to be in the labor force at all. This was unfortunate for women who wished to organize because it deprived them of help from the largest body of collective working-class opinion.

"The great principle for which we fight," said the AFL's treasurer in 1905, "is opposed to taking . . . the women from their homes to put them in the factory and the sweatshop." "We stand for the principle," said another AFL member, "that it is wrong to permit any of the female sex of our country to be forced to work, as we believe that the man should be provided with a fair wage in order to keep his female relatives from going to work. The man is the provider and should receive enough for his labor to give his family a respectable living." And yet a third proclaimed, "Respect for women is apt to decrease when they are compelled to work in the factory or the store. . . . More respect for women brings less degeneration and more marriages . . . if women labor in factories and similar institutions they bring forth weak children who are not educated to become strong and good citizens." No language was too forceful or too dramatic. "The demand for female labor," wrote an official of the Boston Central Labor Union in 1897, is "an insidious assault upon the home . . . it is the knife of the assassin, aimed at the family circle." The AFL journal, *American Federationist*, romanticized women's jobs at home, extolling the virtues of refined and moral mothers, of good cooking, and even of beautiful needlework and embroidery.[25]

These arguments from home and motherhood had several effects. They sustained women's sense of themselves as temporary workers—a self-image on which their exploitation rested. In so doing they inadvertently aided employers, who relied on the notion that women were marginal to the work force to pay low wages and limit training. Trade unionists thus contributed to segmenting the labor force and crowding women into a few areas. Perhaps worst of all, the notion that women constituted a different kind of worker created barriers between the sexes that inhibited cooperation in a common struggle with employers.

The perception that women belonged in the home translated into the desire that they be eliminated from the work force entirely. "Every woman employed," wrote an editor in *American Federationist*, "displaces a man and adds one more to the idle contingent that are fixing wages at the lowest limit."[26] "It is the so-called competition of the unorganized defenseless woman worker, the girl and the wife, that often tends to reduce the wages of the father and husband," proclaimed Samuel Gompers.[27] The Federation's fears, grounded in the new technology and the specter of Taylorization, found expression in anger directed against women. The Birmingham *Labor Advocate*, voice of the AFL in the South, declared in 1903 that woman owed "an incalculable debt to the labor movement. It has done for her everything that it has done for men." And yet, the paper went on, "despite the fact that the labor movement has worked through the trades unions incalculable benefit to the woman wage earner in every industry, it is one of the ironies of the labor agitator's life that women have ever been and do still remain their most uncompromising opponents. . . . Could the woman wage earner be eliminated—suddenly and absolutely eliminated—from all consideration in the labor problem, that problem would be more than half solved."[28]

Skilled members and leaders of the AFL who might appropriately have directed their energies at challenging the uses of technology chose instead to lash out at women who dared to work. Gompers offers a good example. "The ingenuity of man to produce the world's wealth easier than ever before," he wrote in 1904, "is utilized as a means to pauperize the worker, to supplant the man by the woman and the woman by the child. . . ."[29] The *American Federationist* was filled with tales of men displaced by women and children. "One house in St. Louis now pays $4 per week to women where men got $16," snapped the journal in 1896. "A local typewriter company has placed 200 women to take the place of unorganized men," announced an organizer in 1903. Some companies, Gompers editorialized, took on women "not so much to give them work as to make dividends fatter." Some of the least appropriate bitterness was expressed by Thomas O'Donnell, secretary to the National Spinners' Union whose constituency, once largely female, had been replaced by men after the Civil War. The advent of simple electric-powered machinery caused him to complain that "the manufacturers have been trying for years to discourage us by dispensing with the spinning mule and substituting female and child labor for that of the old-time skilled spinners. . . ."[30]

These sentiments did not entirely prevent the AFL from attempting to unionize women. Although the grim realities of exploitative working conditions and the difficulties of caring for children while working ten or more hours a day sustained the argument for eliminating women from the work force, this goal was impossible to achieve. So the AFL, supported by well-intentioned social reformers, continued to organize women and to demand equal pay for equal work. Gompers editorialized on the subject frequently: "We . . . shall bend every energy for our fellow workmen to organize and unite in trade unions; to federate their effort without regard to . . . sex." He and others conceded the "full and free opportunity for women to work whenever and wherever necessity requires," but Gompers did not address himself to the problem of how to determine which women were admissible by this standard, and his actions revealed that he thought their numbers relatively few.[31]

The limited commitment implied by the wish that women would get out of the work force altogether was tinged with the conviction and perhaps the hope that women would, in the end, fail. The AFL granted a charter to Chicago's Ladies' Federal Labor Union in 1888, for example. But "federal unions—amalgams of workers unrelated by skill—had little power, and this one was kept alive only by the efforts of some exceptional female organizers.[32] Mary Kenney, one of these women, became the AFL's first female organizer in 1892. The Federation supported her only half-heartedly and allowed her position to expire within five months. Not until 1908 did the organization appoint another woman, Annie Fitzgerald, as a full-time organizer. In the meantime, the AFL relied on the Women's Trade Union League—an alliance of middle-class sympathizers and female labor activists—to organize women. But genuine ambivalence tempered its efforts.

The AFL repeatedly called for an end to discriminatory pay for women and men: "Equal compensation for equal service performed." But the demand was a double-edged sword. While it presumably protected all workers from cheap labor, in the context of the early 1900s labor market its real purpose was often to deprive women of jobs; equal compensation for women typically meant that employers would as soon replace them with men, who were not governed by such regulations, and were thought to be stronger. The Boston Typographical Union, noted one observer, saw "its only safety in maintaining the principle of equal pay for men and women. . . ."[33]

When the AFL did organize women, its major incentive was often the need to protect the earning power of men. Women were admitted to unions after men recognized them as competitors better controlled from within than allowed to compete from without. "It has been the policy of my associates and myself," wrote Gompers in 1906, "to throw open wide the doors of our organization and invite the working girls and working women to membership for their and our common protection."[34] *American Federationist* articles that began with pleas that women stay out of the work force concluded with equally impassioned pleas to organize those who were already in it. Alice Woodbridge, writing in 1894, concluded an argument that women who worked for wages were neglecting their duties to their "fellow creatures" with the following statement: "It is to the interest of both sexes that women should organize . . . until we are well organized there is little hope of success among organizations of men."[35] The AFL officially acknowledged competition as a primary motivation for organizing women in 1923. "Unorganized they constitute a menace to standards established through collective action. Not only for their protection, but for the protection of men . . . there should be organization of all women. . . ."[36]

These were not of course the only circumstances in which men suspended their hostility toward women's unions. Occasionally in small towns female and male unions in different industries supported each other against the hostile attacks of employers. Minersville, Pennsylvania, miners, for example, physically ousted railroad detectives who tried to break up a meeting of female textile workers.[37] The women in this case were the miners' daughters, sisters, and sweethearts. Far from competing with them for jobs, the women were helping to support the same families. Similarly, women and men in newly established industries could cooperate more effectively in unionizing together. The garment industry saw parallel but equally effective organization among its various branches. Though female organizers complained bitterly of the way they were treated, male leadership depended on the numerical majority of female workers to bargain successfully with employers and did not deny women admission. Yet, even here, union leadership successfully eliminated "home work" without offering those involved—grossly underpaid and often needy females who could not work outside their homes—a way of recouping their financial losses.

Such occasional exceptions notwithstanding, the general consequence of union attitudes toward women was to isolate them from the male work force. Repeatedly women who organized themselves into unions applied for entry to the appropriate parent body only to be turned down or simply ignored. Pauline Newman, who had organized and collected dues from a group of Philadelphia candy makers in 1910, offered to continue to work with them if the International Bakery and Confectionery Workers' Union would issue a charter. The International stalled and put them off until the employers began to discharge the leaders and the group disintegrated.[38] Waitresses in Norfolk, Virginia, suffered a similar fate. Mildred Rankin, who requested a charter for a group of fifteen, was assured by the local AFL organizer that she was wasting her time. "The girls were all getting too much money to be interested," was his comment on denying the request.[39] New York's International Typographical Union refused to issue female copyholders a charter on the grounds that they were insufficiently skilled. When the group applied to the parent AFL for recognition, they were refused on the grounds that they were within the ITU's jurisdiction. They got little satisfaction when the issue came before the AFL's Executive Council the following year. Though the Federation had agreed to issue charters to black male workers excluded from all-white unions, it refused to accord the same privilege to women. Gompers's assertion that he would "bend every energy" to help women organize notwithstanding, the parent body agreed only to "take up the subject with the trade unions and to endeavour to reach an understanding" as far as women were concerned.[40]

A strong union could simply cut women out of the kinds of jobs held by unionized men, a form of segmenting the labor market that sometimes contradicted the interests of employers who would have preferred cheap labor. A Binghamton, New York, printing establishment, for example, could not hire women Linotype operators because "the men's union would not allow it."[41] This tactic excluded racial minorities as often as it restricted women; and, like appeals to racist beliefs, arguments based on the natural weakness of women worked well as a rationale. Mary Dreier, then president of the New York Chapter of the Women's Trade Union League, recalled a union of tobacco workers whose leaders refused to admit women because "they could only do poor sort of work . . . because women had no colour discrimination."[42] A Boston metal polishers' union refused to admit women. "We don't want them," an official told an interviewer. "Women can only do one kind of work while men can polish anything from iron to gold and frame the smallest part to the largest." Besides, he added, "metal polishing is bad for the health."[43]

Less direct methods excluded women from unions equally effectively. The International Retail Clerks' Union charged an initiation fee of three dollars and dues of fifty cents a month. Hilda Svenson, a local organizer in 1914, complained that she had been unable to negotiate a compromise with the International. "We want to be affiliated with them," she commented, "but on account of the dues and initiation fee we feel it is too high at the present time for the salaries that the girls in New York are getting."[44] Sometimes union pay scales were set so high that the employer would not pay the appropriate wage to women. Joining the union could mean that a female printer would lose her job; so women simply refused to join.

But even membership in a union led by men guaranteed little to women. Unions often deliberately sabotaged their female members. Detroit's Amalgamated Association of Street Railway and Electrical Employees had agreed under wartime duress to admit women who were to be employed as conductors into their union in 1918. Just as their probationary period ended, men began returning from overseas and the union refused 250 women regular cards. Only an appeal to the National War Labor Board, which ruled in the women's favor, saved their jobs.[45] Supporting union men was not likely to benefit women either. Mary Anderson, newly appointed head of the U.S. Department of Labor's Women's Bureau, got a frantic telegram from a WTUL organizer in Joliet, Illinois, early in 1919. The women in a Joliet steel plant who, in return for the promise of protection, had supported unionized men in a recent strike were fighting desperately for jobs that the union now insisted they give up. The company wanted to retain the women, but union men argued that the work was too heavy for them.[46]

In addition, such well-known tactics as holding meetings in saloons, scheduling them at late hours, and ridiculing women who dared to speak deprived women of full participation. Italian and southern families disliked their daughters going out in the evenings. Married and self-supporting women and widows had household duties at which they spent after-work hours. Women who attended meetings usually participated reluctantly. They found the long discussions dull and were often intimidated by the preponderance of men. Men, for their part, resented the indifference of the women and further excluded them from leadership roles, thereby discouraging more women from attending. Even fines failed to spark attendance. Some women preferred to pay them rather than go to the meetings.[47]

Cultural patterns that derived from a patriarchal society joined ethnic ties in hindering unionization. Wage-earning women, anxious to marry, were sometimes reluctant to join unions for what they felt would be a temporary period.[48] The role conflict implicit in a young wage-earning woman's assumptions about future family life emerged in ambivalence toward unions. "No nice girl would belong to one," said one young woman. An ILGWU organizer commented that the reluctance of most women who did not want to unionize reflected the obedience they owed to fathers. "The boss is good to us" they claimed; "we have nothing to complain about and we don't want to join the union."[49] A woman who resisted unionization told an organizer that she knew "$6 a week is not enough pay but the Lord helps me ont. He always provides. . . . I won't ever join a union. The Lord doesn't want me to."[50] A recent convert to unionism apologized for her former reluctance. She had always scabbed because church people disapproved of unions. Moreover, she and her sister, she admitted to an organizer, had only with difficulty overcome their fear of the Italian men who were organizing their factory.[51]

For all their initial reluctance women could be devoted and successful union members, convinced that unionism would serve them as it seemed to be serving their brothers. In the words of a seventeen-year-old textile worker, "We all work hard for a mean living. Our boys belong to the miners' union so their wages are better than ours. So I figure that girls must have a union. Women must act like men, ain't?"[52] Such attitudes occurred most often among women whose ethnic backgrounds encouraged both wage labor and a high level of social consciousness, as in the American Jewish community, for example. Young Jewish women constituted the bulk of the membership of the International Ladies' Garment Workers' Union in the period from 1910 to 1920. Their rapid organization and faithful tenure was responsible for at least one-quarter of the increased number of unionized women in those years. And yet they were unskilled and semi-skilled workers, employed in small, scattered shops, theoretically among the least organizable. These women, having unionized at their own initiative, formed the backbone of the ILGWU, which had originally sought to organize the skilled male cutters in the trade.

They often served as shop "chairladies" and reached positions of minor importance in the union structure. Faige Shapiro recalled that her union activity began at the insistence of a business agent but quickly became an absorbing interest. The commitment of some women was such that when arrested on picket lines, they offered to spend the night in jail in order to save the union bail costs before returning to the line in the morning.[53]

Whether in mixed unions or segregated by sex, women often outdid men in militancy. Once organized, they could more easily rely on the families they lived with to support them in a pinch. Since women as a group tended to have fewer dependents than men, they could hold out longer in a strike. Examples abound. Iowa cigar makers reported in 1899 that striking men had resumed work, while the women stood fast. Boot and shoe workers in Massachusetts were reported in 1905 to be tough bargainers. "It is harder to induce women to compromise," said their president; "they are more likely to hold out to the bitter end . . . to obtain exactly what they want."[54] The great 1909 uprising in which 20,000 women walked out of New York's garment shops occurred over the objections of the male leadership, striking terror into the hearts of Jewish men afraid "of the security of their jobs."[55] Protesting a rate cut in the textile mills of Chicopee, Massachusetts, Polish "spool girls" refused their union's suggestion that they arbitrate and won a resounding victory. Swedish women enrolled in a Chicago Custom Clothing Makers local lost a battle against employers' attempts to subdivide and speed up the sewing process when the largely male United Garment Workers' Union agreed to the new conditions. The management promptly locked out the women, forcing many to come to terms and others to seek new jobs.[56] These militant characteristics enabled women who overcame the initial barriers to organization to run highly successful sex-segregated unions. They account for the early success of such turn-of-the-century unions as those of female garment workers in San Francisco, of telephone operators in Boston, and of tobacco strippers, and overall and sheepskin workers elsewhere.

Militance was less effective where trade union ambivalence left women at the mercy of employers who were particularly eager to discourage organization among women. In these instances, employers pressed their advantage. Sometimes they used crude techniques familiar to men. Department store employees were commonly fired when their union membership became known. Many stores had spy systems so that employees could not trust each other. Blacklists were common. Members of the Retail Dry Goods Association refused jobs to women whose names appeared on lists of troublemakers. The Association itself kept a complete record of all employees, including where they were employed and why discharged. Records were passed on to prospective employers, with no right of appeal by the employee.[57] For fear of retaliation, a representative of the year-old Retail Clerks' Union, testifying before a congressional committee in 1914, refused to reveal the number of members in her union. To undercut trade union activities, department stores formed their own employee associations. Filene's in Boston and Bloomingdale's in New York set up welfare funds to make loans to employees in distress or to distribute turkeys at Thanksgiving. Although these funds required employee contributions, and representatives to the boards that controlled them were technically elected by the workers, no employee had ever sat on the Filene's board when one worker described it to an investigative committee in 1916.[58]

In the garment industry, owners of New York's garment shops, fighting what was by 1910 a losing battle against unionism, frequently discharged employees who were thought to be active organizers or union members. They also played on ethnic and racial tensions. Rose Schneiderman, who formed the Hat and Cap Makers' Union in 1903, fought against bosses who urged immigrant workers to stick to the "American shop"—a euphemism for an antiunion shop. Jewish owners sometimes hired only Italian workers, who were thought to be less prone to unionization than Jews.[59] Others hired *landsmen* from the same old country community, hoping that fraternal instincts might keep them from uniting.

Blacks were played off against whites. Waitresses picketing Knab's Restaurant in Chicago were met with counterpickets paid by the employer. A representative of the waitresses' union reported indignantly that the restaurant "placed colored pickets on the street, colored women who wore signs that proclaimed, 'Gee, I ain't mad at nobody and nobody ain't mad at Knab.' " When the nonunion pickets attracted a crowd, police used this as an excuse to arrest the union members. The waitresses were further discouraged by trials engineered by the restaurant employers' association, which had previously given "every policeman a turkey free."[60]

Police routinely broke up picket lines and outdoor meetings. Women were accused of obstructing traffic or incited into slapping provocateurs and arrested. More importantly, women who might have been interested in unionization were intimidated by police who surrounded open-air meetings or by department store detectives who mingled obtrusively with potential recruits. Department store owners diverted workers from street meetings by locking all but one set of doors and channeling the after-work flow away from contact with organizers.

Alternatively, they might send trucks, horns honking full blast, to parade up and down the street in which a meeting was scheduled.[61]

Small employers formed mutual assistance associations to help them resist their employees' attempts to unionize. The Chicago Restaurant Keepers' Association, for example, denied membership to any "person, firm or corporation . . . having signed agreements with any labor organization." Garment manufacturers in both New York and Chicago created protective associations to combat what they called "the spreading evil of unionism."[62]

In small towns, where wage-earning women were still subject to a debilitating paternalism, the power of town officials was called into play. A town sheriff told Ann Washington Craton, organizing textile workers in Minersville, Pennsylvania, just after the war: "You are to let our girls alone. . . . Mr. Demsky will shut the factory down rather than have a union. . . . The Town Council brought this factory here to provide work for worthy widows and poor girls. We don't intend to have any trouble about it."[63] The most extreme form of this kind of paternalism still existed in the boarding-house system. The president of the Nonotuck Silk Company of Northampton, Massachusetts, reported proudly in 1901 that his company required "the girls to go to their rooms at half past nine, and lights to be out at 10; but if they want to go to a concert or the theater, they are to notify the boarding house keeper, who is always up to let them in. . . . We do it for their benefit. Then we say to parents and brothers who live at a distance, 'You can safely let your sister or your daughter come down here to the Nonotuck mills. She is looked after, and is required to be in at suitable hours. We have an interest in her.' "[64]

New ideas about corporate welfare and Taylor's notions of scientific management encouraged some managers to handle disciplinary problems through personnel and welfare work. Personnel management was of course the ideal tool for intervention and control. This newly founded science purported to be able to select employees judiciously and to assign them to the work they could do most effectively. Its techniques ranged from diagnostic interviews that attempted to choose likely candidates for each job, through careful juxtaposition of workers, with due consideration for race and ethnicity, and formal procedures for promotion and termination. Welfare work promised to keep workers contented by enhancing their sense of general well-being. Plants engaged in welfare work might offer employees incentives to purchase houses, to suggest innovative techniques through formal channels, and to participate in company-sponsored recreation. As a government report on textile mills concluded: "Parks, skating rinks, baseball teams, bands, and other welfare work doubtless have as one of their objects the creation of a contented class of mill employees who will not move about."[65]

To workers and trade union organizers, welfare work appeared as an attempt to undermine their roles. One active union organizer described welfare work as "the last stand of the intelligent employer before doing business with a trade union. . . ."[66] The focus of such work varied, but often it seemed to workers just another form of charity. The president of the Retail Clerks' Union, employed by Bloomingdale's Department Store, complained that only married workers and male employees got turkeys at Thanksgiving. "You have got to apply for it and ask for it, say that you need it. It is given out just as a charity is handed out . . . and the turkeys are paid for out of the money of the employees."[67]

To create uniformity and the appearance of content, personnel managers took unusual liberties with the lives and tastes of their employees. Mary Gilson recalled her attempts to dictate the amount of make-up and the style of clothing that workers could wear. "We had a yen to remove stockings worn as rats in huge pompadours," she remembers; or again, "the girls who wanted to express themselves (and had a right to) in gay clothes were frowned upon as the climate of the shop became more frigid toward powder and jewelry and fancy coiffures." Nor did such intervention stop at the factory gate. Gilson's account of her interest in workers' affairs bears repeating. "There was no facet of life we did not touch," she remembered.

> The woman with a job at the factory and an equally onerous one at home, the spirited young girl who was impatient with her "old country" parents and whose discipline she resented; the man who drank too much on Sundays and stayed at home on Mondays. When we visited the latter's home and saw his slattern wife we wondered why he ever was sober. One such woman told us she hated and loathed housekeeping and her husband was "good at it." We suggested when next we saw him that he try shifting the tables and letting her go to work while he stayed at home. When he finally acknowledged that he would really like to try it, she went to work in the factory and he gave up his job. They had four children under seven, and we suggested to him that if he was going to let her work that meant no more children and it meant he was really to take over and not allow her to do two jobs, one at home and one at the factory.[68]

The paternalism, benevolence, and welfare employers offered in compensation for foregoing unionism proved to be particularly useful tools for diverting women from organization. They promised to alleviate some of the harsh conditions under which women worked—conditions long viewed by reformers and investigators as detrimental to the preservation of home and family. These voluntary employer programs, in conjunction with government regulation, seemed to many an adequate alternative to unionism. What was more, trade unions, by allying themselves with regulators and sometimes with employers, could use appeals to women's "natural roles" to restrict their labor force participation. James Armstrong, representing Moulders' Union No. 22 of Brooklyn, New York, told a state investigating commission trying to decide if women should be excluded from jobs in foundries that they would have no need to debate "if we could get together, that is the foundry bosses and us." When asked where women already employed would go, Armstrong's colleague Edward Parker of Buffalo replied, "all you would have to do would be to look at our Buffalo *Evening News* and see the Want Ad column for girls in housework where they belong. I don't think they should be employed in factories. I think the men should be left to make living wages to support the girls and their families."[69]

In their capacity as workers, women might have been left to fight alone. But as women, they got the sympathy and assistance of a variety of reform groups made up largely of non-wage-earning women. Unlike trade unionists, these reformers accepted without question the continuing necessity for poor women to earn wages. Unlike the earlier reformers, this generation attempted to create alliances with the trade union movement and among working women. But their attempts to act as "allies" foundered on the precarious position of female wage earners.

The new reformers shared the progressive notion of faith in the individual. They came, more often than not, from the social settlements that dotted American cities by the 1890s and acted as a training ground for young college-educated women and men who wished to devote a few years of their lives to reducing the gap between urban, immigrant poverty and democratic values. The settlement reflected the tension between the egalitarian ideals of a democratic society and the dawning recognition that poor immigrants might be unable to rise for reasons entirely beyond their control. For women, the tension emerged in a special way. Family life, for which they were held responsible, was considered an essential underpinning of good citizenship. Yet women's work was so utterly degraded as to effectively prevent them from fulfilling their family responsibilities. Later settlements would emphasize ways of alleviating degradation at work through factory inspection and the drive for protective labor legislation. But in the 1890s and early 1900s, settlements operated in two conflicting directions. They reinforced women's home roles by providing cooking and sewing classes and community activities intended to teach domestic skills and American values. And they sustained women's ability to work by providing meeting places for unions and kindergartens for working mothers. Some settlements offered mediation between bosses and striking workers; others housed talented women like Florence Kelley, Julia Clifford Lathrop, and Ellen Gates Starr, who conceived and nurtured legislation to regulate child labor and provide safe and sanitary work places.

Among other offspring, settlements gave birth to the Women's Trade Union League, which took a giant step toward organizing wage-earning women.[70] Conceived by Mary Kenney (now Mary Kenney O'Sullivan) and William English Walling, the WTUL was founded in 1903 at an AFL meeting in Boston. O'Sullivan, a book binder by trade and an organizer of the Chicago Bookbinders' Union as well as the Chicago Ladies' Federal Labor Union, had lost her job as women's organizer for the AFL when the Executive Council refused to renew the position. She had earlier been befriended by Jane Addams and indelibly influenced by the community of women at Hull House. When she married a fellow union leader and moved to Boston in 1894, she continued her organizing activities through Dennison House, a settlement noted for its union proclivities. Walling, in contrast, was the scion of a wealthy New England family. An early settlement house resident, he witnessed the British WTUL and brought the idea of cross-class cooperation back to the United States. Together these two solicited the aid of social settlement leaders like Jane Addams and Lillian Wald of Henry Street and the cooperation of AFL leaders to produce the combination of wage-earning women and middle-class allies who constituted the backbone of women's trade union organizing in the early 1900s.

In its first twelve years the WTUL concentrated on organizing. Led by a national policy-making unit and supported by local leagues in cities like New York, Boston, Chicago, and St. Louis, the group provided money, publicity, tactical advice, and political support for women attempting to unionize around work place issues. Working with the AFL, it offered financial aid to induce the Federation to pay attention to women thought to be too expensive or difficult to organize. League members put up bail bonds for arrested strikers, marched on picket lines, and published a monthly paper called *Life and Labor*. In short, the WTUL, convinced that women had to be integrated into trade union structures if they were to be taken seriously as workers, did for women what male unions had long done for male workers. They gave the lie to bold assertions that women could not be organized. The League created its most spectacular success in the 1909–10 strike of women in New York's garment industry. But it also played important roles in winning strikes in Chicago, Philadelphia, among Kalamazoo corset workers, and elsewhere.

These important successes should have paved the way to further achievements in organizing women. But the WTUL became mired in tensions with the AFL. These erupted spectacularly in 1912 when textile workers in Lawrence, Massachusetts, walked out to protest an effective reduction in wages that followed on a legislative mandate to shorten hours from fifty-six to fifty-four per week. Strike activity, dominated from the start by the radical syndicalist leadership of the Industrial Workers of the World, included some WTUL leaders. O'Sullivan, for example, had traveled from Boston to Lawrence to see what she could do. Then the AFL, ambivalent about the unskilled immigrants who constituted the bulk of the strikers and uneasy with the IWW, negotiated a settlement for its skilled members and withdrew, asking the WTUL to leave the scene. The national WTUL, seeking to maintain organizational unity with the AFL, complied. But Mary Kenney O'Sullivan, angry at the callous disregard of unskilled immigrant women, stayed on the scene. Explicitly refusing to obey AFL directives, she presented the strikers' case to a state investigating commission and interceded at a crucial point with the American Woolen Company, against which the strike had been called. She subsequently quit the WTUL, leaving its members to debate the degree to which they would be subservient to the AFL. The incident reflects the difficulty the WTUL had in operating within ambiguous territory. In the end, the League acquiesed to trade union conceptions of women's place. In 1915, it turned away from direct organization, seeking to solve the problems of women at work by involving state and local government in regulatory activities.

This transition brought the WTUL in line with most reform groups concerned with protecting wage-earning women around the turn of the century. The National Consumers' League, arguably the most influential, attempted through its state and local branches to bring purchasing power to bear as a weapon for improving the conditions of sweatshop workers and sales clerks. Founded in 1892 by Maude Nathan and Josephine Shaw Lowell, the National Consumers' League agitated for seats for saleswomen in department stores, promoted clean, ventilated lunch rooms, published white lists of stores that treated employees well, and issued labels to be attached to items made under sanitary and healthful conditions. In 1899, the NCL hired Florence Kelley, former resident of Hull House and Illinois factory inspector, as its director. Kelley led the organization into a campaign for legislation to regulate department store conditions and to prescribe sanitation and safety measures on the shop floor. Influential until after

The marginal existence of "women adrift" remained a subject of concern until World War I. Above: An illustration from an 1899 book on classes in New York and their ways of living embodies a middle-class conception of dreary, poverty-stricken, lonely lives. *(Museum of the City of New York)* Below: Unemployed homeless women line up at the women's alms house on Blackwell's Island, 1903. *(Photograph by Byron. The Byron Collection, Museum of the City of New York)*

To remedy their situation, women, like these eight delegates to the Knights of Labor convention in 1886, joined unions. Front and center is Elizabeth Rodgers, with her two-week-old baby, Lizzie. *(Courtesy of the Library of Congress)*

By 1903, wage-earning women got the help of the Women's Trade Union League. Depicted at their first convention in Richmond, Virginia, in 1907 are, left to right, Hannah Hennesey, Ida Rauh, Mary Dreier, Mary Kenney O'Sullivan, Margaret Dreier Robins, Margie Jones, Agnes Nestor, Helen Marot. *(Courtesy of the Library of Congress)*

Efficiency techniques and scientific management, like those introduced by the telephone companies after the turn of the century, required special attention to women's welfare. Above: Telephone operators in 1901. *(Brown Brothers)* Below: The Edwards Sanitarium for Chicago Telephone Company employees suffering from telephone shock, March 1919. *(Courtesy of the National Archives)*

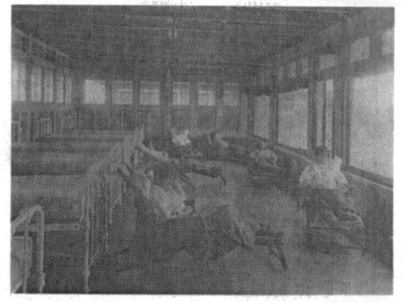

Vocational schools trained women for newer occupations while attempting to ensure their continued loyalty to the home. Above: A course in typing and stenography at the Bryant High School, New York, in 1906. Note the male giving dictation while the woman types from a dictaphone. *(Photograph by Byron. The Byron Collection, Museum of the City of New York)* Below: A domestic science cooking class, 1918. *(Brown Brothers)*

World War I, the NCL was not alone. The YWCA, for instance, set up an industrial division to provide (among other services) an analysis of industrial problems and training for women to face them. These paths reflected a growing consensus that acknowledged women's place in the work force, as long as that place remained clearly defined.

The Women's Bureau institutionalized the consensus. For years, women's reform groups like the WTUL and the NCL had agitated for special representation for women in the Labor Department. When the Department created the Women in Industry Service during World War I to streamline the insertion of female labor into war industries, reformers seized their chance. They successfully lobbied for a continuation of the Service, persuading a grudging Congress to fund a permanent Women's Bureau within the Department of Labor in 1919. Headed by former Chicago shoe worker and WTUL activist Mary Anderson, the Bureau set out to investigate the needs of women workers and to recommend legislative solutions.

If women were not to unionize, how were they to overcome low pay and exploitation at work? Training women in the skills appropriate to their sphere seemed like a plausible answer. Such activists in women's rights as Anna Dickinson and Mary Livermore had advocated training as a solution to women's problems for years. Early commentators on female labor—Virginia Penny, Caroline Dall, and later Annie McLean —repeatedly urged vocational training for girls.[1] These women argued that the changing sex ratio—women already made up more than 51 percent of the population in such urban states as New York, Connecticut, Massachusetts, and New Jersey—would necessitate life-long work for many women, and that widowhood, desertion, and even divorce would force still others to fend for themselves. But acceptance of their proposals turned on the critical question of whether training would break down, or contribute to, sexual segmentation in the job market.

Skilled trades had traditionally been a province of unionized crafts-men who jealously guarded access to training in their fields. Though women frequently taught each other, and occasionally managed to "steal" a trade from a willing male relative, they were rarely admitted to the requisite apprenticeships. Where they managed to acquire skills and posed a threat to male workers, craft unions sometimes grudgingly helped women to form separate, affiliated unions. We have seen, for example, how New York Typographical Union No. 6 used the union structure first to help organize women separately, then to absorb and control them. To allow outsiders to train men or women, but especially women, in skilled areas posed an unending threat. When, in 1872,

cigar makers faced an influx of skilled female Bohemian cigar rollers
into their union, they responded by excluding the women altogether,
provoking their use as strikebreakers a year later.

By the late 1890s employers began to move toward manual training
programs in the public schools as a way of breaking craft monopolies.
Manual training—which encouraged general skills useful for industrial
work—quickly gave way to vocational education, which emphasized
the skills specific to particular jobs. Such developments reflected a
general shift in attitude toward all education. Initially education had
been seen as useless in terms of vocation. Agnes Smedley's father expressed a general prejudice when he pronounced it worthwhile "only
for women and men who were dudes."[72] But the urban and industrial
nation that had emerged out of the Civil War demanded disciplined
workers with positive attitudes toward their jobs. In the words of one
supervisor, the best educated of his workers were "the most capable,
intelligent, energetic, industrious, economical, and moral . . . they
produce the best work and the most of it, with the least injury to the
machinery."[73] Youngsters, employers thought, should be taught in
school to work with their hands so that when they left school they
could fit easily into an industrial framework.

For men, the issue of vocational education centered on the problem
of control. But for women, it became ambiguous. To some well-meaning
reformers, vocational training assumed the aspect of a panacea. Teaching women a trade opened tempting possibilities of financial security
for them as well as a way out of overcrowded women's fields and up in
the occupational structure. "Girls do not become apprentices or learn
a trade thoroughly, and consequently they lagged behind man in the
race of life," argued Ernestine Rose in 1869. "Teach girls to learn a
trade as well as boys," she continued, "and then they would be independent."[74] Jennie Cunningham Croly, feminist and socialist, concurred. To a congressional committee investigating capital and labor
she declared in 1883: "Wherever a person can do anything, can *do* it
in a proper sense, they can always earn a living by it; they can always
get a certain amount for it."[75] Sewing women earned only 50 cents a
day because they were not properly competent. Even a washerwoman,
who could wash, might make $1.25 a day. Raise "the standard of useful
work by education and training," Croly argued, and women would
earn more. The U.S. Department of Labor added fuel to the movement
in 1909 when it documented what everyone already suspected. A New
York City investigative committee had discovered that the average
annual wage for girls without training approximated one-third of the
wage of those who were trained as stenographers, and less than half of
those trained as nurses.

Training would also provide access to jobs previously closed. If women "want to do a man's work," argued New York *Tribune* publisher Whitelaw Reid, "they must prepare."[76] She would, Croly suggested, "supplement . . . common school education with technical or industrial schools where they would be made thorough mechanical draughtsmen, engravers, modelers, designers, dressmakers, embroiderers, laundresses, cooks, and tailors."[77] Training would provide skills for middle-aged women who had worked for years. It could even, Leonora O'Reilly proposed, "act as an incentive to unionization." O'Reilly, who would later supervise machine operators for the Manhattan Trade School for Girls, wondered in 1898 whether training might not give to "working girls" that "force of character which will secure them desirable conditions of life and work."[78] As jobs became increasingly mechanical, she touted trade schools as a way of preventing the "numbness of mind that comes with doing rote work." A trade school taught a girl "the relation between the brain and the hands."[79]

But in practice, vocational education for women was fraught with problems. Widespread opinion held that homemaking was sufficiently complicated that all women should train to become efficient and effective housekeepers. Women entered the labor force briefly—too briefly, some thought, to be worth the time or energy of adequate training. To provide training appropriate to rewarding jobs threatened to undermine women's investment in home roles. Female college graduates, fully half of whom never married, provided a specter of the future. Should social institutions, public or private, lend themselves to such an aberration?

Advocates of vocational education for women tried to meet this objection by praising the home-related aspects of their program and obscuring its job-training potential. "Industrial education," in the words of a noted authority, should be designed "to meet the needs of the manual wage workers in the trades and industries, and in the household."[80] Conceptually this meant that a notion of household labor as a woman's real work underlay every aspect of her vocational training. An insistent refrain accompanied preparation for even the most difficult jobs. Training would prepare female workers "for right living and right spending" in the future, said the Women's Educational and Industrial Union, whose purpose was "the advancement of women."[81] It could teach them to be good consumers, "intelligent, discriminating, purchasing agents for themselves and their homes," said the Federal Board for Vocational Education.[82] Out of training for a job, in short, would come not workers prepared to cope with the job market, but better house tenders. The National Society for the

Promotion of Industrial Education, a coalition of small manufacturers, educators, social workers, and representatives of organized labor, waxed eloquent on this theme. "Will not the woman who has learned to systematize, to go forth rain or shine to work an eight-hour day, to stand on her own feet, taking the consequences of her own mistakes, and expecting no indulgences, have developed a respect for method, a sense of responsibility, and a discipline that are among the best gifts she could bring into the home?"[83]

In this conspiracy to disguise what job training could accomplish, the representatives of interest groups ranging from educators and trade unionists to feminists concurred. Every plan of education for women, the manual training committee of the National Educational Association argued, should be tested "not merely with questions of immediate expediency or of personal advantage, but always with the thought of the larger contribution to the common good, and the higher functions which women can never surrender." The committee insisted that women could not only "lead happier and richer lives and will be more successful as the future homemakers of our cities" if they had some early training, but that industrial education would provide a skill with innumerable advantages. It would raise their parents' standards of living, as well as afford them protection and support if they were to lose their own partners.[84]

Even those who sympathized most with women's needs for saleable skills defended vocational training as an adjunct to normal expectations of marriage. A national committee on women in industry, reporting on ways to educate women at the end of the war, offered a sweeping vision: vocational education would provide training for "the period previous to marriage, or if she does not marry, for the period of her working life, or for the married woman, who, because of widowhood, desertion, childlessness, or some other deviation from normal married life, returns to industry as a wage-earner."[85] "The qualities needed in trade," wrote Mary Woolman after five years as director of the Manhattan Trade School for Girls,

> are the same as those which elevate the home. Employers ask for workers who are reliable, who respect authority, who are honest in time, in work, and in word. The development of a sense of responsibility is a difficult task to accomplish, but it is not impossible at least to lay the foundation, even though the poverty of the students necessarily limits the period of instruction. A trade school can develop character, and consequently the better homekeeper is born from the better trade worker.[86]

Opposition to training women for exclusively wage-earning roles led to schools and curriculae that appeared distinctly defensive. Those

who developed trade schools played down the remunerative aspects
of the skills they were teaching. Witness Florence Leadbetter, principal
of Boston's Trade School for Girls: "We have always said that we
would not admit to our trade school any trade which would not help
the girl in her highest vocation—homemaking—but we believe that
any trade, well-taught . . . will give that discipline . . . needed to
make her the ideal wife, mother, sympathetic helpmate and resourceful
adviser."[87] What had begun in the 1870s as a movement to train
women in saleable skills had become a major adjunct to training for
the home by 1900.

Students enrolled in vocational courses received double messages.
To entice them in, they were promised higher wages and advancement.
The WTUL journal *Life and Labor* printed the following lesson, for
example.

> My sister is fifteen years old.
> She is in a trade school.
> She is learning a good trade.
> She left school last month.
> She wanted to go to work.
> She could earn $6.00 a week in a box factory.
> Box-making is a bad trade.
> It is not a skilled trade.
> It has a short season.
> No girl can earn more than $8.00.
> It is better for my sister to learn a good trade.
> She will not earn much money at first.
> But she will earn more later on.
> She will always have work.
> I am glad that my sister will learn a trade.
> I went to work at fourteen.
> I did not learn a good trade.
> I earn very little money.
> Often I have no work at all.
> I am sorry that I did not learn a trade.

Programs were often advertised as ways of making it in the business and industrial world, which suggests that students may have
been a good deal more ambitious than some leaders of the vocational
movement would have liked to admit publicly. The New York City
School of Filing indicated that supervisory jobs might reward those
who completed its four-week program.[88] Proponents of schools for
sales clerks insisted that "more efficient work could compel better
wages. . . ."[89] Mary Gilson, who had once been a vocational coun-
selor at Florence Leadbetter's school, reports her own disillusionment

with the double-talk: "Stress was always laid on loyalty, cooperation, conscientious work, honest workmanship, and other virtues which were advocated as guarantees of success in the business and industrial world. Never were any flies pictured in the ointment, no mention of the routine jobs women were expected to do and the small chance of emerging out of them. Nor was any consideration given to the possibility that a girl might be paid less than she was worth. No one mentioned equal pay for equal work. Sometimes employers spoke at the assemblies and they always said there was a place at the top for hard workers."[90]

But if the advertising appealed to ambition, the content was unequivocally designed to train women only for jobs already perceived as theirs. This was perhaps a logical by-product of the need to defend vocational education as home-related. The NEA minced no words: "the courses of instruction should train for work in distinctly feminine occupations."[91] A glance at the offerings of a half-dozen public and private vocational schools for girls in Boston in 1910 suggests their intent for the young women enrolled. Typical courses included household service, cooking and housewifery, dressmaking, sewing, millinery, straw machine operating, textiles, laundry work, machine sewing and embroidery. In 1910, Boston boasted two schools for household servants, two schools to train nursery maids, one for hospital attendants, one for cookery, and one for painting pottery. In addition, the city housed twenty schools that offered commercial subjects, of which seventeen admitted women. The Girls' Trade Education League published ten bulletins on opportunities open to fourteen-to-eighteen-year-olds who left school. The bulletins covered such subjects as telephone operating, book-binding, dressmaking, stenography and typewriting, being a nursery maid, millinery, straw hat making, nursing, salesmanship, and manicuring and hairdressing.[92]

Fear of trespassing beyond the bounds of femininity did not discourage a variety of industry-related training programs from providing courses that would maintain sexually stratified jobs. Manufacturers of office machines offered day or evening courses to students for whom they provided employment after completion. These courses, which did not become part of the regular day high school curriculum until after World War I, were short and to the point. They rarely exceeded six months in length, and more frequently ran from four to six weeks. They offered little in the way of general business knowledge, attempting only to develop specific machine skills such as typewriting or the use of adding machines.

Perhaps the best-publicized example of short vocational training courses consistent with women's role was created by Lucinda Prince for Boston's Women's Educational and Industrial Union. The WEIU compromised less than most groups in its aim of educating women for the industrial and commercial worlds. Perceiving retail sales as a rapidly expanding field with many opportunities and few women able to take advantage of them, Prince approached Boston's department store managers with a unique proposal in 1905. Training saleswomen, she argued, would enhance the dignity of retail sales, compel better wages, and bring greater happiness to the lives of sales clerks. For the employer, training would sharpen employee efficiency, contribute to work force stability, and improve service to the customer. Early attempts to offer courses in salesmanship to young women had failed for lack of store cooperation in providing on-the-job experience. But Prince proposed that stores select their most promising young women, allow them to work part time at partial pay, and, after a month of training, rehire them first as probationers, then as permanent employees. Her training program offered to "teach right thinking towards the work as a profession, and rouse a feeling of responsibility," to "instill a regard for system and cultivate the habit of attention to details," as well as to "develop a pleasing personality." Students normally worked from 11:00 to 4:30 daily and spent the early morning and late afternoon hours in class. Promotion to better jobs as head of stock or as assistant buyer and even buyer, though never promised, was implied.[93]

The program took root, running three sessions per year within two years of its founding. By 1920, the Federal Board for Vocational Education was urging local communities to include training for retail sales in their public high schools. But the mobility promised by Prince's original conception still remained disguised. "Training for retail selling is not only a legitimate course for high schools," the Board argued, but "also a valuable educative course for training young people, who will be the customers of the future, to be intelligent, discriminating purchasing agents for themselves and their homes."[94] And although young women were being enticed to enter training programs by explicit suggestions of potential upward mobility, retail selling had become a stereotyped female occupation, so the advance upward posed little threat to existing job divisions. The route from inspector to cashier to stock girl, marker, or office clerk, like that from stock clerk to floor clerk to floor manager to division superintendent, placed women in competition only with other women. The promise of higher income provided sufficient incentive. The Board suggested five years as a typical transition period during which a young girl with training would reach an earning capacity of thirty dollars per week.

By 1920 the nation had at least 3,553 public and private all-day training schools and 6,731 part-time and evening schools for women.[95] Despite this proliferation, there is no evidence that they offered a solution to the low-pay problems of the unskilled. One 1906 study indicated that only 36 percent of the young women who took courses at five different Boston schools ever practiced their trade. Economist Helen Sumner concluded in 1910 that the schools had "done little or nothing . . . to make women wage-earners in mechanical industries more skillful or more efficient."[96] Characteristically states passed vocational education legislation requiring home economics or domestic science courses for girls as part of every publicly funded manual training program. And in some states, legislatures mandated domestic science for girls and manual training for boys in every public high school. New Mexico, for example, suggested that each school replace two periods of academic subject matter a week. Boys were to have manual training and agriculture while girls received domestic science and sewing. A fifth- or sixth-grade girl might learn about different kinds of stitchery, making aprons, mending, darning, making bags and pillow cases, and so on. Indiana's legislation, passed in 1913, established a system of state aid for training in industries, agriculture, and domestic science. Pennsylvania, like Indiana and New York, included home economics as part of its vocational training package.[97]

The Smith-Hughes Act, passed by Congress in 1917, merely confirmed the compromise that opened vocational education to girls only in female areas. Boys were to receive industrial education, while girls could learn to be dieticians or dressmakers. The act, designed to provide federal funds for vocational education in public schools, subsidized full- and part-time training in manual, industrial, and agricultural arts and in domestic science. It allocated no funds for commercial, office, or business training for young women, leaving these to communities or to private initiative. For a while, World War I provided an incentive to open industrial training courses to women and masked the discrimination inherent in the act. But by 1920, these opportunities had all but disappeared. The Women's Bureau reported that only 3 of 104 trade schools surveyed offered women training in auto mechanics, 16 offered training in mechanical drawing and drafting, and 12 in printing.[98] Wary activists could see the handwriting on the wall. In the spring of 1919, the National American Women's Suffrage Association convention in St. Louis resolved that in view of the danger that "wider opportunities may not be assured to women now that the war emergency is past," it was "of the utmost importance that women shall be free to choose their occupations without restriction through custom or prejudice." To which end it asked "that girls shall be given the same opportunities as boys in all vocational training." The NWTUL echoed these sentiments less than a year later. "We urge upon the Federal Board of Vocational Education," it declared, "the necessity of giving to girls and women full opportunity for education along industrial lines. . . ."[99] Such resolutions did not conform to traditional expectations of women's roles, so they got little attention.

In accepting the condition that homemaking be part of the educational process, and in acquiescing to existing job segmentation, advocates of vocational education for women fell into a predictable trap. For the new programs perpetuated familiar characteristics among women workers. They trained women expected to stay in the labor market briefly to expect little upward mobility and to deflect their ambitions into marriage. A Women's Bureau argument illustrated the tenacious effect of old prescriptions. After making the point that women were, after all, capable of doing these jobs, the Bureau said, "The increase in the use of mechanical devices in the modern home renders a knowledge of mechanics essential, if not more so, to the average woman who eventually leaves industry to take up household duties as is a knowledge of sewing, because the manufacture of clothing has ceased practically, to be a profitable household industry."[100] If the Woman's Bureau could resort to such logic, it was small wonder that Anna Lalor Burdick, who worked for the Federal Board of Vocational Training, found it easy to argue for training women for garment and hat work, the hosiery industry, and soap-making, on the grounds that "women's small and agile hands are especially adapted to the work of certain industries."[101]

Despite the influx of married women into the work force, and the clear evidence that their jobs offered inadequate pay and opportunity, vocational education perpetuated the assumption that married women's work was, and would remain, peripheral. Yet for daughters of the working class, it involved a breakthrough of sorts. While denying that individual women could be permanent workers, it acknowledged a permanent role for women in general in the work force. It took women's work seriously enough to provide a few women with access to decent training and a real possibility for creative work force participation. But vocational education did not yield access to upward mobility. Rather, the skills provided more often than not led to a fixed, if slightly more comfortable, labor force position.

7

Protective Labor Legislation

In various incarnations the search for protection extends over an astonishingly long period of time—longer than the battle for woman suffrage itself. Its origins encompass laws that applied to all workers, male and female, as well as to women and children and to children alone. Legislation based on women's special position derived directly from the search for general protection and was alternately rejected, then supported, then rejected again by the organized women's movement as well as by wage-earning women. Positions fluctuated with the changing meaning of "protection" as well as with changing labor force circumstances. Because the idea of "protection" appeared in different guises at different times, it drew support from new coalitions of supporters on each occasion. It pitted working women against working men, and employers against legislators. Just as often, it aligned unionists with manufacturers and set women in unions against those outside them.

The rubric of protection encompasses a huge variety of laws whose scope differed from state to state. Two intentions emerge clearly. Both rested on a perceived need to redress what labor economist Elizabeth Faulkner Baker called "inequality of bargaining power."[1] The first kind of labor legislation aimed to preserve the worker's independence by providing safe and clean working conditions, minimizing health hazards, putting a floor under wages, shortening hours, and eventually by compensating workers for job-related accidents. The struggle over this so-called regulatory legislation is part of the history of the progressive period. The often arbitrary laws that resulted had long-range consequences for men and women in the labor market. The second kind of labor legislation—restrictive or prohibitive laws—aimed at excluding some workers from certain kinds of jobs altogether. These jobs might be defined by the time and place where they were performed or by the nature of the task. This second series of laws applied almost exclusively to women. Between the two categories, no rigid lines existed. Laws that regulated lighting, seating, and ventilation arrangements under which women could work often served in fact to prevent women from being offered certain kinds of jobs.

By and large, this legislation, because it confirmed changes in the number and kinds of women earning a living and simultaneously regulated their opportunities to work, tended to reflect the prevailing sense of women's proper roles and the tension and the conflict in their work lives. Protective legislation divided workers into those who could and could not perform certain roles. It therefore bears some of the responsibility for successfully institutionalizing women's secondary labor force position.

Not that legislation to regulate the relations of capital and labor was new. Its history goes back to the colonial period and beyond. Colonial law, in its attempt to protect the well-off against the potentially exorbitant demands of skilled craftsmen, benefited the less-skilled common laborers and bound servants as well. The long tradition of concern for general welfare, of institutional protection for indentured servants, of minimum wages, just prices, stipulations about adequate food and sufficient clothing for apprentices preceded later developments that allowed workers and employers to battle out their relationships. Late-eighteenth- and early-nineteenth-century ideas of individual liberty and freedom of contract and the decline of mercantilism undermined the earlier notion. A nation of "free" laborers individually contracting with employers to sell their labor replaced those bound by custom and law. Theoretically, each laborer could negotiate with an employer and make the best possible bargain for the sale of his or her labor power.

Far from protecting laborers, courts now held—in a series of decisions beginning in 1802—that craftspeople who united to seek better prices for their work could be prosecuted for conspiracy. Their actions were punishable by fines, deprivation of jobs, and even prison sentences. Judicial decisions took for granted a rough equality of bargaining power between employer and employee. The employee in theory could withdraw his or her labor if the conditions of work were not satisfactory. But in fact, equality hardly existed, and as we have seen the nineteenth century was riddled with worker protests about the deteriorating quality of conditions of labor.

Workers who realistically perceived their unequal status in the wage labor bargain sought by various means to weight the scales. They failed in attempts to control the labor supply through trade union access routes and to regulate the distribution of products through cooperative schemes. But the idea of shortening the working day in order to "merely supply the demand" and thus command higher wages proved more pervasive. One finds proposals for the ten-hour day as early as 1827. The first recorded strike for shorter hours seems to have been led by Boston carpenters in 1825. A six-hour day did not seem unreasonable to a speaker at the Boston Trades Union in 1834 who suggested that to work more than that should be a crime.[2]

Initially, the search for shorter hours was not sex-linked. Rooted in the mercantilist tradition or a Jeffersonian sense of justice, it incorporated the Tudor and colonial ideas of a balanced society that offered fair rewards to all its members. Shortening hours would serve the general welfare in two ways. It would ensure that available jobs were shared, and it would make possible, as the Lowell mill operatives had pointed out, an educated and aware citizenry. These demands for shorter hours became the cornerstones of the movement for protective labor legislation.

Before the Civil War, workers' movements for shorter hours made some gains as trade associations consisting of skilled male workers successfully negotiated ten- and eleven-hour days. Organized mechanics pressed President Van Buren into issuing an executive order that instituted a ten-hour day for federal employees in 1840. Ohio and Wisconsin agreed to give state employees ten-hour days in 1857. And the legislatures of eight states declared ten hours a legal working day in the absence of a contract to the contrary.[3]

Massachusetts was not among them. Its negligence resulted in the petitions signed by thousands of mostly female textile workers who asked for a ten-hour law in the 1840s. Like other workers in the pre–Civil War period, they argued that long hours contradicted "the great principles of justice, equality and republicanism . . . so essential to . . . the existence of a free and virtuous people. . . ." These workers wanted shorter days so that they could find time "for general reading and information." "Are you willing that your sons, aye, and your daughters, too, shall thus go out into the world?" asked Sarah Bagley, berating the readers of the *Voice of Industry* for condoning ignorance in workers. The lawmakers rejected the petitions, taking refuge behind the "privilege of contract," and arguing that they would not "deprive the citizen . . . the employed as well as the employer" of its benefits.[4]

But wage earners continued to argue from notions of general welfare.

They insisted that justice stretched beyond defining an appropriate working day. The savings in labor time made possible by improved machinery, they argued, ought rightly to be passed along to them. The *Daily Evening Voice* eloquently summarized this position: ". . . we believe that when the creator, through the invention of labor saving machines, gives to the laborer a means whereby a saving is made of a large portion of the time formerly required to meet his physical necessities, he intended that the workingman should have the privilege of devoting the time thus saved to the development and improvement of the rational and religious faculties with which he has been endowed. . . ."[5]

Even after the Civil War the possibility of justice without gender distinction persisted among working people. When the Knights of Labor introduced demands for the eight-hour day in 1871, its founder, Uriah Stephens, argued the advantages of shorter hours for workers who would "have time for social enjoyment and intellectual improvement, and be enabled to reap the advantages conferred by the Labor-saving machinery which their brains have created."[6] A sprinkling of states responded to such pressure. South Carolina and Maryland passed laws mandating a ten-hour day for all industrial workers. Eleven more states declared eight- or ten-hour "legal" days—but without enacting enforcement machinery. Some states asserted the right to regulate working relations on the most general grounds of health and police power regulation.[7]

But states that tried to legislate working conditions for adult males found their laws unceremoniously struck down in the courts. The New York State Supreme Court decision that voided an 1884 act prohibiting the manufacture of cigars in tenement houses illustrates the point. The court could not see how "the cigarmaker is to be improved in his health or his morals by forcing him from his home and its hallowed associations and beneficent influences to ply his trade elsewhere."[8] It left open the question of whether states had special interest in the health of their citizens, and subsequent legal battles turned on the issue of whether the state's police power could properly be used to protect workers.

The U.S. Supreme Court dealt this doctrine a mortal blow in 1905 when it decided against a New York state law limiting the hours of bakers to ten per day. The issue was not the hours of labor, the Court argued in *Lochner* v. *New York*, but the bread itself. "Clean, and wholesome bread does not depend upon whether a baker works but 10 hours per day," said the Court, concluding that the statute was therefore "an illegal interference with the rights of individuals to make contracts."[9] The decision reflected prevailing opinions. It decisively rejected the idea that a shared sense of justice ought to influence working hours and conditions. Legislators and courts by and large agreed that freely negotiated contracts were necessary to success in a society that offered readily attainable upward mobility.

Under these circumstances only skilled trade unionists managed to achieve significant reductions in hours or to play a role in determining their own work practices. By the 1890s, such groups as cigar makers, builders, and machinists regularly worked only fifty hours a week. But there were precious few women among them. Textile mills, laundries, and the garment industry, all heavily women-employing, still averaged twelve-hour days, and five-and-a-half- or six-day weeks.

While the use of state power to limit hours and to regulate work conditions in the interest of the general welfare was still in question, special arguments based on notions of female domesticity began to emerge for restricting women workers. Since the courts rejected the assertion that the general welfare demanded regulation for all workers, proponents moved to the position that women in their capacity as child bearers and rearers served the state's welfare in a special way. The idea that their service to the state entitled women to special protection spread rapidly.

Tactically, the argument grew out of the difficulty in getting any kind of protective legislation past lawmakers and courts. Much of the energy behind attempts to limit the hours of women and children in the 1880s and 1890s came from those who believed that women could be an "opening wedge" in obtaining laws for all the unorganized. Shorter hours for some, they argued, along with adequate factory sanitation and safety devices, would inevitably lead to better conditions for all workers. Economist Elizabeth Brandeis acerbically concluded that Massachusetts workers had decided to "fight the battle behind the women's petticoats."[10] But a substantial amount of pressure for such legislation came from those who genuinely felt that women's peculiarly vulnerable position demanded special protection. When this argument was made by unskilled workers competing with each other for jobs, it carried conviction. Their pressure, for example, encouraged Massachusetts lawmakers in 1874 to limit the labor of women and children to sixty hours per week.

Arguments for special protection for women were marked by sympathy and genuine concern. But there was ideological danger in asserting women's weakness. Originally the organized feminist movement staked its claim to women's rights, including the suffrage, firmly on the conviction that women were more like men than unlike them and were therefore entitled to all human rights. By the 1880s, an important wing of the woman suffrage movement had reversed its position. Woman's special sphere, her special sensibilities nurtured in the home, feminists like Lucy Stone argued, developed unique attributes that required representation in the political process. Reformers like Helen Campbell and Annie McLean held that these same attributes—compassion, nurturance, a better-developed sense of morality—unfitted her for the competitive economic struggle. In the unfortunate event that women were forced into the wage labor force these special sensibilities must be preserved.

The argument provided justification not merely for regulating, but for prohibiting altogether, the work of women in certain occupations. If wage work was necessary it had to be bounded by regulations that would preserve woman's body, mind, and morals for home roles. The argument was implicit in all the official investigations of this period, and became the articulated basis of legislation after 1900. Agitation for protection of wage-earning women now rested squarely on the assumption that all women were homemakers without sufficient skill to compete in the labor market. Proponents of protection did not declare all workers in need of it. Rather, they claimed special privilege for the home and motherhood.

A growing eugenics movement and concern about "race suicide" provided additional ammunition around 1900. No selfish employer could be allowed to undermine the strength of the race by threatening the health of future mothers or tempting the morality of future homemakers. All semblance of the class solidarity that had informed the search for protective legislation in the mid–nineteenth century disappeared. By 1900 special protection for women was the rule.

In this climate, legally imposed limitations on the kinds of work women could do took form. Elizabeth Faulkner Baker assigns the first such law to California; in 1881 that state passed a measure denying women the right to work in places that sold alcoholic beverages. The state Supreme Court quickly invalidated it. The state constitution, it ruled, prohibited legislation "either directly or indirectly incapacitating or disabling a woman from entering or pursuing any business, vocation, or profession" open to men. But courts in Ohio and Washington upheld similar statutes as valid exercises of police power, and other forms of prohibition emerged quickly. Most were based on physical and moral grounds. Selling liquor might expose women to lewd men and threaten their innocence. Grinding and polishing metal might clog women's lungs with dust. Work in underground mines (never prevalent in the United States) would coarsen women's gentle natures. Later women were denied work as messengers because Western Union could not guarantee who might open the door to them. Operating elevators, reading meters, becoming letter carriers, and driving taxis were among the erratic series of occupations sporadically denied to women.[11]

A surprising absence of controversy about such legal prohibitions reveals the strength of popular beliefs in women's assigned roles. More often than not, such legislation merely confirmed custom, and courts readily upheld it. Protests tended to be individual—like those of women who disguised themselves as men in order to obtain jobs—and quickly stifled. When successful, such instances never found their way into the public record. But once caught, women who had tried to pass as men received stiff punishments. One young woman drew six months' imprisonment in New York's Blackwell's Island for dressing like a man. A contemporary noted that "the indictment in her case said that 'she wore men's clothes, she being a woman,' as if the offense she had committed was that of being a woman."[12]

More controversy surrounded legislation that attempted to regulate the conditions under which women could earn wages. Ohio passed the first maximum-hour law for women—a ten-hour day—in 1852. Minnesota, Massachusetts, and Illinois followed after the Civil War. The first legal restrictions against night work for women appeared in Massachusetts in 1890. These were at first isolated instances which state judicial opinion generally upheld. The Pennsylvania Superior Court, in an 1896 decision, the first on the sixty-hour week and twelve-hour day for women, declared: "Surely an act which prevents the mothers of our race from being tempted to endanger their life and health by exhaustive employment can be condemned by none save those who expect to profit by it." The court went on to say, "Adult females are a class as distinct as minors, separated by natural conditions from all other laborers, and are so constituted as to be unable to endure physical exertion and exposure to the extent and degree that is not harmful to adult workers."[13]

In rapid succession, legislators in Nebraska, Washington, and Oregon passed statutes limiting the workday for women. State courts upheld them. Shared assumptions about women's natural weakness underlay their actions. "That which must necessarily affect any great number of women who are the mothers of succeeding generations must necessarily affect the public welfare and morals," argued Washington's Supreme Court in 1902.[14] It was no surprise to many and an enormous relief to proponents when in 1908 the U.S. Supreme Court set its seal on the motherhood argument in response to the famous Brandeis brief in the case of *Muller v. Oregon.*

Louis Brandeis and his sister-in-law Josephine Goldmark, working at the time for the National Consumers' League, correctly reasoned that to persuade the court that shorter hours for women were in fact conducive to the general welfare required evidence that long hours were inimical to health and safety. In their carefully prepared argument, presented to the Court in defense of Oregon's ten-hour law, they asserted that woman's "special physical organization," her child-bearing and maternal functions, and the need to prevent "laxity of moral fibre" which "follows physical debility" all required restricting her hours of labor to ten per day. The authors used strong language: "women are fundamentally weaker than men in all that makes for endurance: in muscular strength, in nervous energy, in the powers of persistent attention and application." Quoting extensively from state and federal labor officials, the brief argued: "They must have vacations, and they break down in health rapidly." It cited physicians who asserted "the periodic semi-pathological state of health of women" and their greater predisposition to disease. It dwelt on "pale, crooked, and sickly-looking" women and children who worked sixty or more hours per week. It pointed to women who spent "a good part of their Sundays . . . in bed and recuperating for the next week's demands." Neurasthenia, back troubles, pyrosis, constipation, vertigo, and headaches were the least of the problems identified. Edema, varicose veins, displacement of the uterus, throat and lung diseases were said to follow from excessive work.

The brief thus combined arguments for woman's role with data on her relative lack of physical stamina. And the Court, in affirming Oregon's statute, found this a comfortable resting place. "Women's physical stature and the performance of maternal functions place her at a disadvantage," it declared, and went from affirming woman's essential role in maintaining the "strength and vigor of the race" to accepting the notion that women might legally be wards of the state. "It is impossible to close one's eyes to the fact that she still looks to her brother and depends on him," said the Court. Protecting her "from the greed as well as the passion of man" justified legislation.[15] But the court did not decide by how much the state could limit women's contractual rights to negotiate their hours of labor. What was a reasonable working day for women? Ten hours? Nine? Eight?

The decision electrified the field of protective legislation, reviving long-dormant restrictive measures. Hours were the first and prime target. Between 1909 and 1917, nineteen states passed laws restricting women's working day.[16] Regulations differed not only from state to state but from industry to industry within each state. Manufacturing and mercantile enterprises were the first statutory targets, with laundries and telegraph and telephone companies running a close second.

Hotels, restaurants, and cabarets often escaped regulation entirely. Domestic service and agriculture, still the two leading female occupations and the most arduous, remained untouched. Limits on hours ranged from an eight-hour day and forty-eight-hour week for some industries in Arizona, California, and Washington to ten or twelve hours a day and sixty or more hours a week in most southern states.

By 1914, twenty-seven states had some form of regulation, and three years later, only nine remained without any limitations on hours for women. Six states had an eight-hour day and a forty-eight-hour week for most women. Thirteen states limited the work week to fifty-four hours with no more than nine hours per working day. The remaining states varied maximums from fifty-five to sixty hours per week. By 1924, four more states had enacted such restrictions on hours. Of the five still without restrictions, three—West Virginia, Alabama, and Florida—were in the South. Iowa had virtually no industry to speak of, and Indiana regulated night work, though it did not restrict daytime hours. But some of these restrictions were hardly "protective." North Carolina, for example, forbade women to work more than eleven hours per day, six days per week. Vermont, Tennessee, and New Hampshire had limits of between ten and a quarter and ten and a half hours. Fifteen states, including such heavily women-employing states as Pennsylvania, Connecticut, New Jersey, and Rhode Island, had ten-hour limits.[17]

Even these limits were often evaded. Employers, especially those in small and seasonal businesses, developed a variety of devices for circumventing law enforcement. "Emergency" provisions were built into many laws. Tactics such as stopping clocks and adding time when machinery needed repair protected manufacturers against lost time and enabled employers to extract extra work from women, even in states with stringent laws. For fear of losing their jobs, women often colluded in the evasion, sometimes agreeing to clean machinery on their own time, for example. But the most common form of evasion was simply to build exceptions into the law to serve the interests of special categories of employers. A state might allow women to work a long day where work was seasonal or exempt certain classes of workers from the law altogether. Cannery workers at harvest time, retail clerks at holiday time, night club dancers were routinely exempt from the law's encircling restrictions.[18]

The paradox in approaching women's work-related problems this way was quickly apparent, and especially to wage-earning women. Shorter working hours and more comfortable working conditions were dearly sought after. Yet the price was steep. If women's freedom of contract was to be limited because they were "weaker" than men, what next might be taken away? To be sure, freedom of contract was a worthless privilege, as some argued: one that had been used far more often to justify exploitation than as protection.[19] Yet since only women were denied the freedom to make their own contracts, the limitations that ensued restrained them in a labor market that remained otherwise competitive. More immediately pressing was the fact that protected hours without minimum wages meant less money in the weekly pay envelope: a disaster for those who lived on the margin. Since the justification for regulating women's conditions of work derived from the community's perception of their roles in families, it left little room for meeting the real needs of workers who happened to be women. Economist Sophonisba Breckenridge, writing in 1906, pointed this out. "It is obviously not the women who are protected," she wrote; ". . . the object of such control is the protection of the physical well-being of the community by setting a limit to the exploitation of the improvident, unworkmanlike, unorganized women, who are yet the mothers, actual or prospective, of the coming generation."[20]

If protective legislation handicapped women who needed to engage fully in wage work, it enabled married women who were not entirely dependent on their own earnings to work more easily. In the period after World War I, when the movement had taken deep root, increasing numbers of married women began to handle the "double burden." Their recorded comments are unambiguous. In the 1920s, the Connecticut Consumers' League and the Women's Bureau surveyed women wage earners in some of the poorest occupations to ask them how they felt about shortening hours from ten to nine per day. Interview schedules reveal a grateful relief at the additional time: "I have my work to do at home," said one. And another, "A woman has work to do at home. It does you all out. When I had small children I have hung out clothes at one o'clock at night"; and again, "I think ten hours is too much for a woman. I have four children and have to work hard at home. Make me awful tired. I would like nine hours. I get up at 5:30 when I wash. I have to stay up till one or two o'clock."[21] A Woman's Bureau interviewer described what might have been the typical working day of a fourteen-dollar-a-week Virginia tobacco roller in 1919.

> Mrs. Trainum does all the housework and cooking. In order to get breakfast and prepare the lunches for all three she must get up at 5:30 a.m. and it is always 10 p.m. before she gets through doing dishes, cleaning, mending, and washing, etc. Consequently she is very tired and

cannot get rested up for the next day's work. She believes that an 8-hour
day would help as it would give her a little more time at home and she
could finish her house work a little earlier and get some rest.[22]

For manufacturers, restrictive legislation may have been a relatively
small price to pay in return for the ability to attract married women
into their factories. They argued that long hours were inefficient for
those with two jobs, that things didn't "run so well" after a certain
number of hours, that the turnover rate dropped dramatically among
married women when hours were cut, and that shorter hours enabled
them to hire a "better class of worker."[23] Employers in states with
short-hour laws declared, perhaps reflecting prevailing ideology, that
they would not use women more even if the law allowed it. One
superintendent asserted that without a law he would not work women
more than eight and a half hours, "just enough to make a 48-hour
week." But the Women's Bureau uncovered enough discrepancies
between employers' insistence that they did not and would not work
women long hours and women's reports that they frequently worked
overtime to create suspicions about employers' honesty.[24]

For women the critical issue involved the trade-off between time
and money. For the poorest workers, relief at shorter hours was
accompanied by notes of caution: "I would like to have my daughter
work 9 hours if she could earn as much." Or, in the words of an
immigrant, "I think more better if I have the same pay." Would wages
be reduced? Or, perhaps more important, would greedy employers
speed up the rate of work to try to get as much production out of
nine hours as they had got from ten? Women on piecework felt caught
between the fear that they would be pushed beyond endurance and
their desire not to see incomes reduced by shorter hours. "I cannot
do as much in nine hours as ten. I am on piece work." "I am on
baffing. I could not make any more than I do. I work hard all the
time."[25]

Some women would willingly have given up their shorter hours
for a larger salary—a trade-off they were not free to make when
legislation restricted their hours. Two female employees who decided
they could not make enough paper boxes in ten hours to earn
their keep challenged the constitutionality of Illinois's limited-hours
statute. In a dramatic sequel to *Muller* v. *Oregon*, Pauline Goldmark
(Josephine's sister) of the National Consumers' League prepared a
610-page brief which Louis Brandeis used to convince the Illinois
Supreme Court of the constitutionality of limited hours.[26] Other
women seemed contented with the trade-off. One union leader described these as "older women with family responsibilities and earning

$30 or so a week of [a certain] class of society. . . . They think more of their short hours," he argued, "than of their overtime pay." And to some, a shorter basic day offered an opportunity to earn overtime pay. Most states, however, did not permit overtime for women, protecting them from exploitation on the one hand by locking them into prescribed schedules on the other. Rhode Island women who would have preferred to work one hour more each day in return for a free Saturday could not do so.[27] Both workers and employers resorted to subterfuge to disguise overtime work.

Legal prohibitions on night work initially emerged in order to defend the gains won by restricting hours. Massachusetts, the first state to pass such a law, did so in 1890, in an effort to stop unscrupulous textile mill employers from hiring for a second shift women who had already completed a ten-hour day in a neighboring factory. The law set a 6:00 P.M. limit on women's working hours. Before the Brandeis brief raised the moral issue, only three states—Massachusetts, Indiana, and Nebraska—prohibited women from working at night. New York's law, then being tested in the courts, was in a state of constitutional limbo. Thereafter, the issue became a favorite of reformers. Its legislative history reflects the diverse interests involved. South Carolina, Pennsylvania, Delaware, and New York passed new laws between 1909 and 1917. Other states followed suit. Kansas, New Hampshire, and Wisconsin permitted night work as long as employers observed an eight-hour limit. Others exempted certain job categories from their restrictive laws. New Hampshire excluded nurses, household workers, and, for seven days before Christmas, department store workers. Maryland, Wisconsin, and Delaware exempted the canning industry. Telephone operators could work at night in New Hampshire and Kansas, but not in Delaware. In Massachusetts, textile mills could employ no women after 6:00 P.M.; in Wisconsin no manufacturer could employ women after that hour. But in Pennsylvania, not only could factories run late, but their female clerical force could continue to work too. Seven states declared that the night began at 10:00 P.M.; others were less clear. Oregon prohibited Portland's female department store clerks from working after 6:00 P.M., but allowed those who lived elsewhere to work until 8:30.[28]

Like arguments against long hours, the case for prohibiting night work stemmed from two traditional sources: health and morals. Women who had families and household duties were unable to rest properly in the daytime. And the factory, in the words of one auto-parts factory supervisor, was "no place for women at night."[29]

Repeated investigations affirmed that night hours left women tired and worn, unable to care for children and without a chance for adequate sleep. The Consumers' League drew gruesome portraits of weary women who slept only two or four hours a night, of neglected children and squalid homes. Thinly veiled hints pointed to rampant immorality. One candy company supervisor declared he would never run an evening shift because he "could not get the same class of girls he has in the day time and would not lower the standards of . . . employees." An Oswego, New York, textile manufacturer who employed fifty-five men and seventy-five women rejected the idea of using women at night "for moral reasons." It was, he thought, "absurd to consider it."[30]

But a close look at the kinds of women who worked at night and why they did so reveals a number of family, economic, and skill-related reasons for night work that immediately raise questions about the morality argument. The Connecticut Consumers' League, which consistently opposed such work, reported in a 1917–18 study that the unmarried tended to avoid night work because it interfered with social life. Married women, on the other hand, undertook night work in far higher proportions than their numbers in the work force. Some wished to work on the same shift as husbands who worked at night. Those with children chose shifts when they could arrange for help at home. That could mean waiting for a father to return from his daytime job, or an older sibling to finish school. Nearly half of those who worked all night did little or no housework. Others reported help with some household tasks such as laundry. And some appreciated night work because it meant extra time during the day to spend with children or in outdoor recreation. The Women's Bureau, which interviewed tobacco-factory night workers in 1919, reported a variety of ways in which night work solved problems. One woman with a husband and six children, who needed to help out financially, worked for a month or two at a time, then quit for a while before need brought her back. Another who could not leave her children in the daytime found it easier to get help for them at night.[31]

For workers, the issue was not so much day or night work but the total number of hours worked, day or night. The Consumers' League of Connecticut, after breaking down responses by the number of night hours worked, found a marked difference in health and attitude among women who worked ten or more hours as opposed to those who worked around eight hours. A third of the former complained of poor health compared to only a fifth of those whose hours were limited. Women who worked between six and seven and three-quarters hours at night were most enthusiastic about their schedules. "You can't imagine how good it is," one responded. "Five to one o'clock is grand." "Five to one is ideal. Whoever put that up did something good." "It is better than a 10 hour day for married women and single ones too."[32] In contrast, those who labored long hours at night complained bitterly about tiredness: "pretty tough, to tell the truth"; "awful hard work."

Women with families who worked long hours during the day complained of overwork just as did the married women who worked long hours at night, according to the CLC's investigations. One worker who put in a ten-hour day moaned, "Have to get up so early to get the work done and go to sleep so late at night. I have 2 children—10 hours too much in the shop makes you tired."[33]

Solid work-related reasons also encouraged some women to seek jobs at night. Pay rates were often higher, hours usually shorter. Occasionally the differential was such that, as some Pennsylvania book binders protested, they could earn as much in three nights of work as they could in six days.[34] Waitresses made most in tips at the dinner hour; although state lawmakers demonstrated some inconsistencies in legally excluding them from night jobs while leaving hat check girls, cabaret dancers, and actresses free to work.

Depriving women of the possibility of night work simultaneously eliminated them from some highly skilled and relatively well-paid jobs. Where seniority rules prevailed, for example, women who were forbidden to work at night or on certain shifts could not compete for jobs for which they were otherwise perfectly qualified. Female employees on New York's street railways discovered what that meant in 1919. World War I had provided an opportunity for women to move into the relatively well-paid jobs vacated by conductors, ticket agents, and "choppers" (who worked at stations taking tickets) when men became soldiers. Over the objections of unionized men who argued that employers were "profiteering," the street railway companies hired women because they could then count on stable wage rates instead of competing for increasingly expensive male workers in a period of inflation.[35] The large numbers of women who applied between the end of 1917, when the jobs were first opened to them, and early 1919, when men returned from overseas, enabled employers to adopt stringent health and age requirements and still satisfy their need for workers. But to those concerned with propriety the job of conductor, which required women to push through crowded cars, to swing on the outside of moving trolleys, and to hang around the "barn" in off-periods, posed problems. In this unionized industry women, who were the last hired and ranked lowest in seniority, got the least attractive and most time-consuming jobs. Men could not be asked to violate seniority rules. Yet adhering to these rules left women with more than their share of late-night work and travel, of "dead" hours between rush periods, and of unpleasant runs through unsafe areas with minimal sanitary facilities.

By the time New York City's male street railway employees came home from the war, companies had already begun laying off women to rehire their former workers. Nevertheless, the Amalgamated Association of Street and Electric Railway Employees used the rubric of protective legislation to lobby for a state law that would eliminate all women under twenty-one from these jobs and limit the number of hours women could work to a consecutive nine hours per day, to occur between 6:00 A.M. and 10:00 P.M. In a case notorious for pitting male and female union members against each other, the women, all dues-paying union members, complained that the proposed law would prevent them from working the swing shift—a very desirable short stretch of five or six hours in the evening between the day and night shifts. When the men persisted, the women resigned from the union and formed their own organization, sending women from throughout the state to Albany "to show them that they . . . were able to take care of their own health and morals."[36] To no avail. The law went into effect on May 1919, and 800 of the 1,500 women lost their jobs. The remaining 700, all ticket agents, as opposed to more highly paid conductors and guards, continued to work at reduced hours until, in 1921, they managed to get statutory exemption from provisions of the law.

New York's skilled women printers belatedly discovered that the night work law would mean the loss of their lucrative jobs. It took two years of struggle to persuade a reluctant legislature to exempt them. One astute female printer pointed out the two "kinds of opposition to equality before the law for men and women." One came from those who simply objected to women learning the trade as they "might object to colored men or yellow men . . . because they want to keep for themselves their own industry"; the other "have the idea that women are physically inferior to men, and they want us to have a nice easy time and get lots of money for it. . . ." But, argued Mrs. Ella Sherwin, a forty-seven-year-old widow, "We are forced to compete with the worker who is not restricted as we are, and that is one of the things that we object to."[37]

The struggles of printers and railway clerks illustrate how women fought night-work legislation that could exclude them from good jobs. In 1924 the U.S. Supreme Court undermined their resistance by validating a New York State law that prohibited women from working in restaurants from 10:00 P.M. to 6:00 A.M. Justice Sutherland, speaking for the majority, ruled that "night work so seriously affected the health of women, so threatened and impaired their peculiar and natural functions, and so exposed them to the dangers and menaces incident to night life that the State felt impelled to take cognizance of the situation by enacting the statute attacked, and that in so doing it was clearly within its rights."[38] The court did not find the exemption of singers, actors, and cloakroom attendants unreasonable, leaving women to wonder at the hypocrisy of a state that held female morality in less regard than male need for entertainment. Jane Norman Smith, leader of the New York division of the militantly feminist National Women's Party, angrily wrote to the New York *Times*, "To carry the plea of restriction on the grounds of general welfare, to a logical conclusion would require prohibiting women doctors and nurses from working after 10 o'clock at night, actresses from appearing on the stage after that hour, stage and cabaret dancers from performing. . . ."[39]

Because limits on hours created an urgent need to address the problem of wages, reform groups like the National Consumers' League and the National Women's Trade Union League began to push as early as 1908 and 1909 for minimum-wage laws that approximated what was popularly known as the "living wage." The Women's Bureau put the problem succinctly in a 1920 pamphlet. Eight-hour days, it argued, were "of questionable value to a worker if to obtain an adequate wage she is obliged to seek supplementary work or to speed up her work in the factory, until, because of her increased efforts, the sum total of her fatigue is as great as under the longer hours."[40] Wages could be increased through organization—a method so far ineffective. Or they could be legislated.

Manufacturers had been known to raise wages to compensate for shorter hours in states where hours for women were reduced. The International Harvester Company granted a two-and-a-half-cent-per-hour wage increase in 1912 when New York State instituted a mandatory fifty-five-hour week. More often employers speeded up the work process, hoping that by driving workers harder they could increase productivity and thus avoid a wage cut. On this basis, Lawrence, Massachusetts, textile owners had maintained weekly wage rates when the state limited women's hours to fifty-six per week in 1910. But when a new fifty-four-hour law was passed in 1912, mill owners refused to raise hourly wages, effectively reducing the take-home pay of operatives already living at the edge of poverty. It took a three-month strike to resolve the issue in favor of wage increases. A 1920 Women's Bureau investigation reported that only half the establishments it studied increased time and piece rates after state-mandated reductions in hours. Some others increased the rates they paid to those who worked by the hour, leaving piece workers to speed up if they wanted to maintain their former wages.[41]

Such evidence heightened demand for minimum-wage legislation. Massachusetts passed the country's first minimum-wage law in 1912. Ohio followed, and within two years ten states had set up mechanisms —usually boards or commissions to determine minimum wages for women and children. But the numbers are deceptive, for as a National Consumers' League study indicated in 1914, up to that date minimum-wage determinations had been "confined with one exception to states whose wealth is concentrated chiefly in man-employing industries."[42] Only Massachusetts, of all the great industrial states, had any legislation on the books by 1920. In effect, states where rural interests far exceeded industrial and mercantile concerns passed such legislation. Others held out. With the notable exception of the International Ladies' Garment Workers' Union, trade unions that pushed for maximum hours remained ambivalent to or negative about minimum wages.

Even in Massachusetts, the promise held out by such legislation quickly evaporated. That state's Minimum Wage Commission was empowered to recommend "living wages" for women and minors. But its enforcement powers were limited to publishing the names of employers who did not comply. The Commission could create wage panels, specific to each occupation, with a mandate to consider not only the needs of the wage-earning women but "the financial condition of the occupation and the probable effect thereon of any increase in the minimum wage paid, and . . . to determine the minimum wage . . . suitable for a female of ordinary ability."[43] The Commission did not hesitate to exercise its judgment in these matters. After carefully calculating a weekly budget for millinery workers at $11.64 a week, it recommended a wage of $10.00 per week for experienced employees. In explanation the Commission said, "The successful working of the law and justice to the employers do not permit of a higher minimum wage." It set an even lower wage for apprentices ($7.50 per week)—a sum which by its own estimate was not even sufficient for board and lodging; and it declared that "the board does not look with favor upon higher wages for young girls in the millinery trade."[44]

Some of the eight states that passed minimum wage laws in 1913 had stronger provisions. Oregon stated that "it shall be unlawful to employ women in any occupation . . . for wages which are inadequate to supply the necessary cost of living and to maintain them in health." Yet the "necessary cost of living" was to be determined by face-to-face negotiations between employers and employees: a process that left unschooled, unorganized, and easily intimidated young women at a decided disadvantage. Minnesota's Minimum Wage Commission suggested in 1914 that "the idea of getting men employees to represent women might be worth trying."[45] In practice the living wage thus negotiated never rose to a level adequate to provide the necessities of life for a single, self-supporting woman, much less for one with dependent children.

Nor were adequate enforcement provisions built into these state laws. Massachusetts threatened evaders only with adverse publicity, and exempted from compliance all those who could prove that they would be unable to conduct their businesses at a reasonable profit. Rates, even when reasonable to begin with, quickly diminished in the face of inflation, and an endless round of hearings and investigations was required to raise them. Even outright refusal to comply with an order normally produced only the proverbial rap on the knuckles. Laundry owners who were fined $100 and ordered to pay thousands of dollars in back wages appealed the order. Ethel Smith of the WTUL complained:

> The back pay is collectible when the court decision comes if it is favorable, and *if the women individually bring suit*, but aside from the fact that the women are intimidated, it is a well known fact that laundry workers, whose pay is only $4 to $10 a week, are constantly shifting and the employers refuse to keep accurate records even of their present addresses. In fact, their counsel is advising them not to keep the records which are necessary for the Minimum Wage Board to have in future if the law is sustained. By the time the decision comes the employers may easily have had a complete turnover of force. Their turnover is always high, and in the present season of unemployment they can hire and fire as rapidly as they wish.[46]

Clearly the minimum wage-requirement could not be relied upon to offset income potentially threatened by shorter hours. Although occasional employers acquiesced, they did so only after studies showed that minimum wages soon paid for themselves in improved public opinion and greater productivity. As a representative of the California Consumer's League argued in 1923, by then even employers supported that state's minimum-wage commission.[47]

By then it was too late for such laws. Although a series of state courts had upheld the validity of minimum-wage laws, the U.S. Supreme Court would have none of it. Oregon's Supreme Court had provided the justification accepted by most states. "Women and minors should be protected from conditions of labor which have a pernicious effect on their health and morals," said the court, echoing the rationale for shorter hours, "and inadequate wages have a pernicious effect."[48] The argument underlying the abrogation of a woman's freedom of contract in favor of the state's interest in her health and morals was held to apply to wages as much as to hours. But when the issue got to the

Supreme Court, the majority, striking down a District of Columbia law in 1923, declared, "It is quite simply and exclusively a price fixing law, confined to adult women . . . who are legally as capable of contracting for themselves as men." At the same time the freedom that women had to negotiate their wages was not held to extend to their hours, a conclusion reached by such tortuous logic that Chief Justice Taft was moved to dissent. He supported, he said, the view that "a sweating wage has a great and as direct a tendency to bring about an injury to the health and morals of workers, as . . . long hours."[49]

Issues that emerged as moral questions for feminists and courts of law took on a different aspect for employers. Embattled as they were through the early part of the twentieth century by demands to regulate work conditions, employers' resistance was natural. Agnes Nestor, a glove maker and trade union leader, proudly recalled her experience in winning Illinois's short-hour legislation in 1909. "The trade union girls, almost singlehanded," she recalled, "secured the passage of the women's ten-hour law with all the forces of the employers allied against them. It was our first legislative experience and we battled a long number of weeks to outwith the employers and win votes for the bill."[50] But resistance was neither blind nor unchanging.

Employers, of course, had an infinite number of reasons to oppose any attempt to legislate the conditions under which they could use their male or female labor. But when courts began to accept women as wards of the state, employers' main concern revolved around the issue of equalizing competition. Carroll Wright, respected and knowledgeable analyst of labor statistics for Massachusetts and the United States, argued that there was a far greater sympathy with operatives' desires for a shorter workday then "the operatives imagine or could be made to believe." But, he continued, employers in each industry wanted all their competitors, nationwide, to be subject to the same restrictions: "if all worked but 10 hours, then it would be the same for all, and so everybody would have just as fair a chance for success under 10 as now under more hours."[51] It was simply not "competitive" for one state to regulate conditions if another did not. That had been a persistent argument. Some Pittsburgh textile mill owners had used it as early as 1845 to convince their striking workers to abandon demands for a ten-hour day. They would be driven out of business, they claimed, unless the New England mills followed suit. Seventy-seven years later Harry Parsons Cross, a textile manufacturer's representative fighting a Rhode Island bill that set a forty-eight-hour week for women, protested, "We would welcome the law if it were made universal."[52] Otherwise, employers threatened, stringent laws would drive their plants into states with more lenient laws. "If we should pay as much for 54 hours labor as our competitors in other states pay for 56, or even 60, we should soon have to quit," the president of the American Woolen Company told the striking workers in Lawrence, Massachusetts, in January 1912. "I am not criticizing our Massachusetts law, but for the present, you see, it puts us under a handicap."[53]

Wright, who favored protective laws and believed employers could be encouraged to go along with them, immediately disputed this argument. There had not, he thought, "been a single instance of the removal of capital from one state to another on account of restrictive laws." Rather, it was the proximity of raw materials that encouraged movement.[54] Yet the threat had power, for in fact textile and garment factories, both heavily female-employing, began to spring up in the South after 1900 replacing an old physical plant that had ceased to expand in the older northern states by the first World War. The situation encouraged employers to threaten removal in order to fend off legislation. Florence Harriman, chairperson of the Industrial Relations Commission of 1914, reported to Congress that "employers who believe the conditions of labor to be more restricted in their own state than in competing states threaten an exodus," leading legislators to "amend restrictive measures in deference to the threat."[55] Rhode Island manufacturers argued in 1922 that they would be driven from the state if women's hours were reduced to forty-eight. A California cotton mill owner with more than 700 employees declared he was moving out in response to eight-hour and minimum-wage legislation. And Pennsylvania textile manufacturers claimed that a proposed forty-four-hour week would drive textile mills into the South and supplant women with men.[56]

Employer resistance diminished under the impact of new ideas that made it easier to accept change. Large manufacturers such as the influential business leaders represented in the National Civic Federation could not escape the pressure of progressive era reform by the early 1900s. The general climate of opinion that demanded solutions to issues of poverty and degradation emerged in special ways in relation to women. Enlightened businessmen saw attacks against them for destroying health and home as having some validity. After all, they shared the sense that the family was the keystone of social order, and self-interest called attention to women's social role in the family unit. Sometimes they responded defensively, turning family and morality arguments inside out. An Indiana paper box manufacturer, for instance, defended long hours on the grounds that "life on the streets" after work was more harmful than regular employment. A

California cotton manufacturer with 267 female employees believed long hours would allow for the increase of savings.[57] But most often businessmen attempted to structure their own worlds by instituting welfare work within the corporation or by channeling women into office jobs where hours were already short by custom and complaints about health and overwork would be minimal.

Not infrequently employers hired women in factories and for hours that reinforced a sense of where women belonged, irrespective of laws on the subject. When interviewed, employers or their representatives frequently made comments such as "It's no place for a woman at night" or "men's jobs do not employ women at night." Others, asked how the eight-hour day had affected them, responded that they "would not hire women for long days even if there were no restrictions, as a matter of policy rather than law," or that certain kinds of work were simply too hard for women. One articulate superviser, responsible for 760 employees, nearly one-third female, acknowledged that restrictive legislation deprived women of some jobs. Yet he enthusiastically approved of laws as social measures that "indirectly benefited men and the community as a whole."[58]

These compromises were made easier by dramatic increases in labor productivity—the results of scientific management techniques that commanded maximal output from each worker and reduced possibilities of independent thought and error. A worker properly selected and supervised could produce as much in ten hours as a poorly supervised worker in eleven or twelve. And beginning in 1912, scientific studies of the relationship of fatigue to efficiency added ammunition to the arsenal. Josephine Goldmark's pioneering 1912 book demonstrated that long working hours actually decreased productivity. Increasing a worker's speed when hours were reduced did not work either: the faster they were used, the more quickly the muscles tired. Production would actually rise with a short, evenly paced workday. Some employers testified to the truth of these assertions. An Indiana manufacturer of kitchen cabinets with twenty-eight female employees who had voluntarily reduced hours to fifty per week in 1916 said he had maintained production and increased pay after the reduction in hours. The argument from fatigue became so persuasive that it threatened to overshadow other pleas based on women's special position by the late 1920s. A Harrisburg newspaper, editorializing on Pennsylvania's proposed forty-four-hour bill in 1929, objected when proponents asserted that women needed increased leisure and opportunity for the improvement and culture that would make them better mothers. "Better than the leisure-for-culture arguments are those related to industrial efficiency, industrial fatigue and health. A tired worker is a poor worker. Fatigue causes accidents and so costs money. Toxins due to overstrain cause disease and decrease productive power."[59]

Still many smaller employers had a hard time of it. Often unable to afford new equipment and dependent on a local labor force, they resisted legislation that would reduce their ability to use workers as they wished. Factory inspectors, reformers, and Bureau of Labor statisticians believed that "unscrupulous employers" had to be compelled by law "to do what others are willing to do."[60] But spreading custom and the pressure of unionization seem to have been as important as legislation in improving working conditions in their plants.

By the 1920s, the emerging legal structure seemed merely to confirm patterns that had already been established by large employers and enlightened managers. Massachusetts did not pass its fifty-eight-hour law in 1897 until it was clear, in the words of one authority, that "very few factories were working women and minors the full time allowed by law. . . ."[61] By the time the campaign for a forty-eight-hour week took shape in a half-dozen industrial states in the early 1920s, employers had already complained that a prevailing labor shortage made women reluctant either to work long hours or for lower wages than they wished. "We can't get the girls to come in any earlier," said one Indiana cigar manufacturer whose 549 female workers had a forty-seven-hour week in 1926. "They are independent and won't work any longer than these hours."[62] More than half of the small New Jersey plants visited by the Women's Bureau in 1919 had reduced their hours without legal compulsion. Managers said they would not get labor without shortening hours since neighboring plants had shortened their day. A Cambridge, Massachusetts, candy manufacturer whose 300 women employees worked forty-five and three-quarters hours a week in 1916 said he could never run an evening shift because he "could not get the same class of girls he has in the day time. . . ." The idea of minimum wages, even where they were only recommended, also had an influence, educating women, as one California cotton mill owner complained, "to expect it" and to "refuse to work for less."[63]

Within trade unions, different economic pressures forced a similar conclusion. Fear of competition from women and reluctance to invest in organizing them led trade unionists to distinguish sharply between men and women when it came to legislation. To legislate for men, who were theoretically organizable, would undermine their commitment to unionization. But for women, whose stay in the labor force was expected to be brief, legislation could provide an attractive alternative to the expense of organizing while it controlled the way in which women could enter the labor force and compete with men. Regulatory legislation would limit women's access to jobs by discouraging employers from hiring them. Prohibitive or restrictive legislation would eliminate competition from women altogether. As John R. Commons, a noted labor economist, put it, "the wage bargaining power of men is weakened by the competition of women and children, hence a law restricting the hours of women and children may also be looked upon as a law to protect men in their bargaining power."[64]

AFL leaders, who represented 80 percent of organized workers in 1900, understood the value of labor legislation to their members. "We cannot drive the females out of the trade," argued Adolph Strasser of the Cigarmakers' International, a founding member of the AFL, in an often-quoted 1879 annual report to the members of his union, "but we can restrict their daily quota of labor through factory laws. No girl under 18 should be employed more than 8 hours per day; all overwork should be prohibited, while married women should be kept out of factories at least 6 weeks before and 6 weeks after confinement."[65] To justify this position, Strasser used the argument of woman's weakness. Testifying before a congressional committee in 1882, Strasser concluded a diatribe against the number of women entering the trade with a plea to restrict them. "Why?" asked his interrogator. "Because," replied Strasser, "I claim that it is the duty of the government to protect the weak, and females are considered among the weak in society."[66]

A trade union movement distressed at expanding competition from women thus entered into uneasy agreement with reformers seeking legislation to protect them. Reflecting the position the reformers had arrived at, trade unionists adopted notions of women's weakness. ". . . Women may be adults," argued one AFL columnist in 1900, "and why should we class them as children. Because it is to the interest of all of us that female labor should be limited so as not to injure the motherhood and family life of a nation."[67] In a piece entitled "The Kingdom of God and Modern Industry," economist Ira Howerth wrote:

> The highest courts in some of our states declare that a law limiting the hours of labor for these women is unconstitutional. It may be so, but if it is so, so much the worse for the state. The state or nation that permits its women to stunt their bodies and dwarf their minds by overexertion in insanitary [sic] stores and mills and factories is thereby signing its own death warrant. For the degeneracy of women is the degeneracy of the race. A people can never be any better than its mothers.[68]

This rationale encouraged the AFL to join the campaign for protective legislation early in the 1890s. Proposals such as limiting women's working hours to eight per day, eliminating them from jobs where foot-power machinery was employed, and denying them government jobs entirely appeared repeatedly at the Federation's conventions. By 1900 the Birmingham *Labor Advocate* was publishing articles urging women's removal from a variety of industries. "Girls under 18 should not be allowed in commercial or industrial establishments. Four states forbid women to work in mines; these laws," the journal intoned, "should be extended to about 100 of their present occupations which are too severe and too unhealthy."[69]

Because their ends appeared to be the same, trade unionists and reformers supported each other in getting legislation passed. Together, such groups as the WTUL, the NCL, and the AFL succeeded in pushing through the bulk of progressive period legislation. As useful as such legislation could sometimes be, a healthy dose of skepticism about trade union motives persisted. Women's Party activist Jane Norman Smith claimed, for example, that trade unionists acknowledged openly that in public "we must talk about 'humanitarian' laws for women and that sort of sob stuff, but when we get into committee, we just come right down to brass tacks and say to the men, 'We had better drive the women out of the trade as fast as possible, and the quickest way to do it is through a special 8-hour law for women.' "[70]

Whatever the real benefits offered to women by regulatory legislation, trade unions did nothing to dispel this fear. The actions of a variety of trade unionists demonstrated their capacity to use regulatory legislation in their own self-interest. New York State's male grinders and polishers in the machine tool industry, for example, asked in 1894 for legislation to force manufacturers to provide local ventilation systems to remove dust and grit from the working area. They received no response. Some years later, legislation prohibited women and boys from these jobs on the grounds that the jobs were detrimental to their health. In 1913, new factory legislation finally provided the needed ventilation for all workers, but women were still denied access to the jobs. They protested in vain. In 1921, they managed to secure an amendment that permitted women over twenty-one to operate wet grinding machines, but despite the existence of dust-removal mechanisms, not even endorsement by the Women's Bureau could persuade lawmakers to lift the prohibition on women's use of dry grinding equipment.[71]

Iron molders demonstrated equal tenacity in their fight for legislation to eliminate women from "core rooms." Women had been employed at making the "core" from which molds were taken since 1884.

At first only a curiosity, they had increased steadily in number since 1903 when plant consolidations made their use profitable. In 1907, the molders' union decided to take action to eliminate them. Declaring that "heavy, dangerous, grimy and dusty work is physically injurous to women and incompatible with their finer nature, and that the lower labor standards generally acceptable to women constitute a menace to the standards obtained by men," the union agreed to fine members up to fifty dollars for instructing women and to expel any member caught doing so a second time.

In 1910, the iron molders appealed to New York State for a law prohibiting female employment. Union leaders told a factory investigating commission that the work was too rough for women, that noxious fumes injured women far more than men. The commission reported ventilation in foundries that was unacceptable for both sexes, and numbers of workers, male and female, who suffered from rheumatism, kidney trouble, and pulmonary disease. Although concluding that women faced no worse conditions than did men, it asserted that "it would have been far better if women had never been originally allowed to enter this employment" and argued that "its suppression would be beneficial to the race." The report continued, "We cannot at this time recommend an entire prohibition of work that would result in throwing the three hundred women now in the industry out of employment. We believe that work by women in core rooms . . . should be discouraged and ultimately suppressed." The bill that emerged from the legislature prohibited women from working in the same rooms as men and forbade them altogether from core rooms where the ovens that emitted fumes were located in the working space. It also regulated the size and weight of cores women could handle. The result, in the words of a union official, was "practically to exclude women from the foundry."[72]

By the 1920s, most union officials viewed protective legislation for women as a complement to unionization for men and avidly promoted it. The AFL supported reformers' efforts to establish a permanent Women's Bureau within the Department of Labor with this end at least partially in mind. The Bureau could be expected to promote government intervention to defend the interests of wage-earning women, releasing trade unions from that task. Upon investigation the Bureau found that many union officials viewed unionization and protective legislation as alternate means to the same goal: better working conditions for all workers. Sara Conboy, United Textile Workers official and a WTUL activist, told a Women's Bureau interviewer that she believed in "legislation to limit long hours of work for women where and when the union [was] not strong enough to limit hours."[73] Some unionized workers thought legislation surer and faster or believed that it was more dependable than possibly untrustworthy union leaders. A. J. Muste, then secretary of the Amalgamated Textile Workers' Union of America, preferred unionization, but was said to believe that legislation did not hinder organization and might be essential in industries with many women and minors.[74]

But female union officials displayed a strong streak of skepticism. The ILGWU's education director, Fannia Cohn, only reluctantly acquiesced to the need for protective legislation. "I did not think the problems of working women could be solved in any other way than the problems of working men and that is through trade union organization," she wrote in 1927; but, she continued, "considering that very few women are as yet organized into trade unions, it would be folly to agitate against protective legislation."[75] Cohn ascribed the problems of women workers to the absence of organization. A woman printer, one of two who fought the ultimately successful battle to exempt printers from New York State's night-work law, rejected this argument out of hand. With only one-quarter of the labor force organized, she argued, women were "not competing with the organized aristocracy of labor; on the contrary they are competing in the labor market with unorganized and unorganizable men, and so legislation which might be truly 'protective' if applied to *workers* becomes a cruel handicap when applied to women only."[76] Few female trade unionists, however, opposed the strong consensus for protection. And their voices were lost in the din of approval that arose from women reformers both before and after suffrage was achieved in 1920.

All the largest women's reform groups enthusiastically advocated protective labor legislation—first as a device to entice wage-earning women into the suffrage movement, then as a panacea for their ills. The Women's Trade Union League turned from organizing to legislative action in 1912, and by 1915 legislation was its major priority. The national and state consumers' leagues, whose activities had ranged from providing labels to identify products made by well-treated workers, to compiling "white" lists of stores that sold them, to inspecting factories for health hazards, debated for a year whether its efforts could not better be spent seeking legislation. Finally turning toward restriction in 1918, the National Consumers' League urged its general secretary to "actively oppose everywhere the employment of women under twenty-one years as messengers, letter carriers, elevator or street railroad employees, or as meter readers and bell girls in hotels, restaurants, and men's clubs."[77] The League of Women Voters, successor to the National American Woman's Suffrage Association, similarly turned to protection as its goal.

All of these groups offered the same double-pronged rationale. Women, they argued first, "were inadequately organized" and therefore had been unable "to obtain the better conditions enjoyed by the men who have obtained them through the power of their labor unions." To prevent women from becoming, in the words of a NWTUL pamphlet, "underbidding competitors" who would "drag down the standards of all industry," they needed labor laws. And, second, women had special need for these laws "to permit efficient motherhood and healthy children."[78]

The continuing paradox of this appeal from women's weakness contributed to splitting feminist ranks. For the organizational energy and skill required to pass protective legislation conflicted with the continuing struggle toward women's equality. In opposition to advocates of legislation, an important group of feminists argued, "If you demand equality, you must accept equality." Led by Alice Paul's National Women's Party, the militant wing of the women's suffrage movement, these women began to urge a constitutional amendment guaranteeing equality—which they finally got submitted to Congress in December 1923. The so-called Lucretia Mott amendment declared, "Men and women shall have equal rights throughout the United States and every place subject to its jurisdiction." It rested, as had the original arguments for women's rights made in 1848, on the assumption that women, who were basically similar to men, were entitled to all human rights.

Consistent with this viewpoint, the NWP insisted that the benefits of industrial legislation extend to all workers and that occupation, not sex, be the basis of legislative restriction. Jane Norman Smith explained the Women's Party's position. "If . . . a law is passed applying to women and not applying to men, it will discriminate against women and handicap them in competing with men in earning their livelihood." She dismissed arguments of moral danger and biological inferiority. "This is a philosophy that would penalize all women because some women are morally frail and physically weak."[79] An Equal Rights Amendment, explained Crystal Eastman, lawyer, writer, and pioneer in developing workmen's compensation laws, would "establish the principle that industrial legislation should apply to all workers, both men and women, in any given occupation and not to women workers alone."[80]

It was, on its face, a reasonable position. It had already been adopted by the International Labor Organization's 1919 International

Congress of Working Women, where it was bitterly opposed by Women's Bureau head Mary Anderson. It represented the predominant position of British and Western European feminists. It had been articulated by a variety of women's groups before 1923, and was to emerge again in the early years of the New Deal when optimists believed that protective labor legislation for all workers might yet prevail.

In the United States some of the leading proponents of special legislation in the 1920s had earlier taken a more flexible stance. Lillian Wald and Florence Kelley, veterans of campaigns against child labor and for factory inspection, had believed in 1914 that protective legislation should cover all workers. In a lengthy exchange of letters with Florence Harriman, resident commissioner of the Industrial Relations Commission, they strongly dissented from the Commission's attempts to separate women from men in the legislative arena. "Miss Kelley and I," wrote Lillian Wald, "both hope very much that your Industrial Relations Commission will find it wise to make your recommendations for industry itself, rather than for women and children as distinct from boys and men." An ambiguous reply produced a joint response: ". . . it is becoming more obvious every day that it is unwise to segregate women and children in the field of industrial legislation."[81] In those early days, others had concurred. Mary Van Kleeck, who had headed the Women in Industry Service and was Mary Anderson's good friend, told the first International Congress of Working Women in 1919: "We seek not only the protection of women against the evils of industry, but we seek such a position in industry in relation to its controlling forces as will enable women to remove the evils of industry as they affect either men or women workers."[82] Women, in short, had to mobilize to fight poor industrial conditions for all workers, not only for themselves.

But when, after some vacillation, the National Women's Party chose to pursue a constitutional amendment as the means of achieving equality, reformers feared that the gains of decades of struggle to improve working conditions for women might be lost. National Women's Party officials, floating various versions of a proposed amendment, knew that protective legislation was vulnerable should the amendment pass. Maude Younger, the Party's national legislative chairman, wrote to Ethel Smith of the WTUL agreeing to accept changes in the ERA. "We would be glad to find any other form of wording which would better accomplish the object we have in view, namely the removal of all legal discriminations against women without at the same time injuring the eight hour law and other social legislation in which as you know, I am personally deeply interested."[83] Ethel Smith rejected the olive branch. "I have found no one yet . . .

who believes it possible to draft a blanket *Federal* constitutional amendment which would not jeopardize our social legislation."[84] Still the NWP would not give up. Though most legal opinion claimed that minimally an amendment would mean court fights over existing legislation, there were occasional dissenters. Albert Leavitt, one of the amendment's drafters and a professor at the University of North Dakota School of Law, wrote to a Labor Department official: "When it is in final shape, I am of the opinion that it will not jeopardize the legal protection given to women workers. Indeed it is the purpose of the National Women's Party to safeguard protective legislation to the utmost extent."[85]

But unlike the Women's Party most advocates of protection were not willing to risk hard-won legislation for an abstract commitment to equality. Faced with the possibility of seeing all protective labor legislation collapse, Kelley, Wald, and Mary Van Kleeck, among others, became fierce opponents of what they called a blanket amendment. By 1924, Van Kleeck was Mary Anderson's staunchest supporter for special legislation for women, and Crystal Eastman called Florence Kelley "the leading spirit" in opposition to the ERA and "a passionate advocate of protective laws for women and children in industry."[86]

The NWTUL officially called on the NWP to "discontinue its efforts for blanket legislation."[87] The best legal minds in the country, including Felix Frankfurter, agreed. Frankfurter wrote to Ethel Smith in 1921 of his "shock" at learning of the amendment, which "threatens the well-being, even the very life of these millions of wage-earning women."[88] The WTUL pulled out all the stops in its fight. It publicly chastised women who favored the ERA, solicited and published the support of union leaders, and asserted its exclusive right to speak for wage-earning women.

The state and national consumers' leagues also strongly opposed the amendment: the 1922 national board meeting resolved that "since the Board of Directors are advised by counsel that the effect . . . of the amendment proposed by the Women's Party which, in its present form, abolishes all political, civil, and legal disabilities and inequalities on account of sex or marriage, would be to wipe out protective legislation for wage earning women, Mrs Kelley be directed to inform the protagonists of the proposed amendment that unless its wording is so changed as to safeguard the validity of the legislation for women, such as the NCL had advocated throughout its existence, the NCL would be constrained actively to oppose the amendment."[89]

Male organized labor joined in the attack. Having long since arrived at the position that protective legislation was more effective than organization as a way of keeping women in their place, Gompers, in 1922, came out unequivocally against the ERA. The International Typographical Union, notorious for its antifemale stance, unamimously adopted a resolution condemning the NWP's amendment as a threat to protective legislation and stating, "We deplore and condemn the acts of members of this and other labor organizations cooperating with interests engaged in a constant effort to break down beneficial legislation after years of effort."[90] *Justice*, organ of the ILGWU, treated ERA as anathema. "To destroy industrial laws for women merely because the same laws do not exist for men is . . . the same kind of thing we would have been doing had we sought to deprive men of suffrage because women did not have it."[91]

The conflict admitted of no resolution. Women could not be both wards of the state entitled to special protection and equal to men unless men were also protected. Max Danish, editor of *Justice*, bluntly phrased the dilemma: "The organized labor movement of this country, while in sympathy with the aims and principles of full equality of men and women, can, however, under the curcumstances, hardly give its sanction to such blanket legislation," he wrote of the ERA.[92] Yet if it came to a choice, women effectively had none. Lacking such protection as a trade union might offer, they were dependent by now on legislative protection, their jobs so constituted as to rely on it. Labor, having done its best to turn women into children, now pleaded that they needed the fatherly care of government intervention on their behalf.

The Women's International League for Peace and Freedom debated the issue of equality endlessly at its 1924 Washington meeting. But in the end, it too found that it could not support both equality of the sexes and protective legislation. So it chose to ignore the issue of protection in order to support equality. Even the WTUL had its fifth column. In 1926, its executive secretary, who had supported protective legislation in the past, changed her mind. Equality, she now felt, would come only if wage-earning women could struggle alongside men. Men who supported an amendment that would effectively separate women from that struggle, she believed, were "putting it over on the women. . . . the only way in the future to obtain desired results," she argued, "would be through organization of women instead of legislation."[93]

As feminists began to polarize, the Women's Party position hardened to the point where the Party withdrew its tacit support for protective legislation and became intent on passing an ERA at any cost. The Women's Bureau—freshly created, and seeking a more secure place in the Department of Labor—entered the fray. Mary Anderson, its director, had always stood squarely on the side of legislation and therefore opposed equal rights. Her position certainly made political sense, since the Bureau's viability depended on the support of trade unions and women's organizations—both of which opposed the ERA. And Anderson felt grateful to close friends who as leaders of the National Consumers' League and the WTUL had joined with her to protest artificial salary limits and salary cuts for Bureau personnel in the early years.[94] Anderson, who had begun her working life as a shoe worker, argued that "theoretical" feminists were "talking about things and conditions entirely outside their own experience or knowledge." She urged that "rights must be interpreted for women workers as something concrete, and we must start with the world where it is today. . . ."[95]

The Women's Party, supported only by the National Federation of Business and Professional Women's Clubs and other organizations of well-educated career women, finally provoked a confrontation on the issue. At the 1926 Conference on Women in Industry it pushed through a special resolution asking the Bureau to explore the effects of labor legislation. Hoping that the results would prove that women were disadvantaged by such legislation, the Party insisted that the investigation be guided by an advisory committee representing both sides of the question. Mary Anderson, anxious, as she wrote to her friend Mary Van Kleeck, for "everyone to feel, including the Women's Party, that I am keeping the faith," was equally anxious not to "arrest progress in getting laws." Van Kleeck responded reassuringly. "The Women's Party has asked for an investigation which implies that they do not feel that the information is already at hand. Moreover, they will be consulted regarding its scope, and it will be the occasion when they must produce facts or have their case fall to the ground. The whole matter will be opened up for scientific procedure, and I cannot but believe that it will prove to be a check upon the characteristic activities of that group which they themselves have not foreseen."[96]

To undercut the expected opposition from the Women's Party, Anderson created two committees to support the work: one, which would be sensitive to all the political interests, to offer advice, and another, made up of her supporters, to direct the work. The advisory committee included representatives of the Women's Party, the League of Women Voters, and the WTUL, as well as the AFL. The technical committee that was to design and direct the investigation included Mary Van Kleeck and Lillian Gilbreth, the efficiency expert. Both committees met with the Women's Bureau in the fall of 1926. The meeting proved to be a fiasco, ending when the two sides disagreed as to how the investigation should be conducted, and the advisory committee broke up.[97]

But the investigation continued under the direction of the technical committee. Its results are presented in a 1928 Bureau publication: *The Effects of Labor Legislation on the Employment of Women*. Not surprisingly, it held the effects of legislation to be overwhelmingly positive. "With practically no exceptions," announced Mary Winslow, assigned by the Women's Bureau to head the investigation, "the few handicaps resulting from protective legislation have occurred only in a small number of special occupations—in which normally few women are employed—and in semi-professional work, such as that of pharmacists, proof-readers, etc." Instead of finding that legislation had a pernicious impact on women, the Bureau found that it had often improved not only women's conditions and hours of labor but men's as well. It found no significant instances in which legislation had tended to deprive women of jobs. Indeed, it asserted, legislation in most cases merely confirmed and rationalized custom to everyone's benefit.[98]

Circumstances surrounding the investigation, as well as the way it was thereafter publicized and used, raise doubts about its validity. Politics masqueraded behind a facade of statistical data. The Women's Bureau had clearly proved what it set out to discover from the beginning, and then issued its findings amid carefully arranged publicity. The Bureau underplayed some important data. Measuring the effect of prohibiting night work, it concluded that this did not limit the daytime jobs available to women, and it was comforted by finding that employers in any event had "astonishingly strong feelings against hiring women at night" and would probably not do so regardless of legislation. By its own estimate, some 60,000 women had lost their jobs as a result of restrictive legislation—a number it dismissed as insignificant next to the eight million women working for wages. Yet it neglected to point out that these 60,000 were frequently at the cutting edge of job opportunities, that it was precisely where few women were employed that women tended to lose their jobs, and that evident constraints discouraged women from taking risks and attacking barriers to equality. The data did not measure the extent to which legislation prevented employers from opening new jobs to women. The Bureau offered no insights about the degree to which legislation retarded the progress of women already working, or about the numbers who, discouraged by such long legal battles as those of the printers and the conductors, never applied for off-limits jobs.

Accusations and counteraccusations notwithstanding, when the dust cleared, protective labor legislation stood unscarred. In 1929, the Women's Bureau circulated a triumphant poster. "Does your daughter face her young years with carefree zest and ambition?" it asked, and then went on to urge parents to insure that their cities and states had appropriate legislation guaranteeing that "her work is laid in pleasant places, with hours that leave time for continuation study, for recreation and exercise; fair wages that make for fair living, and a light, airy, and clean building in which to earn that living." None could oppose these objectives, yet they told only part of the story.

Of all the potential solutions to the "problem" of wage-earning women, protective legislation satisfied more interests than any other. Widely accepted views of women's primary responsibilities to the home governed its development and guaranteed its acceptance. A world view shared by trade unions and employers alike and acknowledged by most women—wage earners as well as reformers—made protective legislation only the final seal on already accepted behavior patterns. In a period when the notion of equal opportunity for women at work had virtually no popular approval, ameliorating their work conditions seemed wholly to satisfy perceived need. The body of legislation that emerged undertook to help women without violating traditional female roles and in accord with labor market needs and trade union sensibilities. As Mary Anderson put it, "I consider myself a good feminist, but I believe I am a practical one."[99]

In a period when family restrictions and limited availability of jobs perhaps doomed in advance such solutions as cooperatives, education, and training, legislation appeared as the most plausible solution to problems of overwork. It came at the cost of affirming the relative labor force positions of men and women. Protective labor legislation joined with limited labor force opportunities and virtual exclusion from labor unions to institutionalize women's isolation from the mainstream of labor. This translated into special behavior on the part of women workers that isolated them still further from male workers. What was more, legislation ignored the poorest women such as agricultural workers and domestics who had perhaps the most tiring jobs. At the other end of the spectrum, it did not deal with "brain workers," exempting thousands of office workers and professionals from its mandate. These workers were thought to be strong enough to protect themselves. While it acknowledged, by restrictions, the increasing place of women in the work force, legislation attempted to avoid changes in their social roles that more freely available economic opportunities might have permitted. It recognized that women had two jobs, one of which had to be limited if the other was to be performed adequately. By denying that women were full-fledged, equal wage earners, legislation institutionalized social reproduction as women's primary role. It thus extended a version of the ideology of domesticity to working-class people. Since it acknowledged the possibility of wage labor for women, however, it simultaneously loosened the bonds of propriety from around some middle-class women.

As they affected both the work place and the home, protective statutes provided a continuing device for dividing workers along gender lines and stratifying the work force at a time when the number of skilled jobs was declining and the resulting homogenization of the work force threatened to lead to developing class consciousness and thence to class conflict. Neither protagonists nor critics ever lost sight of the possibility that legislation could both ameliorate the worst abuses against women and simultaneously confirm their status as a separate group of workers.

Most critics of the emerging body of legislation feared that it would inhibit women's access to good jobs. A few feared that such legislation might ease harsh conditions too much, and so provide an incentive for women to work. When this seemed to be happening, protests instantly emerged. In 1916, for example, the president of the American Association of Labor Legislation presented a national health insurance plan to its members that included a provision to pay hospital expenses and cash benefits to women who withdrew from the work force during the weeks immediately before and after childbirth. Critics protested that such generosity would give potential mothers an incentive to work. And the proposal was withdrawn. The Women's Bureau responded negatively to Roger Babson's 1924 book *Recent Labor Progress*. According to Mary Anderson, Babson claimed that "the Bureau is making the work of women in industry too attractive. . . . He feels we ought to work to reduce the number of women in industry and to increase the numbers who became mothers of good families."[100]

In fighting for protective legislation, working women perhaps bowed to the inevitable, accepting for themselves the objectives favored by employers who preferred not to see them in unions, of male workers who hoped both to limit competition and to share in the advantages gained, and of middle-class reformers who felt they were helping to preserve home and motherhood. Echoing the arguments of twenty years earlier, Mary Anderson defended protective legislation in 1925 on the grounds that such laws were necessary to conserve the health of the nation's women.[101]

Legislation contributed to channeling young women into the rapidly expanding white-collar sector. Safe, clean secretarial and clerical work, with its short hours and decent pay, confirmed the marginality of women's positions in the labor force, positions that continued to be bounded by obeisance to marriage and the family. As WTUL activist and author, Alice Henry said of an earlier group of working women, "they did not realize that women were within the scope of the labor movement."[102] Fannia Cohn understood what that meant. That hard-headed and clear-sighted official of the ILGWU preceded a call for a revolution in society's view of women with a plea for an end to competition between men and women. "This competition must be abolished once and for all, not because it is immoral, yes inhuman, but because it is impractical, it does not pay."[103] In the first two decades of the twentieth century, however, traditional views of women prevailed—releasing some women from some of the misery of toil, but simultaneously confirming their places in those jobs most conducive to exploitation.

III

Transforming the Notion of
Work for Women: World
War I to the Present

8

Ambition and Its Antidote in a New Generation of Female Workers

In 1927 the Consumers' League of New York surveyed 500 working women. Would they favor a law reducing hours from fifty-four to forty-eight, the League asked. Overwhelmingly, women answered affirmatively. "I want more time to live. You get old fast enough without working yourself to death," responded a young worker. One added, "I go to 'Y' classes twice a week and am studying stenography. When I worked nine hours a day I was too tired to go anywhere."[1] Their answers differed dramatically from those the Connecticut League had received when it asked women about their working hours just ten years before. Now, women worried less about adequate incomes; they cared more about "living." This was a new kind of woman wage earner, with different expectations and new demands.

She came from a new kind of home, which had produced a shift in the composition of female labor. And she reflected new pulls in the work force, which led her to alter her expectations. Different women were working for different reasons. They had different marital profiles and came from different age groups. The women who had held the old jobs did not qualify for the new ones. And some of those who could have continued to work chose not to.

Helen and Robert Lynd pointed to the origins of change when they described the slow improvement in living conditions of Middletown's poorer housewives.[2] Easy-to-clean linoleum replaced floor boards; coal fires displaced wood that had to be chopped first; running water, even electricity, came directly to the flat. As household work diminished, families began to have choices. Whereas in the nineteenth century the changing nature of household work might have released a daughter from the home to continue her education or to bring in wages, the changes that followed World War I affected wives. They could take advantage of the reduced work load and of generally shorter factory hours to earn money for additional amenities. Alternatively, pride in the family dwelling and a husband's wish to keep his wife at home encouraged some women to cease wage work. If a wife took in a boarder or two, the family could enjoy the benefits of full-time care. Statistics for the 1920s show a relative decline in the proportion of immigrant and black women working for wages. In part this reflected an increase in other wage-earning women. And in part it reflected exercise of the option not to work. For, given the kinds of jobs available to older, poor women, and to young women with neither skill nor education, the possibility of not working must have seemed like freedom indeed.

But for every woman who wished to shed the "double burden" and to choose a single job in her own household, another felt the pull of opportunity. Shorter hours and better working conditions enabled some women, tempted by the array of new products, to work for family extras. "Who would pay for it, if I didn't work?" a mother might ask of her daughter's education, her new piano, or the family's annual holiday.[3] Well-educated daughters of the middle class moved into the labor force looking for the promise of wartime opportunity and the economic freedom that would surely accompany the vote. Married and unmarried, women with high school diplomas, college training, and graduate degrees came from different social backgrounds and had different expectations than those pushed into wage work by material necessity. A new generation of female wage workers emerged whose job-related hopes extended beyond economic survival, challenging the social organization of women's work that had once reinforced custom and attitude by exerting control over women's labor force possibilities.

Life for the two groups of women differed. Production workers, domestic servants, and the poor, whose survival depended on their wages, still faced the old problems of arduous labor. More fortunate women faced new problems of exclusion. The line that divided the two was not always rigid. Between the jobs that nobody would consider giving to a woman because they violated some unspoken sense of what women were all about, and the jobs that clearly belonged to women because time and low pay had by the twenties stamped them so, was a no-man's land into which the luckier women moved, seeking to carve out an economic place in the new world, still unsure of the terrain.

·   ·   ·

Like the Civil War that preceded it, and the second World War that was to follow, World War I allowed women to demonstrate aptitudes for certain "inappropriate" jobs. They took advantage of the wartime emergency to move up a notch on the occupational ladder into jobs previously closed to them. "It was not until our men were called overseas," recalled one female banking executive, "that we made any real onslaught on the realm of finance, and became tellers, managers of departments, and junior and senior officers."[4] The Women's Bureau concurred. The war "forced the experiment of woman labor in the craftsmanly occupations," it argued in a 1920 bulletin. In entering new fields, women challenged the physiological and social assumptions that justified discrimination against them. Employers registered surprise at women's ability to do jobs previously denied them. The Women's Bureau repeatedly quoted supervisors who declared themselves astonished at what wage-earning women could accomplish. "We believe that there is hardly a line of work in which a woman cannot adapt herself . . . ," said one furniture manufacturer. "One of the lessons from the war has been to show that women can do exacting work," commented an auto manufacturer.[5]

From a structural perspective, job shifts during the immediate prewar and postwar years appear insignificant. The Federal Civil Service opened new categories of jobs to women, but continued to pay them less than men. Some women moved into men's jobs in chemicals, automobile manufacture, iron and steel. Others, lower on the scale, moved into jobs vacated by women moving up. Still others, who had never worked, entered wage work often as menial laborers, or on occasion to fill office jobs vacated by men. The Women's Bureau estimated that less than 5 percent of all women workers in these years were new to the labor force. But a substantial number of black women who had been closed out of industrial jobs entirely now found niches for themselves.[6] When the war ended, the entire structure slipped back down nearly, but not quite, to where it had started.

Census data describing women's involvement in industry reveal two patterns. In those parts of the productive sector where jobs had been steadily and slowly opening for women, the pattern continued during the war decade, sometimes with a temporary rise reflecting increased female employment in the war years. When hostilities ended, the numbers of women declined, leaving the residual gain that might have been expected in any event. This was true in such female-employing industries as tobacco and food processing, but it was also true in industries only marginally dependent on female labor such as leather goods, metals, iron and steel. On the other hand, in sectors like chemicals and electrical goods, where women had been losing

New, if temporary, opportunities opened with World War I. Here young women operate stock boards at the Waldorf Astoria in November 1918. *(Courtesy of the National Archives)*

The Women in Industry Service described this 1919 photograph of Nellie McGrath delivering mail to a Washington family as "the first instance in which a woman has been employed to deliver the mail." *(Courtesy of the National Archives)*

Women's work as common laborers is not frequently recorded. Above: A McKees Rocks, Pennsylvania, brickyard, 1919. "They *are* girls," wrote a Women's Bureau agent on the back of the photo. Below: Women railway workers at Busch Terminal, Brooklyn, New York. On the back of this one someone wrote: "Note: Specially prized picture. Do not give out the original UNDER ANY CIRCUMSTANCES." *(Courtesy of the National Archives)*

This young woman operating a drill press at the Packard Motor Car Co. was still employed in February 1919. *(Courtesy of the National Archives)*

Assembling the framework of a plane at Standard Aero Corp., Elizabeth, New Jersey, during World War I. *(Courtesy of the National Archives)*

ground, they gained jobs briefly in wartime and then continued to lose them thereafter. Heavily women-dependent industries followed this pattern as did those that employed relatively few women. The declining proportion of women in knit goods momentarily ceased and then continued. In other industries, as in textiles and clothing manufacture, women lost ground continuously between 1910 and 1930, regaining it briefly during the depression years. In sum, the emergency expansion of industrial production, and the momentary absence of men, did not alter patterns of employment in manufacturing beyond the war years.[7] With few exceptions, jobs returned to male control when the conflict ended.

But in expanding sectors of the war economy, women began to make real gains that persisted thereafter. The country's new place in world affairs, its concern for international finance and worldwide markets, permanently transfigured the business landscape. Corporations and the communications industry embarked on their rapid expansion, gobbling up legions of telephone and telegraph operators as well as clerks and bookkeepers, virtually all female. Advertising and sales became a part of the design for prosperity, demanding a renewable supply of saleswomen, buyers, designers, decorators, and copywriters. What women as a group failed to gain in manufacturing, they more than made up for in white-collar areas that encompassed office staff at all but the highest levels. By 1920, in a process accelerated by the war but not caused by it, a larger percentage of employed women worked in these jobs (25.6 percent) than in manufacturing (23.8 percent), in domestic service (18.2 percent), or in agriculture (12.9 percent).[8]

But a structural perspective obscures what the experience of work meant for women. For women who had once received reasonable wages, the idea of good wages remained. Having been in a position to choose among a variety of jobs, women who found their choices limited protested. Black women, who had been confined to domestic and menial jobs, resisted returning to them after the war, especially when the conditions of even those jobs deteriorated. Women who had driven ambulances and organized relief for the country were less likely to remain contentedly in their households than their mothers had been.

Job-related demands gathered steam as women tested out a new freedom in their personal lives. The vote, newly won, brought no immediate political victories, but it did provide a sense of freedom and of endless possibility. "The time has come now," declared veteran suffragist Anna Howard Shaw, in the glow of victory, "when we women have a right to ask that we shall be free to labor where our labor is needed, that we shall be free to serve in the capacity for which we are fitted."[9] "Emancipation in the industrial field," predicted Everett William Lord, dean of Boston University's College of Business Administration, "will follow as a natural sequence the equalization of men and women politically."[10]

Smaller, less permanent families encouraged a search for work outside the home. Fewer boarders, fewer live births per family, fewer adult children living at home, and more readily available birth control aids contributed to a sense of freedom and of control over one's life. Films became the models, automobiles and radios the visible symbols, of a new affluence. The divorce rate began its unremitting climb, reflecting a search for more satisfying affective relationships. As one woman, married in 1920, said after fifty-six years of living with one husband, "Marriages were expected to last. Even so, I would have sought relief in divorce if I had found myself mistaken and caught in a destructive situation."[11]

Loosening sexual inhibitions contributed to the sense of greater freedom. Companionate marriage, trial marriage, divorce, still the province of a minority, all augured a new search for satisfaction. For the first time significant numbers of women challenged male sexual dominance and rejected their subservient positions. Like Mae West's aggressive ability to use her body for her own ends, sexual freedom was an assertion of the self: bursting the bonds of societal constraints and affirming an autonomy that transcended economic independence. Sexual freedom and the possibility of choices in life mingled freely, though not without discomfort.

In the prewar years, privileged women and the daring had already carved out paths toward autonomy. Political radicals like Emma Goldman and Elizabeth Gurley Flynn dramatized the struggle for sexual independence as part of their fiery defense of working-class interests. Less dramatically, "new women" like Crystal Eastman and her friend Henrietta Rodman, a committed feminist, writer, and political activist, managed to arrange life styles that included husbands and children as well as serious commitments to their vocations. Before the war less privileged women had ordinarily assumed not that marriage meant giving up wage labor, but that creative, satisfying, and important work was not compatible with domestic bliss. Examples of painful choices are the stuff of American legend. Rose Schneiderman, the daughter of a widowed immigrant mother who went to work at thirteen, chose to devote her life to trade unionism, knowing that to do so probably meant giving up the possibility of marriage. Anzia Yezierska, poverty-stricken child immigrant, learned to write English expertly so that she could satisfy her burning desire to tell her tale to

America. When she discovered that housekeeping interfered with her struggle to "make herself for a person," she left her husband and then her infant daughter in order to pursue her career.

There had, of course, always been a number of women who had chosen not to marry—whose restless energy had turned toward social settlements or the YWCA or found outlets in Greenwich Village rebellion. While the very talented, the very rich, and the determined had long been able to shape the minds of Wellesley girls or pioneer their way into medical school, the war promoted a more general sense that enormous possibilities were there for the taking. The postwar period encouraged an acquisitive individualism on the part of achieving Americans. Women, like men, demanded their share of the world's rewards. Ambition crept into their vocabulary. To aspire, to achieve, not merely to do a job, became at least a possibility for daughters as well as for sons.

The image of the flapper stymied these heady notions to some extent. Glamorous, economically independent, sexually free, and of course single, the flapper represented what a business community would have liked its young women workers to be. In return for limited economic and sexual freedom, women were encouraged to adopt a flighty, apolitical, and irresponsible stance. The image was meant to guarantee only peripheral involvement in the task of earning a living: an extension of women's supportive functions in the male world without the threat of competition. By masking women's real possibilities, the guise of the flapper enabled them to emerge from their homes and into the business world. In practice, however, the flapper image contained the seeds of every woman's freedom. Once having escaped their father's houses, young women leapt beyond temporary secretarial jobs into graduate and professional schools. Access to the business world legitimized the goal of independence. Once present, it could neither be confined to the unmarried nor removed from those who took husbands.

Graphic illustrations of the release of pent-up latent talent appear even during the war years. Mary Gilson, for example, went to Washington to recruit twenty-five women for management training courses. Their jobs were to be in the new personnel departments needed to cope with an influx of female workers in an era of corporate welfare and scientific management. She was deluged with applicants. "Thousands of letters poured in from every quarter of the country and from every class and occupation. All sorts and conditions of women applied. . . ."[12] And although many women simply tried to get footholds in better-paying jobs during wartime, the war and postwar shakedown that followed opened a larger arena.

File clerks who normally began work at twelve dollars per week could aspire to run offices, where they might create classification systems, index, and keep records at eighty dollars per week. Cash girls could become sales clerks or even buyers. Telephone operators could be supervisors. Job mobility became plausible even for the uneducated. Employment placement officers, dissatisfied now with placing clients in dead-end jobs, wondered out loud whether factory workers had better chances for success than stenographers. Women moved into new jobs in sales, marketing, publishing, accounting, credit, and life insurance. They began their rapid takeover of the human services fields, including social work, personnel work, and counseling.[13]

Advice on how to "make it" flowed freely. Selling life insurance, an executive told high school girls, would provide the "surest as well as most convenient means of providing for an independent old age." A woman who became an officer of the Guarantee Trust Company told an interviewer that a woman looking for a good entry into banking ought not to think of stenography. "If she does she is likely to remain a stenographer for years, if not for all of her business life." The advantage of filing, wrote another female banker, "lies in its being the best means of studying business itself, and of suggesting work that is both congenial and promising."[14]

In 1916, New York's Bureau of Vocational Information gave a series of lectures full of advice to women bound for success. In tones reminiscent of Horatio Alger, lecturers told women, "If you expect to get to the top, believe that you can get there, and then climb with all your might and main. Perseverance is also essential. . . . If you have in mind that you . . . are going to do this for . . . years, perhaps all your life, you will be more likely to succeed." Others echoed the advice. The main essential for success in civil service was "serious purpose rather than using it as a stopgap. . . ." Women entered actuarial training convinced, in the words of one young candidate, that "there is absolutely no sex limitation in this field. . . ."[15] By 1922, only one-third of women college graduates intended to be teachers compared to three-quarters a generation earlier. The remaining two-thirds had their career sights firmly fixed in business, the social services, and the professions. Nearly every graduate expected to obtain a job.[16] They found support in expanding networks of professional women. Clubs like Zonta and the Association of Business and Professional Women did for these women what women's clubs had done earlier for those who donated their labor to good causes.

Among factory workers, notions of satisfaction and relative freedom manifested themselves differently. Women now seemed to accept more readily their ability to work for wages at will. Available jobs and lessening desperation meant changes in the family economy. In one family, two sisters could take turns, one staying at home to help with the housework while the other went to work. In another, a young woman whose work tired her out could choose to stay at home temporarily and help her mother. Helen and Robert Lynd described a working-class mother of five who decided to earn extra money to buy her daughters' clothes when they refused to wear homemade garments. And young women who did not have to contribute to family support felt free to choose jobs they liked over those that paid well.[17] Some women reported that they preferred mill work to housework and hired "colored girls" to take care of their children, or left them with mothers-in-law while they worked in the mill.[18] Teenage daughters of all ethnic groups still turned over their pay envelopes intact to their mothers. But the twin influences of relative affluence and consumer pressures began to erode even this pattern in the twenties.

The possibility of mobility affected women and their daughters. Former household workers found jobs in candy factories, while candy dippers told their daughters not to "come with me to learn dipping" but to work in an office or department store where employment was more certain and the pay steady. Southern mill families urged their daughters to take "business courses."[19] Young garment makers studied typing and bookkeeping at night. Teaching jobs opened as possibilities for the offspring of Colorado miners like Agnes Smedley, or for immigrant children like Anzia Yezierska.

To significant numbers of women, marriage and work no longer seemed like mutually exclusive alternatives. The same heady freedom that encouraged young unmarried women from comfortable families to enter the labor force also encouraged them not to give up their careers when they married, or to shun marriage if they had careers. A certain desperate eagerness to do both characterized the most adventuresome. Crystal Eastman epitomizes it best; her life style allowed her to pursue a legal career while she mothered two children. To socialists like Theresa Wolfson, child of immigrant parents who became a labor economist and college professor, the dual role emerged naturally from a political ideology of equality. Rhoda Elizabeth McCulloch, Smith College professor, repeated an argument that would soon become familiar. Men, she claimed, "have not understood that it is impossible to make a home within four walls. The doors and windows of a modern house are the open doors and windows of the community itself, and a woman cannot create the spirit of a home save as she shares in creating the spirit of the community in which she lives." "Women needed to work," argued McCulloch, for "personal satisfaction."[20] The WTUL's Mabel Swartz agreed. For professional women, work was "a development of their personalities, an enlargement of their lives."[21]

McCulloch summed up the issue. "What questions about marriage do women want settled?" she asked. "The right to work, the right to an independent income, the right to a growing mental life." She neatly laid out the pros and cons for each of these "rights." First the negatives: women who worked undermined male pride in supporting them; they tended to be less tractable if they had independent incomes; and they remained content to have no children, or to have small families. Then the pros: the present economic system demanded women workers; large families were no longer desirable; children needed intensive care less and less; economically independent women would "elevate [the] present conception of marriage." And finally, McCulloch articulated the risks of combining marriage and wage work. Encouraging women to have careers with or without marriage offered them something more than child bearing It raised a woman's expectations of herself as a "personality," it might change "moral standards"—it might even lead women to prefer independence to the "burdens of marriage."[22]

Marriage and career, ambition and independence: if they spread to most women, these goals would be nothing less than revolutionary. It was one thing for tiny numbers of the avant-garde to try to create new lives, quite another for one-quarter of the women who earned wages to have husbands and children. And yet, already, paid work for women seemed to be becoming pervasive. In 1920, less than two million of the eight million wage-earning women were married. By 1930, more than three million of the ten million women who worked for wages were living with husbands—the proportion of married women had jumped from 22.8 percent to 28.8 percent of the female work force—an increase of more than 25 percent.[23]

If these figures underrepresent the numbers of women who worked at home, as census data commonly did, they nevertheless reflect new attitudes toward women's work. Large or small, the increase represented a growing shift in social realities that made it possible for women to acknowledge wage work of which they had formerly been ashamed. The men in the Amalgamated Clothing Workers of America, wrote an irate member, "still cherish the old theory that women are transient in industry. . . . But less and less frequently does a woman leave the industry when she marries."[24] Even traditional trade union attitudes were beginning to change. The Birmingham *Labor Advocate*, which had approved of men "marrying the women" to get them out of the labor force twenty years earlier, now acknowledged women's need to work. In 1922, it reprinted an article from the New York *Herald* which, while asserting the necessity of women's contribution to the home, nevertheless argued, "In these days the home job doesn't usually fill the whole time of a woman," a situation "responsible for the restlessness among modern women and the increasing tendency among many of them to take jobs outside the home."[25]

Acknowledging women's changing labor force participation raised questions about the constraining ideology of the home. The new kinds of jobs women were entering tended to sustain or create gender-free illusions of mobility—a mobility that had little to do with family life and could best exist parallel to, instead of in support of, women's primary family roles. For it was in the jobs that hinted at upward mobility that the dangerous potential of an ambitious womanhood posed the greatest threat.

In the 1890s, the glittering temptations of department stores were said to spoil saleswomen for marriage. Now, with the advent of alternative means of economic survival, all work might be suspected of doing that. A Baltimore *Sun* reporter commented quite accurately that "the harm has been done when a young girl who doesn't have to work goes out into the business world. She has formed certain habits and tastes that will not contribute to the happiness of a life lived under the stress of poverty."[26] Anzia Yezierska echoed the same thought. In her unpublished story "Rebellion of a Supported Wife," she wrote, "Women who have known the independence of earning their own livings before marriage are the ones who feel most poignantly the humiliations they have to live through while being 'supported.' "[27]

Was there no way to nip the bud of ambition without cutting off the supply of necessary women workers? As always, assumptions about women's social roles clashed with the need for cheap labor. Confronted with a postwar end to massive immigration and a consequent increase in male wages, women's labor became by contrast too attractive to disregard. Throughout the twenties the earnings gap widened, until at its end women's wages averaged only 57 percent of men's. Tempted by the possibilities of a less expensive labor force, some employers increased their demand for women. Sporadic shortages of female labor occurred in states as disparate as Virginia and Massachusetts, as well as in some kinds of jobs. By 1924, the New York *Times* reported shortages in all categories of office workers.[28] To attract workers to these areas, employers offered monetary incentives, heightening women's impression of wider choices available. A Richmond, Virginia, tobacco factory, for example, offered each young woman who brought in a friend a two-dollar bonus and an additional five dollars if the friend worked for one month.[29]

This increased demand for female wage workers ran afoul of the desire to regulate women's aspirations. To induce women to take jobs while simultaneously restraining their ambition to rise in them required a series of socially accepted constraints on work roles. Unspoken social prescription—a tacit understanding about the primacy of home roles—remained the most forceful influence. This is most apparent in professional jobs where the potential for ambition was greatest.

Elizabeth Kemper Adams published a volume entitled *Women Professional Workers* in 1921. Part of the Chautauqua home reading series, the book described women's new opportunities in a manner calculated to justify them to a traditional rural audience. Adams argued that women belonged in all professions because professionals sold "experience, judgment, and advice." They were "not working for profits." Rather, they could be viewed as "agencies of social regulation and improvement." Professional workers therefore had no "personal or partisan ends" but were, instead, motivated by "intellectual and moral devotion."[30] Defined that way, professional jobs took on the luster of women's assigned task. Women would bring "a free, resourceful, and unhampered intelligence" to social problems.

Translating these functions into the reality of jobs, Adams cited the special opportunities women could find in nearly every profession. Acknowledging the value of a comfortable income, she also noted how readily women could do good. In law, "their relative detachment from vested interests and large property transactions left them free to devote themselves to the human and preventative side. . . ." They were "of course especially needed in matters concerning the protection and welfare of women and of children . . . in legal aid societies . . . as judges in juvenile courts, municipal work, courts of domestic relations, small claims court, and so on." Medicine, too, offered "widening and increasingly varied opportunities for women, especially in connection with promotion of the health of children, of girls and women in industry, of the community, of the home." Personnel service, a growing job category for women after 1910, made particular use of their "resourcefulness and determination. It has to do with the promotion of satisfactory relations, the adjustment of difficulties and grievances, and the maintenance of proper standards of working and living—matters with which women are supposed to be especially qualified to deal."[31]

For employers, these unspoken constraints derived from a set of assumptions rooted in women's supposed contribution to family stability. Bankers, for example, hired women for their "neatness, deft

handling of money and papers, tact, and a certain intuitive judgment" and kept most women out of courses in investment and away
from paths to policy-making positions. Foremen and supervisors expressed the same tacit assumptions when asked why they did not hire
women for certain jobs. They were "not even considered," they
replied, or they were "just not right."[32]

Where employers succumbed to the temptation to hire the cheaper
labor of women, workmen sometimes took action on their own—as,
for example, in the street railway battles of the immediate postwar
period; or in the iron foundries where molders insisted, "You would
not let your daughter or wife go into it, neither would I, neither
would any other of these people"; and as in the printers' support of
legislation whose net effect was to eliminate women workers from
their industry.[33] Banker Elizabeth Cook's matter-of-fact assessment of
men in finance might apply to all these fields. "They are friendly,
tolerant and not very radical. They are willing to admit that they
are not violently prejudiced against women in certain lines, but they
have a terrific fear that they will eventually take the place of men."[34]

Some jobs continued to be seen as inappropriate for women—for
reasons that clearly had little to do with the work itself. A woman
could not be a court reporter, a well-paid job requiring superb shorthand skills. Employers argued that court reporters were under great
strain and it was "doubtful whether a woman could 'stand the gaff.' "
But others insisted that the real reason was because "the testimony
is so revolting that the courts will not permit a woman to be present."[35]
Neither of these explanations satisfies, and one is tempted to be as
suspicious of real motives as was the reporter who asked why only 12
of the 300-odd members of the Court Reporters' Association were
women—when the "art of court reporting is only a big brother to
stenography, which is almost an all woman's business."[36]

Such comments reveal a pervasive and unshakable sense of women's
place on the part of men. The *Newark Star Eagle* expressed some of
the tension in 1925. "AWAY GOES ANOTHER MAN'S JOB," it screeched.
"SHE'S FIRST OF HER SEX TO HOLD A SENATE POSITION." It then chronicled
the tale of a young woman who had become "secretary to the president
of the state senate, who happens to be her father. . . . The position
hitherto has been considered too trying for anyone but a member of
the hardier sex."[37]

Managerial insistence on limiting women's mobility and the potential for women to aspire to success confronted each other most
directly in newly expanding offices. The best managerial principles,
as well as the most efficient use of paid labor, demanded that jobs go
to those who could do the task at the cheapest price. Assembly-line

techniques in production had pulled women into factories. Now, as the service and distribution sectors of the economy expanded, they, too, created routine work that demanded repetitive skills. These new jobs beckoned women on every hand. Expanding corporations, then the growing educational and social service networks and the spreading medical facilities, offered work that had none of the exhausting and unhealthy conditions that still surrounded women employed in factories. These rapidly expanding occupational sectors begged for women who were, it was said, grateful for decent jobs. They learned fast, commanded little pay, did not expect rapid promotion, and quit to marry and have children before they became eligible for expensive pensions and paid vacations.

Employers could comfortably offer women these jobs because they demanded not much more in the way of imagination and initiative than did factory labor. Any of the series of skills into which office work had broken down after the Civil War could be learned at the growing network of publicly supported vocational training schools. Hired because employers needed a transient, yet educated, labor force, female typists, receptionists, clerks, and stenographers were expected to find their rewards not in high pay and promotion but in glamour, paternalistic amenities, and the opportunity to serve.

In the climate of the 1920s, women were not easily reconciled to these limits. Secretaries interviewed in the early part of the decade reported that though they liked their jobs, they were discouraged about not being able to "get ahead" in them. One secretary described her movement from one job to another: "I had become dissatisfied with my slow advancement," she explained, but in the new job "advancement has not come as rapidly as I expected."[38] So great was the desire for promotion to executive positions among secretaries and stenographers that a barrage of literature directed toward them in the early and mid-1920s attempted to persuade them that secretarial work was a satisfactory occupation in itself. Advancement, they were told, would come by way of higher pay and more responsibility. Employers were advised to steer clear of college graduates who "resent being directed and told what to do." The message seems to have taken hold. The secretaries who responded to a Bureau of Vocational Information questionnaire in 1926 expressed appreciation of the job's limitations. Some liked secretarial work because it had fixed hours. Others objected when job responsibilities took precedence over the home.[39]

Whatever resistance remained competed with the stringent requirements imposed on a secretary's personality. Office work, as we have seen, emerged in the twenties in a way that sustained women's roles by extending their home functions to the job. Women could gain experience in caring for men in the office before they were required to do so at home, perpetuating the illusion that a job could serve as training for the rest of a woman's life. The qualities required for a good wife and a good secretary, as sociologist Margery Davies has observed, complemented each other. "The very nature of secretarial work," commented one office manager, "is self-effacement. . . . the secretary develops an obedient and slavish type of mind, rather than a vigorous and constructive one."[40] Among her most valuable qualities, tact, and even disposition, quick work, endurance, and a winning personality ranked high. A secretary, noted one observer, "thinks *with* her employer, thinks *for* her employer, thinks *of* her employer."[41]

When women married they lost some of their value, presumably because they put these qualities to the service of someone other than their boss. Executives would not consider married secretaries, argued one female employment agent, because "a man wants a [sic] unmarried woman of attractive appearance. . . . a married woman's attitude toward men who come to the office is not the same as that of an unmarried woman." Married women were "very unstable in their work," said another; "their first claim is to home and children." Some thought widows made the most attractive of all possible employees because they were the "best investment." Others claimed that a woman over thirty was the hardest of all to place. A secretary could be mother or sweetheart, but not wife.[42]

The ideas were self-reinforcing, rewarding personality traits considered feminine and punishing others. One employment manager put it this way: "Select a woman who you think could be married at any time if she chose, but just for some reason does not."[43] Women who displayed inappropriate personality traits found themselves put down. Thus one interviewer described a very successful real estate saleswoman as "rather showy and overdressed and slightly aggressive."[44] In contrast, those who chose the limited success available by utilizing their feminine characteristics were appropriately rewarded. College women for example, could do better in banks if they helped homemakers deal with savings, budget, and family problems that affected financial stability.[45] The wifely qualities thought to be essential to business and secretarial careers effectively eliminated any possibility of promotion. For, as one career secretary noted, "the more efficient she became and the more indispensable she is to him in a secretarial capacity, the less likely will he be to run the risk of crippling or inconveniencing himself by recommending her promotion to an independent position in the business."[46]

The occupational stereotype that prevented women from moving up in the office and business world, and that simultaneously affirmed personality patterns and social roles consistent with the home, cast a broad shadow. It extended to expanding administrative and professional occupations equally consistent with home roles. Careers in nursing, libraries, teaching, and social work drew on years of socialization and a consciousness bred to serve. They fitted the demand for personal satisfaction, yet met the criteria for women's work. They were careers in the sense that they paid relatively steady salaries instead of poor and intermittent wages, but they explicitly limited possibilities for advancement. Some states and municipalities fired women teachers, as well as librarians and social workers, who married, not because they then became incompetent, but because they might set bad examples to other women. Because it was thought that executive positions in all these areas ought to be filled by men, the search for male talent was intense, and the monetary rewards disproportionately high compared to those offered to women. "Well-equipped women," who, as Mary Van Kleeck noted, were "very much easier to find," were simply passed over.[47]

Women who escaped or transcended the prevailing social constraints drew mixed admiration and doubt. Even the sympathetic felt drawn to comment on the unusual capacities required to combine career and home roles. A Bureau of Vocational Information typescript recounted the tale of the First Woman's Bank of Tennessee, an institution entirely controlled and managed by women, where "all of the officers including the directors are married and all but three have children."[48] The press emphasized the dual role of such women. "WOMAN PRESIDENT OF BANK DOES HOUSEWORK IN HER HOME," proclaimed one headline.[49] Another paper captioned a photograph of the woman who invented tea bags: "Gertrude Ford proves that it is possible to maintain a house, be a Devoted Mother and conduct a Successful Business."[50] If the press was to be believed, success at work ought to be buttressed by a satisfying home life. A New York *Herald* reporter described the ascent of a young Scottish immigrant girl to an executive post at Western Union: "In spite of her sustained contact with the business world," the reporter noted, "she remains conspicuously feminine in dress and demeanor and believes in marriage and children for the average woman above all the rewards of the business world."[51]

Beyond the newspaper headlines, professional opinion still tended to deny the possibility of combining the two spheres. In 1927, the *Nation* ran a series of articles on women who had rebelled against convention. John B. Watson, a psychologist of the behaviorist school well known for his advice on child-rearing techniques, responded to them. "The great weakness of women who seek careers," he argued, is that they have never been trained to work like men." For women to succeed would require a transformation in personality: work must become their "first nature" as it was men's.[52] But if that happened, what would become of commitment to the home? In 1929, the debate team at New York's Hornell High School discussed the question "Resolved: that the emergence of women from the home and into business and public life is a deplorable feature of public life."[53]

For all the attention given it in the twenties, the danger of ambition taking over was more apparent than real. A careful look at what was happening to women in that decade provides no grounds for assuming that they were on the way to equality. The proportions of lawyers, bankers, religious leaders, and editors who were women continued to increase. However, there were warning signs. While the *American Banker* reported in 1928 that 2,000 women held executive positions, at least one woman banker commented in response that they had "not yet penetrated the innermost precincts."[54] And the rate of increase in all the higher professions slowed in the 1920s; in some areas, such as medicine, science, and dentistry, the proportion of women began to drop. Even the proportion of teachers who were women was beginning to fall after decades of steady growth.

Most women did not have the kinds of jobs that suggested the possibility of personal growth and satisfaction, and their daily lives were filled with the same pressures that had characterized the lives of their mothers a generation earlier. Twenty percent of all wage-earning women still worked in other people's homes as servants, cooks, and laundresses, and more than a third were engaged in some form of personal service. In the mid-1920s, a typical commercial laundry worker in New York State worked more than forty-eight hours a week and took home less than fifteen dollars in her pay packet.[55] Bath maids in New York hotels often worked seven days a week, seven hours a day, and chambermaids routinely worked more than fifty-four hours a week. These women worked so hard that one report described "even strong young Polish girls . . . so tired out at night that they spent their evenings lying on their beds." In these jobs, there was "no such thing as a transfer or promotion policy." The nearest thing to it, one investigator reported, "was found in one hotel where in the housekeeping department women were sometimes taken as bathmaids at $25 a month and later became chambermaids at $28 a month."[56] A typical waitress in a state where hours were not limited might work from eleven to three and then again from five to eleven or twelve at night. She was rarely allowed to eat on the job and was charged for what her customers ordered but would not, for whatever reason, pay for.

Paralleling the new world of apparent opportunity in offices lay the old world of harsh conditions in factories, where nearly three out of ten wage-earning women still worked. Speedup and bonus systems sapped the energy of many factory workers by increasing the pressure for job performance, though hours might be lowered a bit and wages raised slightly. Along with "a terrible strain" women complained of being too tired to enjoy leisure time. One twenty-four-year-old Virginia weaver complained that on Saturday afternoons and Sundays she usually stayed at home—too tired to go anywhere. Even a movie, she said, tired her eyes.[57] Yet the effects of shorter hours and the impact of factory legislation had begun to raise expectations in this group as well. Spot shortages among factory workers and demands for female labor in other sectors increased women's sense that they too should have some of the amenities. What employers called "a better class of girls" could be obtained only by structuring jobs to fit women's needs. To attract these women and to ensure that they remained contented workers, corporations had, as we have seen, begun to develop their own control mechanisms before the war. Some provided possibilities for promotion. Others structured their hiring practices to open more technical jobs to women.

As in offices, higher expectations required management to set upper limits on women's aspirations. Their earnings, for example, might be restricted to a sum that fell far below the levels for even low-level managerial jobs. One candy factory reported a fifty-dollar weekly limit for forewomen.[58] Women who earned too much in production jobs found themselves shifted to other jobs that lowered their rates.[59] Other factories discouraged transfers from one department to another. Labor laws colluded. "It would not be possible for a woman to reach a more executive position," said a candy company executive, "because of the fifty-four-hour law limiting women's work in New York State. The manager may at times be called upon to supervise two shifts of women and this effectually bars a woman from this position."[60]

Given limited possibilities for promotion or for significantly higher wages, women in factory jobs continued to pay attention to more pleasant surroundings and more congenial workmates. This accounts for the preference of some employers for "American-born" women and the rigid restriction of occupations in which black women could work. Agricultural labor, domestic service, and laundry work accounted for 75 percent of all black women who worked in 1920. In some cities the proportion of wage-earning black women in domestic service rose to 84 percent, while 30 percent of all employed black women worked on the land. But during the war black women had managed to push open doors they could not easily see closed against them. And the need to replace immigrant labor in the twenties enabled black women to replace immigrant women in unskilled jobs in candy factories, for instance, and men in some heavy jobs.[61]

To do so, they had to accept less pay than a white person doing an equivalent job would have received. One observer commented that as soon as Washington, D.C., laundries realized they might have to pay a minimum wage, they "began to ask the employment bureaus about the possibility of obtaining white girls" to replace the Negro women. Married women could be hired to do the heavy unskilled work of men for up to one-third less than employers had to pay the latter. Yet these jobs were attractive to women who had few options.[62] Wages, however, were never the key differential. Employers continued to offer a rigidly segregated labor force as an incentive to native-born white women to work, and in most of the South white female employees got privileges not offered to black women. Working days sometimes started an hour later. The Women's Bureau found amenities such as lunchrooms, cloakrooms, fresh drinking water, and clean toilets, if offered at all, available primarily to white women. Black and white women who worked at the same process at the same wage commonly worked in separate rooms. The menial jobs, the dirty and heavy work, consistently went to black women along with foreign women of "low grade."[63]

When the women employed in these poor jobs began to demand better wages and job conditions, employers resorted to a new kind of paternalism. Because factory jobs negated the idea of glamor, and poverty mooted appeals to motherhood, their efforts to undermine women's demands were rooted in notions of efficiency that had by now become endemic to American factory production. Nineteen-twenties paternalism had particular appeal in the South and for small industries, as well as for plants employing large proportions of women. It had originated in the prewar attempt of "welfare capitalism" to maximize efficiency. Undermining worker resistance to managerial prerogatives, these tactics thrived in the pressure of war production and burst into bloom thereafter. At the same time that employers, eager to take advantage of efficiency techniques in order to maximize output, pushed workers to the limit, they counter-acted anticipated resistance with a variety of trade-offs: restrooms for the fatigued; recreation areas; suggestion boxes; social workers and counselors in the plant; committees to set up rules, and so on. The Indianapolis Telephone Company offered its female employees "a large restroom . . . furnished with rugs, easy chairs, writing tables, bookcases, piano and Victrola, where during noons and rest periods the girls may dance, chat, or read."⁶⁴ The trappings of welfare varied from plant to plant. Some employers provided hot lunches and Thanksgiving turkeys; others, occasional Saturday afternoon picnics. A Virginia tobacco company gave white women fifteen minutes off—with pay—every Tuesday and Friday to dance to a three-piece band.

Companies expected such techniques to produce tangible benefits. In addition to encouraging employees to work more quickly and efficiently and to put up with conditions against which they might otherwise protest, they expected additional loyalty and consequently lower turnover. Ideally, appreciation for the plant's interests would discourage efforts toward unionization before they got started. Sometimes, as in the mine-mill towns of the Schuylkill Valley, Pennsylvania, or in the South, paternalism extended to the entire community: houses, stores, recreation areas, and so on, all belonged to the mill corporation. Its officers supported the local church and paid the salary of town police, extending the deferential work relationship to community life.

Paternal forms had special value in relationships with female workers. They confirmed a social relationship to which women were in any case expected to conform. In addition to denying women sufficient wages to achieve economic independence, paternalistic techniques reinforced a sense of obligation. One young metal worker who complained to an investigator about uneven rates of pay for women said she liked her job anyway. The foreman "lets the piece workers come and go almost as they wish. He permits girls to sing on a chorus at their work."⁶⁵ A power machine operator in Petersburg, Virginia, reported that she earned far less at her present job than she could elsewhere. But her forelady was "very nice" and "always considers those who have to take care of others." She assigned an employee to a new machine with good piece rates, telling the other workers that she "has two babies to support so none of you girls ought to want to take it away from her."⁶⁶

Concessions to married women with children in some southern towns encouraged them to feel grateful to the management. They were allowed to stop work fifteen minutes before the noon whistle so that they could warm up the family dinner before everyone else got home. Occasionally a mill dependent on married women agreed to allow them an extra hour off on Monday mornings so that they might do the family wash.⁶⁷

The women hired to implement personnel policy—a fast-growing field—operated in an ambiguous role. When asked, they indicated that their jobs required such characteristics as sympathy, love of people, buoyancy, tact, and understanding—qualities consistent with wifeliness.[68] But they used these qualities to serve a management policy designed to build a sense of loyalty to the mill "family," and thus to undermine the workers' ability to resist exploitation. The Bureau of Vocational Information surveyed directors and members of factory and store welfare departments in 1918 in an attempt to find out if personnel was a suitable career for women. The questionnaire asked respondents to indicate how they conceived of their jobs. The answers are revealing. The welfare worker was engaged in "all work concerning the building and maintenance of human equipment," answered the personnel officer of General Electric's Erie, Pennsylvania, plant. Female equipment obviously required careful handling: "A warm welfare worker could . . . engage her sympathy" by measures "that a man could not obviously use."[69] Ruth Pope Galt, who worked for a Louisville, Kentucky, flour processor, described her job as "old-fashioned housekeeping, and the care that any mother would give to her household." Ada Trevor Fox, whose employer manufactured batteries, was more specific. Asked about her most important achievements, she replied: "Getting all labor laws complied with." Others mentioned "getting the confidence of the girls and women" and "keeping girls from public dance halls and back rooms in saloons" as their most important functions. Sadie Gross summed it all up. A seventy-dollar-a-month secretary to the welfare director of Cleveland's Hydraulic Pressed Steel Company, she described her greatest achievement as "creating a family spirit among the men, and making them attached to the company so that they bring all their troubles to the Welfare Director, who takes care of them."[70] What more could a company ask?

Voluntary concessions and paternal techniques could be withdrawn when the "children" began to flex their muscles or when they no longer served business interests. Mary Gilson quit her job with Joseph and Feiss when the depression of 1923–24 created a labor surplus and the company curtailed many of the activities she had instituted.[71] In Rhode Island, female employees of the Automatic Gold Chain Company, who had welcomed the company's picnics and parties, walked out on strike against a longer work week. Mary Newman, a supervisor, told a Women's Bureau interviewer that the manager had declared he would now "treat the girls as they treated him." He was particularly offended because "the very girls he entertained most frequently were the ones who walked out."[72]

Paternalistic techniques within the factory did not spread everywhere. In most of the South and in small towns throughout the United States, they remained more matters of rhetoric than of substance. A northern spinner who moved south hoping to find a job in 1930 wrote of a Marion, North Carolina, mill:

> The sanitary conditions were ghastly. When I desired a drink of water, I had to dip my cup into a pail of water that had been brought into the mill from a spring in the fields. . . . Often I saw lint from the cotton in the room floating on top of the lukewarm water. . . . When I needed to use a toilet . . . I did not find the running water system such as the factories of the North have, but just six holes cut into a plank. The waste matter dropped into the river, and this same river provided the bathing place for the village.
>
> The married women of the South . . . arise about five to take the cow out to the pasture, do some weeding in the garden, and they always have hot cakes for their husband's breakfast when he arises. Then they prepare their children for school and finally start work in the mill at 6:30 to work eleven hours. Upon their return to their homes they have housework to do. Instead of a sink to wash the dishes in, they have a board stretched across one corner of a room. . . . the refuse is thrown out of the back door. . . . I could see outside thru cracks in the wall.[73]

Such sordid conditions particularly rankled in a world where the radio and popular magazines introduced examples of more leisured life styles into even the poorest household, and where much of urban America had already begun to absorb the values of consumerism. As the world changed around them, female factory workers increasingly began to demand their share of material benefits. Women's industries like clothing and textiles became centers of strike activity.

In the garment factories that dotted the Appalachian Mountains, employers relied upon women who had little experience in industrial work and whose ambitions were limited to higher incomes. Manufacturers seeking to escape the influence of the Amalgamated Clothing Workers of America and other unions in the clothing trade had begun to move their factories away from urban centers and into rural areas in the early part of the twentieth century. There they hoped to find cheaper and less militant labor sources. These "run-away" shops relocated in places like the beautiful Schuylkill Valley of central Pennsylvania's Appalachian Mountain region. The wives and daughters of miners in the small anthracite coal mining towns of this area seemed an ideal labor supply. Unskilled, they were often Polish, Lithuanian, and Slavic immigrants whose menfolk earned wages low enough to make an extra income welcome and necessary. Miners' high rates of injury and death forced many women into the labor market. And, except for occasional domestic work, the garment trade provided the only other employment available.

Even before World War I, New York and Philadelphia manufacturers of men's clothing used skilled cutters to lay out patterns and cut garments and then shipped the cut goods to factories scattered in West Virginia and the Appalachians. They had not been the first to see the advantages of the labor supply available there. Manufacturers of cotton and woolen textiles, men's underwear, and women's house-dresses and kimonos had been setting up mills and factories in the coal towns since the turn of the century. Militant trade union tactics in the big cities accelerated the process after the war. Soon every mine had its factory. Unskilled women and girls sewed and finished clothing.

Though women at first welcomed the income generated by these jobs, they soon found themselves caught in a collective nightmare. Wages, initially high enough to attract workers, were continually re-duced as families became dependent on the extra income. Employers, who paid by the piece, rotated their workers so that a person who acquired skill at one job and could earn reasonable pay was trans-ferred to another where she had to learn a new process before her pay once again increased. To earn even a pittance required cruelly long hours of labor, and to support a family on factory or mill wages meant sending every child to work. Most owners lived in faraway Philadelphia or New York and never saw their factories in operation.

In 1919–20, the Amalgamated Clothing Workers' Union sent several general organizers to this area to test out the ground. They found young female workers—often the daughters of organized mining families—receptive to unionization, but facing a variety of pressures. Town leaders warned them not to jeopardize the community's liveli-hood. Firemen and local sheriffs refused to rent meeting spaces to women in attempts to keep them from "making trouble." One woman reported a conversation with her boss, who "told us it was a no good union—a Bolshevik Union. He talked to the priest about it and the priest told us not to join." But the most significant barriers came from among women themselves. They divided along several lines. Those who attended church regularly refused to join an organization that admitted people who did not attend and were therefore considered of dubious character. Protestants (Methodists in many mining towns) had difficulty joining with Irish and Polish Catholics. And young women sometimes resisted joining when they feared the leadership was too free sexually. When organizer Ann Craton asked a young church-going worker why women failed to respond to a strike call, she was told, "It's because you let the 'whores' run the union . . . people say you should keep the bad girls out of the union and let the nice girls run it. . . ."[74] The "whores" in this case were two eighteen-year-old sisters, said to have the "bad disease."

The particular difficulties of organizing woman workers led a group of trade union women to join with M. Carey Thomas, then president of Bryn Mawr College, and Hilda Smith, an instructor at Bryn Mawr and a WTUL member, in setting up a new kind of training institute: summer schools for women workers. Education for union women had precursors. The ILGWU began to offer evening classes and cultural programs to its members in 1915. The female leaders of Local 25 who organized them aimed at developing union spirit among women members. And the NWTUL sponsored short training sessions in leadership for trade union women from 1915 on.

But the new summer schools offered something more. They aimed to train women wage earners in union leadership skills by removing them from their jobs for several weeks of serious education in such areas as economics, politics, and trade union history. They would do this on college campuses or in quiet country homes, settings that the organizers hoped would create a convivial atmosphere and encourage shared experience. With the financial support of some trade unions and after consultation with female trade union leaders, the first school opened at Bryn Mawr in 1921. It offered a residential program lasting from six to eight weeks each summer to sixty or more wage-earning women selected for their already demonstrated commitment to trade union principles.

Women attended these sessions at substantial cost to themselves. They gave up eight weeks of pay, and risked losing their jobs altogether. One student wrote her version of a dialogue with her employer when she asked for time off:

EMPLOYEE: Mr. M., I would like to ask you to give me a leave of absence for two months, which I want to spend in attending school.

EMPLOYER: What did you say? A leave of absence! In the time when the season starts, in the time when I need you most; No such thing—A leave of absence! What kind of school is it that you want to go to?

EMPLOYEE: It is the Bryn Mawr Summer School for Women Workers in Industry.

EMPLOYER: Oho! Now I know. You want to attend a school, which teaches workers how best to fight bosses.

EMPLOYEE: Not at all. This school's aim is to enable workers to think more clearly on problems that they are confronted with.

EMPLOYER: I hope you don't intend to become a philosopher. And what will it be if you get so educated there, that after you return, you won't want to work any more in a tailor shop?

EMPLOYEE: If I did not want to work for you any more, I would not want you to keep the job for me.

EMPLOYER: What for do you want education? Can't you stitch coats without having any? And to become a professor—it is too late anyhow.[75]

Trade unions, like the ILGWU, sometimes helped workers to negotiate time off, and occasionally larger companies held jobs for
workers who attended the school. This had been the case in some
southern textile mills, until a series of strikes persuaded mill managers
to alter the policy. In June 1930 an observer noted that "the company
this year wouldn't keep jobs for girls if they went to summer school.
So girls who go lose insurance, etc. May be taken back, but if so, as
beginners. . . . One girl has gone to Bryn Mawr anyhow; one may
go to Southern Summer School."[76]

Once at the school, young women found a largely female instruc-
tional staff which encouraged participation and discussion and urged
them to try their minds at creative writing as well as at more traditional academic areas. In the first years at Bryn Mawr, the staff
included such well-known labor leaders and economists as Amy Hewes,
Caroline Ware, Hazel Kyrk, Agnes Nestor, and Alice Henry. The
Barnard College Summer School described itself in its 1927 brochure
as giving "a wider understanding of industrial and social problems,
a more scientific attitude toward them and a deeper sense of sound
responsibility, increasing the workers' ability to study and to enjoy
more creative activities in leisure time."[77] Intellectually the experience
left its mark: "What an unfolding of surprising facts took place in
those first economic lessons," wrote a 1927 student; "gradually there
seemed to dawn an understanding of the relation of myself and my
job to society as a whole."[78]

Summer schools for women workers achieved notoriety and mixed
success in the twenties. Students took the injunction to participate
seriously, demanding courses critical of capitalism and insisting on
discussions of trade union issues. At Bryn Mawr some of the faculty
objected to such radicalism and ignored student pressures, leading
others to set up a new school at West Park, New York, on land donated
by Hilda Smith. These problems did not prevent the model of residential training for women workers from spreading to locations in
the South and West until financial support diminished in the depression thirties. The schools then closed or were transformed into one-
or two-week-long, mixed-sex union training programs. Sustained frequently by one or more trade unions, the transformed schools lacked
both the educational breadth and the vision of the earlier model.

Before this happened, however, several hundred women managed
to spend part of a summer reading, writing, and studying subjects that
expanded their general cultural awareness as well as their particular
knowledge of trade unionism in the United States. They were then
expected to go back to their shops, and lead women into active
attempts to change their lives. The unique experiment produced

contradictory responses from students, who loved the unexpected leisure and freedom to learn and were simultaneously stymied by what to do with it. Some, like Rose Pesotta, attended for two years running. She went on to become an organizer and a vice president of the ILGWU. The absence of instruction in socialist theory disappointed others. Many wrote about the tension produced by the contrast between their daily lives and the idyllic quality of the summer. For those who came with a revolutionary vision, the quiet and lovely campus produced culture shock. "I work, you play," wrote one young woman at a conference of working and college women.

> You have everything,
> I have nothing.
> Why should I sit here, afraid to take my coat off?
> Is it because I smell so strong of acid?
> Why don't I take my gloves off?
> Is it because my hands are so rough and dirty looking?
> Why do I keep my hat on?_
> Is it because my hair smells like a wet dog?
> Acid again. Acid that smells like burning sulphur.
> There are fumes of sulphur in Hell.
>
> You daughers of the rich,
> You walk so easy and sure of yourselves,
> You don't smell at all.
> Your hands are well kept,
> Your hair shines with cleanliness,
> Your eyes are bright and eager looking.
> But who makes your sweetness, your cleanliness possible?
> Is it not workers like me?
> I work, you play,
> You have everything;
> I have nothing.[79]

Despite such difficulties, the learning had its effect. "I believe," wrote a student, "workers' education will lead to a new social order. The workers will be enlightened. Well-informed and intelligent labor leaders will take the place of those who have not had the advantage of workers' education classes. Best of all, workers' education will help to develop a social order where all men realize that they are brothers, and love, not hate and greed will be the desire of all people."[80]

These kinds of understandings, deepened by experiences acquired at the spreading summer schools, encouraged organizing among women. The bitter textile struggles of 1929–30 included trained female organizers as well as men from the AFL and the Communist Party–affiliated Textile Workers' Union.

The strikes that began in 1929 in Henderson, North Carolina, and spread through that state to Tennessee and Virginia by 1930 reflected deteriorating economic conditions. Like the garment factories of the Appalachians, the textile mills had paid well during World War I and shortly after. But unlike the garment industry they attracted whole families of subsistence farmers to give up land for work in mill towns in the expectation of high wages and education for their children. When the war ended, southern mill owners, eager to retain their share of industry, campaigned for northern capital on promises of cheap labor. As the market declined at war's end owners reduced wages, to the point where entire families had to work to support themselves. The promise of education disappeared. Matilda Robbins, a Textile Workers' Union organizer in Greenville, South Carolina, recorded the words of a woman whose family had taken the promises at face value.

> They came and told us how easy we'd have it in the mill. The young 'uns 'ud sho be give an ejicatiòn in them there schools and make good money. We didn't have to be po' white trash no mo'. And pap he was right smart and told them agents how he'd sho' like to see the boys get up in the world. And I, too, was a'thinkin' how nice mebbe the girls 'ud look in city clothes. Our'n was a big [fifteen] brood—eight of 'em— and the oldest oney ten or so. Well, we come 'long to the mill and pap and me and Tommy we was took right in. Po' Tommy he aint never been able to get nuff schoolin' to read proper. Purty soon me and pap and four young 'uns was duffin' and spoolin' and spinnin'. But they aint yet git ejicated, or has they the fine clothes 'n all them things the agents were a'promisin'.[81]

Once a family had moved to the mill town, its members had little choice but to conform to mill owners' requirements. Frequently work and housing went only to families in which several members put themselves at the service of the mill, and in any event wages remained low enough to drive husbands, wives, and children to work. This situation proved barely tolerable until the mid-1920s, when reduced rates of profit put pressure on the industry to reduce wages even further. Absentee owners introduced the "stretch-out" (adding more hours to the working day) or "speedup" (demanding greater productivity in the same number of working hours). And they relied more heavily on efficiency techniques designed to minimize waste motions and so maximize a worker's output without increasing either wages or hours. Desperate workers rebelled. In one plant after another, they walked out.

In April 1929, Mary Heaton Vorse, a well-known journalist and sympathizer with labor, traveled to Gastonia, North Carolina, to investigate the second major strike of what had already become a series of eruptions in southern textile mills. *Strike*, the novel Vorse produced, stands as a monument to the confused rush of events that had solidified southern wage-earning men and women in defense of traditional wage and living standards.

This strike and those that surrounded it demonstrated once again women's capacity to organize and sustain struggle; for it was women who bore the brunt of picketing and of family survival. And they also developed their own techniques of relating to strikebreakers. Vorse captures women's special role as she illustrates the paradoxical relationship of mill to community in her fictional description of the Gastonia struggle. When the young boys who constituted the state militia entered the town to restore order, two of the strikers confronted them:

> "Boy," said Ma Gilfillin, "what you all reckon you goin' to do yere? Yore goin' to guard the mill agin me, boy?"
>
> The boys shuffled uneasily, and one of them said, "Why, no, Ma, I don' reckon we're agoin' to do no guardin' agin you all."
>
> "Her an' me is strikers, son, and if yore aguardin' yore guardin' agin me. Look out you don' run no baynit into no old lady."
>
> "Oh, no, ma'am," said the boy, "don' you worry, Ma."
>
> "Thar's a good boy," said Mis' Gilfillin. "Reckon you all don' know what fer we're strikin', do you?"

And as the boys shuffled and laughed, the old ladies shouted, "Now you be good boys, an' be keerful with yore baynits."[82]

In this way women could contain some arbitrary violence. Yet in the same town, a rampage of sheriff's "deputies" resulted in the death of Ella Mae Wiggins, a young mill worker and charismatic strike leader whose ballads are still sung. One of them recalls the double burden of the working mother:

> We leave our home in the morning,
> We kiss our children goodbye,
> While we slave for the Bosses
> Our children scream and cry.
>
> And when we draw our money,
> Our grocery bills to pay,
> Not a cent to spend for clothing,
> Not a cent to lay away.
>
> How it grieves the heart of a mother,
> You everyone must know.
> But we can't buy for our children,
> Our wages are too low.[83]

.   .   .

Wage-earning women in the twenties learned a new militancy from
the experience of struggling for better living conditions in a society
that took them for granted. This lesson emerges clearly in an exchange
of letters that appeared in the *Advance*, organ of the Amalgamated
Clothing Workers of America, in 1926 and 1927. When female union
members accused the Amalgamated of discriminating against them by
giving preference to men in the best-paid jobs, demanding disproportionate wage reductions for women in slow season, firing women first,
and denying women access to important union posts, the editor replied
that if women wanted to participate fully in the union, they had to
behave like men: "If women do not find their way to the front this is
due to their lack of aggressiveness. . . . Our women ambitionists," he
advised, should "do what men do, if the game seems attractive enough
to them."[84]

But the women who hurried to reply to the editor's barbs would not
be drawn into his trap. As half the members of the union, they declared, they were entitled to treatment that met their specific needs.
"We hope that we'll never learn to adopt the same methods as some
of the men use to come to the front," replied one. It was in the union's
self-interest and therefore up to it to "counteract the kitchen mind"
that was women's historical legacy, they insisted, asking for female
organizers, a women's bureau, and attention to women's social needs.
They had not so far made a public fuss, they claimed, because they
had "developed along with the present leadership, and their loyalty
to the present leadership is surpassed only by their loyalty to the
union itself." And they went on to threaten, "Is it really necessary to
stir up a mess and with it the consequent hatred toward union
officials, before you responsible people realize that the situation is
important enough to warrant attention?"[85]

These women, committed to their jobs and aware of their importance to the industry, did not hesitate to call attention to their special
needs. Like other wage-earning women in this period, they challenged
the continued existence of a doctrine of separate spheres; but at the
same time they failed to perceive the depths of its social and psychological roots. So, while working-class women broke some barriers, the
portion of the marketplace allocated to women became increasingly
credentialized, segmented, and hierarchical. That was the paradox of
the twenties. Even those women who fought for equality had not yet
mastered the mechanisms for making it stick. Women were invited
into the work force and again invited not to expect too much of it.
They got a national Women's Bureau to investigate their conditions,
summer schools to increase understanding and militance, and birth

control to regulate family lives. But they did not get access to equal economic opportunity.

Overall, between 1910 and 1940, from 86 to 90 percent of all women worked in only ten different occupations—an occupational concentration that contributed to the ability to assign low wages and poor status to these jobs. Occasionally women managed to work their way through the formal and informal discrimination patterns. By and large, however, it was understood that women would stay in the lower ranks and drop out after marriage. To be sure, ambitious women and married career women flourished among the privileged and the well-educated. Still, by the end of the decade, only one out of every fifteen married women worked for a living, and most of these were still poor and black. Young women found their rewards in glamor, leisure, and the relative freedom of the flapper. What looked like upward mobility to the growing middle class reflected a shift in occupational structures, easing life, providing more things to consume, and offering higher incomes to female workers without altering their relative positions in the wage labor force. For the moment, these satisfied. And, curiously, women soon discovered that the labor force segmentation that had restricted them in the affluent twenties protected them in the depression thirties.

9

Some Benefits of Labor Segregation in a Decade of Depression

An anonymous author writing in *Harper's Monthly Magazine* in the spring of 1933 described what the depression had done to her. She had, she wrote, worked in the early years of her marriage; her husband's income, with hers, reached a very comfortable $7,000 a year. There were savings, stocks. Then came the crash, unemployment for her mate, and psychological readjustment. She continued in her job, and for more than two years the pair subsisted on her income alone. The husband assumed household tasks, cooking, mending, and shopping. The marriage, blessed with a sense of humor, survived.[1]

This was only one of many such tales—of instances in which the depression challenged life styles developed in a period of seemingly unlimited material affluence. The crash came after a decade of debate in which new forms of companionship were tested, new sexual relationships developed. And then the world buckled. The volume of industrial production dropped the first year by 17 percent and the next by another 17 percent. By the end of 1932 it had declined by nearly half, and the gross national product by nearly one-third. Four and a half million people were listed as unemployed in 1930, eight million in 1931; by 1933 nearly thirteen million people—a quarter of the work force—who would gladly have earned an honest living could not find work.[2] Things got a bit better after that, but with the exception of 1937, when the rate of unemployment dropped a bit, one of every five potential workers remained unemployed until World War II revived production.

The depression turned what had been the previous decade's joyous discovery of freedom to work into a bitter defense of the right to a job; it buried the options and choices for which women had struggled beneath the relentless pressure of family need. Individual and personal responses were no longer meaningful. In the depression, every woman discovered that her own decision to undertake wage work, or not, rested on a larger set of social issues. Ideas and structures once used to keep women in the family and out of jobs now emerged as mere rationalizations for idleness. And ideas that once had consigned women to inferior places in the labor force now preserved for them jobs that menfolk could not get. Their status as cheap workers and their marginal wages could, and did, keep whole families alive.

Husbands and wives who had managed to negotiate the challenges of the twenties found themselves attacking deprivation with guidelines developed for an optimistic future. The response was bewilderment. Women accustomed to relative affluence had not asked for a transposition of roles—only for a respite from the household, a foothold in a career, a chance to make some money. And suddenly they found themselves bearing the psychic, and sometimes the full economic, burdens of their households. Women who had worked out of economic necessity had expected to marry or to share the burdens of household support. They encountered men devastated by the crisis and discovered the difference between making a contribution to household maintenance and being responsible for parents as well as children.

The immediate readjustment required by the Depression resulted from its curious double message. While it imposed on the family pressures that pushed women into wage work, it fostered a public stance that encouraged family unity and urged women, in the interest of jobs for men, to avoid paid work themselves. The discordance intensified when the economy began to restore itself in ways that made room for an army of brand-new workers, heavily female, while it left experienced soldiers, often male, standing in breadlines.

To explain why a slowly rejuvenating economy could not provide jobs for men required a scapegoat. Who better than the women who seemed simultaneously to be taking jobs away from the male breadwinners and destroying the family? For the ability of women to retain and even expand their job potential played havoc with the cherished set of ideas about home, hearth, and women's place in it. It produced crisis and confusion, locking men and women into rigid attitudes, stifling a generation of feminist thought, and intensifying hostility to women wage earners. At the same time, the depression brought invisible opportunities for women that few dared to mention and no one to gleefully enjoy.

· · ·

The heart of the matter was what the depression did to the family: it provoked a series of changes that sparked a continuing debate about how women could best serve under conditions of economic crisis. The broad outlines of these changes hint at the dimensions of what contemporaries eventually called a "crisis" in the family. The divorce rate fell: a relief to many who had feared the moral laxity of the twenties. But there seemed to be a tendency to postpone marriage. Families were doubling up in a single household. And the birth rate dropped precipitously, down to seventy-four live births per thousand women of child-bearing age in 1933. To those who feared the disintegration of American values that the depression seemed to be causing, the details were far worse. For while overall marriage rates dropped—a manifestation, some thought, of economic prudence—the rates for blacks, Jews, and Italians, among the poorest members of society, continued to rise. The children of the native-born and of Northern and Western European immigrants seemed more comfortable in putting off marriage—their rates dropped fastest of all. One Philadelphia study attributed these differences to cultural values: members of older, more established groups preferred to maintain their status and "plane of living." Those who came from poorer groups, "whose minimum plane of living is more or less passively accepted," tended to marry "regardless of its implications for the plane of living."[3] And though the birth rate was dropping, the wrong sort of people seemed still to be having babies. Dorothy Dunbar Bromley, a pioneer investigator of sexual behavior, cited a Milbank Foundation survey that reported 48 percent more births in families with no employed members than in those with at least one working member. Those who had been poor in 1929 and continued to be poor in 1932 had the highest birth rate of all. Malnutrition, illness, public relief were all more common in these families than elsewhere.[4]

Did these shifts in marriage and birth rates presage further shifts in the nation's racial and ethnic composition? What would be their implications for cherished familial values? A host of other questions emerged. What happened to a man's self-image when he could no longer support his family? What of male/female relationships, or the dependence of parents on half-grown offspring, or the respect of young children for nonproviding parents? What of the quintessentially American presumption that "if a man cannot find work . . . he is a rather worthless individual"? Would this go by the board? Would families look down upon men who could no longer support them? And what would be the permanent effect on the "tens of thousands" of boys who took "to the road" to relieve parents of having to support them?[5]

The prevailing response was a surge of institutional support for families. The array of activities uncovered by one scholar included "marital clinics, child guidance clinics, home economics education, parent education, the birth control movement, the public health movement, maternal and infant hygiene, the visiting housekeeper. . . ."[6] The first marital clinic opened its doors in Los Angeles in 1930. The New York State Conference on Marriage and the Family began in 1936. The National Conference on Family Relations appeared in 1938. The depression led the National Council of Parent Education to change its name to the Association for the Advancement of Family Life.[7]

The effect of so much attention was to confirm the sense of traditionalists that women ought to be at home, to which a group of Chicago sociologists added rational confirmation. Their study of one hundred families in 1934–35 concluded that well-organized families tended to pull together to surmount the crisis; families whose members had a poor adjustment to each other fell apart. The depression exaggerated whatever tendencies were already present.[8] Eminent sociologists like William Ogburn and Joseph Kirk Folsom noted somewhat pessimistically that most of the family's historical functions had been made obsolescent by an industrial/urban world. Outside agencies had assumed control over economic, educational, religious, recreational, and protective tasks. There remained one all-important function: the "affectional." The family's "chief remaining tasks was to provide happiness for mates and to provide the desirable personality for the young." To save the family required enhancing its affective capacity, or insisting that women pay attention to nurturing and caring.[9] Traditionalists interpreted this remaining function as a mandate for women to stay in families to help them develop sufficient affective and inner strength to withstand economic buffeting.

Popular culture portrayed husbands who endlessly hunted for jobs, while wives sat by poignantly wringing their hands in despair. The opening scene of a 1935 social commentary film, King Vidor's *Our Daily Bread*, offers such a picture. Mary says to her husband, who has come in after yet another fruitless day of job-hunting, "Oh, Jack, what shall we do?" And indeed the image of the loving, supportive wife who took no active part in the family's economic survival evoked a certain amount of nostalgia among the middle classes. "Would we not all be happier," asked writer Frank Hopkins, "if we could return to the philosophy of my grandmother's day when the average woman took it for granted that she must content herself with the best lot provided by her husband?"[10] Women's magazines published articles with titles like "You Can Have My Job: A Feminist Discovers Her Home" and "The Return of the Lady."[11]

But the fact was that women had long since given up doing what their grandmothers did, and the depression was not the time to retreat. Unemployment and the fear of unemployment conspired to motivate women to seek jobs. They could not sit idly by watching families recede into despair while jobs, even meager jobs, existed at all. Those who had always earned wages tried to continue to work. Others looked for jobs for the first time.

The women who went to work during the depression were more often married, they tended to be slightly older, and they were probably better educated than wage-earning women as a group in 1929. Among them were greater proportions of the native-born. This statistical shift reflects the need to maintain family incomes during hard times by sending a second wage earner out to work.[12] Changes such as having fewer small children and doubling up of households provided opportunities for shared household and child care and sustained the search for work.

The simultaneous need for women to make economic contributions and to strengthen affective relationships in the family produced predictable tensions. Issues involving male and female roles, allowed to pass unnoticed for generations because they affected mostly poor, immigrant, and single women assumed central importance when they touched on the respectable middle class. Students of the family protested women's desertion bitterly. Women committed to feminist positions and understanding the need to work insisted on equal rights in the work place. Those who had to work simply found jobs if they could, leaving the experts to debate the impact of their desertion. The tension surrounding these choices coalesced into three interrelated issues. The clearest was whether married women with employed husbands should ever work—a question of salving male egos as well as of acceptable social roles. A spinoff of this was the issue of whether the competition of women for men's jobs would destroy male economic opportunity—a question of security. And both of these were subsumed into the more abstract but equally painful question of whether wage work was a gender-based privilege or a human right.

A broad popular consensus agreed that women's access to wage work should be conditioned by family needs. "Americans," said author Norman Cousins, "are home-minded. They are for anything that tends towards preserving the family against anything that might weaken the family as the traditional unit of our civilization. . . ."[13] The debate centered on whether the wage work of married women inevitably jeopardized the family, an old issue that now prickled with new thorns. Wage work, argued some, denied women sufficient time to cultivate the womanly arts: leisure, gracious living, gardening, and social contacts went by the board. Children were all but abandoned; their antisocial behavior was laid on the conscience of the working mother. "Truancy, incorrigibility, robbery, teenage tantrums, and difficulty in managing the children," concluded one study, all resulted from a "mother's absence at her job."[14] And the very existence of job opportunities encouraged women to feel independent and therefore contributed to marital unhappiness.[15]

Women as well as men, it was said, would have to develop new personalities in families where wives held down jobs. And if husbands became dependent, and wives the providers, both faced what our anonymous author called a problem "vastly more terrifying than the economic wolves howling at the apartment door."[16] What would be the impact of these inverted roles? Would women's personalities change? Would they become what one writer described as "swift, hard, poised, incisive" businesswomen without "a song or a skip in them"[17] When the *Ladies' Home Journal* asked its readers if a woman who held "an important position in business" would lose her feminine qualities, more than a third of those who responded feared that she would.[18]

The question of whether the roles of worker and of wife/mother were not mutually exclusive was on everybody's lips. According to *Good Housekeeping*, a brilliant career was obtained only by sacrificing husband and family. Ninety percent of women scientists were single. Eight of America's twelve "greatest living women" had never been married. Only two were mothers. The seven "famous" women interviewed—who included an astronomer, an illustrator, a political activist, a college president—all noted that they lived happy, fulfilled lives. Yet each added a qualifier: "To marry and have children is the ideal life for a woman." Said one, "What career could ever be as fine?" "A caress is better than a career," said another. A few suggested that technology and modern civilization no longer required a choice. But for all their public consensus about the value of motherhood, each of these women described her own single life as totally satisfactory. The interviewer, Sarah Comstock, commented as if surprised that with or without a husband, each had managed to make herself a home. Her parting shot revealed her own bias: "May not some of them have hidden a longing that hurt like a wound . . . as they bent above some crib and listened to the heavy sleeping breath that rhythmed from rosy lips . . . ?"[19]

Not everyone thought work for women bad for the family. There were those who believed that by forcing family members to share tasks and thus contributing to less authoritarian child-rearing methods, women's wage work would strengthen the democratic personality.[20] Boys and men might benefit from study and practice in homemaking and child care, from undertaking more nurturing roles.[21] And wage work would even help the family directly. It would provide some couples with sufficient income to set up house, and therefore offer them an incentive to marry. It would give others the means to save for children, an expense increasingly avoided.[22]

But these were more abstract questions than that of competition. Were women who took jobs depriving husbands, or potential husbands, of them? Imbued with a world view that gave the male responsibility for economic sustenance, parents, dependent wives, and unemployed men all wondered why women were working at all. Norman Cousins articulated the simplest version of a panacea that was offered repeatedly. "There are approximately 10,000,000 people out of work in the United States today," he wrote in 1939; "there are also 10,000,000 or more women, married and single, who are jobholders. Simply fire the women, who shouldn't be working anyway, and hire the men. Presto! No unemployment. No relief rolls. No depression."[23]

Feminists responded by noting that only one-quarter of America's adult women worked for wages anyway. They pointed to the segmented labor market. Do men, they asked, "pine to slave in somebody's kitchen, to work in beauty salons? . . . to supplant the distaff side of society at its traditional jobs. . . ."[24] Competition in industry was "between one man and another, rather than between men and women," argued Women's Bureau statisticians.[25] But the nub of the attack was directed at married women. The Women's Bureau responded with studies indicating that less than a third of wage-earning women were married— that only one married woman in ten held a job. Many of these had unemployed or disabled husbands with incomes too low to provide even basic necessities. Feminists cited Women's Bureau studies indicating the overwhelming proportion of women who, alone or with others, supported families. Nearly one-third of married women who worked were entirely responsible for their families, while 55.6 percent shared the responsibility with others.[26]

The question of wage work for married women, argued feminists, "must not become a smoke screen to hide the real unemployment problems of providing work by shortening hours and increasing the consumers' purchasing power by sharing the earnings of industry." NWTUL leaders insisted that "the only fair dismissal policy with reference to women, as to men, is to consider . . . not the marriage status but the economic status of the worker."[27] To single women who joined the attack on the married, feminists pointed out that they jeopardized their own jobs should they marry in the future: if marriage became an acceptable reason for firing a woman, all women would be penalized. The result, argued economist Marguerite Thibert, would be the "progressive disappearance of all vocational training for women." Single women would flood low-skilled occupations and pull down wage standards; women's union ties would loosen, and the state would be required to provide full maintenance for all widows and orphans.[28]

Arguments to the contrary notwithstanding, married women seeking work held an unenviable position. Virulent campaigns to eliminate them from the labor force persisted throughout the depression. State and municipal governments began to press married women to leave the civil service as early as 1930 and 1931. Section 213 of the federal government's 1932 Federal Economy Act decreed that in the event of personnel reductions, married employees should be fired first if the spouse also held a job with the federal government. Unsympathetic supervisors used the act to fire women, and within a year more than 1,600 female employees had been dismissed. Seventy-seven percent of the nation's school systems refused to hire married women as teachers, and half of them dismissed female teachers who married. Railroads, notorious for discriminating against married women even before the depression, now began to fire women who married. Texas instituted a means test for women in transportation jobs—wives whose husbands earned more than fifty dollars a month had to go. Unions acted prejudicially as well. The Brotherhood of Railway and Steamship Clerks declared that no married woman whose husband could support her was entitled to a job.[29] Discrimination did not abate in the course of the decade. As late as 1939, legislatures in twenty-six states were considering bills to bar married women from state jobs.

The defense of a married woman's right to work typically centered on the issue of need. Most moderates would have agreed with the leadership of the NWTUL. "Married or unmarried," said the NWTUL, "it is safe to assume that most people work for their living because they have no other means of support for themselves or others."[30] But those who defended women's work on this basis created a new kind of divisiveness. Against the wealthy who did not need additional income, they proclaimed it a social duty for all those who could afford to live without jobs to do so. They noted and deplored an increasing tendency in shops and department stores to employ "the society girl with a following."[31] One personnel officer declared that "unemployment can be solved to a great extent, for women, at least, if the daughters of the rich and well-to-do will keep out of the business world. . . . I tried to point out," she went on, speaking of an interview with a well-off young woman, "that if such people as she, with so many opportunities, did not feel it was their duty to preserve the culture and refinement of the world and advance our arts and sciences no one else would."[32] Barnard College's dean told the class of 1931 to consider their needs before they entered the job market. "Is it necessary for you to be gainfully employed? If not, perhaps the greatest service that you can render to the community . . . is to have the courage to refuse to work for gain. . . ."[33] Mary Robinson of the Women's Bureau demurred. If need were to be the basis of the right to a job, then men as well as women should be hired and fired on those grounds. Would lawmakers, she asked, "rule out of lucrative positions bachelors, spinsters of independent means, all men who get a fat living from cutting coupons, and their own wives on public payrolls?"[34]

Dividing women by class and marital status could not but provoke debate on the issue of whether *any* woman had a right to work. Here was where the most radical women entered the fray. Was work, as some asked, the "exclusive prerogative of the masculine portion of humanity" or was it "a fundamental right of every human being"?[35] The astute recognized that defending the rights of all women to work touched on larger issues than income. Lorine Pruette articulated them neatly in a book on women in the depression. "The structure of the family and the state," she argued, "cannot develop as it should in a society that denies women the right to function according to their abilities, needs and desires."[36]

Pruette need not have worried. Whatever society did or tried to do, women did not give up their jobs, nor did they stop searching for work. Despite private and public policy, and notwithstanding depression and unemployment, women's proportion of the work force inched up slightly. They had been 24.3 percent of all workers in 1930. By 1940, they were 25.1 percent. Wages for all workers declined in the early depression years. But the unchanging ratio of women's wages to men's which historically had swung between 55 and 63 percent moved now toward its upper extreme. Women's wages moved to between 60 and 63 percent of men's.[37] The data suggest that women may have been pulling men's wages down, but for a change their own wages were not tumbling quite as quickly.

Was it in response to available jobs, or out of a need to support their homes, that women entered the work force? One study suggested that both factors were operative. Economist John Parrish examined the nation's labor supply at the end of the depression and discovered some startling facts. Why, he asked his readers, did high unemployment persist in the years from 1932 to 1937 even though industrial activity by 1937 came close to 1929 levels? Part of the answer lay in the numbers of college-age young people who could not afford to continue their education. But repeatedly, overwhelming proportions of the "new" workers— those applying for jobs for the first time—were women. They were twenty-five years old and more, and often married: reentry workers who had given up paid employment earlier. More than 75 percent had never worked. They entered the labor market at twice the rate of men. By 1940, 2.5 percent of all wage-earning women were "new" workers, as opposed to 1.2 percent of men. The large number of married women working suggested that the excess of new female over new male workers came from the ranks of married women. In 1930 28.8 percent of all wage-earning women were married. By 1940, the figure reached 35 percent.[38]

This figure represents only a small increase over the rate at which married women could have been expected to enter the labor force. What is surprising is that in the face of immense hostility and male joblessness, married women continued to find jobs at the same rate they might have done had there been no depression at all. We are faced then, with two seemingly opposite questions: given the enormous economic pressure of the depression on families, why did so few married women choose to seek jobs; and given the need of jobs for married men, why did so many married women insist on wage work? The answer to the first question lies in the ideological constraints that continued to operate even in this period of crisis; the answer to the second can be found in the needs of the labor force. And both were equally powerful in the 1930s.

In the first three years of the depression, women's employment rates, by all accounts, dropped more rapidly and more heavily than those of men. The Women's Bureau observed in a 1933 report on unemployment that fluctuations and declines had frequently affected women to a greater extent than they had men. It attributed this to occupational segmentation. Manufacturing and domestic and personal service were among those women-employing sectors with the most extreme employment fluctuations.[39] Despite high unemployment, demands for women proportionally outran demands for men, and outran proportions of women engaged in some occupations in 1930, indicating that employers were choosing women for certain jobs, especially in domestic, clerical, and manufacturing areas.[40]

The turning point seems to have come in late 1932. Technological rationalization and then the National Recovery Administration contributed to expanded opportunities for women. Light industry and the service sectors recovered more rapidly than heavy industry. Jobs in domestic service became available (albeit at lower rates). The clerical and human services sectors began to expand as federal funds poured in to relief agencies. By 1937, official Women's Bureau reports reflected these changes. About one-fifth of normally employed women were out of work, the Bureau concluded. But the proportion of unemployed was larger among men than among women. States with heavy declines in mining, metal work, and the building trades showed huge discrepancies between the male and female employment rates. In Michigan, for example, overall employment in 1935 dropped about 7 percent. But when the figures are broken down by sex, women—who constituted 25 percent of the work force—lost only 2 percent of their jobs; men lost about 8 percent. Pennsylvania saw a total drop of 6.2 percent in employment from January to December 1934. But the rate of employment for women actually rose marginally, while that for men dropped more than 8 percent. In states like Rhode Island, however, where men as well as women were engaged in light industry, the rate of male unemployment did not exceed that of female unemployment.[41]

These relative gains occurred despite the rising numbers of women entering the work force. Parrish estimated that, in absolute numbers, fully two and a half million more people were available for work in 1937 than would have been the case had there been no depression. Most of these were women who, having not yet returned "to their former positions outside the labor force," swelled the totals of the unemployed. They added to the ranks of unskilled workers, offering a large labor pool from which employers could draw. Parrish noted, in a puzzled footnote, that the pool was not about to "return to normal," for by 1937 there was "little detectable tendency for these 'new' workers to return to their former status outside of the active labor market."[42]

And why should they do so? Many of the jobs available to them were no worse than those they might have had before the depression. It was true that women lost some ground in professional areas that had always been theirs. In teaching, social work, accounting, practical nursing, and librarianship, small numbers of men began to encroach. Women also lost some ground in occupational categories they had always shared with men: bookkeepers, telegraph and radio operators, insurance agents all had trouble keeping their jobs. But by and large, women demonstrated enviable tenacity not only in hanging on to jobs they had long held, but in moving into new areas.

Women's relative strength seems to have been a function of three factors: their absence from industries suffering most from cyclical unemployment after 1933; their location in industries where the secular trend was upward; and the technological rationalization, abetted by the NRA, which refined machine processes. The depression did not create these trends but it did accelerate all of them, enabling us to trace what were to become permanent shifts in labor force demands.

In heavy industry, where the depression hit hardest, women seem paradoxically to have benefited from previous discrimination. Having consistently been denied jobs in heavy industry, they were present only in tiny numbers in those sectors most severely affected: building, transportation, autos, and steel lost heavily and only slowly lumbered back to health. Again John Parrish's work is helpful. In 1940 he calculated that women constituted less than 2 percent of all workers in the five hardest-hit industrial groups. In contrast, they were 30 percent of all workers in the groups with the least decline.[43] Simultaneously, the clerical and social service sectors, in which women were heavily employed, recovered rapidly. The promotion of the social services, education, and recreation, with their attendant clerical needs, and a rapid expansion of government bureaucracy at the lowest levels opened jobs in sectors defined as "female." All the ground women lost in male/female-employing industries such as laundries, hotels, restaurants, and bookkeeping and accounting they more than regained in new areas.

Finally, women benefited from the ongoing streamlining process. Caught with an outdated physical plant, some manufacturers used the depression-caused cessation of business and the accompanying government incentives to retool their plants. Hoover's Reconstruction Finance Corporation offered guaranteed loans for this purpose. NRA codes sometimes restricted production by setting limits on hours each plant could operate. This provided additional incentive to maximize output. When, to ensure their survival, corporations replaced old machinery with new, refined machine processes, and converted skilled jobs to routine production processes, they created jobs for women. The Women's Bureau, investigating, discovered that men not only avoided these newly simplified jobs, but rejected the lower wage rates that often accompanied them.[44] Technological unemployment was not a new phenomenon. But what was new in the thirties was the accelerated pace with which technological innovation was incorporated into manufacturing processes and establishments.

Industrial changes challenged a trade union structure, weakened by membership losses in the 1920s and by internal political struggles, to develop new ways of handling difficult situations. At first unions floundered. Although AFL president William Green declared the labor movement's support for "the installation and extension of the use of machinery in industry," the Federation in fact had developed no policy. For while the manufacture of new machines would provide jobs for those who made them, it threatened to displace the skilled workers whose jobs were mechanized. Defending union members jobs ran counter to the larger community interest which generally supported government and industry re-tooling efforts. In the early years of depression unions, too weak and divided to develop alternative policy, did not respond, allowing displacement of their members precisely when they had fewest options for other jobs.[45]

The 1933 National Industry Recovery Act offered a solution, sanctioning industrial rationalization on the one hand and intervening in the "free market" to regulate employment and encourage unionization on the other. The National Recovery Administration created by the act encouraged industrial firms to band together in every area in order to create a series of codes to regulate production, wages, and prices for each industry grouping. Intended to represent all the manufacturers in a given area, the 537 codes that eventually emerged in fact reflected the influence of large industrialists who captured disproportionate shares of the market. The NRA effectively suspended antitrust laws to provide incentives to produce. But it was felt that if industries were to be allowed to benefit from self-defined limits on competition, they must at least be forced to consult with workers about the wage provisions of the codes. Section 7a of the act encouraged workers to join bargaining units. Under the slogan "The President wants you to join a union," union membership blossomed. Already sickly in the 1920s, trade union membership had declined to less than three and a half million by 1929. The early years of the depression were nearly fatal. By 1933, another half-million members had fallen by the wayside, leaving less than 6 percent of American workers unionized. Then came the NIRA, followed by the Wagner Labor Relations Act, which offered some minimal protection to workers who wished to organize. Millions upon millions took the opportunity: by 1939, nine million workers, 17 percent of the labor force, belonged to unions.[46]

On the face of it, the wage agreements negotiated by unions and corporations and incorporated into NRA codes were not favorable to women workers, yet they were destined to make it easier for women to work. To encourage consumption, the NIRA mandated minimum wages—forty cents an hour under most codes, then a drop to 25 cents in the Fair Labor Standards Act of 1938. NRA administrator Hugh Johnson, Secretary of Labor Frances Perkins, and Eleanor Roosevelt all opposed differential wages. Yet about a quarter of the codes, covering nearly 17 percent of the workers in code industries, provided for lower rates for women. The garment industry code was notorious. "Jacket, Coat, Reefer and Dress Operators, Male," it declared, a $1.00 an hour." "Jacket, Coat, Reefer, and Dress Operators, Female, 90¢ an hour." "Skirt Operators, Male" were entitled to ninety cents an hour, those who were female to eighty cents.[47]

Wage distinctions made on the basis of arbitrary job classifications were more widespread and harder to detect. They reflected and perpetuated the male bias that had always existed. Again the garment industry offers a good example. Dress cutters, almost universally skilled males, were entitled to forty-five dollars per thirty-five-hour week by the NRA code. Sample makers, almost all female, but at least equally skilled, got thirty dollars per thirty-five-hour week. In semiskilled categories, operators, who were largely female, received ninety cents an hour, while pressers, who were always male, got a dollar an hour.[48] These rates varied with the quality of the garment and the kind of work, but wage differentials always appeared as part of an accepted notion of what men and women ought to be earning.

The actual effect of the codes, Mary Anderson concluded, was to institutionalize low wage rates for women. Some codes permitted lower rates for light, repetitive work, regardless of the skill and dexterity required. Others allowed persons who had been paid below the code minimum in July 1929 to continue to be paid at the same rate.[49] In 1937 the Women's Bureau quoted a presidential commission: "Practically every significant industry which employed women at low wage rates or in which labor was unorganized, requested a female wage exception, or a minimum rate so low as to allow for a differential without providing a specific female wage exception."[50] Even the Civil Works Administration and Works Progress Administration projects systematically discriminated against women. Male WPA workers got five dollars a day; women, three dollars a day. One observer recorded the protests of married women and widows with children who earned thirty cents an hour while unmarried boys got fifty cents an hour for similar work.[51] The results showed up in a comparison of men's and women's wage levels in November 1936. In women-employing industries, wage levels rarely exceed an average of $20.00 a week. Textile and boot and shoe workers averaged less than $16.00, clothing workers $17.50; but in male-employing industries like steel, autos, lumber, and building, wage levels were always at least $20.00 per week and usually around $30.00.[52]

Despite these significant wage differentials, the codes succeeded in raising minimum-wage levels dramatically. Since women had been heavily concentrated in the lowest-paid sectors, their wages rose faster than those of men. In New York State, women's wages rose 16.6 percent from July 1933 to November 1934, right after the codes went into effect. Men's wages rose only 3.4 percent. In Pennsylvania, wages in manufacturing went up an average of 11.6 percent, but in such heavily women-employing industries as textiles, women's clothing, and cigar and tobacco making, the increases more than doubled the average.[53] Women's wages still remained low enough so that employers were not tempted to substitute men. And because regulation now applied to both sexes, employers who had been discouraged from hiring women and children because their states had tried to enforce laws on their behalf found no reason to continue to discriminate against these groups.[54]

No one could claim that these marginal improvements in wage levels changed women's position in the labor force relative to that of men. But one could argue that relative to where they had been before, women had gained something. The results were immediately evident. The industrial department of Chicago's YWCA reported in December 1933 that wages for new women workers in 200 of that city's firms had doubled in three months—rising from fifteen to thirty cents an hour. Simultaneously the working week had declined from seventy and sixty hours in some industries to forty-eight and forty hours. Benefits to the poorest workers were especially high: NRA described them as "nothing short of phenomenal" and cited female labor as a particular instance.[55] Black workers in the cigarette industry received average wage increases of 73 percent, while wages for white workers went up by 46 percent. Real weekly wages jumped 16 percent in the South and 7 percent in the North. Likewise, a 1936 Women's Bureau survey of the dress industry demonstrated that under the NRA the median wage of workers on the cheapest dresses (traditionally the poorest paid) went up 75.2 percent, as compared to around 50 percent (44.3–55.7 percent) for those on the next grade and only 47.5 percent for the more highly paid workers on the highest-priced lines.[56]

The Depression-born codes also succeeded in doing what years of agitation had failed to do, namely reducing the average number of hours worked for all workers, but particularly for women and other low-skilled, poorly paid hourly employees. A forty-four-hour week had been a privilege in 1929; forty-eight was standard, and unskilled women frequently worked up to fifty-four hours weekly. In 1933, forty hours became the NRA standard for the normal work week, and a thirty-five-hour week appeared occasionally. The Women's Bureau estimated that more than 80 percent of female-employing industries reduced their hours by a minimum of 16 percent. In the textile industry, where hours had been particularly long, they declined by 25 to 28 percent.[57] Women in the forty-three states that had had maximum-hour laws in 1930 now found that men had similar restrictions. The effect of removing this disadvantage to hiring women remains unclear, but the Women's Bureau felt so confident that regulations had equalized the situation that it abandoned its campaigns to strengthen legislation in states where it was weak and to institute legal restrictions on women's working hours in the other five states.

Shorter hours raised the complementary issue of lower wages. Although minimum-wage provisions defused the problem for some workers by raising hourly rates, the question of how much hours could be shortened without eating into wages remained. The NWTUL leadership, which in 1935 called for a forty-four-hour week for those not covered by NRA codes, was concerned when the AFL requested support for a thirty-hour-week bill. Could workers, wondered Secretary-Treasurer Elizabeth Christman, really make enough in such short hours to live on? "I am not one of those who argue that you can earn as much in 30, 35 or 40 hours as you can earn in 60 hours."[58] Some workers echoed these anxieties.

Fears of insufficient wages were not irrational, as an informal study by social researcher Amy Hewes demonstrated. Hewes asked her students at Bryn Mawr Summer School for their collective experiences under NRA. What she discovered surprised them all. These young women workers reported that shorter hours and higher wages for the least skilled came at the expense of the better-paid, who were sometimes laid off or continued at reduced pay, and at the cost of speedup. Employers, it turned out, tended to offset the increased weekly wages of the lowest-paid workers by reducing the wages of the better-paid. One worker-student reported, "Before the N.R.A. came into effect, I was getting thirteen dollars and a half a week. I was also receiving, besides my usual weekly salary, one dollar a week for carfare. Just as soon as the concern got its Blue Eagle our carfare was taken away from us, and we who received thirteen-fifty were cut so the employer could make up twelve dollars for those who had not been getting that much."[59] Speedup enabled employers to make up for wage gains by increased production. Hours might drop, as they did for one woman, from forty-eight to forty per week, but if wages dropped proportionately and production demands increased by as much as 50 percent, where was the gain? Such techniques were not the only ways of manipulating the NRA. Employers routinely abused apprenticeship systems, paid less than minimum wages to learners, and refused to recognize outside unions.

Whatever the exceptions, it seems clear in retrospect that despite the losses of large groups of women, the condition of the aggregate benefited from the accelerated process of economic rationalization. Opportunities for most women increased. Repeatedly, occupational shifts created possibilities for women, and custom could not long resist economic demand. Efficiency tried to be sex-blind and sometimes succeeded. Workers and the public fully expected that in a crisis jobs ought to go to male breadwinners; however, efficiency responded to its own imperatives, consistent with its own traditions.

Some illustrations from the thirties point up how women benefited from the kinds of changes occurring. In the cigar industry new machinery, invented in the 1890s, created new methods of bunching and rolling to replace skilled old-fashioned hand rollers. These methods offered the potential of reducing the work force by 80 percent to produce the same number of cigars. The International Cigar Makers' Union at first tried to bar from the union those who worked in this new way, or left to local option the decision to accept them. It refused to organize the machine workers, allowing the jobs to be given to nonmembers, mostly female, and depriving its own skilled members of the possibility of any work at all. For three decades the union fought a slow losing battle against converting to the new equipment, gradually giving up jobs and members. Predictably, union membership declined as manufacturers converted to machine-made cigars. Finally in 1927, the union agreed to accept machine tenders as members. By then it was too late. The depression speeded adaptation to machinery so that by 1933 more than 50 percent of cigars were machine-made. Union membership dropped from 23,400 in 1925 to 7,000 in 1934.[60] Less than 10 percent of the 70,000 workers in the industry were now organized. And an industry whose workers had been 25 percent female in 1890 was nearly 60 percent female in 1930. Then came the NRA with its permission to organize and its special encouragement to organize the unskilled. Membership among women cigar workers climbed. By 1939 there were more than 12,000 members, one-fifth of the now 60,000 workers in the industry. In the twenty years from 1920 to 1940, the number of cigar workers had declined more than 40 percent, but women retained a slowly increasing share of the newly unionized work force.[61]

In the textile industry, overproduction and intense competition among manufacturers had kept prices low and profit margins narrow for years. The problem was complicated by a shift in the industry from the relatively expensive labor of New England to the relatively cheap labor of the nonunion South. Cheap labor and the absence of other industrial opportunities for labor led southern mills to rely more heavily on men than the New England mills, and consequently the shift in location, even in an expanding industry, meant steady erosion in women's share of the industry from 1910 through the early years of the depression. By 1933, women made up one of every two northern textile workers, and nationwide two of every five cotton textile mill workers were women. But in South Carolina only one in every three workers was female, and their proportions were steadily falling.[62] The depression altered the pattern. In order to raise prices, the southern manufacturers represented in the Cotton Textile Institute tried to limit production in 1931 and 1932. They shortened hours to fifty-five daytime and fifty for the night shift and agreed to eliminate women and children from the latter. Simultaneously they introduced efficiency measures, cut wages, and attempted to reduce operating costs. Women lost jobs at night, but new openings occurred in the daytime as children were fired and wages fell.

The NRA codes worked out by the industry in 1933 reflected these practices. In an attempt to lower production, textile manufacturers agreed to limit the number of hours any factory could be operated to two shifts of forty hours each a week. They discouraged the entry of new firms into the industry, providing an incentive for owners to modernize their plants and make the best use of available hours. While the continuing shift in plants from North to South benefited men, modernizing most often helped women, and on balance women came out ahead. The absolute numbers of women employed rose as the industry recovered, and women's share in cotton textile mill jobs ceased its twenty-year decline.[63]

The garment industry provides yet another example of how the depression offered incentives to hire women. Here aggressive unionization, before and after the advent of the New Deal, had ensured women a place in the shops. By 1931, the ILGWU had recognized that dressmaking (almost wholly female) was replacing cloakmaking (heavily male) as the major garment division. *Justice,* the ILGWU's newspaper, pointed to the additional impact of the crash: ". . . in the past two years since the current industrial stagnation has robbed so many men breadwinners of their jobs, a new element of women workers has entered the dress trade whom the employers find even easier to exploit and intimidate."[64] Women's share of the jobs in the industry increased from 64.4 percent to 74 percent—reversing a nearly fifty-year decline.[65] Threatened by this influx of new, easily exploitable workers, the union chose to organize. Long before Section 7a stimulated unionization, and often led by women themselves, the ILGWU's aggressive policy began to pay off in increased membership, heavily female, and in its greater voice in the industry. When the NRA opened wide the doors against which the ILGWU had been pounding, union leadership was ready with new demands and compromises. They wanted shorter hours and a voice in setting rates. Like the Amalgamated Clothing Workers of America the ILGWU, which had fought the piecework system in the twenties, now considered returning to it. Hourly rates in a period of labor surplus encouraged employers to fire all but the fastest workers. Piecework meant that available jobs could be equitably distributed, and since the employer stood to lose little, it protected less efficient workers. With rates per piece negotiated by the union and insured by a guaranteed minimum-wage floor, piece-work proved to be an incentive for workers to speed up their work and aided in a rapid recovery of the industry. The national reach of the NRA codes strengthened the ILGWU's grasp on the industry and provided regional protection for women operatives. A thirty-five-hour week, no overtime, and standard rates in force everywhere reduced incentives for owners to move from place to place in search of cheap and captive labor, and for most workers substantially increased job security.[66]

In every industry where women worked, the tendency to hire women implicit in occupational changes encouraged unions to include them in organizing drives. This occurred regardless of the feelings of individual union leaders. Section 7a, the Wagner Labor Relations Act that followed, and the mass unionization drives spearheaded by the Congress of Industrial Organizations, all implicitly recognized the need for industry-wide organizing to protect jobs. As we have seen, women had never constituted more than a tiny fraction of the unionized workers in the United States. In 1930, less than 9 percent of the AFL's members were women, despite the fact that women made up more than a quarter of the wage labor force. Less than 3 percent of wage-earning women were union members. Some unions like the glass blowers and metal workers still refused to admit women. These discrepancies resulted from the AFL's historical organization by craft. More than two-thirds of AFL members worked in the building trades or in transportation, communications, mining and quarrying, machinery, metal, and ship building—fields that employed only minuscule numbers of women. In contrast, textiles, leather, and clothing—manufacturing areas which had huge numbers of women—accounted for only 6 percent of AFL members.

The introduction of NRA codes not only directly provided some of the benefits of organization to unorganized women but forced the AFL to reconsider organizing practices. Women's unequal pay, always a drag on male wages, became a visible problem in a period where job shifts occurred so rapidly that men felt both reasonably and unreasonably threatened. It was no accident, then, that in the spring of 1934 William Green announced a campaign to bring women into unions; nor that he chose this moment to bitterly condemn discrimination against women. At the same time, the AFL debated and reversed its policy of condoning new technology. Instead, it passed a resolution calling for an investigation of the displacement of labor by machines.[67]

Industrial unionism saw even greater numbers of women organized. The automobile, rubber, metal trades, glassware, and leather industries all had a small but growing share of low-paid women who eagerly joined CIO unions in the mass drives of 1936–39. For the first time substantial numbers of women could expect to benefit from seniority, adequate pay, paid vacations, and the principle of organization.

But unions were reluctant benefactors, at best. Male-led and male-oriented, unions managed in their own way to retain traditional job classifications by sex, to discriminate in wages by refusing to reclassify jobs to reflect the skill rather than the sex of the worker, and to practice internal discrimination in bargaining for benefits. A particularly revealing exchange illustrates the tension between union officialdom and the women it now represented. The newspaper of Local 2, UAW-CIO, published a letter on November 15, 1939, from the wife of a union member. Why, she asked, didn't the union "eliminate the working wife from the Murray Corporation and why aren't others laid off immediately upon getting married?" Mike Mannini, the local's vice president, responded. The answer is worth quoting at length.

> . . . I do not condone husband and wife working. . . . When our union began to function in 1937, many women were employed by the Murray Corporation, consequently, these same women are protected (regardless of their working husbands) by our seniority clause, a clause as a ranking officer of Local 2, I am pledged to enforce to the very best of my ability. Then, too, in order for the Murray Corporation to survive in the automobile industry, women must be employed on certain highly competitive work. I reiterate that the working wife, whose husband is employed should be barred from industry. This isn't possible for the following reasons: The union must protect their seniority; many women must work to support large families because their husband's income is inadequate—many pose as single girls. . . . Some day, Dear Sister, I hope we will reach that economic ideal where the married woman will find her place in the home caring for children, which is God's greatest gift to women and her natural birthright. Hoping you understand my futile position in this dilemma. . . .[68]

Trade union organizing and the NRA codes benefited primarily women who were regularly employed in the industrial sector. When the codes were declared unconstitutional in 1935 these women were covered by industry-wide, union-negotiated wage agreements that provided a basic thirty-five-hour week and twenty-five-cent-an-hour wage. But two large groups of women, located in areas untouched by technology or organization, found themselves excluded by everything. They were the home workers and the domestic servants.

Everybody except the home worker agreed that taking piecework into the home was an evil. By the 1930s, industries still resorted to many out-work tasks. Among them, the Women's Bureau in 1937 included stringing toys; carding buttons, hooks and eyes, bobby pins and safety pins; shelling nuts; addressing envelopes; hooking rugs; knitting; embroidery; crocheting; decorating postcards; making garters; and work on cheap jewelry, lampshades, paper boxes, bags, and toys. The Bureau estimated that 80 percent of the women employed at home earned less than twenty cents an hour and that of those who put in a forty-hour week, the vast majority earned less than five dollars for their labor.[69] Out of these small wages, the home worker covered the costs of lay-offs, spoilage, or illness. In addition to the direct suffering it caused, home work competed with factory-made products, forcing the factory owner to cut corners to meet his competition and thus reducing the wage of the factory worker.

Seeking to eliminate the exploitation of home workers and to protect factory operatives, most codes either severely regulated home work or abolished it entirely. They made no provision for those dependent for survival on this meager living. Stung by the outcry that resulted, President Roosevelt issued an executive order allowing handicapped people and those who cared for invalids to work at home if they were paid the going factory rate.[70] The order did not exempt from the code provisions women who earned their livings or contributed to household expenses. Nor did it exempt married women with small children, forcing the needy to choose between home and work.

In 1940, one of every five women who earned wages—two million in all—worked as a servant in someone else's home. Half of these women were black and Hispanic. Even among women workers, they stood out as among the most poorly paid and hardest-working, yet neither NRA, nor the blanket agreements, nor the Fair Labor Standards Act touched them. Given the extent of unemployment, one would expect their wages to have tumbled and their working conditions to have become measurably worse. In fact that does not seem to have happened.

Most domestic workers were forced to rely upon market factors for protection against wage decreases. And here, the forces that had favored them since the turn of the century continued to hold out. Early unemployment rates among this group seem to have averaged about 30 percent. Then the tide turned. Increasing industrial opportunities for women continued to attract many who would otherwise have been forced into domestic work. And a rising demand for servants came from middle-income women anxious to replace their own work at home when they entered the labor force. Consequently wages, already low, did not decline further.

Still, domestic servants were poor. Newspaper advertisements offered around $33.34 a month in March of 1934 for a live-in domestic. If to the $7.77 per week that averaged we add room and board expenses (generously estimated at around $4.50 weekly), the average New York

City house worker must have been earning something like $12.25 per week. That was the nation's highest rate. The YWCA suggested $9.00 a week as an appropriate wage for live-in servants—should they ever be included under an NRA code. The Women's Bureau thought that $6.00 for a seventy-two-hour week was typical for Lynchburg, Virginia, domestics in 1937.[71] Low as such wages were, however, they seem to have been at least as high as those offered to domestics before the depression.

If the market sustained a general level of wages, it did not prevent competition among workers. The depression witnessed a small influx of white women into domestic and public household service. At the upper levels, white women replaced nonwhites, setting off a ripple effect that resulted in real suffering among the poorest workers at the lowest wage levels characteristic of day workers. One result was an informal hiring practice known as a slave market. On designated urban corners every morning of the week, black women waited for potential customers. Prices were subject to individual bargaining and ranged from ten cents an hour to a lucky thirty cents. Although many of the women who thus sold their labor had seen better days, not everything about the scene was discouraging. The advent of relief payments enabled some to refuse to work for less than a minimum, and when their labor was in special demand, these women managed to unite on their street corners and collectively and successfully demand a higher rate of pay.[72]

Such gains were hardly remarkable. But they illustrate how the depression created opportunities of which women took full advantage and of which they would not soon let go. A few sociologists, Women's Bureau officials, and journalists tried to defend women's choices. But the campaign of legislative harassment, newspaper vilification, and social work pressure revealed the extent to which women's failure to respond to the crisis by giving up jobs to men threatened the society as a whole.

Could they have withdrawn from the work force even if they had wanted to? Perhaps not. The evidence indicates not only that women felt they had to work, but that segmentation had proceeded to the point where women were unlikely to be replaced by men. Those who argued that driving women out of jobs would produce only an insignificant number of jobs for men were probably right.

Even before the 1920s, convictions that women's place was in the home had become harder to maintain next to the increasing reality of their work lives. World War I and the 1920s had laid bare the pulls on women to enter the work force. But friction was contained by relatively plentiful work opportunities, stringent sex segmentation, and a panoply of laws and social customs designed to prevent all but the most daring from transcending their place. The crisis of the 1930s eroded the mechanism of containment. It reduced the barriers between male and female jobs and carried progressive era protection for women to men as well. Together, real possibilities in the labor market and the irrefutable needs of families offset public insistence that women fulfill their family responsibilities at home. The Depression that should have driven women back to the home instead solidified their positions as workers. It emphasized the feeling, already planted in the twenties, that under some conditions women could carry out family functions as effectively outside the home as inside it.

10

"Making History Working for Victory"

Depression and war have opposite effects on the economy. One prompts efficiency, constraint, cautious investment; the other encourages industrial expansion—even a spirit of reckless gambling. If the 1930s depression sloughed off workers, making every fourth one redundant, the war gobbled them up, then searched for more. Where workers had to plead for jobs in the thirties, in the early forties industry begged for workers. And when the army had soaked up the residue of unemployed men, employers turned to women. Unprecedented opportunity now confronted women who months earlier had pleaded for work. Was this to be a breakthrough?—a turning point that would signal the end of discrimination against women in the labor market?

It certainly looked like it. In many ways, this war duplicated the experience of World War I. Women found jobs in areas previously closed to them and, once there, proved to be effective workers. The statistical data reveal a dramatic influx of women—five million between 1940 and 1944—into the labor force and new openings in the heavy industries that had been tightly defended against them. Historians like William Chafe, Chester Gregory, and Sheila Tobias and Lisa Anderson have concluded, as a result, that World War II was, in Chafe's words, "a milestone for women in America." From that perspective, the war serves to explain and justify the new expectations of the fifties. Tobias and Anderson see demobilization as the central issue raised by the war years.[1] The war, they argue, opened doors, changed attitudes, made women aware of possibilities they had not previously considered.

To some extent this is undoubtedly true. As in World War I, women who had always worked fought hard to retain their gains when the war ended. But viewing the war this way places too much weight on the role of a single unpredictable event in altering women's behavior. And, whereas women came to the first war out of a lengthy period of struggle for minimal wages and working conditions, they entered the second from a depression-fostered certainty of their economic importance. In fact, women had already begun to change their working patterns in the two preceding decades. They responded to war not as shiny new instruments honed to do their bit in a larger design, but out of the continuity of their own historical experience. In the twenties and thirties different women had struggled to participate in the labor market in their own ways—some seeking the challenge of a career, others organizing for higher standards of living. The war provided opportunities for both kinds of women to continue these struggles. It did not relieve the tensions surrounding their dual roles, but did cast a different light on them.

The second World War provides a place to see these tensions from a different perspective than the depression. Asked their reasons for wage-earning in both periods, women offered the same explanations. Wage work contributed to family life; financial need justified potential neglect of the home. Wartime appeals to patriotism turned the defensive posture these arguments had in the depression into an aggressive stance. Where the depression had prompted women to apologize for paid work—to present it as a last resort to preserve family life—the war focused attention on women's positive contributions to labor force needs. Satisfying family requirements, once a seemingly insurmountable barrier to wage work, became a practical problem to be solved quickly so that the nation could meet the war machine's insatiable hunger for personnel.

The changed perspective made all the difference in the reception women met in the labor force, and there is no doubt that the war raised the level of their material well-being. But whether it permanently altered their relation to wage work is another question. Women would not willingly have given up their family roles even if social sanctions were lifted and support services helped them to do so. And employers and male workers could not readily overcome a tradition of segmentation so closely related to masculinity. Economist Theresa Wolfson put it this way: "It is not easy to forget the propaganda of two decades even in the face of a national emergency such as a great war. Women themselves doubted their ability to do a man's job. Married women with families were loath to leave their homes; society had made so little provision for the thousands of jobs that a homemaker must tackle. And when they finally come into the plants, the men resent them as potential scabs."[2] The resulting ambivalence led women to weigh the tremendous pressure to take jobs against the sacrifices required of their time and by their families. It penetrated every facet of women's work force experience.

As the European war stimulated production in 1940 and 1941, the residue of unemployment began to lessen, though men, not women, benefited from the early build-up. Women were told to "Do the home job better" or channeled into volunteer jobs. As one jocular civil defense official put it, "Give the women something to do to keep their hands busy as we did in the last war—then maybe they won't bother us."[3] As government programs began early in 1941 to "warm up" the unemployed to heavy industry, twenty men were offered places to every woman. Some 700,000 workers received training in industrial skills in the last half of 1941. Only 1 percent of these were female. Employers believed women were not suited to most jobs and declared themselves unwilling to hire women for 81 percent of available production jobs.

Attitudes began to change after Pearl Harbor. Early in 1942, it became clear that the draft would decimate the ranks of production workers. The government issued a nondiscrimination directive. For the first time, employers sought out women, for nontraditional jobs, and occasionally offered the kinds of services that made wage work more viable for those who had households and children to care for. They sometimes provided day care centers on site. Shopping and banking facilities appeared in plants. Convenient transportation and hot lunches attracted women to factory work. As men left jobs for the armed services, women entered them. Still, from September 1942 to September 1943, the number of people in the work force remained at the 1940 level.[4]

By mid-1942 planners recognized that this was not enough. Calculating that only 29 percent of America's fifty-two million adult women had jobs, the War Manpower Commission started a campaign to recruit women in areas of labor shortage. Journalist Eleanor Herrick accused half the women in New York City of shirking their war obligations. The federal government lowered the age limit for the employment of women from eighteen to sixteen years. Patriotic appeals to women accompanied tales of their special stake in winning this war in order to stop Hitler from reducing women to "sex slaves" or driving them back to their kitchens. The Women's Bureau described desperate entrepreneurs who harangued women at street corners to come to work, or bribed high school principals to send workers to their plants. The radio did its bit, popularizing tunes like "Rosie the Riveter," which told listeners about "red, white and blue" Rosie who was "making history working for victory." Rosie kept

> . . . a sharp lookout for sabotage
> Sitting up there on the fuselage
> That little frail can do,
> More than a male can do,
> Rosie—(Brrrr) the riveter.
> Rosie's got a boyfriend, Charlie;
> Charlie, he's a marine
> Rosie is protecting Charlie
> Working overtime on the riveting machine.

By February 1943, *Fortune* magazine declared the margin for victory to be "woman power" and suggested drafting them if they did not come forward voluntarily to work in industry. And in July 1943 the War Production Board declared itself in-need of a million and a half more women within a year.[5]

Women responded to these appeals in large numbers but not with the kind of unthinking enthusiasm that the statistics seem to demonstrate. Fully three-quarters of the women who worked for pay during the war had worked before, and one and a half million more would have entered the labor force anyway in the normal course of events. Less than five million of the nineteen million women who worked for wages at some time during the war emergency had not been in the labor force before the war began.[6]

What looks like massive mobilization of women in the war years breaks down on examination to something less startling. Nearly 11.0 million women held jobs in 1940. At the peak of wartime production in 1945, 19.5 million women were actually earning wages: an apparent increase in absolute numbers of nearly 8.7 million people or 80.5 percent. But a closer look at the figures forces us to modify our assessment of the real change this number implies. In addition to the women actually working in 1940, the Census Bureau counted some 3.0 million unemployed and looking for work. An additional number, unknown except by estimate, were discouraged but would have worked if they thought jobs were available. A million such workers seems a safe guess.[7] The difference between the resulting figure of 14.8 million and 19.5 million reduces the increase in women workers to 43 percent or 4.7 million new workers in the war years.

But we need to make still further modifications. What percentage of the 4.7 million would have entered the labor force anyway as a result of population growth and maturity? And what percentage would have entered as a product of the continuing twentieth-century trend of women moving into the work force? The first figure can be calculated on the basis of population growth. In 1940, 27.6 percent of the female population over fourteen was in the labor force. They constituted 25.3 percent of all workers. If the same percentage had been in the labor force in 1945, when the population of women numbered 52,860,000, an additional 750,000 workers in round numbers would have joined the labor force, war or no war. But the proportion of women wage earners had been increasing steadily since 1900 and in all likelihood would have climbed in this decade as well. From 1900 to 1940, the female labor force participation rate had increased 23.5 percent, or an average of nearly 6 percent each decade—though there were in fact wide fluctuations from decade to decade. For the half-decade from 1940 to 1945 we can safely add another 3 percent, or 400,000 women, to the 1940 figure as normal growth. In fact, the figures would in all likelihood have been higher, given the possibility that the depression, having discouraged women from wage work, had created a backlog of women eager to try their wings. Subtracting these two groups, then, one might argue that only 3.5 million workers who might not otherwise have entered the labor force did so in the war years—an addition of 25.28 percent to the female work force above the natural and expected increases. Seventy-five percent of these new female workers were married.

Wartime figures reflect the latent tendency of women to seek wage work when normative pressures to stay at home are removed. Considering the unusual (if still inadequate) child care and food services available; the absence of men to whom women ordinarily catered; attractive wages and job opportunities; and a temporary suspension of overt animosity, these data may represent a peak of the number of women willing to work for wages in that period. In the two years after the war ended, women's participation in the work force dropped by a factor of 19 percent—a figure only a trifle lower than the estimated "additional" women who entered wage work as a result of the war.[8] In other words, after the wartime emergency receded, most of the women who remained in the labor force would have been working for wages anyway. There is no way of knowing if the three and a half million new women workers were the same women who dropped out, or were forced out, of the labor force when the war ended. But it seems clear that wartime surveys reporting that 75 to 85 percent of wage-earning women wanted to keep their jobs at the war's end probably reflected the normal proportion of wage-earning women. Of the two million additional women (above the 1940 level) still in the labor force in 1947, the Women's Bureau estimated that all but 250,000 would have been working in any event.[9] By 1950, the rate of women's participation in the work force had increased to 32 percent—for a net gain of 16 percent over the entire decade. The Census Bureau estimated that without war, natural factors would have yielded seventeen million wage-earning women in 1950. There were in fact eighteen million in that year—only a slight increase above expected growth.[10]

Much has been made of the number of women who entered the work force as an indication of changes in attitude and breakdown of traditional socialization patterns. But from another perspective the figures reflect continuity with previous attempts by some women to break out of traditional roles. Married women had entered the work force during the depression. In the war years, older married women contributed most of the increase that occurred among female workers. Despite publicity given to children left in locked cars while their mothers worked, a government report noted in 1943 that "practically no net expansion occurred among women between 20 and 30 years of age, and only a 6 percent increase of actual over normal employment is estimated for women in the next five year bracket." In contrast, women over forty-five appeared in the labor force in numbers about 20 percent above what would normally be expected.[11] And of the nearly five million women at work in the spring of 1945 who had not been in the labor force five years earlier, three million were over thirty-five.[12]

These rapid rises in participation rates exceeded those of any other age group in the labor force. They were more rapid for the married than for the unmarried, indicating both the degree to which single women had already been engaged in paid labor and the latent trend for the married with no children at home to want to work. This tendency continued after the war. By November 1946, half of all wage-earning women were over 34.8 years old. And the inclination of younger married women to leave the work force when husbands returned home meant that the proportion of older workers in the labor force would continue to rise. By 1950 there had been a net drop in the rate at which married women aged 25–34 went out to work. Correspondingly, half again as many women aged 45–54 were working for wages as had worked in 1940.[13]

Given the high level of previous work experience among most women in the labor force during the war, it is not surprising that the emergency presented itself as an opportunity to get ahead. Memories of the depression urged women wage earners to get what they could while they could. So for those who had been accustomed to working, war-born opportunities encouraged an aggressive stance and resulted in real gains, at least for the duration of hostilities. Black women, older women, and professional women all took advantage of a reduction in discrimination to enter well-paying jobs.

For black women, the change was especially dramatic. For generations, they had been denied access to good, skilled jobs that now opened to them. The proportions who entered the labor force did not expand as rapidly as those of white women reflecting high prewar participation rates. But black women took advantage of their previous work experience and the labor shortage to move into more desirable jobs. About 20 percent of those who had been domestic servants found work in areas that had previously snubbed them. Where white women moved from laundries into factories, especially in the South, black women readily took the jobs they vacated. But it took effort to move up into factory jobs. The threat of a mass demonstration in Washington in 1941, while the United States was building up its armaments in preparation for war, drew public attention to discrimination against all blacks. To head off demonstrations, the federal government created the Fair Employment Practices Commission in July 1941.

Sustained by the FEPC as well as by rulings of the War Manpower Commission against discrimination, and actively aided by the National Council of Negro Women, black women pressed for lucrative factory jobs. In cities like Detroit, where defense work was widespread, large factories imported huge numbers of rural whites to fill jobs for which they initially refused to hire blacks. Black women there led a series of demonstrations, beginning early in 1942 and lasting for nearly two years, to force local authorities to hire them. These demonstrations—for housing as well as jobs—culminated in the storming of a Ford plant by two busloads of women protesting discriminatory hiring policies.[14] Progress was slow. Yet for once, protesters had the active support of union locals, some civic agencies, and government policy. Members of UAW locals threatened to walk out of one plant in 1943 unless black women got jobs. At another plant, union representatives took nine months to win an agreement to hire black women, and then only after a threat of citywide action. The War Production Board and the U.S. Employment Service repeatedly urged employment of blacks in Detroit and elsewhere.[15]

By war's end the position of black women workers had improved substantially. They never got some of the best-paying jobs—in steel mills, as welders, ship fitters, and riveters. But the numbers involved in low-paid and low-status domestic work dropped by 15 percent while the number of factory operatives more than doubled, and clerical, sales, and professional workers substantially increased.[16] Ninety percent of the black women at work after the war had been in the labor force in 1940. Their movement into better jobs reflects not changed attitudes but their ability to take timely advantage of enlarged opportunities.

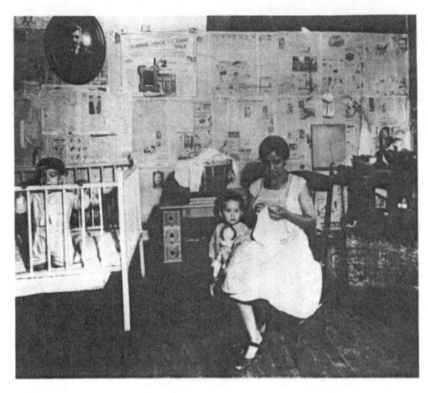

The depression hit the poorest families hard. Here a Mexican woman does home-work in 1932. *(Courtesy of the National Archives)*

While the depression helped to rationalize some, particularly unionized, sectors of the garment industry, it left others untouched. The Women's Bureau took both these shots in 1937. Above: Sweatshop conditions. Below: A model work-place. *(Courtesy of the National Archives)*

CIO pickets jeer mill workers, Greensboro, Georgia, 1941. Photo by Jack Delano for the Farm Security Administration. (*Courtesy of the Library of Congress*)

World War II brought new demands for women. Above: Three women employed at the Pacific Parachute plant in San Diego, California. Photo by Russell Lee. *(Courtesy of the Library of Congress)* Below: Assembling motors at the Douglas Aircraft Company in Long Beach, California. *(Brown Brothers)*

Involving women in production created new demands, as this cartoon from the Federal Works Agency demonstrates. *(Courtesy of the National Archives)*

Permanent employment raises new consciousness among many women and leads to a more active participation in unions and the work place. Above: workers at the Lerner shops participate in a negotiating session. *(Courtesy of the Tamiment Institute and District 65, United Automobile Workers)* Below: Workers in a newly unionized industry demonstrate for higher wages. *(Courtesy of Public Employee Press, District Council 37, American Federation of State, County and Municipal Employees)*

Professional women were equally aggressive. Historian Susan Hartmann has documented the extent to which they worked through their clubs and organizations to press for economic equality. Groups like the American Association of University Women and the National Federation of Business and Professional Women's Clubs met with the Women's Bureau to design "programs to promote the training, equal treatment and full utilization of women in war production," as well as "to plan for the retention of women's gains after reconversion." These organizations had little understanding of, or sympathy for, the economic problems of poor women or the racial discrimination faced by black women. Rather, they pushed to get women into policy-making positions in war agencies, even denying the need for special black representation on the Women's Advisory Committee—the only direct pipeline for women into the wartime agencies concerned with utilizing labor effectively. Despite the opposition of organizations representing poorer women, business and professional women continued to support the ERA and paid little attention to such mundane issues as day care.[17] For them, the important thing, as always, was not resolving the home and family issues that might equalize work force opportunities for all women, but improving their own relative economic positions. They became entrenched in civil service jobs at the federal and state levels, made inroads into banking and insurance, and moved into administrative jobs in education and health. Though gains remaining after the war ended were relatively small, professional women had nevertheless succeeded in moving out of the holding pattern in which the Depression had placed them.

Two other pieces of evidence suggest that what happened in the war and immediate postwar years represented a response to emergency rather than a shift in attitude. The first emerges from a look at what women did when hostilities ceased; the second, from examining what happened to them in the demobilization period.

When war production ended, large numbers of women simply quit their jobs. The rate at which women chose to leave jobs was at least double, and sometimes triple the rate at which they were discharged. And it was consistently higher than quit rates for men. In the food, clothing, and textile industries, where they had traditionally been employed, women quit jobs at an incredible pace. Women in well-paid jobs—chemical, rubber, and petroleum—quit more slowly than from any other manufacturing jobs.[18] Apparently, more experienced workers who had moved into better-paid jobs wanted to keep their jobs. More newer workers who had spent the war in traditionally female sectors willingly gave their places up.

Employers countered low quit rates by laying off women in the heavy industrial sectors where returning soldiers wanted jobs back. In the two months immediately following V-J Day, women were laid off at a rate of 175 per 1,000, double that of men. As the rate of layoffs slackened, women still lost their jobs at a slightly higher rate than men—especially in some durable goods industries. The biggest involuntary reduction came in the jobs where they had made the biggest gains in wartime and which presumably represented the biggest shift in social attitude—the durable heavy goods industries. Iron and steel manufactories, automobile and machinery makers fired women faster than they fired men. On the other hand, employers clearly sought to retain female employees in the nondurable goods sectors, where they were laid off more slowly than men.

Women's net gains in the war years were, therefore, negligible. They managed to retain a slightly greater share of manufacturing jobs, especially in the durable goods industries, but the general pattern of their employment remained the same as before the war. Even within manufacturing, the big gains occurred in electrical goods, where the task of assembling tiny parts was said to be suited to nimble fingers. The shift to clerical and office jobs continued. Few women retained skilled crafts jobs. The Women's Bureau concluded a study of Bridgeport, Connecticut, after the war sadly: "Only a few women have been allowed to continue in the newer fields of employment, and thus to continue to use skills learned during the war."[19] Older women, married women, women without at least a high school education, and black women again had a hard time finding jobs.

Wartime necessity required women's wage work. But it did not release women who worked from the pressure to adhere to old social roles. Women's own urges for better jobs and wages met their match in the pleas for patriotism and service to the community that came from employers, the Labor Department, and the War Manpower Commission. These rationales for wage work produced policies that effectively skirted women's desires for work for its own sake. The neverending fear that women might be unwilling to leave when the war ended led government policy makers and employers to make it clear that women ought to work only temporarily. And this too required continuing patterns of behavior that perpetuated the divided labor market with all of its psychic underpinnings.

Because of the ambivalence surrounding women's work, policies designed to make it easier for them to enter the labor force emerged erratically. Women found themselves without representation on the influential War Manpower Commission. Instead, the Commission created a Women's Advisory Committee in September 1942. That committee was authorized to recommend policy regarding women. But its recommendations were channeled through a Management-Labor Committee and thence to the WMC. The commission turned down Mary Anderson's request for one or two representatives on the Management-Labor Committee, offering instead a seat without a vote to Margaret Hickey, who chaired the Women's Advisory Committee. Three steps removed from the seat of power, the WAC operated in a vacuum. According to the Women's Bureau, it took seven months "before the WMC and its staff advisers sat down to consider the problem of how to improve communications."[20]

While confusion persisted in administrative ranks, women in good jobs found themselves facing male pressure to be feminine, and sometimes hostility for violating traditional roles. To keep women's images of themselves as intact as possible, administrators focused attention on the ways women managed to remain feminine despite hardships. The director of War Public Services for the Federal Works Authority—in charge of expanding facilities for the war effort—told an interviewer in 1943 that women war workers deserved special commendation for the attention they paid to grooming. "They bring glamor to the job," she said. The personnel manager of a plant confirmed the importance of grooming: "We like the girls to be neat and trim and well put together. It helps their morale. It helps our prestige too."[21] Women workers sustained and supported this stance. They struggled to be able to wear their own clothing, even where it might be dangerously floppy. One plant posted drawings of scalped women to get them to tuck hair into bonnets or nets. Overt hostility kept women in their places too. Nell Giles, a reporter for the Boston *Herald* who worked in a defense factory for a period of months, described being hooted down for carrying a black tin lunch box. Only men, it seemed, carried lunch boxes. Women used paper bags, even though they couldn't put soup or milk in them. Giles didn't have the courage, she admitted, "to buck that line."[22] Catcalls, whistles, and hisses faced women who walked onto the production floor for the first time. Young girls who became pages on the floor of the New York Stock Exchange met wolfish whistles.

Employers adopted promotion and training policies that played into these role divisions. At the suggestion of the War Department, female training included frequent analogies to household work. Supervisors attempted to convince new recruits that any woman who could use a needle could handle a welding rod, or that cutting out sheet metal resembled cutting a pattern for a dress. Employers' willingness to use women was governed by immediate needs. They refused to integrate women into training programs that might provide access to skills beyond those essential for their initial tasks. For temporary help, management reasoned, that would have been a wasted investment. One group of women complained in late 1944 that "management is engaging in a vicious and deliberate campaign to induce women to quit by transferring them from one department to another, by assigning women the least desirable jobs, and by an unceasing psychological drive to harass women out of the plants."[23]

The struggle for equal pay illustrates another level of ambivalence. For years, trade unions had argued for equal pay for women only when the jobs of unionists were threatened by women's lower wages. Women's quest for equal pay on the grounds of equity had met little response. Now women were literally taking men's jobs, as earlier it had been feared they would do. To pay them at a man's scale undermined the barriers that divided women's work from men's. To pay them below it undermined the value of the job and threatened men's wage scales when they returned to reclaim their jobs. Manufacturers under contract to the government, and paid on a cost-plus basis, could readily agree to raise wages. Those in the private sector preferred to retain barriers. Trade unions concerned with job protection tended to fight for equal pay (although only the left-wing unions espoused genuinely egalitarian values). Wishing to avoid chaos in the labor market as well as to promote "mobility of the labor force and maximum utilization of women workers," government agencies agreed to support labor and attempted to persuade management to go along with equal pay. A Bureau of Labor statistician acknowledged the realities involved when she wrote in 1947 that there were three reasons for granting equal pay to women: justice, sustaining men's wage rates, and increasing purchasing power. The second, she argued, was by far the most powerful.[24]

Recognizing the pressures to sustain wages in a period when wage rises were strictly limited, the National War Labor Board issued General Order No. 16 in November 1942, permitting employers to "equalize the wage or salary rates paid to females with rates paid to males for comparable quality and quantity of work."[25] But the Congress failed to pass a companion bill that would have prohibited wage differentials based on sex. And only five states with about a quarter of the nation's female wage earners enacted their own laws. Furthermore, since these laws were concerned primarily with the issue of sustaining men's wages, they addressed themselves only to preventing women from wage-cutting that could depress men's earnings, not to the major source of discriminatory wages for women—the historic differentiation of male and female jobs, where jobs defined as female carried a lower wage rate. As a result, the gap between men's and women's wages increased during the war. Women were earning far more in dollar terms than before the war, and more than they would earn thereafter.

Still, the average full-time woman worker earned only 55 percent of what her male co-worker earned: a drop from the 1939 figure of about 62 percent.[26]

Women protested the vagueness of federal guidelines and agitated for additional protection. In Dayton, Ohio, angry women told Elizabeth Christman of the Women's Bureau that despite federal guidelines on equal pay embodied in General Order No. 16, the Frigidaire plant in which they worked continued to hire women at lower rates than men would be paid for the same jobs, and to violate their seniority. Book binders in the Government Printing Office complained of getting thirty to fifty-two cents an hour less than men for the same work.[27] Christman reported that hundreds of grievances had been filed by female employees of General Motors in Ohio against rate discrimination. The same women objected to the War Labor Board's use of "comparable" to define work that should be paid equally. They wanted to substitute "same pay for same work" in order to avoid misunderstanding and confusion.[28]

Like the struggle for equal pay, the struggle for access to trade unions suffered from the ambiguity of women's presence under sufferance owing to wartime emergency. Unions that had never had women members, like the International Boilermakers, Iron Shipbuilders, Welders and Helpers, continued to deny them membership until it was clear that the war emergency necessitated it. Unionized men complained that women would "spoil the job" or "break the morale of the plant." Women who did not understand informal work rules tended to exhaust themselves in rapid bursts of work and to work without stint. Some unionists struck to prevent women from being hired. Others, like those in steel, auto, rubber, and machine tools, accepted or actively recruited women into their ranks but denied them upgrading and frequently continued discriminatory job classifications.[29] Most trade unions maintained separate seniority lists of men and women and tolerated job classifications and job rates on the basis of sex. They bypassed issues of particular interest to women workers. Women complained that men were not fighting hard enough for such things as equal pay. And they wanted maternity leaves without loss of seniority, good day care centers, and time off to care for sick children.

Yet the women who joined unions benefited nonetheless. In the aftermath of the great organizing drives of the 1930s, unionization had spread over the industrial Northeast. Union shops and maintenance of membership agreements—under which incoming workers automatically joined the collective bargaining unit—provided unions with a steady influx of members as war industry expanded. Recruiting three and a half million women into heavy industry where they had not previously been employed increased fourfold the number of female union members within two years. Economist Gladys Dickason estimated that at the beginning of the war only 800,000 wage-earning women were unionized. They made up 9.4 percent of unionized workers. By 1944 more than three million women constituted 22 percent of trade union membership.[30]

Whether they fared well or ill was a matter of union politics. The strongest voice for egalitarian policies came from the left wing of the union movement. The United Electrical, Radio and Machine Workers, whose membership was 35 percent female by 1944, had an equal proportion of women on its executive council and managed to end discriminatory pay entirely. The United Rubber Workers included an equal pay clause in 142 of its agreements.[31] The United Auto Workers developed perhaps the most complete policy-making apparatus. It attempted to get women involved in the union administrative structure. It held rallies where it encouraged women to be active in their shop committees as well as in their communities. In the spring of 1944, the UAW War Policy Division set up its own Women's Bureau to serve the union's 300,000 female members. R. J. Thomas, UAW president, announced that the new bureau was to "give special consideration to seniority, safety standards, maternity leave practices, and other problems relating to the employment of women. In addition, the Bureau will develop techniques for interesting women in general union activities and in developing their sense of union citizenship."[32]

From the beginning, the Bureau concerned itself with the tricky issue of how to involve women in general trade union issues while it prepared them for inevitable postwar layoffs. Mildred Jeffrey, at its head, began studying "the effects of cutbacks on unemployment of women workers" as early as May 1944. She described the situation then as "already acute in some areas" and urged a national conference to defuse their objections to being fired. She wanted "our women," she wrote, to "fully understand the problems which the International faces. . . ."[33]

The conference that met in December covered a wide variety of issues. Its 150 representatives passed resolutions asking for "in-plant" cafeterias to sell hot food and requesting counseling services that would include advice about family problems as well as work. Women complained that company counselors often attempted to "inculcate anti-union attitudes" or acted as spies "to see if women are loitering about in rest rooms, smoking, or wearing improper clothing." Members asked for maternity leaves without loss of seniority, insurance plans that included maternity benefits, improved child-care facilities designed to continue after the war emergency, a guaranteed annual wage, and unemployment benefit policies that did not discriminate against women.[34]

For all these ambitious long-range goals, when it came to the issue of layoffs, women workers acquiesced. They readily acknowledged that the union faced a difficult problem in reconciling the competing interests of returning veterans with those of newly hired women. Female representatives recognized that women would be "the first to feel the impact of reconversion lay-offs" yet went on to endorse a seniority system that gave job preference to a man who had worked under UAW jurisdiction for even the briefest period before the war over a woman who had been in the union for the duration.[35] Better than most unions, the UAW attempted to serve its female members. It protected and extended their rights as union members. Yet, though it supported federal bills for full employment, it too succumbed to a pattern that saw most unions unceremoniously discard their female members at war's end.

Ambivalence toward women working during the war showed up even in the provision of support services necessary for them to work effectively. While almost everybody acknowledged the difficulties involved when a woman undertook wage labor in addition to household chores, few offered concrete suggestions for lightening the load. In fact, the opposite happened. Defense contractors asked for, and routinely got, permission to suspend maximum-hour legislation, and a woman with children to care for might be coerced into working nine or ten hours a day in a six-day week. If she took a day off for family needs, she was berated as unpatriotic. In its concern to attract "womanpower," *Fortune* sympathized with the working mother who had "marketing, cooking, laundering and cleaning to attend to" and wondered how long she could "stand up under a twelve- or fourteen-hour day."[36] Yet when it came to setting up services, only a few plants extended more than limited help. Lest women become accustomed to amenities and too comfortable at work, little attempt was made to accommodate them even at the peak of national need. Communal kitchens and shared cleaning were rare. Most factories provided hot lunches only after a struggle. And though occasionally one reads of banking services brought to the door, only the model plants of Kaiser Industries offered anything like the British experience of factory-delivered laundry services, packaged ready-to-eat foods, and special shops. For fifty cents, Kaiser's "Home Service Food" program allowed a mother to order a family's evening meal two days ahead of time and pick up her order along with her child at the end of a day's work.[37]

Provision of even limited services stopped short when it came to help with mothering. The WMC declared its policy to be one of actively recruiting women without children under fourteen and then added that "this principle should not be construed to mean that women who are responsible for the care of young children and who desire to work are to be deprived of an opportunity for training or employment."[38] But such language militated against an active campaign for child-care facilities. And the Commission went on to appeal to mothers of young children to remain at home and to ask employers not to recruit them until "all other sources of local labor supply have been exhausted in order that established family life will not be unnecessarily disrupted."[39] The Commission never spoke consistently, however. In one critical industrial area, the War Production Board noted, the WMC pleaded with women to get into the war plants, while local leaders urged them to leave the plants and stay home with their children.[40]

The women who worked in industry had no direct influence on developing federal child-care policy. The Children's Bureau in the Department of Labor included female early-childhood experts, and professional women and social workers sat on the Women's Advisory Committee, but much of their advice was simply ignored. The Women's Bureau later commented wryly, "It seems sound, in any case, to permit a voice in their own affairs to one-third of the working population, especially when that one-third carries a far greater proportion of responsibility for the maintenance of family and community welfare."[41] Left almost entirely to bureaucrats, child care became a political football, tossed about in the public press as it became the focal point of hostility to women earning wages. "Experience has shown that the surest and quickest way to disrupt a family," wrote a trade union chaplain, "is to take the mother out of the home. . . . Too many mothers of families are working in war plants, not because of necessity nor for reasons of patriotism but because they are drawn by the lure of huge wages."[42] Behind the specter of the disrupted family followed that of juvenile delinquency. In the spring of 1943, a seventeen-year-old was arrested for paying thirteen-year-old girls twenty-five cents apiece to "play" with men. Had all their mothers been at home, it was argued, this could never have happened. As if to underscore the concern, the Senate Subcommittee on Education and Labor held hearings on juvenile delinquency in the winter of 1943.[43]

Confused by the mixed messages and divided over the child-care issue, Congress vacillated. At first it seemed satisfied to leave the problem in the hands of local communities—a solution approved by the Children's Bureau, but which completely failed to provide facilities for all those who needed them. Not content to leave child care in such disarray, and prodded by publicity about inadequately supervised children, President Roosevelt freed emergency construction funds, under the 1941 Lanham Act, to build facilities for child care. The Federal Works Administration, which supervised the funds, was to allocate them in consultation with community officials and with the Federal Security Administration, under whose charge fell most health and welfare policies.

Problems of coordinating separate federal and state agencies combined with ambivalence at all levels to produce an underfunded and entirely unsatisfactory program. The first project under the FWA's child-care program was approved in August 1942. But funds were "slow and insufficient" and even when the flow started, limited staffing reduced the numbers of children centers could care for and limited their hours. So inadequate were they that rumors circulated about executives in war industries who wanted to set up their own child-care centers. They planned to petition the Navy for permission to charge the cost to production.[44] By August 1943, although 53,000 children were enrolled in FWA centers, reports began to spread that they were underutilized: the Chicago *Times* ran a story headlined "WAR NURSERIES LACK CHILDREN: TWO MAY CLOSE."[45] The centers were spottily and inconveniently located. Their hours were too short. Their fees were often too high (up to six dollars per week per child). And the FWA admitted that it had made no attempt "to sell the mother on the idea that nurseries give the child the advantage of trained care and excellent supervision." Nursery workers, often rapidly selected and poorly trained, were identified in the public mind as poor people more interested in income than in children. School boards with the facilities and expertise to implement programs had been openly hostile.[46] By September, the FWA acknowledged that the centers were operating at only a quarter of capacity.[47]

Interoffice squabbling finally stopped in October after the Senate had passed, and a House committee killed, a bill to provide day care funding jointly administered by the Office of Education and the Children's Bureau. The bill, sponsored by Senator Elbert Thomas, would have set aside twenty million dollars for federal grants to communities that built their own centers. It was effectively scuttled by Roosevelt, under whose leadership Congress finally gave the FWA sole prerogative over building federal centers.[48]

But they never worked well. Those who sought to provide services for working mothers did so apologetically. "We have," said Florence Kerr, then director of the FWA child-care project, "what amounts to a national policy that the best service a mother can do is rear her children in her home. . . . But we are in a war. . . . Whether we like it or not, mothers of young children *are* at work. . . . So we do need care centers."[49] Because they reflected the conviction that mothers of young children had no business in the labor force, the programs were geared not to the needs of mothers but to those of employers. They were, as one panel of educators and union leaders reported, "not intended as a substitute for the home, but rather as an aid to parents who face unusual problems arising from the war emergency."[50] A proponent of the Thomas bill declared, "While none of us like the idea of mothers of infants working, many of them have essential skills and many of them, particularly soldiers' wives, need the money."[51] The FWA came up with a most appealing slogan to handle the contradition implicit in seeking funds for children whose mothers really ought to have been at home. "Men are needed on the battle front. Women are needed at the home front. Men are needed with minds clear and steady. Women are needed with attention for their work undivided. . . ."[52] To help their husbands, mothers needed day care.

Insistence on maintaining feminine roles had serious consequences. Since their right to be at work was never fully asserted, women were left vulnerable, after the war, to the removal of such pitiful services as existed. And this insistence accounts for the reluctance of many women to help out during the war. Faced with the failure of a massive campaign to recruit women in the Detroit area in the fall of 1942, the WMC turned to the Women's Advisory Committee to help find "the reasons for the slow response." The Committee replied swiftly. Women would not leave their homes, they argued, "in really large numbers until they had assurance that supplementary community adjustments in the form of child-care centers and other community facilities would be provided, and also, in some instances, until they had better assurance of employer acceptance."[53]

The evidence offers little support to those who suggest that the war was either a turning point or a milestone. Neither the lives of women nor the way industry responded to them in the immediate postwar years suggests such a conclusion. Questions the war had brought to the fore—like equal pay, child care, and community services for wage-earning women—lost immediacy as women faced the reality of poorly paid jobs or none at all. The question of whether women should or should not work once again assumed ideological proportions as the labor market offered women more limited opportunities and taking advantage of them created some family stress.

Reactions to the end-of-war layoffs varied. Young women tended to accept cuts philosophically. On Wall Street, sixty-six young women who had worked as pages and clerks on the floor of the stock exchange for the first time all expected to lose their jobs as the war ended. A

sympathetic reporter commented, "Most of the girls really don't care.
. . . they have learned that Wall Street is not yet adjusted to the
presence of women between 10 A.M and 3 P.M."[54] Experienced women
who lost good jobs were not as quiet. They stormed employment agencies, wrote angry letters, demanded action from the Women's Bureau,
and queued endlessly for jobs. To no avail.

Women who had never worked before tended to move back to the
home. It came as no surprise to them, according to Frieda Miller,
who had succeeded Mary Anderson as director of the Women's Bureau
in 1944, that they were the first to be fired, nor did they particularly
want to "get ahead at the expense of veterans."[55] Women of child-
bearing age gave birth to the baby boom. But the normal increase in
the number of women eager to find jobs was enough to rekindle the
old debate as to whether or not they ought to work. As in the thirties,
even those who supported wage-earning for women made sharp distinctions between the need to work and the desire to do so. A 1946
Fortune survey asked if "a married woman who has no children under
16 and whose husband makes enough to support her should or should
not be allowed to take a job if she wants to." Only a third of the men
and two-fifths of the women queried believed they should be allowed
to take jobs. *Fortune* noted a sharp class division—more than half of
the prosperous women answering favored women's freedom to work.
But only 35 percent of the poor women agreed. They cited two main
reasons in explanation: people who needed jobs would be deprived
of them, and a woman's place was in the home.[56]

But which women needed jobs? asked Lucy Greenbaum in the *New
York Times Magazine*. They were, she answered, those whose husbands
would not return from the war, or who would return injured; or those
who would never marry because the war had decimated the ranks of
men. Then she added a new category. There were those who *wanted* to
work: those who found happiness in a job, who found the child-rearing
role unduly restrictive or who, having experienced the relative independence and responsibility of wage earning, would simply refuse
"to retreat to the home."[57]

Against the women who wanted to work, traditionalists directed a
stream of vituperation in the immediate postwar years. Family life
depended on their staying at home, so it was morally wrong for such
women to seek jobs. Women, argued Agnes Meyer in the *Atlantic
Monthly*, were needed "to restore a security to our insecure world."
She called on them to resist pressure to enter the labor market and
to renounce any job except that of housewife and mother. "What ails
these women," she asked, "who consciously or unconsciously reject
their children? . . . The poor child whose mother has to work has

some inner security because he knows in his little heart that his mother is sacrificing herself for his well-being. But the neglected child from a well-to-do home, who realizes instinctively that his mother prefers her job to him, often hates her with a passionate intensity."[58] This was, according to Marynia Farnham and Ferdinand Lundberg, authors of the best-selling *Modern Woman: The Lost Sex,* as it should be. Women, they suggested "would do well to recapture those functions in which they have demonstrated superior capacity. Those are, in general, the nurturing functions around the home." To women who chose to enter "fields belonging to the male area of exploit or authority —law, mathematics, physics, business, industry and technology—government and socially minded organizations should . . . make it clear that such pursuits are not generally desirable for women."[59]

If women, despite their natural bent, insisted on entering such fields, the consensus held that they deserved to be discriminated against. The psychic maladjustment that led them to leave their homes made them intrinsically poor risks in the office. They were emotionally unstable, quarreled too much, and fomented feuds in the office. They lacked the "gift for teamwork that makes for coordinated research" and did not have "the focused imagination that makes a man work steadfastly on a long project." As professionals they were indecisive, as unionists they were disloyal. Worst of all, their interest in work distracted attention from what should have been a primary concern with the home."[60]

Few advocates of jobs for women engaged in debate at that level. Instead they responded in two ways. Women's Bureau and government policy makers proposed retraining and counseling to channel women into jobs expected to have little attraction for men. Frances Perkins, then Secretary of Labor, urged that some doors through which women had passed during the war be kept open after it ended. She advocated public health and welfare work "as professions in which 'excellent' opportunities should be available to women."[61] Frieda Miller argued that women "would like to retain, some if not all, of the gains" made during the war. But the Women's Bureau was pragmatic about the possibilities. In 1944 it prepared a policy statement describing what would happen to women's jobs in power laundries, where they had taken over virtually all operations. "Work as washman and extractor operator may be crossed from the list for women unless the pay is so low as not to attract competent men. The Army has given many men training in these jobs, and servicemen should have first chance at the work if they want it. But since at present women are being paid less than men for washing, and the new machinery is calculated to require much less physical strength it is possible that women will be kept on in the washroom though the danger is that this will be at depressed wages."[62]

For other women the fight to retain wartime gains revolved around their pay. By war's end, as we have seen, equal pay had been accepted in principle by some trade unions and five states. In Congress, representatives Mary Norton, Claude Pepper, and Wayne Morse introduced a bill in 1945 to insure equal pay and opportunity to women. The Women's Bureau and the WTUL waged aggressive campaigns for this bill, the Women's Equal Pay Act, and for similar legislation, from 1945 on. But opposition from chambers of commerce and management associations prevailed. By the early 1950s, equal pay was as distant as it had ever been. Maurice Tobin, then Secretary of Labor, demonstrated to an Equal Pay Conference how little progress had been made. "Dear Mr. Blank," he read, quoting a little from a company manager to an employment agency,

> We have an opening here for a combination program director and salesman. This position can be filled by either a man or a woman. We will pay a woman $20 a week for doing the office work and give her $10 a week drawing account, thus guaranteeing her $30 a week. We will pay her 20 percent commission on all sales.
>
> We will start a man at $30 a week for doing the office work, and $30 a week drawing account, and also pay him 20 percent on all sales. . . . the person who fills this position must have at least a year or two of business and office experience.
>
> . . . The gal especially should be attractive.[63]

More radical feminists asked for full employment. The real issue, argued writer Edith Efron, was not one of turning a woman into a sort of pseudo-man who "talks, works, thinks, acts, reacts like a male." The real question, the woman worker suspected, was not " 'How come no jobs for women?' but 'How come not enough jobs?' "[64] Women's situation, argued Lucy Greenbaum, "will depend to a large degree on the extent to which the nation's entire economy can develop a high level of employment and the extent to which the industries that require the type of work women do best can expand."[65] *The Independent Woman*, organ of the National Federation of Business and Professional Women's Clubs, raised the issue of the right to work again. "We think that it is a right that belongs to the individual, man or woman, to decide whether or not he or she wants to work. Industry, business or government should not make that decision. If there is a job to be done, the worker should be accepted according to training and ability."[66]

But most of the American public did not agree. Less than 22 percent of the men and 29 percent of the women interviewed by *Fortune*'s pollsters thought that women "should have an equal chance with men" for any job. Only 46 percent of the men, and less than 50 percent of the women, thought even women who had to support themselves should have an "equal chance." And substantial numbers of both sexes thought men should always have the preference no matter what the woman's economic position.[67]

As in World War I, men who worked next to women grudgingly conceded their ability to do a job. But demonstrations of effectiveness at tough jobs did not change attitudes about women's work in general or about their primary role at home. At best, militant women staged a holding action—slightly increasing the numbers out at work as they returned to stratified jobs and continuing to struggle for equal pay. The strength of the propaganda campaign to get women out of the work force reflects the extent to which perceptions of family needs still governed women's work, paid or unpaid. As family members eager to enhance economic security, women fought to retain paying jobs; but as family members anxious to preserve jobs for male breadwinners, both men and women fought to return women to the sanctity of the home.

The war turned out to be less a milestone than a natural response to the call for patriotism, to lucrative jobs, to husbands' absences, and to more readily available household and child-care services. The milestone came after. It was marked by the dawning recognition within families that women's functions of cushioning depression and fighting inflation, traditionally performed by economies within the household, might be more effectively handled by wage-earning. A woman's income, still supplementary, and her job, still less than a career, could make the difference between sheer survival and minimal comfort. If the entry of women into war work was a response to opportunity, the continuing rise in their work force participation after demobilization reflects a response to increasing economic demands on the family. Briefly, a reordered set of ideas—what Betty Friedan called the "feminine mystique"—managed in the 1950s to reconcile the competing interests of home and work. Though middle-class and working-class communities responded to postwar ideology differently, the home remained central to the aspirations of most women. It took a new set of pressures on the family and a dramatic shift in the labor market to challenge that ideology.

11

The Radical Consequences of Incremental Change

The typical housewife with a blue-collar husband entered the 1950s on the watch for a bit of income to help the family out. Concerned about saving or paying for the family's first home and its fittings, she would have agreed with one assumption of the White House Conference on Effective Uses of Woman-power held in 1955: "The structure and the substance of the lives of most women are fundamentally determined by their functions as wives, mothers, and homemakers."[1] But the same conference that so blithely reiterated the traditional notion of women's roles simultaneously heard a contrary message. Called together to assess women's actual and potential contribution to the economy, conference participants heard speaker after speaker suggest that women ought to be encouraged to participate more fully in the occupational world. Roland R. Renne, president of Montana State College in Bozeman and a member of the National Manpower Council, identified the major problem. What were the ways, he asked "by which we can significantly increase the effectiveness of our woman power?"[2]

This was the central contradiction of the fifties. Beside the overwhelming popular assumption—the certain knowledge of women's fundamental obligations to the home—lay a subtle shift in government policy that insisted on women's capacity to take jobs as well. On the surface, the fifties reflected work force patterns of the years before the war. But underlying these visible patterns lay an accelerating trend that hinted at new and irreversible roles.

In contrast to earlier decades where, at any one time, wage-earning women were a relatively small, if significant, minority, in the fifties their proportion crept upward, to the point where in the sixties women who did not work for wages became the exception. Women were 29 percent of the work force in 1950, 35 percent in 1965, and 40 percent by 1975—a percentage increase equal to that of the entire sixty years preceding 1950. And where earlier wage work had been merely a short phase of many women's lives, in the fifties it began to assume a more central position. Instead of quitting work after marriage, even women with adequate incomes stayed on. And women who stopped working when they began having children tended to return to jobs after the youngest child began school. Instead of choosing part-time jobs to fit family styles, more women worked full time. A third of all women worked in 1950—only half of them full time. By 1975, nearly half worked, more than 70 percent at full-time jobs.[3]

The increase astonished everyone. Yet in view of the sturdy mechanisms regulating how women worked, its implications seemed minimal. Nearly all the growth was in the clerical and service sectors. Said the Detroit *Free Press*, "Rosie feels something like Typhoid Mary when she applies for a factory job."[4] Among white married women, wage work was still conditioned by the rationale of household need. Women, according to myth, "helped out" their mates by bringing in a little income. In the absence of the depression notion that every wage-earning wife deprived a breadwinner of a job, popular sentiment validated this idea.

But for how long would the vast majority of women continue to work without recognition of their contribution on the job? A carefully regulated labor market rooted in conceptions of women as homebound had consistently denied women access to jobs with responsibility, decent pay, promotion, and policy-making power. But in the past, most of the women subject to such discrimination had been poor, immigrant, and black. To a dominant white society, racism and the trappings of poverty seemed self-evident explanations for the failure of these workers to rise in the occupational structure. To some extent, these more blatant forms of discrimination obscured the sexual bias that inhibited the progress of women in general. If wage work spread to most women, could job-related restrictions continue? For how long would women continue wage work without attempting to shed some of the responsibilities of the home? And for how long would they earn wages without taking some of the freedom that their new economic status offered: the freedom not to marry, not to play submissive roles, the freedom to express their own sexuality? These questions, which were to have such explosive impact in the seventies, took form in the fifties.

At first glance, the fifties was the decade of the family. To make a woman completely content, headlined a 1962 *Saturday Evening Post*

article, "it takes a man, but the chief purpose of her life is motherhood." George Gallup and Evan Hill, the authors, based their observa-
tion on a scientific sample of interviews with 2,300 women. Their
results confirmed what everyone already believed. "Our study," they
wrote, "shows that few people are as happy as a housewife." Ninety-
six percent of married women reported that they were either extremely
happy or fairly happy. The American woman of the fifties said she was
uninterested in either business or politics. She didn't want equality,
and if she had a job she awaited "the day when she could assume the
full-time role of housewife and eventually mother." Her "strongly
rooted purpose" was "home and family—motherhood. . . . She rarely
loses her protective family-mother instinct even when the children
are grown for when motherhood is gone, grandmotherhood replaces
it."[5]

But already the family was flashing warning signals. Vested as it
was in the trappings of a consumer economy, to sustain the household
at what the Bureau of Labor Statistics called "a modest but adequate"
level increasingly required women's wage work. As blue-collar workers
and a growing corps of bureaucrats moved into postwar suburban
communities, household needs expanded dramatically. Homes and cars,
refrigerators and washing machines, telephones and multiple televi-
sions required higher incomes. Keeping children at school beyond the
age of sixteen and sending them to college meant foregoing their income, and sometimes paying tuition as well. Higher real wages of male
breadwinners could pay for some of these, but as the level of consumer
aspiration rose, wives sought to aid husbands in the quest for the good
life. The two-income family emerged. In 1950, wives earned wages in
only 21.6 percent of all families. By 1960, 30.5 percent of wives worked
for wages. And that figure would continue to increase. Full- and part-
time working wives contributed about 26 percent of the total family
income, a figure that had not changed since the twenties.[6]

These figures do not necessarily reflect a breakdown of notions of
social role. At least in the fifties, two of every five employed wives
came from families that would otherwise have had incomes below
"modest but adequate" levels. Some of these worked part time, and
many were young women without children or mature women whose
children had grown. Families used additional income earned by wives
in the same way as if it had been earned by the husband alone. In
addition to extra work-related costs such as clothing, transportation,
and taxes, families spent it to purchase appliances and to increase their
standard of living.[7] The bulk of the increase in labor force participation
in the fifties occurred among women over forty-five—past the years
when they would normally have young children at home. These women

accounted for most of the jump in the proportion of married women working for wages. But even in the family-oriented fifties, the proportion of women with small children who sought to go out to work increased by one-third and that of those with children under six by more than a quarter.[8]

But the ideas that insisted that even women who worked for wages derived their social value from home roles were powerful. Partly as a result of them, increasing work force participation did nothing to reduce the segmentation that defined the occupational structure. As jobs in the clerical sector mushroomed, the demand for women to step into them grew apace. By 1960, one-third of all wage-earning women held these jobs. And though the number of women employed as domestics declined, those who earlier would have been domestics tended to move into blue-collar "service" jobs as health care aides and technicians, beauticians, waitresses, and office cleaning ladies. By 1960 nearly 80 percent of the women who earned wages worked in jobs that were stereotyped as female.[9]

There was a difference, however. In contrast to the depression, when women who helped sustain families faced hostility, a persistent shortage of workers in some areas encouraged employers to seek female help. Unlike the wartime emergency when some female workers and most male employers viewed women as temporary help, the fifties saw a permanent shift in the work force. Large numbers of men remained in the armed services. High military spending boosted the economy. And the spinoff effect of restrained domestic spending during the war contributed to a period in which consumer spending and production all exceeded predictions. As the Korean War produced spot labor shortages in key areas, women gained new and unexpected opportunities. The demand for clerical and service workers continued unabated after the war, yielding predictions of shortages in these areas. Young women, in short supply because of low depression birthrates and high postwar marriage rates, were especially sought after. By 1953 the Women's Bureau complained of insufficient numbers of stenographers and typists and of shortages in nursing, teaching, social work, and medical fields that approached the critical level.[10]

From Seattle, Women's Bureau investigator Elsie Wolfe sent back urgent reports about shortages of labor in skilled jobs, lack of nurseries and the scarcity of women in training programs. The situation there benefited black women, normally among the last hired. Full employment in this community meant that black women could get jobs with defense contractors and state and local government. And Wolfe predicted in August that by Christmas of 1951, department store sales jobs would open to them. Even clerical jobs began to open to women from minority groups, though access to industrial training programs in skilled crafts remained limited for all women. Despite the serious labor shortage, male prerogative persisted. "Many women are enrolled in the training programs for new employees," reported Wolfe, "but there are very few women in the more advanced training programs."[11]

The Cold War mentality gave the Women's Bureau the wedge it needed to open some of these programs. It would be a disaster, argued Frieda Miller, if another war occurred while the skills acquired by two and a half million women in wartime got rusty. Plans should be made to recruit and train "the millions of women who may be needed in war production work."[12] Alice Leopold, Miller's successor as head of the Women's Bureau, continued the argument: "We can never hope to compete with the slave world in terms of numbers of workers, but we can and do compete with them very definitely in terms of the strength, morale, and skill of our work force. Women are becoming increasingly important in the development of our country's industry, in scientific research, in the education field, and in the social sciences."[13] Dr. Irving Siegel, member of the powerful Council of Economic Advisers, argued for women's entry not only into the so-called humanitarian occupations but into "occupations typically staffed with men and occupations newly defined" as well.[14]

In response to these pressures some of the policies that discouraged women's entry into the labor market began to come under question. The Women's Bureau supported proposals to offer women paid maternity leave. Frieda Miller testified in favor of a Senate bill that would give married employees of the federal civil service up to two months of paid leave. The Bureau reported renewed pressure for adjusting community resources "to meet the needs of working women" by "various types of housekeeping services, meals on wheels, and properly licensed and supervised day care facilities for children." The Labor Department suggested enticing mature women into the labor force by means of part-time work, orientation courses, and "action" programs. The practice of retiring women earlier than men came under fire, and the Women's Bureau attempted to work out a plan to raise the reduced benefits offered by Social Security to married women and those who retired early. The Bureau began aggressively to attack the association of wage-earning mothers with juvenile delinquency. "All the statistical evidence that we have seen," wrote Alice Leopold, "would indicate that the employment of the mother is not directly correlated with juvenile delinquency."[15]

The new climate encouraged wage-earning women to raise again the question of equal pay. Despite widespread support for equal pay to protect the jobs of male workers replaced by women during World War II, the policy did not, as we have seen, carry over into the postwar period. The 1945 federal bill for equal pay in all private employment failed to get through Congress. By 1952, women were ready to begin fighting again. A coalition of civic groups, women's organizations, labor, and employer organizations that year formed a National Committee for Equal Pay. Progress remained slow. Not until 1956 did the now-united AFL-CIO commit itself to equal pay, undertaking a three-year campaign at the local level. In a pamphlet issued in December 1956, the AFL-CIO urged its officers to study a bill "providing equal pay for comparable work with a view to taking whatever action seems appropriate."[16] Falling wage rates for women's jobs, as compared to their wartime highs as well as to average men's wages, stimulated these efforts. By 1960, the median annual earnings of full-time women workers had fallen to 60 percent of the rate for male workers—a figure that reflected their increasing occupational segregation.

At the same time, shortages of workers led to recommendations for new kinds of training and even the creation of educational opportunities for women. The Department of Labor created programs to entice married women with college degrees into teacher education. A presidential commission recommended lower college tuition and conveniently scheduled classes to encourage mothers to prepare for future jobs. And proposals to train women in nontraditional areas emerged. "There isn't a chance in the world of our closing the gap between the supply and demand," declared Frieda Miller, "unless we do persuade more women with aptitudes for this kind of work to receive training in the field of engineering." Miller advocated breaking down "arbitrary restrictions" and creating "training opportunities" for older women to solve the problem.[17]

The push for equal pay and for new educational opportunities rekindled demands for an Equal Rights Amendment. Although organizations like the League of Women Voters, the National Consumers' League, the National Congress of Negro Women, the CIO, and major trade unions in the AFL remained firmly opposed to an ERA, limited support emerged within the Women's Bureau. The Bureau, which had staunchly opposed the amendment since 1923, found itself in the early 1950s in a different position.[18]

In Mary Anderson's day, the Women's Bureau had been an outspoken advocate for the legal protection of wage-earning women. A product of the combined pressure of trade union and women's groups, the Bureau responded to these constituencies by interpreting its congressional injunction to improve the lot of female wage earners as a mandate to fight on their behalf. It operated therefore on the margins of the Department of Labor, to which it formally belonged—a step-child nurtured not so much by the Department as by a network of women's groups. The New Deal expansion of legislative protection to all workers, together with the spread of trade unionism during the depression and the war to encompass many more women, undermined the argument for special protection for women. Frieda Miller responded by altering the Bureau's focus in the 1940s, advocating an extension of the New Deal's social benefits to agricultural and domestic workers—groups she felt had not shared in generally improving conditions. For the same reasons that led Miller to shift the Bureau's emphasis, the women's networks that had for years supported the Bureau in its battles with the Labor Department began to drift away. The influence of the WTUL and the NCL waned, and the WTUL finally disbanded in 1950. The League of Women Voters concentrated on electoral politics. Trade unions—their membership increased and solidified—no longer required an alliance with the weak Women's Bureau.

By the time Alice Leopold took over the Bureau's direction in 1953, its constituency and its purposes had changed. No longer sustained by women's groups or the labor movement, Leopold became much more the bureaucrat eager to serve the Department of Labor. Her new title—Assistant to the Secretary of Labor for Women's Affairs—reflected the Bureau's altered position. Like the Labor Department itself, the Bureau became a data collection agency whose major task was to organize the available labor force in the service of national economic well-being. Lacking outside support for advocacy positions independent of the Labor Department, or for ameliorating the lot of women whose wage-earning lives had vastly improved, the Bureau focused on the issue of how women's skills as workers could be more effectively deployed. From its original position of helping women who happened to hold jobs, the Bureau had now shifted to a stance of helping a nation decide how to use women better. An Equal Rights Amendment, which would end special restraints against women workers, would serve this new position effectively. But an ERA would also reject the social values implicit in women's labor force position and in protective labor legislation. Caught in a dilemma, the Bureau and the Department of Labor withdrew their opposition to an ERA in 1954, without endorsing it. Letting that issue lie, Leopold engaged the issue of women's social roles.

This new direction pushed the Bureau into activities like the 1955 White House Conference on Effective Uses of Womanpower, which Leopold described as "the beginning of new efforts on the part of the

U.S. Department of Labor to develop our country's manpower to the fullest." To this end, the Bureau became concerned with how assumptions about sex roles limited opportunity for women. The Labor Department hoped to resolve such issues by answering questions like whether "fear of male resentment" handicapped women so much that they "hesitate to seek job advancement."[19]

An internal memo in 1954 revealed how far the Bureau had moved from its initial advocacy position. Planning the White House Conference on Womanpower, one staff member wrote: "It was suggested at a staff meeting that unions be included along with women's civic organizations. If this is done I think that management representatives should be included also in order to make the group tripartite in character. . . . This time I would like to see us invite some of the trade associations in industries employing large numbers of women. . . . I believe it would be very useful for the Bureau to establish a cooperative working relationship with certain of these groups, especially those that have a definite connection with state legislation."[20]

The conference's keynote speaker, Roland Renne, offered the 567 participants a series of specific suggestions for increasing women's labor force participation. Two or more women might fill a single vacancy; jobs might be structured to meet the demands of those who wished to work part time or in the evening hours. He urged women to work more efficiently at home so they would have time for outside jobs, rejected any correlation between the increase in working mothers and rising juvenile delinquency, and suggested that even wives of prominent men might willingly work part time if "the proper cultural environment" could be developed. Turning to education, he decried early marriages that prevented women from acquiring professional training. The government, Renne thought, ought to foster policies to encourage women who did "marry young and have families to get started on their formal education and professional training before their children are fully grown." Finally, he urged greater economic incentives for women who worked as teachers and nurses and in other traditionally female jobs.[21]

These suggestions evoked at least one alarmed response. What was deplorable, wrote Bob Senser, a reporter for the weekly newspaper *WORK*, was not that the conference speakers hailed women's rapid entry into the work force as progress, "but rather that the hallelujahs were shouted with almost no dissent." The idea that "men and women should go forward together shoulder to shoulder in working life" was "a new crusade" conducted "under the auspices of the United States Government." And "hardly anybody said a word in protest. . . . No need to overthrow the established order. No reason to proclaim 'Women of the U.S. arise.' The beginnings of the new order are already here."[22]

Whatever his distress, Senser accurately gauged the conference's mood. It reflected a major turnabout in official thinking. Except in periods of national emergency, women's home-centeredness had been taken for granted by policy makers, the Labor Department, the Women's Bureau, and most women. Regardless of women's expanding participation in the wage labor force, ideology and practice had concurred in the assumption that women's future role was in the home. But slowly a new mentality was dawning. As government policy began to encourage women to move into the labor market, and women began to accept their status as permanent wage workers with the right to a job, they became eager for the rewards of that status.

Complaints of various kinds of discrimination flooded the Women's Bureau. And though it was sympathetic to the notion of equal access for women, the Bureau, tied into the Labor Department bureaucracy, no longer had the political capacity to act on their behalf. A letter from Mrs. W. B. McPherson of Jacksonville, Florida, was typical. "Women are not being assigned work . . . they could do," she wrote to the Bureau. And the Bureau replied that laws "do not usually prohibit discrimination on a sex basis in hiring or promotion of workers . . . moreover the Federal regulation applicable to Government contractors does not prohibit discrimination in employment on the basis of sex."[23]

The Bureau consistently held to the position that where the law did not explicitly forbid discrimination, it could do nothing. Baltimore postal service workers wrote bitterly to complain that though they had passed the appropriate civil service exams, their names were on a "female register which the postmaster does not wish to open for appointments" and they would therefore "never be given the same security of status that is given the men with whom we work. . . . Please help us to abolish this INSULT TO THE WOMANHOOD OF AMERICA!" they concluded. Leopold waited a month before writing identical answers to all four women. The Bureau had received assurance," she wrote, "that the Post Office Department is doing everything within its power to see that qualified individuals receive career status."[24] But in fact a woman's sex disqualified her from civil service jobs in the Post Office until the mid-sixties. To the wife of a disabled veteran who documented consistent discrimination in a Kentucky naval ordnance plant, the Women's Bureau declared itself powerless to intervene even though the plant decision on the woman's complaint stated flatly that "the *appointing officer has the authority to specify sex in making selections for positions*."[25]

The federal government was among the worst offenders. Not only did it permit supervisors to specify the sex of civil service appointees until 1962, it promoted unemployment policies that discriminated against women. Two female officers of Local 301 of the United Electrical Radio and Machine Workers of America in Schenectady complained that special works projects to aid the unemployed consisted of "construction projects of one type or another" which women were "not able to handle." Since women, they argued, "are at this moment the major group . . . suffering from lay offs in this area . . . it is . . . important for us to be able to suggest a program of work projects which also meets the needs of unemployed women workers." The Bureau did not reply to the letter.[26] But it did raise the issue of unemployment insurance for married women who left their jobs to move with their husbands to a new location and found themselves denied benefits. Under pressure from activists like CIO staff member Katherine Ellickson, it continued to agitate for more equitable Social Security benefits for married wage-earning women. But the time for change had not yet come.

Women's new sense of place in the job market yielded protests— not always unsuccessful—against trade unions too. Female union members complained that trade unions colluded with employers in eliminating female workers. "While accepting the women's dues, the union takes the attitude that women should not work anyway."[27] Three women sued the Ford Motor Company and the UAW. The Detroit *Free Press* reported that these women, who claimed to represent "105 others who had assigned claims to them . . . said they were laid off in 'flagrant breach' of the UAW Ford contract." The women protested that males "were hired shortly after, with no seniority. And . . . male workers laid off at the same time—with less seniority—were quickly rehired. . . . Union officials rebuffed all their attempts to file a grievance."[28]

And yet slowly the principles of seniority were beginning to work for women as well as against them. In response to a complaint from members of the Port Arthur, Texas, local of the Oil Workers' International Union, the Women's Bureau cited three cases where arbitration boards had held that women with seniority could not be bumped by males of lesser standing. In each instance, the boards ruled that sex was not a barrier to seniority, even where female seniority meant promotion into jobs customarily held by men.[29]

Hints of a changing mentality in the fifties—a new impatience— find their clearest expression in women's new understanding of the constraints of gender in a supposedly meritocratic society. "As I have been a stenographer for some fifteen years," wrote Hester Staff of Pleasant Ridge, Michigan, to the Women's Bureau, "I have pondered considerable [sic] about the unequal struggle that women have to support themselves in our society. The Roosevelt and Truman administrations made great strides in removing inequalities due to 'race, creed and color' but there seems to have been little improvement in the earning capacities of the female part of the population." What, she wanted to know, was being done about it?[30] Others were more strident. "I believe justice demands that we receive the same rights, privileges and protections as male workers," wrote a female union member from Missouri, who asked that the word "sex" be included in codes that banned discrimination on the grounds of race, color, or creed. She was not interested in the "so-called equal rights legislation" and she did not believe mothers of small children should work. But "those of us who are forced to support our children alone need help to save our jobs."[31]

Where justice was not forthcoming, a Brighton, Massachusetts, woman concluded, disillusionment would set in. Cathryn Crowley, a Michigan secretary, wrote to Alice Leopold: "We are brought up to believe in a democracy; we are told that if we have talent coupled with ambition we will go far; those of us who accept this challenge are at a definite disadvantage. We are not told that undemocratic elements are at play and that we still be hindered in our efforts simply because we are women. Someone should have told me years ago that I'd have to be content with half a loaf. . . . I wouldn't have tried so hard."[32]

These ideas may have been on the cutting edge in the 1950s. Yet they were forcefully articulated by some policy makers as well as by ordinary wage earners—and they reflected the language of meritocracy so popular in that decade. Women asked for equal access to employment not as a special favor to help them maintain their fitness to perform home roles, but as their right as members of a free-market economy that theoretically offered the opportunity to compete to all who wished to try. They defended their request in the language of individualism, insisting that every person had a responsibility to live up to her own capacities. Frieda Miller clearly articulated this notion in a series of postwar speeches. "I believe," she said shortly after the war, "that if opportunity to work on the basis of capacity is justice in war time, it is no less justice in peace."[33] In 1950 she insisted that even mothers of small children should have free choice as to whether they wished to enter the labor market. And a year later she encouraged women to work by appealing to them to distinguish between "essential family values and . . . the more or less incidental and customary surrounding circumstances." Changes in women's right to paid employment, she argued, were "not willful individual excursions but a phase of historical economic development of mass production by factory methods which took away from women in homes their old production activities for family welfare."[34] Florence Kluckhohn, sociologist and author of articles on employed mothers, drew the logical conclusion at the conference on womanpower: "We either make it easier for women to take their places in the occupations and accept their right as individualistic, achievement oriented Americans to be there, or we give to all the other activities she might pursue outside the home better organization and higher evaluation."[35]

Born when the stringent barriers to wage work broke down, ideas about women's right to work took shape in the decade that followed. The freedom that had been demanded by a few daring women in the twenties and pursued by the persistent in the fifties became in the sixties an objective sought by many.

At the beginning of the decade change seemed remote. The ideology of the home still successfully contained most women's aspirations. But as women with permanent commitments to work increasingly sought jobs, the seeds planted in the fifties germinated. Responding to the new climate and to incentives to acquire professional credentials, a new generation of young women began to emerge from colleges and universities. A relatively affluent middle sector, young and well-educated, entered the job market, doubling the number of female lawyers, doctors, and dentists in the space of a decade. For most, the initial commitment was a job until children came. As for the generation of young mothers who joined them, wage work itself presented new possibilities. With children safely off in school and suburban households sustained by labor-saving appliances, the extra income and involvement of wage work seemed attractive.

Poverty shaped the work force in another way. Earlier in the century it had been the common characteristics of women seeking jobs. In the postwar period, that was no longer true. But women still remained poorly paid, the median wage of full-time female workers dropping to 59, then 58 percent of the average man's wage by the mid-sixties. For women wage earners who were married—more than half had working husbands—the wage supplemented the husband's income, so their relative poverty was disguised. But single women and the one out of every five who headed a household—black or Hispanic, divorced or widowed—found themselves in the same situation as all women wage earners in the past: they could qualify for jobs only in the poorly paid women's sectors, and such jobs did not pay enough to cover child-care costs. Anxious to reduce the costs of maintaining poor families, Lyndon Baines Johnson began his "War on Poverty" programs to offer job training and child care for mothers. Such policy changes encouraged women to break out of traditional jobs. If they were to be trained, then why stay in poorly paid occupations? At the same time, women already in the job market started to demand jobs in nontraditional sectors.

By 1970, these pushes produced statistically visible changes. The number of women in skilled, predominantly male, trades rose to almost half a million: an increase of nearly 80 percent over 1960, twice that for women in all occupations, and eight times that for men in the skilled trades. Increases occurred in all kinds of jobs—among carpenters, construction workers, mechanics, electricians, plumbers, tool and die makers, machinists, and typesetters. The numbers still added up to only small proportions of women in these trades as a whole—no more than 2 or 3 percent in most—but they are significant because they predated or paralleled the rising women's movement and the federal regulations that emerged in that decade.

Important as the gains were, they diminished when looked at from a perspective that considered most women's lives. Still caught in the belief that the home came first, about one-third of the married women who earned wages took part-time jobs, and many took jobs for which their education and skills overqualified them. They chose work for the convenience of being close to home or for hours that suited children's schedules. Nevertheless, by 1970 more than 40 percent of wives worked for wages, and the rate among younger women with children had begun the dramatic acceleration that stunned analysts in the seventies.[36] It was too much to expect that women would continue to look on jobs as temporary. Even women who had entered the work force for their families soon began to seek jobs in which they could use their skills to achieve appropriate rewards.

As wage earning became the life style of all kinds of women—the educated, the married, the affluent as well as the needy—old patterns changed. No longer could it be said, as a presidential commission had claimed in 1957, that "the labor force behavior of women is characterized by part-time work." The pattern of female labor force participation had long been drawn as a pair of peaks with a valley representing the drop in participation rates when women quit to rear families. In the seventies the peaks flattened as women entered the labor force to stay. Yet women as individuals did not seem to benefit from the increased commitment to wage work of women as a group. They wondered why. The relatively low wages of female workers had historically been attributed to their attachment to the home. The attachment had diminished, but women's labor force position remained the same. Nor could it any longer be said that the high proportions of black workers among females were pulling down average wages for women in general. As the proportion of white women in the labor force climbed—to virtually equal the participation rates of black women by 1979—the rate of female wages stubbornly refused to rise. Black and white wage rates among women drew together by 1979. Yet the rates for women remained only 59 percent of those for men.

The tension implicit in the combination of rising work force participation and denial of egalitarian demands resulted in attempts to seek legislative relief. But the push for such measures as equal pay and fairer access to jobs encountered the age-old barrier of women's traditional sex roles. In the early sixties nondiscrimination measures foundered because policy makers were not yet ready to tackle this leviathan.

The Women's Bureau crept incrementally toward equal rights for women by trying to understand the factors that discouraged wage work among them and to increase opportunities for work. Other branches of the federal executive slowly came around to the same position. President John Kennedy, moved by the extent to which his New Frontier galvanized women into calling for an end to discrimination, created a Presidential Commission on the Status of Women in 1961. The White House statement establishing the Commission committed the Presidency to advance "the full partnership of men and women in our national life."[37] Yet Kennedy thought employment rights could be enhanced only by trying "to expand . . . opportunity generally in the economy." His Secretary of Labor, Arthur Goldberg, tied opportunities for women directly to a healthy economy rather than to human rights. "If our economy grows rapidly," he wrote to Eleanor Roosevelt, "it will be far easier to support enlarged community services. Indeed . . . the continued growth of the American economy will generally enhance the demand for the services which women workers can or do provide."[38]

But women were impatient. In a decade of assertive individualism, ambitious women and those who had always worked were in no mood to wait for what the Report of the Commission on the Status of Women called "expanding opportunities for all working people." The report provided the impetus for what the head of a woman's club called "the second woman suffrage battle." By now the tension had become explosive. Betty Friedan's *The Feminine Mystique* articulated it for many women. The book identified an invisible culture, a "mystique" that pervaded women's lives and continually reaffirmed outdated roles. As Friedan described it, the mystique "arrests their development at an infantile level, short of personal identity, with an inevitably weak core of self." To avoid this fate, Friedan suggested that women attempt to develop their own life patterns, their own sense of self. The book's instant success spoke poignantly of the shattering recognition it brought to many. The social realities that had justified accepting old patterns had changed.[39]

Aware that members of minority groups seemed to be successfully demanding access to pieces of the American dream, young white women absorbed the rhetoric and adopted some of the tactics of civil rights struggles to fight for their own freedom. For some, the struggle was still against simple discrimination, for equality. But for others, the search for equality uncovered an array of sex role stereotypes, an arsenal of cultural values that reinforced the limited self-perceptions that traditional family roles involved. These were heady discoveries, and as yet the idea of challenging them belonged to few women.

Most political activists turned their attention to legislation. In 1962, the Kennedy administration outlawed discrimination in the federal civil service, and in 1963 it pushed through Congress an Equal Pay Act prohibiting differential pay for men and women working at equivalent jobs. The Equal Pay act had its limits. Like the Fair Labor Standards Act, to which it was appended, it excluded domestic and farm workers, and it left employers free to continue simply to refuse women access to jobs. Then came the Civil Rights Act of 1964. Attempting to demonstrate what he considered the ludicrous nature of a clause regulating the hiring practices of private employers, Virginia's Senator Howard Smith threw the word "sex" into Title VII of the bill as a joke. When passage seemed imminent and a committee tried to remove the word, two women, Senator Margaret Chase Smith and Representative Martha Griffiths, threatened to stall the whole bill unless it was left in. Against the will of most legislators, "sex" became part of a clause that prohibited firms with fifteen or more employees from discriminating on account of religion, race, and ethnicity.

To its surprise, the Equal Employment Opportunities Commission created to administer Title VII found itself flooded by complaints of sexual discrimination. In response it created a series of guidelines employers could use to protect themselves against such charges. The EEOC also took seriously the task of harmonizing state protective labor laws with the Civil Rights Act, sometimes to the point of overturning those laws. Unable to handle individual protests, the overburdened EEOC decided to follow through only on class action cases, leaving many women with no recourse for their own problems. But the campaign against discrimination continued. Groups like the National Organization of Women and Women's Equity Action League, which emerged in the mid and late sixties, pushed for action in the courts and through state and local human rights commissions. By 1972 they had pressured every state legislature in the country into prohibiting sex discrimination in employment. Before 1964, only two states had such prohibitions. On the national level, Executive Order 11375, issued by President Johnson in 1968, forbade federal contractors from discriminating against women and, in an aggressive new mode, required them to file affirmative action programs indicating how they planned to improve employment opportunities for underrepresented groups. The goals and timetables demanded by affirmative action became in the seventies a major lever for opening long-closed jobs to women.[40]

The Women's Bureau, which supported and sustained these actions, now found itself caught in a contradiction. For years protective labor legislation had played a critical role in sustaining socially approved gender-based distinctions in the work force, as well as in channeling the labor force aspirations of each new generation of wage-earning women into socially approved areas. Preserving these distinctions— which was the purpose of opposition to an ERA—ran counter to the Women's Bureau strategy of seeking equality incrementally, through legislation guaranteeing equal pay, ending discrimination against pregnant workers, weeding out job discrimination, and so on. By the late 1960s, it became clear to the Women's Bureau and the Department of Labor that they could not both seek de facto equal rights through legislation that prohibited invidious distinctions on the basis of gender and simultaneously invoke the protection of laws that assumed significant gender difference in the work force. In 1970, the same year that the Department of Labor did so, the Bureau finally endorsed the concept of an Equal Rights Amendment. The Congress sent an ERA to the states in 1972, as the question of women's roles was becoming a major public issue.

As it turned out, moving toward, even achieving, equality at work proved to be the beginning, not the end, of the battle. Each step on the road to equality—equal pay, an end to discrimination in hiring and training, access to promotion—exposed a deeply rooted set of social attitudes that tried to preserve women's attachment to the home and hindered a commitment to the job world. To work freely, women required control over their own reproduction and sexuality. They felt entitled to sexual gratification, as men had always been, and to access to birth control and to abortion if necessary. Economic independence encouraged freer life styles, reducing the dependence of women on men and permitting a genuine choice of life partners—

male or female. Women who earned adequate incomes could choose
not to have children or among a variety of child-care arrangements
if they had them. Freedom for women to live without men, to live
with them without benefit of legal marriage, to create two-career families, or to live without families at all posed staggering challenges to
traditional values.

Demands for job equality, no matter how limited, raised serious
questions. The rules of work, for example, seemed incompatible with
a family life that involved two working adults or a single working
parent. "We keep the old male work rules, 9 to 5, 40 hours a week,
and if there's overtime, you do it or you don't keep your job," said
one sociologist. "Neither men nor women can combine working and
parenting under these rules. We need new ways of working."[41] Working by these rules raised questions about family life, child rearing, and
the socialization of children. Work for women, in the words of one
wage-earning mother, "is considered like a luxury. And usually it's
the woman who stays out of work when the child is sick."[42]

The inequality of the job market was rooted in the inequality of
the home, which in turn was rooted in fundamental assumptions about
women's biology, psyche, and social roles. Professional caucuses and
special interest groups examined the complex network of socialization, sexuality, the media, and public policy that perpetuated inequality. For the first time the way in which home and work had
historically confirmed each other emerged into public view. To alter
the conditions under which women worked required a fundamental
reevaluation in sex roles, a rethinking of male/female relations. The
chairman of the National Commission on Manpower Policy described
in 1977 what was happening as "a revolution in the roles of women
that will have an even greater impact than the rise of Communism
and the development of nuclear energy. . . . Its secondary and tertiary
consequences are really unchartable."[43]

The threatening implications of changing sex roles and changing
values encouraged some women to join groups like HOT DOG (Hu-
manitarians Opposed to Degrading Our Girls) and HOW (Happiness
of Womanhood) to fight the ERA and to restore "morality" to American life. HOW, founded in 1971 in San Diego, boasted 10,000 members a year later, and a platform that declared, "There is a distinct
difference in male and female. A true lady will delight in accentuating
that difference, and through the art of femininity, she will inspire masculinity that "with everyone working no one has the time to be
concerned about the problems in our society. Let's strive towards a generation of Professional Housewives."[44] Between 1965 and 1975 more
than 400,000 women paid thirty dollars each for an eight-week series

of classes given by an organization dedicated to male supremacy called Fascinating Womanhood. The classes promised to teach women how to rejuvenate their marriages and to save society and morality at the same time.

Opponents of changing values insisted on the historical legitimacy of the ancient family—appealing to its "biblically ordained nature . . . with the father as head of the household and the other subject to his ultimate authority." People like Paul Weyrich, founder and executive director of the ultra-right-wing Committee for the Survival of a Free Congress, found not only women's liberation threatening, but homosexuality and sexual freedom as well. "Life is a lot more sane and livable," said one traditionalist, "if you know where you stand. Women need to know that somebody will have the authority and make the decision and that your job is to be happy with it."

All these groups targeted the women's movement as the enemy. Confusing the symptom with the cause, they failed to identify the deep roots of change and attacked women for what they defined as self-centeredness and lack of respect for old values. Some took stands against easy divorce and objected to unmarried couples living together. Others organized to stop the separate states from ratifying the ERA. One group suggested a Constitutional convention that would forever prohibit physicians from doing abortions. In 1980, these groups united in a "profamily" coalition unified by a concern for traditional moral values. "We realized," said Phyllis Schlafly, a leader of "Stop ERA," that "if we didn't get out and defend our values, this little feminist pressure group was going to end up changing our schools, our laws, out textbooks, our constitution, our military—everything—and end up taking our husbands' jobs away."[45]

Since social order was conceived of as wedded to the home, it seemed to disintegrate as the family changed its form and focus. An undercurrent of sympathy supported antifeminist positions and rallied in support of traditional values. Clinging to the past as a life raft, many insisted on the primacy of the family for women; for if tradition denied women the opportunity to make independent choices, it nourished old and familiar forms. So the ERA, lacking a handful of votes in three states, stalled. New "Right to Life" forces emerged to legislate away from women the reproductive freedom they had only just begun to exercise. Organized black women remained ambivalent to the political directions of an essentially white women's movement. Having long ago discovered that racism restricted their ability to provide economic sustenance for themselves and their families, they refused now to believe that if problems of sexual bias disappeared, those of race discrimination would not still remain. Nor did issues of sexual liberation touch them deeply, for if race discrimination were to diminish, many hoped that the benefits of economic opportunity would allow them a genuine choice. On the left, Christopher Lasch, among other social commentators, pleaded for a return to the natural authority of the family as a way of opposing what he saw as the atomized self-centeredness of women. Male workers, threatened by the influx of women into traditionally male sectors, resorted to harassment on the job. In government, the Labor Department continued to identify women workers separately, insisting that their presence in the labor force inflated unemployment figures "which used to measure only the efforts of male heads of households to find jobs."[46]

Such resistance inhibited the speed with which alterations in fundamental patterns of sex segregation in the work force occurred. By the early 1980s women still occupied limited kinds of jobs with limited opportunities; and a disproportionate degree of poverty still characterized female-headed families.

But the logic of women's changing economic roles moved inexorably against these old patterns, keeping alive the struggle for equality as families came to terms with change. Rationalizations involving family need had first validated women's work force roles, then kept women at work as the family's needs expanded. When economic imperatives acquired their own momentum so that even an intact family with a fully employed male head-of-household could hardly maintain expected consumption patterns without two wage earners, women were locked into wage labor whether men willed it or not.[47] To remove women from the work force now—a notion embodied in the wishful thinking of traditionalist groups and reflected in the way the Department of Labor presented statistics on unemployment—would require a major change in the national standard of living. It would threaten the health of an economy based on expanding production. If women were to hold jobs permanently, they would inevitably continue to press for some of the rewards of wage labor, and to develop life styles that ensured at least an even chance at them.

With the home no longer the center of their daily lives, and with no expectation, for most women, that it ever again would be, increasing numbers were forced to make difficult decisions about their priorities. MANY YOUNG WOMEN, NOW SAY THEY'D PICK FAMILY OVER CAREER," headlined the New York *Times* in 1980. The college students interviewed hoped to marry men who "would be more involved in child rearing than their fathers" and to take jobs that offered maternity leaves for up to seven years. Confronted with the difficulties of finding cooperative employers and mates with flexible job schedules, these young women exploded angrily at the pressures imposed by feminism "to work, to marry, and raise families without providing answers as to how all of this should be done."[48]

But the pressures were not imposed by feminism. Feminists merely called attention to them in the seventies and began to search for solutions. Their experiences in coping with new roles led them to ask the questions that challenged the ideology of sexual stratification. As more women tried to cope, the questions spread. In every class and racial group, the possibility of decent wages for women pressed upon old stratification systems and pried open educational and vocational training opportunities. To take full advantage of these required of women a different mind-set, a less submissive psychology, a greater ambition. Whether or not any individual woman decided to accept this challenge for herself and her children, few had the luxury of choosing not to choose. Ever-increasing numbers of women found that the accumulated pressures of the postwar period had pushed the ideology of the home from the center of consciousness. In its place women at the edge of change began to search for new perceptions of self and new relationships to power and authority.

Home and work roles, seemingly complementary in the preindustrial period, and tightly regulated thereafter, had by the 1980s burst their constraints. As long as women's social virtue was clearly attached to their home roles, they could go out to work without threatening the assumptions on which family and labor market rested. But when the majority of women moved into wage work—albeit as a way of helping out in the home—the contraditions between the two soon threatened the traditional organization of the family and the power relationships that derived from it.

The generation of women reared in the fifties, who matured in the mid- and late sixties, arrived at the threshold of work more or less conscious of these issues. They moved into jobs and family lives making seemingly individual decisions that, taken together, challenged the historical roles of their parents and would shape the lives of their children.

A Note of Acknowledgment

The notes that follow document fairly completely the particular sources from which I have drawn examples, illustrations, and support for the arguments made in the text. They neglect, however, the intellectual forces that have informed the questions around which this book is built. I began thinking about and researching this volume in the early nineteen-seventies, when the women's movement was at the height of its militance, and a new social history had begun to emerge from the experience of civil rights and antiwar activism. These movements spawned a search for new ways of explaining our past; they posed questions not asked earlier, and they insisted on examining facts that other fishermen (to borrow an analogy from E. H. Carr) would have thrown back into the sea. The fertile decade that followed produced new research—on which, as the reader will find in the notes, I have relied heavily—and a new set of constructs that are not so clearly visible, but are nonetheless critical underpinnings of this book.

The transformation of woman's work over three centuries derives its contemporary significance from attempts to explain continuing sex-role divisions. When such role divisions are justified as part of a "natural order of things" they become immutable and unchangeable. At the other extreme, when they are dismissed as a consequence of particular juxtapositions of historical phenomena, they are seen as relatively malleable. Understanding the historical roots of sexual stratification in the labor force, then, is clearly of importance to all of us.

Initial attempts at exploring this pervasive issue came from feminist theoreticians. Three areas of thought provided fruitful contributions to the patterns of change I have tried to elucidate in this volume. The first is the relationship of woman's unpaid housework to the process of production. Raised by socialists interested in clarifying woman's relationship to class and class struggle, the issue focused attention on the hidden roles of women in sustaining the economy. Woman's unpaid labor, the argument went, was crucial in two ways. By caring for children and socializing them to future work, women reproduced the paid labor force. And in so far as their household work subsidized the paid labor of men as well as of some women who earned wages, it has been crucial to capital formation. A second group of theorists approached the issue of role division from the perspective of a "family wage." The idea that a man should earn an income adequate to support a whole family appears to have become an object of struggle among American workers earlier in terms of industrial development than in Europe. Arguably such an idea sprang logically out of the relative affluence of the New World and the aspirations its immigrants brought with them. The debate is important in any attempt to understand the choices of females in relationship to paid labor, for widespread notions of a "family wage" would influence how they perceived their own roles as workers as well as how other workers perceived them. Such a notion also influences the practices of employers responsible for selecting the wage labor force. It raises a third theoretical issue: whether such ideas and others that spin off from them are agents of change in themselves— or, how the structure of ideas that has influenced women's lives is related to their real economic roles. This question poses particular problems for historians of women since so much of our past has demonstrated the tenacity of cultural frameworks in inhibiting autonomy and choice.

No one has done more to concretize these issues than Gerda Lerner, who has repeatedly insisted on the necessity of examining woman's experience as the center of the historical process. In a series of essays collected in *The Majority Finds Its Past*, she has argued that the definition of history itself must alter in a way that encompasses the forceful activity of half the human race. Less dramatically, labor and social historians have begun the laborious research necessary to translate abstract theoretical constructs into a series of verifiable hypotheses. Of necessity, this work interconnects with other intellectual currents, especially in economics and sociology.

Recent scholarship, for example, has grappled with the pushes and pulls that influenced particular groups of women to seek wages. I think immediately of the work of sociologist Ruth Milkman on the depression of the 1930s, and of that of economist Claudia Goldin and historian Elizabeth Pleck on black women in the late nineteenth century. Such work has led sociologist Veronica Beechey to conclude that women's work has to be seen not as divided between family work and wage work, but as all of a piece. I would agree. The notion that women played two different roles is less useful than that of a continuum between family and wage work. Women may perform one kind of task or another at a given moment of the day, or cycle in their lives. They may choose to reject one or the other role entirely, their behavior and their opportunities indelibly influenced by ideology, culture, and socialization. Thus, shifts in technology and labor force needs, the changing structure and function of the family, and changing ideas about women and their roles are intertwined—as dependent on each other as the separate strands of a braid. Like a braid, these strands may be parted for purposes of analysis, but to look at one without the others is to compound illusion.

The recent good work in women's labor force participation provides the pieces of this analysis. This work, however, lends itself to a variety of interpretations. Historians of the family and some sociologists have used notions of modernization to explain transformations in the kind of work women do. They suggest that the increased per capita output and the transition to mass consumption, normally associated with industrialization and urbanization, loosened family ties, enabling women to move into wage labor. Presented in the context of a debate on the function of the family (in the work of Neil Smelser, for example), such movement seems to free women. But more recently historians such as Joan Scott and Louise Tilly have noted that family ties persisted during the industrialization process and that women normally engaged in wage work not as a liberation from their traditional roles but as an extension of them. This perspective tells us something about why women have remained in consistently disadvantaged labor force positions despite their increasing labor force participation, and it is buttressed by the work of such economists as Michael Piore, Harriet Zellner, and Mary Stevenson, who have addressed the issue of how the labor market is structured. They suggest that crowded labor markets, failure to invest in human capital, and the dual, or segmented labor market all bear some responsibility for women's occupational segregation.

These suggestions surely offer accurate descriptions of the mechanisms that lock women into place. Still, they leave us reaching for explanations of why women are willing that it should be so. To resolve this issue requires an exploration of the conscious determinants of behavior, of women's roles as active agents in their own lives. Here the new labor history has begun to suggest some approaches. David Montgomery has evaluated the changing labor process and the shop-floor resistance that resulted from it in terms of a broad spectrum of ideas and customs on which workers' movements rested. Herbert Gutman has suggested that ethnically derived cultural identity acts as a force of its own to influence workers' behavior and their work choices. Though neither historian places women at the center of his research, both kinds of analysis raise questions about the role of custom in maintaining woman's home-bound roles and in determining the choices she makes in entering the labor force. They encourage us to focus on what Gutman has called the "self-activity" of the woman worker, as well as on the essential role of gender relations in structuring an emerging labor force.

If the scholarship of the past decade has not yet come to terms with the pattern of female wage labor, it has provided important insights and critical questions. Without it, this book could never have been written. Instead of criticizing that work, or analyzing it, I have tried here to incorporate its pieces into a meaningful whole: to explore the interrelationship of ideas and economics and family lives, as they existed separately and together. In so doing, my inability to footnote the specific contributions of developing theory measures the speed with which we have incorporated it into our general knowledge and speaks more eloquently about its value than a dozen footnotes could. It constitutes the foundation stone on which this book gratefully builds.

Epilogue

A generation into the women's movement, and three decades after women began to demand equal opportunity at work, even a casual observer could count the changes in the lives of women and men. Most women—including those with small children—worked for wages. Most men—including those with good jobs—expected that their wives would earn incomes of their own. At first glance the picture reveals a satisfying, even exciting, movement away from the sharply divided gender roles that had characterized the working lives of men and women within living memory to an apparent confluence of roles and attitudes, a greater flexibility in the relations between family and work. But a closer look uncovers a more volatile landscape. As women moved towards parity in many areas of the labor force, they sparked an intense debate about what their expanding commitments to wage work would mean for family life. The debate exposed sharp distinctions in the options available to women and men of different class and racial/ethnic groups. At issue were two questions: whether gendered relationships could be sufficiently re-negotiated to enable women, like men, to become more completely engaged with the workforce, and its corollary, whether achieving success at work would result in sacrificing affective and caring human relationships.

To be sure, the figures suggested that women had breached the major economic barriers to their search for equality. Between 1970 and 2000, women entered the labor force at twice the rate of men with mothers of small children in the vanguard. Astonishing all observers, the proportion of wage-earning mothers of children under six doubled in these three decades—rising from 30 to more than 63 percent. The wage gap between men and women narrowed until full-time women earners, who had averaged less than 60 cents to every dollar earned by the median male worker, hit 77 cents in 1993, before settling back to 75 cents in 1997.[1] Occupational segregation, especially in professional and managerial jobs, diminished rapidly as schools of law and medicine, dentistry, architecture, and business admitted women on the basis of merit.

And yet the numbers did not seem to be adding up to equality either in the home or in the workforce. Skepticism came from the women and men who seemed to be benefiting most. They asked, What would happen to the children? Who would care for the ill and the elderly? How, given that few men chose the stay-at-home role, would a new generation of men fill the vacuum in family lives created by growing demands on women? Would equality in the labor market lead to equality in the home? Or would inequality in the home stymie women's labor market goals? Would women engineer a revolution in the labor market, reshaping it into more family friendly configurations? And what of poor women and single mothers whose efforts to earn incomes could undermine their search for positive family experiences? Was equality worth the price?

In the lives of individuals these questions took concrete form in a series of difficult choices about whether women could in fact "have it all." But there were no easy answers. Many women established high-powered careers in law, academia, and the financial world only to discover that they had put off having children until it was too late. Others—tired of struggling to balance child care, household maintenance, and income-generating jobs—questioned the promise of wage-work and began to drop out of the labor force. And when poor single mothers were forced into jobs without regard for their children's well-being, some questioned the irony of a social transformation that valued women's caring roles so little. In the late twentieth century, the restrictive, tightly twisted braid of family, labor force demands, and old-fashioned ideas about what men and women should do had begun, unevenly, to unravel. And yet its demise produced as much uncertainty as satisfaction.

Most women and men found themselves caught in the maelstrom. While a privileged few sought self-fulfillment at work, expanding consumption, stagnant or declining male wages, and the fear of inflation pushed every family member out of the home. In a competitive global market, where most new jobs paid low wages, few families could get by on one income, so the less fortunate settled for routine, repetitive jobs.

The price of continuing prosperity, of maintaining the American standard of living, was a dual income family, which, paradoxically, undermined the traditional gender roles that the American standard of living was meant to support.

The most unambiguous feature in the rapidly changing picture was the decline of the male bread-winner family. For nearly two hundred years, since the advent of the industrial revolution, American men and women had assumed that the ideal family consisted of a wage-earning male and a non-earning stay-at-home wife. The pattern reflected the lifestyles of middle- income, urban families, remaining only a dream for the majority of black families, and for poor and immigrant families of all kinds. Yet by the 1950s, it was deeply rooted in American culture. The image of the non-earning wife set the standard for masculine and feminine roles, influenced educational options for boys and girls, framed men's and women's expectations of the job market, and provided differential tax benefits to those who hewed the traditional line. It also created a chilling, even hostile, atmosphere for those who remained unmarried for reasons of sexual preference, divorce, or a desire not to partner.

The ideal of a family supported by a male breadwinner came under fire from two directions: the late 1960's women's movement, which supported self-fulfillment and economic independence for both sexes, and the practical needs of an economy fuelled by ever increasing consumer demands. Together they enticed many Americans to try out other family forms. As the twentieth century crept to a close, the Census Bureau reported that a quarter of all households contained one person; one of every seven was headed by a single parent, and one of every 20 consisted of non-family members living together. In 1998, the census reported, married couples constituted just over half (52.9 percent) of all American households. Only a quarter of American households contained a married couple with children.

To sustain household incomes, families of every size found themselves putting in more hours of work. Both partners had jobs in 60 percent of married-couple families, and second income earners, generally wives, contributed a third of all household incomes.[2] The presence of children encouraged women to work, rather than the opposite: of families with children, only about one in five relied on a husband's wages alone.[3] In what is arguably the speediest shift of any industrial nation, the labor force participation rate of married women with small children exploded, passing the half-way mark in 1987.[4] A decade later the Bureau of Labor Statistics reported that more than half of all new mothers returned to the work force within a year of giving birth.[5] By 1995, 70 percent of mothers with husbands earned their own incomes.

Prosperous households with two workers added an average of ten hours to the family's working week in the 1980s and 1990s; less prosperous households added five to six hours.[6] The resulting "time bind" to use sociologist Arlie Hochschild's felicitous phrase, increased stress on family life and provoked a series of debates around questions like were women with two jobs "stressed" or blessed?"[7] "The workforce has changed, Hochschild wrote, "women have changed. But most workplaces have remained inflexible in face of the family demands of their workers and at home, most men have yet to really adapt to the changes in women."[8] The result was a "stalled revolution."

With few exceptions, men resisted efforts to redistribute responsibilities within the family. Surveys showed that as late as 1990 men with wage-earning wives tended to do less household labor than those whose wives did not hold jobs. Especially in low-income families, marginally employed men perceived their manhood as contingent on avoiding household labor.[9] Still most men moved towards sharing child care more equitably. Yet only 40 percent of fathers (compared to three-quarters of all mothers) thought they should sacrifice careers for their children.[10] And up to the end of the 1980s, two-thirds of male college seniors expected, when they married, to put their jobs first. For a man, choosing not to be employed remained a difficult choice. As one father who fantasized about staying at home with his three sons put it, "how do we give up identities that rely so much on what we do at work?"[11]

Given the lack of support at home, it isn't surprising that many women with choices opted to marginalize themselves in the labor force. More than 20 percent of mothers with partners chose part-time work in 1996, compared to only 12 or 13 percent of those without partners.[12] Some women with well-paid partners resorted to the familiar tactic of "sequencing"—establishing themselves in a career, dropping out to have children and then returning at some point to a job that did not conflict with motherhood. Others left the labor force altogether. To mitigate the career effects of these choices, Felice Schwartz, president of Catalyst, a prominent labor force research firm, proposed that corporations develop special paths for their most valuable female employees with families. Feminists angrily accused her of advocating a "Mommy Track." Her solution, they argued, would set a new double standard, holding women alone responsible for the family adjustments necessary for women's workforce participation, and setting precedents that stereotyped mothers as unable to perform in high-powered jobs.[13]

As the choices of well-off women expanded, those of women with poorly paid partners or none at all, narrowed. The incomes of about 70 percent of wage-earning women fended off poverty in their families, sometimes bringing an inadequate single income into the middle-income range.[14] These women, who often worked at the lowest wages, discovered that a slow rise in minimum wages helped them increase their contributions to the family but more frequently poor women found themselves pushed into second jobs. Lone mothers found this especially difficult, sometimes putting together two or even three part-time jobs, none of them with benefits, in order to make ends meet. But dual-income families also resorted to such jobs. One study of Vermont, for example, revealed that wives tended to take a second part-time job when they needed to pay extra bills. In contrast, men who already had good jobs, did so as a way of "righting the gender balance between themselves and their wives when the employment of their wives threatened a kind of rough equality."[15]

Changes in welfare laws increased the pressure on the poorest families. When the Social Security Act became law in 1935, it embodied the prevailing wisdom that children without fathers were best cared for in their own homes by their mothers. To keep mothers out of the workforce, the program gave public assistance to children, and, after 1941, to their mothers or caretakers as well. The children of deceased, male, social security contributors also received state support after 1941—ultimately in the form of more generous non-means tested benefits. But in those early days, state policy reinforced the widespread notion that mothers were best off at home.

In the late 1960s, the same tide that swept well-educated, young women and middle-class wives into the labor force undermined commitments to give poor mothers the opportunity to care for their children without wage work. Disturbed by a rapid expansion of welfare rolls, legislators and an impatient public pressured mothers to take jobs. A new perspective on working mothers encouraged them to label those who stayed at home or relied on inadequate part-time jobs as "lazy" work avoiders.[16] In 1967 and again in 1981, Congress insisted that mothers of school-age children take waged jobs unless there were extenuating circumstances like disability or the absence of child care. Finally, in 1988, the Family Support Act required states to put women to work as a condition of federal support. Cognizant of objections that minimum wages could not support families, fully aware that many children would lose health benefits, and knowing that public child care systems would not have spaces for the children of newly employed mothers, most states complied half-heartedly. Congress responded with the Personal Responsibility and Work Opportunity Act, passed in 1996, which ended welfare entirely and substituted a program called Temporary Assistance to Needy Families. Its five year life-time limit on aid to all recipients of public assistance, including mothers, and its insistence that even during these years all recipients work at assigned jobs trumpeted the assumption that all women, even the mothers of small infants would be better off "out to work."

Very little transitional help accompanied these harsh requirements. States got block grants for child care and job-training: most used only small fractions of the available monies. But when mothers who could not find adequate child care failed to turn up for assigned jobs, they were penalized with reduced stipends.[17] Nor did states adequately plan to train women for available jobs. Instead, they adopted "work first" policies, putting people in dead-end jobs that required little training or education.[18] There were exceptions: Wisconsin implemented innovative strategies for providing good day care and enabled larger proportions of women to work than in most other states.[19] A few communities worked with small businesses to train former welfare recipients for satisfying jobs. Chicago's Greater West Town Development project, for example, received national attention for successfully training dozens of women to become skilled woodworkers.[20]

In the meantime, the private sector faced the challenge of relieving the tensions on working families. Faced with a booming economy and a tight labor market, and sometimes goaded by labor union contracts, corporations began to compete for workers by offering services to families. The "family friendly"' workplace offered maternity and parental leaves with guaranteed jobs on return, flexible working hours to enable parents to come later or leave earlier for family purposes, and sometimes financial support for child care. Some offices welcomed babies and encouraged co-workers to cover for parents besieged by a toddler's tears. Others provided on-site day care, or restructured work to allow parents to do their jobs at home.[21]

While trade unions and a few corporations attempted to ameliorate pressures on working families, investments in public services stagnated. Despite efforts to give tax credits to working families, the United States lagged far behind other countries in its capacity to encourage family life in tandem with wage work. The United States alone, did not require employers to provide paid vacations; nor did it mandate paid maternity leaves or health insurance. In an effort to move slightly forward, feminists proposed legislation to require employers to provide 12 weeks of unpaid leave to their employees. Their first effort successfully passed Congress in 1990, only to be vetoed by President George H. W. Bush. Signed with a flourish by President William Clinton on February 5, 1993—the first significant legislative act of his presidency—the Family

Medical Leave Act mandated that employers with 50 or more workers provide up to 12 weeks of unpaid leave to workers who needed to care for sick children or parents, or for the birth or adoption of a child. In 2002, California became the first state in the union to mandate six weeks of *paid* parental leave.

These initiatives did little to solve the problems of the neediest women. While almost half of more affluent parents chose to pay for organized, and presumably higher quality day care, more than a third of poor women left their children with neighbors or relatives. The workplaces of low-wage workers rarely offered on-site day care, and the neighborhoods in which they lived sometimes lacked the public amenities that made work easier for their middle-class counterparts. Poor public transportation, unsafe neighborhoods, inconvenient shopping and day care, long delays for health care for themselves and their children, all made it difficult for poor women to reconcile wage work with satisfying family lives. Nor did the Family Medical Leave Act provide the poor with much relief. It covered only those who had been employed for at least 25 hours a week, for a full year, and in a company that employed at least 50 workers—conditions that the vast majority of low-wage workers could not meet.[22] Few low-wage workers had enough savings to allow for time out of jobs to meet family needs; most had either no partner at all or one with a low-wage job and many were ineligible for unemployment insurance, so they did not benefit even from enforced idleness. Under the circumstances, many women could not afford to take time off even where the law allowed it.

While women's new roles introduced turmoil into family life, the labor market had not become correspondingly more comfortable for women in 2000 than it had been at the start of the women's movement in 1970. In the year 2000, women constituted 47 percent of the labor force—a figure projected to rise slowly in the following decade, and to reach 48 percent in 2010. Young women entering the labor market in this period faced sharply differentiated prospects. The ambitious and well-educated found few barriers to mobility in new and growing areas like finance, banking, management, and law. Lucrative careers awaited those willing to work long hours and to sacrifice family life for the sake of advancement. For these women, no matter their race or ethnic background, the wage gap narrowed dramatically: Black, white, Hispanic, or Asian, young women averaged more than 90 percent of men's wages. Yet when women hit their 30s, and began to marry and have children, their wages declined relative to men of the same age and in the same kinds of jobs.[23] And sooner or later, most women hit the fabled "glass ceiling" the very top levels of the corporate world to which they could still hardly aspire.[24]

The uneven changes are evident in the military. On its face, the armed services were transformed by the recruitment of women: in 2000 women constituted nearly 12 percent of all the armed services, and 12 percent of officers as well. The Marines and the Navy lifted the last prohibitions against women in combat in 1993. But women constituted only 5 percent of the officers in the highest pay-grades, and as of 1996, only 11 of the 968 generals were female. The numbers raise questions about whether women can be as effective as men, not for genetic or biological reasons, but because the culture of the armed forces—like that of every large corporation—militates against their best performance.

For those less fortunately positioned, the labor market posed greater obstacles. Pulled by the demand for labor in the prosperous nineties, and pushed by restrictions on government support programs, poorly educated and trained women faced a more difficult prospect. Their unemployment rates had dropped, like those of men, but the poorest among them still had twice as much trouble as more educated women in finding jobs. When they did get work, they discovered that the jobs did not bring many advantages. The economic forces that encouraged employers to demand less loyalty of their workers and more productive labor, fostered a huge growth in temporary, contingent, and part-time jobs. These jobs generally paid low wages, lacked opportunities for advancement, and provided no health insurance, paid vacations, or unemployment insurance. One of every five women workers held a marginal job in the year 2000.[25]

In other areas of the labor market, contradictions belie seemingly dramatic improvements in the numbers. For example, in the span of 30 years, women doubled their representation in skilled trades—but the numbers are so tiny as to have had little impact. As of 2000, women made up 2 percent of all licensed plumbers and electricians, and only one and a half percent of carpenters. They still held minuscule numbers of jobs in the construction trades, which employed nearly 40 percent of all men. Similarly, on paper, women significantly improved their positions in sales, rising to 63 percent of the work force. But most of the gains occurred in the retail sector where women had always predominated. And even there, publicly visible lawsuits like those brought on behalf of female employees against giant employers like Sears, Home Depot, and Wal-Mart failed to improve woman's status.

By the spring of 1986, women constituted more than half of the professionals in the country. They continued to make impressive strides in areas like economics and law and among university professors, dentists, and physicians. Still, a breakdown reveals that their strengths remained in their old arenas: as teachers, librarians, social workers, and health care professionals. Men retained their hold in engineering and in the prestigious professions. And if the proportion of female entrepreneurs rose dramatically, they tended to be over-represented in small businesses and scarce in multi-million dollar enterprises.[26]

At the other end of the scale, the majority of women remained enmeshed in household and personal services. They were still 98 percent of all the secretaries; 97 percent of all the child care and domestic workers; 97 percent of nursery school and kindergarten teachers; 93 percent of registered nurses. And, in an ironic bow to equality, the proportion taking second jobs climbed to nearly 6 percent by the mid-1990s—coming close to the falling numbers of men with second jobs.

To break down occupational sex segregation, the government and private employers resorted to affirmative action. Enjoined by a presidential executive order in 1968, and enforced by the Department of Labor, affirmative action was initially conceived to deal with racial segregation in jobs. But in 1970, pressure from women's groups like the National Organization for Women (NOW) and the Women's Research and Education Institute (WREI) pushed the Department of Labor and the Equal Employment Opportunity Commission to extend the strategy to women. Affirmative action, as then conceived, involved encouraging employers to reach out and find members of minority groups and women, and, all other qualifications being equal, to hire members of these groups in preference to others. To put muscle behind the strategy, the federal government required federal contractors to adopt hiring goals for diversifying their workforces, and timetables by which they intended to measure success. The EEOC adopted a similar system to encourage private employers. Federal enforcement lagged in the 1980s, when the Reagan administration concluded that job preferences unfairly discriminated against white men by imposing what it called "quotas" on employers. In 1985, the Reagan administration finally ended the policy with respect to federal contractors.[27]

A promising strategy in the 1970s (sex segregation declined by 10 percent over all in that decade), preferential treatment was responsible for encouraging huge firms like AT&T to train more women for high-paying jobs. Adopted by almost every state, affirmative action laws enabled some women to successfully sue for jobs. In one precedent-setting case, Lillian Joyce got a coveted job as a road dispatcher in California, when she sued under the state's equal opportunity law.[28] And a changing labor market, including shortages of skilled workers, encouraged some companies, to take their own affirmative steps. The

Corning Glass works garnered favorable national publicity when it adopted new mentoring and training programs to pave the path to promotion for black men and most women.[29]

But affirmative action was fiercely challenged by successful lawsuits from white men who claimed that establishing goals for women and minorities discriminated against them.[30]

To discourage women and emphasize their own solidarity, men resorted to what we now call sexual harassment. Their tactics included sexually suggestive remarks, comments on a woman's clothing and appearance, and sometimes threats for refusals to comply with sexual demands. They encompassed more elusive strategies as well, like refusing to mentor women trainees, failing to cooperate with female managers, sabotaging equipment, and even altering work records to make women look incompetent. As legal historian Vicki Schultz puts it, sexual harassment served as "a means for men to claim work as masculine turf."[31]

At first, women swallowed their complaints for fear of losing face and retaliation: "In those early days," recalled land-surveyor, Vali Cooper, "you had to keep it to yourself, not let them see you cry."[32] But a coterie of feminist lawyers, led by Catherine MacKinnon, set to work to alter the legal framework. Partly as a result of their efforts, in 1980 the Equal Employment Opportunities Commission issued guidelines describing impermissible sexual behavior in the workplace. And by the spring of 1986, the Supreme Court had agreed that sexual harassment was a form of sexual discrimination.[33] In the succeeding decade, the courts slowly expanded the grounds on which women (and men too) could sue for discrimination to include negative actions towards all workers on account of their sex, whether or not the actions were sexual in nature. In principle, at least, the Court had signaled its disapproval of behavior that sent negative and unwelcoming messages to wage-earning women.

All the difficulties and the still unsettled decisions about how to adapt the labor force to women, and family life to the demands of dual wage work, reveal profound underlying tensions about appropriate gender norms. Advocates of women's equality applaud changes in household patterns, seeing evidence of a growing acceptance of women's roles beyond the family and the possibilities of real choices for men as well as women. Opponents insist that greater independence for women (including the possibilities for initiating divorce, and remaining unattached to a male partner) mark a deterioration of family values, and threaten the American way of life.

And yet growing legions of wage-earning women in the labor market would be hard put to agree on whether and how earning wages and making a living has affected their lives. For some, the best educated and the most affluent, the gains are palpable: more choices, and happier lives despite, perhaps because of, the challenge that combining two roles reflects. For them, the remaining constraints on melding work and home are cultural, a shift in attitudes that especially transforms notions of masculinity to incorporate shared family responsibilities and might reduce demands of American workers to the more reasonable levels of other industrial countries. For women who are compelled to take poorly paid, dead-end jobs without adequate social and family support systems, the labor market offers neither relief from poverty nor opportunity for them or their children. For them, the constraints are social and economic as well as cultural. They require a dramatic shift in government policies to level the playing field and to permit real choices in both jobs and family lives. Western European models might serve as a starting point, offering subsidized and available quality child care, national health insurance schemes, safe and reasonably priced housing, along with such labor market amenities as shorter working days and weeks, mandated paid vacations, and paid parental and maternity leaves.

To achieve even part of this program requires agreement on the value of work in the lives of men and women, and the value of caring in the lives of men. To date no such agreement exists. Loss of child-custody suits threaten women who earn wages not because they spend less time or devote less energy to their children than divorced fathers, but because once at work, they lose the traditional entitlement embodied in the notion that children are best off with their mothers.[34] Loss of tenure (and livelihood) menaces academic women who invoke pregnancy to demand extensions of time on tenure clocks never adjusted to the child-bearing life cycles of women. At the other end of the scale, loss of unemployment benefits intimidates married women with children who refuse jobs that are some distance from their place of residence. Loss of social security benefits jeopardizes the future of the widow dependent on her deceased husband's earnings record, who wants to re-marry.

At the heart of these debates is whether gender equality in the labor force can best be ensured by treating wage-earning women "differently" with respect to their workforce options, or by treating them just like men. If women demand and accept special treatment, argue some feminists, they will in the end undermine their desirability to employers. But if women do not get special treatment, particularly with regard to pregnancy, argue other feminists, they will be disadvantaged when they willingly take on socially valuable caring and reproductive roles. The debate revolves around what some see as the "essential" difference between men and women: women have babies and men do not, and it extends to the recognition that it is women, overwhelmingly, who care for babies and children as well as the ill and elderly. Its goal is to alter work-force rules created for men in order fairly to accommodate a work force that is now almost half female.

With the goal of a gender integrated work force in sight, the challenges of the twenty-first century require accommodation as much from men as from women, from employers as from workers, from legislators and policy makers as from individuals. Our task now is to find the compromises that will enable women and men to choose to go out to work without sacrificing the families that satisfy affective needs.

Notes

1. Limits of Independence in the Colonies

1. Edmund Morgan, *The Puritan Dilemma: The Story of John Winthrop* (Boston: Little, Brown, 1958), p. 71; John Demos, *A Little Commonwealth: Family Life in the Plymouth Colony* (New York: Oxford University Press, 1970), p. 78.
2. Demos, *Little Commonwealth*, p. 186.
3. Sigmund Diamond, "From Organization to Society: Virginia in the Seventeeth Century," *American Journal of Sociology* 63 (1958): 457–75; Edmund Morgan, "The Labor Problem of Jamestown: 1607–1618," *American Historical Review* 76 (June 1971): 595–611.
4. Quoted in Marcus Jernegan, *The Laboring and Dependent Classes in Colonial America; 1607–1783* (New York: Frederick Ungar, 1971 [1965]), p. 199.
5. Robert Bremner, ed., *Children and Youth in America: A Documentary History*, 3 vols. (Cambridge, Mass.: Harvard University Press, 1970), 1:69; Edith Abbott, *Women in Industry: A Study in American Economic History* (New York; Arno Press, 1969 [1910]), p. 12; Richard B. Morris, *Government and Labor in Early America* (New York: Columbia University Press, 1946), p. 397.
6. Bremner, *Children and Youth in America*, 1: 65–66; Jernegan, *Laboring and Dependent Classes*, p. 91.
7. Abbott, *Women in Industry*, p. 32; Jernegan, *Laboring and Dependent Classes*, pp. 199–200; Bremner, *Children and Youth in America*, I: 66.
8. Alice Clark, *The Working Life of Women in the Seventeeth Century* (New York: Harcourt Brace, 1920), p. 12.
9. Nancy F. Cott, "Divorce and the Changing Status of Women in Eighteenth Century Massachusetts," in M. Gordon, ed., *The American Family in Social Historical Perspective*, 2d ed. (New York: St. Martin's, 1978), p. 129.

10. Arthur Calhoun, *A Social History of the American Family from Colonial Times to the Present* (New York: Barnes and Noble, 1945), pp. 83, 84.

11. This is not to say they were not often dissatisfied. See Mary Beth Norton, *Liberty's Daughters: The Revolutionary Experience of American Women, 1750–1800* (Boston: Little, Brown, 1980) for the argument that by the revolution, women lacked self-esteem. And see Nancy Folbre, "Patriarchy in Colonial New England," *Review of Political Economics* 12 (Summer 1980): 4–13, for the argument that women had little power in the family.

12. Lucy Maynard Salmon, *Domestic Service* (New York: Macmillan, 1911), pp. 30, 31; Morris, *Government and Labor in Early America*, p. 320 n; Bremner, *Children and Youth in America*, p. 13; Winthrop D. Jordan, *White over Black: American Attitudes Towards the Negro, 1550–1812* (New York: Penguin, 1968), p. 77.

13. Morris, *Government and Labor in Early America*, p. 347. This casts doubt on Linda Grant Depauw's notion that "in the pre-industrial period, men and women earned equal pay." See her *Four Traditions: Women of New York During the Revolution* (Albany, N.Y.: New York State Bicentennial Commission, 1976), p. 65. Although it may be true, as she suggests, that among artisans, farmers, and other self-employed persons there was no gender distinction as to the price of goods sold, and although it is hard to find distinctions in allowances of food and clothing to servants and slaves, nevertheless it seems clear that women's wage work was valued at less than that of men.

14. Lois Green Carr and Lorena S. Walsh. "The Planter's Wife: The Experience of White Women in Seventeenth-Century Maryland," in *William & Mary Quarterly*, 3d ser., 34 (October 1977): 548. It was not only servants who indulged in relatively free sexual behavior. See Nancy Cott, "Eighteenth Century Family and Social Life Revealed in Massachusetts Divorce Records," *Journal of Social History* 10 (Fall 1976): 20–43.

15. Morris, *Government and Labor in Early America*, pp. 352, 349; cf. also Eugenie Andruss Leonard, *The Dear-Bought Heritage* (Philadelphia: University of Pennsylvania Press, 1965), p. 334.

16. Leonard, *Dear-Bought Heritage*, pp. 340, 341.

17. Nancy Cott, *Root of Bitterness: Documents in the Social History of American Women* (New York: Dutton, 1972), pp. 89–90; Morris, *Government and Labor in Early America*, p. 444.

18. A point made by Carol Berkin, *Within the Conjurer's Circle: Women in Colonial America* (Morristown, N.J.: General Learning Press, 1974), p. 10. See Norton, *Liberty's Daughters*, pp. 29–33, for a description of household tasks among slave women.

19. Julia Cherry Spruill, *Women's Life and Work in the Southern Colonies* (Chapel Hill: University of North Carolina Press, 1938), p. 11.

20. Mary Ryan, *Womanhood in America from Colonial Times to the Present* (New York: New Viewpoints, 1975), p. 23.

21. Spruill, *Women's Life and Work in the Southern Colonies*, pp. 11, 17;

Richard B. Morris, *Studies in the History of American Law* (New York: Octagon Books, 1963 [1930]), pp. 131, 134.

22. Calhoun, *Social History of the American Family*, pp. 176, 232.

23. Spruill, *Women's Life and Work in the Southern Colonies*, pp. 361–62. Richard B. Morris, *Studies in the History of American Law*, pp. 152, 154, argues that in seventeenth-century Massachusetts married women could, with the approval of the General Court, occasionally convey their own property, but that this possibility disappeared in the eighteenth century.

24. Alexander Keyssar, "Widowhood in Eighteenth-Century Massachusetts: A Problem in the History of the Family," *Perspectives in American History* 8 (1974): 100, 101, argues that the purpose of such laws was to prevent widows from becoming public charges while at the same time protecting the right of the line of succession to the estate. Carr and Walsh "Planter's Wife," p. 280. And see Edmund Morgan, *American Slavery—American Freedom* (New York: Norton, 1975), pp. 166–70, for examples of the problems as well as the prosperity of widows.

25. DePauw, *Four Traditions*, p. 13.

26. Jernegan, *Laboring and Dependent Classes*, p. 105; and see Calhoun, *Social History of the American Family*, pp. 83, 84, for additional examples.

27. Leonard, *Dear-Bought Heritage*, p. 426; Spruill, *Women's Life and Work in the Southern Colonies*, p. 290.

28. Quoted in DePauw, *Four Traditions*, p. 13.

29. Ben Barker-Benfield, "Anne Hutchinson and the Puritan Attitude Towards Women," *Feminist Studies* 1 (Fall 1972): 75–76.

30. Cott, *Root of Bitterness*, pp. 47–48, 54.

31. Barker-Benfield, "Anne Hutchinson and the Puritan Attitude Towards Women," p. 71.

32. Keyssar, "Widowhood in Eighteenth-Century Massachusetts," p. 95. The imbalance was particularly high in Massachusetts as a result of war casualties, but Connecticut and Rhode Island also had significantly higher numbers of women than men. The ratio was, of course, reversed in frontier areas, where women always remained scarce. In Virginia, the sex ratio probably equalized about 1720. Morgan, *American Slavery—American Freedom*, p. 336.

33. Bremner, *Children and Youth in America*, p. 103; Leonard, *Dear-Bought Heritage*, p. 175. Each spinner was required to produce three pounds of cotton, linen or woolen yarn per week for thirty weeks each year. Allowances were made for children and for some women. Leonard does not indicate how this was to be enforced. But families were apparently tithed as if they had produced at least the minimum.

34. Bremner, *Children and Youth in America*, p. 66.

35. Douglas Lamar Jones, "The Strolling Poor: Transiency in Eighteenth-Century Massachusetts," *Journal of Social History* 7 (Spring 1975): 28–55. Jones argues that half of all transients were women. See also Linda K. Kerber, *Women of the Republic: Intellect and Ideology in Revolutionary America* (Chapel Hill: University of North Carolina Press, 1980),

pp. 142–43, for a discussion of why women were particularly vulnerable to vagrancy laws. Gary B. Nash, *The Urban Crucible: Social Change, Political Consciousness and the Origins of the American Revolution* (Cambridge, Mass.: Harvard University Press, 1979), pp. 184–86, explains why Boston was especially poor.

36. Gary B. Nash, "The Failure of Female Factory Labor in Colonial Boston," *Labor History* 20 (Spring 1979): 169–74. Nash suggests that some 1,200, or as many as "30% of the town's married women had no spouse to contribute to the support of their households" (p. 166). Cf. also Nash's *Urban Crucible*, pp. 188–97; and Leonard, *Dear-Bought Heritage*, pp. 189–90.

37. Edith Abbott, "A Study of the Early History of Child Labor in America," *American Journal of Sociology* 14 (July 1908): 21; William R. Bagnall, *The Textile Industries of the United States*, 2 vols. (Cambridge, Mass.: Riverside Press, 1893), 1: 33, 34.

38. Quoted in Abbott, "Study of the Early History of Child Labor," p. 23.

39. Leonard, *Dear-Bought Heritage*, p. 205; Helen Sumner, *A History of Women in Industry*, Vol. 9 of *Report on Condition of Women and Child Wage-Earners in the United States*, Senate Doc. 645, 61st Cong., 2nd sess. (Washington, D.C.: Government Printing Office, 1910; reprint ed., New York: Arno Press, 1974), p. 41.

40. Leonard, *Dear-Bought Heritage*, p. 201, quoted from the Pennsylvania *Pocket and General Advertiser*, December 1775.

41. Quoted from the Massachusetts *Gazette*, Nov. 9, 1767, in Rolla Milton Tryon, *Household Manufactures in the United States, 1640–1860: A Study in Industrial History* (Chicago: University of Chicago Press, 1917), p. 108.

42. Morris, *Government and Labor in Early America*, p. 43.

2. From Household Manufactures to Wage Work

1. John F. Kasson, *Civilizing the Machine: Technology and Republican Values in America, 1776–1900* (New York: Penguin, 1977), p. 10.

2. William R. Bagnall, *The Textile Industries of the United States*, 2 vols. (Cambridge, Mass.: Riverside Press, 1893), 1: 187, 224. See also Helen Sumner, *A History of Women in Industry in the United States*, Vol. 9 of *Report on Condition of Woman and Child Wage-Earners in the United States*, Senate Doc. 645, 61st Cong., 2d sess. (Washington, D.C.: Government Printing Office, 1910; reprint ed., New York: Arno Press, 1979), p. 47, for a similar example from a Baltimore cotton mill in 1808. This one asked for eight- to twelve-year-old boys or girls.

3. Sumner, *History of Women in Industry*, p. 47. See also U.S. Secretary of the Treasury, *Documents Relating to the Manufactures in the U.S.*, House Doc. 308, 22d Cong., 2d sess. (1833) (hereafter cited as *McLane Report*), 1: 173; and Mary Alice Feldblum, "The Formation of the First Factory Labor Force in the New England Cotton Textile Industry, 1800–1848" (Ph.D. diss., New School for Social Research, 1977), pp. 99–104.

4. Alexander Hamilton, "Report on Manufactures," in Samuel McKee, ed., *Papers on Public Credit, Commerce and Finance* (New York: Liberal Arts Press, 1957), p. 193.

5. Mathew Carey, "Address to the Farmers of the U.S." and "New Olive Branch," in *Essays on Political Economy* (Philadelphia: H. C. Carey and I. Lea, 1822), pp. 348, 440.

6. These quotations are from Sumner, *History of Women in Industry*, p. 39, and Hamilton, "Report on Manufactures," p. 193. See also David Montgomery, "The Working Classes of the Pre-Industrial American City, 1780–1830," *Labor History* 10 (Winter 1968): 17.

7. *Niles' Register*, November 18, 1815, p. 190.

8. Carey, "Address to the Farmers of the U.S.," p. 430.

9. Nancy F. Cott, "Young Women in the Second Great Awakening in New England," *Feminist Studies* 3 (Fall 1975): 26; Montgomery, "Working Classes of the Pre-Industrial American City," pp. 19–20, argues that New York in 1820 had 118 women aged 16–25 for every 100 men in that age group; in Philadelphia the ratio was 122 to 100; and in Boston 127 to 100.

10. Rolla Milton Tryon, *Household Manufactures in the United States, 1640–1680: A Study in Industrial History* (Chicago: University of Chicago Press, 1917), p. 253, argues that by 1810 more cloth "was fulled and dyed and pressed in regular establishments than outside them."

11. Bagnall, *Textile Industries of the United States*, 1: 259.

12. *Niles' Register*, September 15, 1821, p. 36.

13. Data on household production comes from *McLane Report*, 1: 78; George Rogers Taylor, *The Transportation Revolution, 1815–1860* (New York: Harper Torchbooks, 1968 [1951]), pp. 212–13; and Tryon, *Household Manufactures*, pp. 304–5.

14. Tryon, *Household Manufactures*, p. 276; Robert Brooke Zevin, "The Growth of Cotton Textile Production after 1815," in Robert Fogel and Stanley Engerman, eds., *The Reinterpretation of American Economic History* (New York: Harper & Row, 1971), p. 141, estimates that the direct cost of power weaving came to one cent a yard as opposed to the three to seven cents a yard paid to hand-loom weavers for each yard of cloth before 1815. In the four-year period from 1823 to 1827, the cost of power weaving was chopped by 75 percent.

15. Quoted from the *Banner of the Constitution*, June 29, 1931, in Sumner, *History of Women in Industry*, p. 51.

16. Cott, "Young Women in the Second Great Awakening," p. 17.

17. Philip Greven, *Four Generations: Population, Land and Family in Colonial Andover, Massachusetts* (Ithaca, N.Y.: Cornell University Press, 1970), Ch. 7, especially p. 203.

18. Alan Dawley, *Class and Community: The Industrial Revolution in Lynn* (Cambridge, Mass.: Harvard University Press, 1976), pp. 138–39; Blanche Hazard, "The Organization of the Boot and Shoe Industry in Massachusetts Before 1875," *Quarterly Journal of Economics* 27 (February 1913): 249, 258–59.

19. Dawley, *Class and Community*, p. 29; Donald Robinson, *Spotlight on a Union: The Story of the United Hatters', Cap and Millinery Workers' International Union* (New York: Dial Press, 1948), p. 141.
20. William A. Sullivan, *The Industrial Worker in Pennsylvania: 1800–1840* (Harrisburg, Pa.: Historical and Museum Commission, 1955), p. 23; Thomas Dublin, *Women at Work: The Transformation of Work and Community in Lowell, Massachusetts, 1826–1860* (New York: Columbia University Press, 1979), p. 18; John Michael Cudd, *The Chicopee Manufacturing Company, 1823–1915* (Wilmington, Del.: Scholarly Resources, 1974), p. 56.
21. Sumner, *History of Women in Industry*, pp. 47–50.
22. Quoted in Nancy F. Cott, *The Bonds of Womanhood: "Woman's Sphere" in New England, 1780–1835* (New Haven: Yale University Press, 1977), p. 39.
23. Quoted in John Andrews and W. D. P. Bliss, *A History of Women in Trade Unions*, Vol. 10 of *Report on Condition of Woman and Child Wage-Earners in the United States*, Senate Doc. 645, 61st Cong., 2d sess. (Washington, D.C.: Government Printing Office, 1911; reprint ed., New Yord: Arno Press, 1974), p. 41, from the Lynn *Record*, January 1, 1834.
24. Gary Kulick describes the process in "Pawtucket Village and the Strike of 1824: The Origin of Class Conflict in Rhode Island," *Radical History Review* 17 (Spring 1978): 6, 12–14, 24–25. For resistance in the shoe industry see the discussion in Dawley, *Class and Community*, pp. 59–66. On machine-breaking and arson see Feldblum, "Formation of the First Factory Labor Force," pp. 261–70.
25. Sarah Savage [pseud.], *The Factory Girl* (Boston: Munroe, Francis and Parker, 1814), p. 4.
26. Aunt Melinda Edwards to Sabrina Bennett, April 4, 1839; Persis Edwards to Sabrina Bennett, April 18, 1840; and Mary Killvie to Sabrina Bennett, October 8, 1834, Bennett Family Letters, Haverhill Public Library, Haverhill, Mass. All citations from the Bennett Family Letters are courtesy of the Trustees of the Haverhill Public Library, Special Collections Department. See also H. E. Bock to Harriet Hanson Robinson, 1846, file 67, box 3, and Lucy Larcom to Robinson, December 1845, file 67, box 3, Harriet Hanson Robinson Collection, Schlesinger Library, Radcliffe College.
27. January 8, 1847, Ann Swett Appleton Letters, Merrimack Valley Textile Museum, North Andover, Mass. These are typescript copies of the originals, which are in the possession of Priscilla Ordway. Edited copies of the originals are in the Manchester Historic Association, Manchester, N.H.
28. April 4, 1839, Bennett Family Letters.
29. May 14, 1843, Bennett Family Letters.
30. *Lowell Offering*, December 18, 1840, p. 18.
31. Quoted from an unidentified newspaper article in Robinson scrapbooks, vol. 30, p. 11; and unidentified news clippings reporting 1888 meeting of the International Council of Women, file 30, box 2, Robinson Collection.

32. Savage, *Factory Girl*, p. 10.
33. Ann to Sarah, February 1847; see also letters of March and April 4, 1847, Appleton Letters.
34. Charlotte S. Hilbourne, *Effie and I, or Seven Years in a Cotton Mill: A Story of the Spindle City* (Cambridge, Mass.: Allen and Farnham, 1863), p. 76; "I hail it with gratitude to the great Father, who is also the orphan's God, that He has endowed men with the means, ability and disposition, to erect such institutions of industry, where any and all may acquire a competence, independent and free from the degradation which charitable obligation demands" (p. 78).
35. Lucy M. Davis to Sabrina Bennett, September 25, 1846, Bennett Family Letters.
36. Mary Killvye to Sabrina Bennett, October 8, 1838, Bennett Family Letters.
37. Aunt Melinda Edwards to Sabrina Bennett, February 23, 1842; see also Olive Sawyer to Sabrina Bennett, September 25, 1836, Bennett Family Letters.
38. Aunt Melinda Edwards to Sabrina Bennett, April 4, 1839, and again, September 25, 1846, Bennett Family Letters.
39. Jemima Sandborn to Richard Bennett, May 14, 1843, Bennett Family Letters.
40. Persis Edwards to Sabrina Bennett, April 18, 1840, Bennett Family Letters.
41. Ann to Sarah, April 1847, May 1847, Appleton Letters. See also Robinson scrapbooks, vol. 30, p. 42, Robinson Collection, for a description of the agreeable life in her boarding house.
42. Sumner, *History of Women in Industry*, pp. 87–88; Vera Shlakman, *Economic History of a Factory Town: A Study of Chicopee, Massachusetts*, Smith College Studies in History 20, nos. 1–4 (October 1934–July 1935), p. 53; Hilbourne, *Effie and I*, p. 45.
43. A portrait of life in the mills can be reconstructed from Dublin, *Women at Work*; Benita Eisler, *The Lowell Offering: Writings by New England Mill Women, 1840–1845* (Philadelphia: J. P. Lippincott, 1977); Philip Foner, *The Factory Girls* (Urbana: University of Illinois Press, 1977); Caroline Ware, *The Early New England Cotton Manufacture: A Study in Industrial Beginnings* (Boston: Houghton Mifflin, 1931).
44. Constance McLaughlin Green, *Holyoke, Massachusetts: A Case History of the Industrial Revolution in America* (New Haven, Yale University Press, 1939), p. 15; "Statistics of Lowell Manufactures" (unpublished, n.d.), Merrimack Valley Textile Museum, North Andover, Mass.; Ware, *Early New England Cotton Manufacture*, pp. 238–47; Henry Miles, *Lowell as It Was and as It Is* (Lowell: Nathaniel Dayton, 1846), p. 68; Shlakman, *Economic History of a Factory Town*, p. 56.
45. Savage, *Factory Girl*, p. 7; unidentified news clipping, file 30, box 2, Robinson Collection. See also Robinson scrapbooks, vol. 30, p. 35; and Ware, *Early New England Cotton Manufacture*, p. 213.
46. April 15, 1847, and June 1848, Appleton Letters.

47. Kasson, *Civilizing the Machine*, p. 76; Miles, *Lowell as It Was and as It Is*, pp. 144–145.

48. Carey, "New Olive Branch," p. 346. See Herman Melville's short story "The Tartarus of Maids," in Richard Chase, ed., *Selected Tales and Poems* (New York: Holt Rinehart, 1960), pp. 215–29. The story, first published in 1855, is an allegory of abused purity.

49. Unidentified news clippings reporting 1888 meeting of the International Council of Women, file 30, box 2, Robinson Collection.

50. Miles, *Lowell as It Was and as It Is*, pp. 132–33; Lise Vogel, "Hearts to Feel and Tongues to Speak: New England Mill Women in the Early Nineteenth Century," in Milton Cantor and Bruce Laurie, eds., *Class, Sex and the Woman Worker* (Westport, Conn.: Greenwood Press, 1977).

51. Dublin, *Women at Work*, p. 118.

52. Ibid., pp. 68, 89.

53. Kulick, "Pawtucket Village and the Strike of 1824," pp. 22–23; Dublin, *Women at Work*, pp. 111 ff.

54. Andrews and Bliss, *History of Women in Trade Unions*, pp. 12, 13; Elizabeth Anthony Dexter, *Career Women of America, 1776–1840* (Francestown, N.H.: Marshall Jones, 1950), p. 178; Sullivan, *Industrial Worker in Pennsylvania*, p. 107.

55. Quoted in Sumner, *History of Women in Industry*, p. 74.

56. *The Factory Girl* (Exeter, N.H), March 1, 1843, cited in Lise Vogel, "Hearts to Feel and Tongues to Speak," p. 76.

57. Andrews and Bliss, *History of Women in Trade Unions*, pp. 25, 28, 30.

58. *Voice of Industry*, January 23, 1846, p. 2.

59. *Lowell Offering*, January 1845, inside front cover, cited in Vogel, "Hearts to Feel and Tongues to Speak," p. 75.

60. Philadelphia *National Gazette*, January 7, 1829, and Boston *Transcript*, February 1831, cited in Andrews and Bliss, *History of Women in Trade Unions*, pp. 23, 26; also Shlakman, *Economic History of a Factory Town*, pp. 62 63.

61. *Lowell Offering*, March and April 1843, inside back covers, cited in Vogel, "Hearts to Feel and Tongues to Speak," p. 75.

3. Industrial Wage Earners and the Domestic Ideology

1. Jemima Sandborn to Richard Bennett, May 14, 1843, Bennett Family Letters, Haverhill Public Library, Haverhill, Mass. All citations from the Bennett Family Letters are courtesy of the Trustees of the Haverhill Public Library, Special Collections Department.

2. U.S. Bureau of the Census, *Historical Statistics of the U.S.: Colonial Times to 1970*, 2 vols. (1975) 1: 12

3. Edith Abbott, *Women in Industry: A Study in American Economic History* (New York: Arno Press, 1969 [1910]), p. 90.

4. Edith Abbott, "Harriet Martineau and the Employment of Women in 1836," *Journal of Political Economy* 14 (1906): 622–624; New York *Daily Tribune*, August 14, 1845; on the continuation of household production

see Joan Jensen, "Cloth, Butter and Boarders: Household Production for the Market," *Review of Political Economics* 12 (Summer 1980): 14–24.

5. Louisa May Alcott, *Work: A Story of Experience* (New York: Schocken, 1977 [1873]), p. 157.

6. Ann Louise Kuhn, *The Mother's Role in Childhood Education: New England Concepts, 1830–1860* (New Haven: Yale University Press, 1947), p. 150. See also William Robert Taylor, *Cavalier and Yankee: The Old South and the American National Character* (New York: Braziller, 1961), p. 140. Ruth Miller Elson, *Guardians of Tradition: American Schoolbooks of the Nineteenth Century* (Lincoln: University of Nebraska Press, 1964), p. 309; Siegfried Giedion, *Mechanization Takes Command: A Contribution to Anonymous History* (New York: Norton, 1969 [1948]), p. 514. For discussions of the nineteenth-century woman, see also Barbara Welter, "The Cult of True Womanhood, 1820–1860," *American Quarterly* 18 (Summer 1964); and Glenda Gates Riley, "The Subtle Subversion: Changes in the Traditionalist Image of the American Woman," *The Historian* 32 (February 1970). Catharine Beecher built her career on developing the notion of domesticity. See especially her *Treatise on Domestic Economy* (New York: Schocken, 1976 [1841]).

7. Bernard Wishy, *The Child and the Republic* (Philadelphia: University of Pennsylvania Press, 1972), p. 28.

8. Aileen Kraditor, *Up from the Pedestal* (Chicago: Quadrangle, 1968), p. 13.

9. Quoted in Elson, *Guardians of Tradition*, p. 309.

10. Quoted in Helen Sumner, *A History of Women in Industry in the United States*, Vol 9 of *Report on Condition of Woman and Child Wage Earners in the United States*, Senate Doc. 645, 61st Cong., 2d sess. (Washington, D.C.: Government Printing Office, 1910; reprint ed., New York: Arno Press, 1974). p. 26.

11. "European Customs," *The Man*, July 5, 1834, p. 68.

12. "Useful Industry in Women," and "The Duty of Women," reprinted from the Boston *Transcript* in *Voice of Industry*, September 14, 1845, p. 4.

13. Olivia, "Women's Sphere of Influence," *Voice of Industry*, December 5, 1845, p. 3; see also the condescending article "How to Treat a Wife," *Voice of Industry*, September 14, 1845, p. 4.

14. "The Truant Husband," *Voice of Industry*, July 24, 1845, p. 4; Emma, "Ally Ray, or First and Second Love," *Voice of Industry*, September 18, 1845, p. 4; also in *Voice of Industry* "Working for a Living," June 19, 1845, p. 3; "Report of the Female Labor Reform Association," November 9, 1845, p. 3; see also "Elsie and Isabel or Truth and Falsehood," June 12, 1845, pp. 1–2, a tale of betrayal and deception whose message is submission to fate, with the reward to be garnered after death.

15. Quoted in Gerda Lerner, *The Woman in American History* (Menlo Park, Calif.: Addison-Wesley, 1971), p. 84.

16. From Benita Eisler, ed., *The Lowell Offering: Writings by New England Mill Women, 1840–1845* (Philadelphia: J. P. Lippincott, 1977), p. 195.

17. January 18, 1847, p. 9, Ann Swett Appleton Letters, Merrimack Valley Textile Museum, North Andover, Mass. These are typescripts of the originals, which are owned by Priscilla Ordway. Edited copies of the originals are in the Manchester Historic Association, Manchester, N.H.
18. Ann to Sarah, June 1848, Appleton Letters.
19. Virginia Penny, *How Women Can Make Money: Married or Single* (New York: Arno Press, 1971) [1870]), p. v.
20. Ibid.
21. Stanley Lebergott, *Manpower in Economic Growth: The American Record Since 1800* (New York: McGraw-Hill, 1964), p. 279; Robert Ernst, *Immigrant Life in New York City, 1825–1863* (New York: Kings' Crown Press, 1949), pp. 66–67; Lawrence A. Glasco, "Ethnicity and Social Structure: Irish, Germans and Native Born of Buffalo, N.Y., 1850–60" (Ph.D. diss., State University of New York, Buffalo, 1973), p. 205; Sumner, *History of Women in Industry*, p. 181. For the distinction between "help" and "domestic" see Faye E. Dudden, "From Help to Domestic: American Servants, 1800–1880," forthcoming from Wesleyan University Press.
22. Quoted in Donald Cole, *Immigrant City: Lawrence, Massachusetts, 1845–1921* (Chapel Hill: University of North Carolina Press, 1963), p. 23. See also Constance McLaughlin Green, *Holyoke, Massachusetts: A Case History of the Industrial Revolution in America* (New Haven: Yale University Press, 1939), pp 32n., 20; and see Michael B. Katz, *The Irony of Early School Reform: Educational Innovation in Mid-Nineteenth-Century Massachusetts* (Boston: Beacon Press, 1968), for a general discussion of schools in this period. Arguments for domestic education for women are widespread, but see especially any of Catherine Beecher's numerous works; Elson, *Guardians of Tradition*, p. 309; and Gerda Lerner, "Women's Rights and American Feminism," *American Scholar*, Spring 1971, p. 238.
23. Larcom to Robinson, April 14, 1857, file 52, box 3, Harriet Hanson Robinson Collection, Schlesinger Library, Radcliffe College. Estimates of teachers' salaries can be found in Elizabeth Anthony Dexter, *Career Women of America, 1776–1840* (Francestown, N.H.: Marshall Jones, 1950), p. 7.
24. See the discussion of midwifery in Mary Roth Walsh, *Doctors Wanted: No Women Need Apply. Sexual Barriers in the Medical Profession, 1835–1975* (New Haven: Yale University Press, 1977), pp. 5–9.
25. New York *Daily Tribune*, September 30, 1845, p. 1. The Irish moved into nursing by the 1880s.
26. Penny, *How Women Can Make Money*, p. 17; and New York *Daily Tribune*, September 30, 1845, p. 1.
27. See Sara Elbert's introduction to Alcott, *Work: A Story of Experience*.
28. William Sanger, *History of Prostitution: Its Extent, Causes, and Effects Throughout the World* (New York: Harper and Brothers, 1859), pp. 524, 473, 488, 456.
29. See Sumner, *History of Women in Industry*, p. 23. Sumner's summary of

contemporary estimates is confirmed by Lebergott, *Manpower in Economic Growth*, p. 547.

30. John Michael Cudd, *The Chicopee Manufacturing Company, 1823–1915* (Wilmington, Del.: Scholarly Resources, 1974), pp. 92, 90, Lebergott, *Manpower in Economic Growth*, p. 543, estimates the average full-time earnings of a Massachusetts cotton worker in 1849 at $199 per year and in 1859 at $203 per year, for men and women. These rates are about 50 cents a week higher than the national average. Ernst, *Immigrant Life in New York City*, p. 77, estimates average wages for women in New York City at $3.50 a week, substantially higher than other estimates for the 1850s. Prices for board rose substantially in the 1850s. Charles Bigelow to R. W. Heneker, Esq., September 8, 1856, Essex Company Letters, Merrimack Valley Textile Museum, North Andover, Mass., indicates that in that year the company added 35 cents to the former board price of $1.25 per week, bringing the total for weekly board charges to $1.60; Green, *Holyoke*, p. 45, estimates that women earned $3.00 per week less $1.50 for board. Cudd, *Chicopee Manufacturing Company*, p. 90, estimates that though women's average wages rose from 58 cents a day in 1840 to 62 cents in 1860, real wages declined.

31. Vera Shlakman, *Economic History of a Factory Town: A Study of Chicopee, Massachusetts, Smith College Studies in History* 20, nos. 1–4 (October 1934–July 1935), estimates daily wage rates in Chicopee's paper and cotton mills as follows:

	Men	Women
1859	.90	.66
1860	.91	.66
1861	.91	.65
1865	1.20	.89
1870	1.58	1.19

Green, *Holyoke*, p. 45, argues that skilled men earned $1.75 a day, or between $9.00 and $10.00 a week, compared to $3.00 a week for women.

32. Quoted from the Cabotsville *Chronicle* in the *Voice of Industry*, June 26, 1845, p. 2.

33. Ibid. On other occasions the *Voice of Industry* warned that as the population increased and other means of livelihood became less abundant, America's working population would become even further degraded. See July 31, 1845, p. 3.

34. "The Ten Hour System and Its Advocates," *Voice of Industry*, January 16, 1846, p. 2. Italics in original. See also "Manchester Operatives Again," December 19, 1845, p. 2.

35. *Voice of Industry*, July 3, 1845.

36. Ibid. February 6, 1846, p. 2.

37. Ibid., Nov. 7, 1845, p. 3.

38. Ibid., May 7, 1847, p. 2.

39. Quoted in *Voice of Industry*, January 15, 1845.

40. Quoted from the Philadelphia *Public Ledger*, February 21, 1839, in John Andrews and W. D. P. Bliss, *A History of Women in Trade Unions*, Vol. 10 of *Report on Condition of Woman and Child Earners in the United States*, Senate Doc. 645, 61st Cong., 2d sess. (Washington, D.C.: Government Printing Office, 1911; reprint ed. New York: Arno Press, 1974), p. 49.

41. *Voice of Industry*, June 19, 1845, p. 3.

42. Quoted in Green, *Holyoke*, p. 31n.

43. Almira, "Stanzas," *Voice of Industry*, February 6, 1846.

44. Shlakman, *Economic History of a Factory Town*, p. 138; Cudd, *Chicopee Manufacturing Company*, p. 88.

45. Caroline Ware, *The Early New England Cotton Manufacture: A Study in Industrial Beginnings* (Boston: Houghton Mifflin, 1931), p. 231.

46. Ibid, p. 234.

47. August Kohn, *The Cotton Mills of South Carolina* (Spartansburg, S.C.: Reprints Company, 1975 [1907]), p. 28; see also Charles Bigelow to J. Pickering Putnam, July 8, 1853, Essex Letters; Cole, *Immigrant City*, p. 22.

48. Shlakman, *Economic History of a Factory Town*, p. 138.

49. A. I. Cummings, *The Factory Girl: or Gardez La Coeur* (Lowell: J. E. Short, 1847), p. 58. Italics in original.

50. Pemberton Mills, Ward Inspectors' Lists, MS 117, Pemberton Company Relief Fund Papers, Merrimack Valley Textile Museum, North Andover, Mass. See entries for Mrs. McCann, January 16, 1860; Mrs. Hannan, January 16, 1860; Catherine Rourke, January 21, 1860; and Mary Moran, January 21, 1860.

51. Ibid., Bridget Gleason, January 28, 1860.

52. New York *Daily Tribune*, March 7, 1845, p. 2.

53. From Edward Zane Carroll Judson (Ned Buntline), *Mysteries and Miseries of New York: A Story of Real Life* (New York: Dick and Fitzgerald, 1849), pp. 26–27.

54. "The Factory Girl," *The Man*, May 17, 1834, p. 4. Robinson remembers singing these verses but argues that she and her friends thought they reflected the conditions of English millchildren. See Harriet R. Robinson, *Loom and Spindle or Life Among the Early Mill Girls* (Kailua, Hawaii: Press Pacifica, 1976 [1898]), p. 21.

55. Quoted from the Allegheny *Democrat and Working Men's Advocate*, December 9, 1836, in William A. Sullivan, *The Industrial Worker in Pennsylvania, 1800–1840* (Harrisburg: Pennsylvania Historical and Museum Commission, 1955), p. 37.

56. Melinda Edwards to Sabrina Bennett, April 4, 1839, Bennett Family Letters.

57. Lucy Davis to Sabrina Bennett, September 25, 1846, Bennett Family Letters.

58. Final Report of the Treasurer of the Committee of Relief, January 10, 1860, p. 14, Pemberton Company Relief Fund Papers.

59. Elizabeth Baker, *Technology and Women's Work* (New York: Columbia

University Press, 1964), p. 17. Sumner, *History of Women in Industry*, p. 51, indicates that the number dropped to 40.6 percent in 1900.

60. Katz, *Irony of Early School Reform*, p. 12; Emilie Josephine Hutchinson, *Women's Wages: A Study of the Wages of Industrial Women and Measures Suggested to Increase Them*. (New York: Columbia University, 1919), pp. 34, 158.

61. Quoted in Sumner, *History of Women in Industry*, p. 38.

62. Ibid, p. 29.

63. Quoted in Andrews and Bliss, *History of Women in Trade Unions*, p. 48.

64. Ibid., p. 35, from the *National Laborer*, January 14, 1837.

65. Ibid., pp. 45, 46.

66. Mary Elizabeth Massey, *Bonnet Brigades* (New York: Alfred Knopf, 1966), p. 7.

67. Ibid., p. 6; Caroline Dall, *Women's Right to Labor, or Low Wages and Hard Work* (Boston: Walker Wise, 1860), p. 69.

68. Andrews and Bliss, *History of Women in Trade Unions*, pp. 39, 41, 46, 47, 57.

69. *Voice of Industry*, October 2, 1846, p. 3. See also Walter Huggins, *Jacksonian Democracy and the Working Class: A Study of the New York Workingman's Movement, 1829–1837* (Palo Alto, Calif.: Stanford University Press, 1960), p. 79.

70. *Voice of Industry*, December 26, 1846, p. 3; Andrews and Bliss, *History of Women in Trade Unions*, pp. 64, 65.

71. New York *Daily Tribune*, August 25, 1845, p. 2.

72. Douglas North, *Growth and Welfare in the American Past* (Englewood Cliffs, N.J.: Prentice-Hall, 1974), p. 170.

4. Why Is It Can a Woman Not Be Virtuous . . .

1. "What the Ladies Think of Our Cause," *Workingman's Advocate*, July 11, 1874, p. 2.

2. Mary Elizabeth Massey, *Bonnet Brigades* (New York: Alfred Knopf, 1866), p. 340. See "The Workingman's Movement," the New York *World*, December 1, 1863, p. 4, for estimates of the number of women added to the labor force as a result of the war.

3. *Fincher's Trades' Review*, "Meeting of Sewing Women," April 23, 1864, p. 2; and *Fincher's Trades' Review*, "Great Demonstration of Working Women," January 28, 1865, p. 2, which provided the following comparisons of prices paid to contractors as compared with those they paid to sewing women.

Item	Contractors' Price (in cents)	Arsenal Price (in cents)
Shirts	7	18
Drawers	7	13
Trousers	17–20	40
Blouses	13–16	42
Calvary jackets	40–50	120
Infantry coats	50–75	125
Great coats	40	90

But lower prices also existed. The *Daily Evening Voice*, Deceember 30, 1864, p. 2, reported that women made entire cavalry jackets for thirty-five cents each.

4. The New York *Sun*, November 17, 1863, p. 1. Women's share of jobs in the clothing industry fell from 45 percent to 38 percent between 1860 and 1870. See Helen Sumner, *A History of Women in Industry in the United States*, Vol. 9 of *Report on Condition of Woman and Child Wage-Earners in the United States*, Senate Doc. 645, 61st Cong., 2d sess. (Washington, D.C.: Government Printing Office, 1910; reprint ed., New York: Arno Press, 1974), pp. 143, 270, for additional descriptions.

5. *Workingman's Advocate*, May 8, 1869, p. 4.

6. *The Revolution*, May 13, 1869, p. 296. The U.S. Commissioner of Labor, *Fourth Annual Report, 1888, Working Women in Large Cities* (1889), p. 72, confirmed Phelp's sense that increasing division of labor lowered female wages.

7. Sumner, *History of Women in Industry*, p. 146 ff, offers numerous examples.

8. New York *Sun*, November 13, 1863, p. 1.

9. *The Revolution*, May 13, 1869, p. 296; and October 29, 1868, p. 259.

10. *Fincher's Trades' Review*, November 21, 1863, p. 2. For other examples, see *The Revolution*, October 29, 1868, p. 259; May 13, 1869, p. 296; October 1, 1868, p. 198.

11. New York *Sun*, November 19, 1863, p. 1.

12. *Fincher's Trades' Review*, May 14, 1864, p. 4.

13. *Fincher's Trades' Review*, March 18, 1865. The contractors in this instance got $1.75 per dozen gray shirts; the women got only $1.00. Philadelphia women seem to have been successful with such a petition in 1864, gaining an increase of 20 percent in wages and getting a commitment that a portion of arsenal work would be given directly to them. See John Andrews and W. D. P. Bliss, *A History of Women in Trade Unions*, Vol. 10, of *Report on Condition of Woman and Child Wage-Earners in the United States*, Senate Doc. 645, 61st Cong., 2d sess. (Washington, D.C.: Government Printing Office, 1911; reprint ed., New York: Arno Press, 1974), p. 95.

14. "The Wail of the Women," *Workingman's Advocate*, April 24, 1869, p. 1.

15. See, for example, the New York *World*, November 12, 1863, p. 8; See also December 3, 1863, p. 4, which echoed the argument that but for the war, these women would have been assisted by their menfolk. The *World* added a class dimension to the argument when it pleaded for new job openings for women: "Heretofore the working women have generally sprung from the ranks of the very poor, and in this country their occupation has been confined almost exclusively to domestic service and sewing. But now, in the new army of working women which the war has already collected, are to be found many of education and ability, who will bring intelligence and a larger capacity to bear upon the work in which they may be engaged. To such as these, new fields of labor must be opened and such remuneration guaranteed as will offer an induce-

ment to sustained effort, and compensate for the expenditure of time and energy."

16. *The Revolution*, October 29, 1868, p. 259; *Fincher's Trades' Review*, January 28, 1865, p. 2.

17. *The Revolution*, October 8, 1868, p. 214. See also Carole Turbin, "Woman's Work and Woman's Rights—A Comparative Study of the Woman's Trade Union Movement and the Woman Suffrage Movement in the Mid-Nineteenth Century" (Ph.D. diss., New School for Social Research, 1978), Ch. 4.

18. A complete account of the development of the Collar Laundry Union and of its cooperative is in Turbin, "Woman's Work and Woman's Rights," Ch. 5.

19. New York *World*, November 12, 1863, p. 8.

20. *Fincher's Trades' Review*, June 25, 1864, p. 2; May 14, 1864, p. 4; *Daily Evening Voice*, March 23, 1865, p. 2; New York *Sun*, November 24, 1865, p. 1; December 9, 1865, p. 4.

21. *Fincher's Trades' Review*, June 6, 1863, p. 2.

22. "Two Heads or One," *Workingman's Advocate*, May 7, 1870, p. 4; see also "A Perfect Wife," ibid., March 19, 1870, p. 1.

23. *Workinghman's Advocate*, April 9, 1870, p. 1; see also "A Wife's Power," ibid., March 11, 1876, p. 1; and November 13, 1869, p. 4.

24. Ellen Butler, "Women and Work," *Daily Evening Voice*, January 12, 1865, p. 1.

25. *Fincher's Trades' Review*, June 16, 1863, p. 2.

26. *Fincher's Trades' Review*, June 24, 1865, p. 2. See also the *Daily Evening Voice*, March 23, 1865, p. 2. Even limited encouragement included patronizing comments. "The Female Operatives Organizing," *Workingman's Advocate*, January 29, 1870, p. 1, reported the organization of 200 women in the following words: "This is certainly a very promising commencement altogether eclipsing the first efforts of the 'Knights,' but then everybody knows that when the ladies make up their mind to do anything in this line, they inevitably mean business."

27. *Workingman's Advocate*, April 29, 1871, p. 2.

28. Ibid.

29. U.S. Commissioner of Labor, *Working Women in Large Cities*, p. 17. See Meredith Tax, *The Rising of the Women: Feminist Solidarity and Class Conflict, 1880–1917* (New York: Monthly Review Press, 1980), Ch. 2, for a description of the Chicago Knights of Labor Local No. 1789.

30. New York *Sun*, November 7, 1863, p. 1; November 12, 1863, p. 1; *Fincher's Trades' Review*, November 21, 1863, p. 2.

31. Every New York paper covered the story, but the *Sun* carried the most detailed account. See especially issues of November 13, 17, 19, 25, and December 17, 1863.

32. Typescript of act incorporating the WWPU in New York State, 1868, in file 298, box 13, Leonora O'Reilly Collection, Schlesinger Library, Radcliffe College.

33. Testimony of Mrs. M. W. Faber, superintendent of the WWPU, in U.S.

Education and Labor Committee, *Report Upon the Relations Between Capital and Labor*, 4 vols. (1885), 2:638. See also *The Revolution*, January 21, 1869, p. 39, for some additional figures on the WWPU's reported accomplishments. U.S. Commisioner of Labor, *Working Women in Large Cities*, p. 40. To protect their own reputations, these institutions typically refused to serve domestic servants, widows, or divorced persons.

34. For biographical information, see the article in Edward James and Janet James, eds., *Notable American Women*, 3 vols. (Cambridge, Mass.: Harvard University Press, 1971), 1: 489–92; and Phyllis Kriegel, "The Daughter of Privilege and the Daughters of Labor: Grace Dodge and the Working Girls' Societies, 1884–1896" (M.A. Thesis, Sarah Lawrence College, 1977).

35. Grace Dodge, "Working Girls' Societies," *The Chautauquan* 9 (October 1888): 223.

36. Maude Stanley, *Clubs for Working Girls* (New York and London: Macmillan, 1890), pp. 17–18. Dodge listed some of the clubs' discussion topic as follows: "When women take men's places and cut down wages, what is the effect upon the home? In what way can women obtain for the same work the same wages as men? How far are we responsible for the bargain counter and sweating system? . . . Are labor organizations among women increasing; what have they accomplished?" See Grace Dodge, "Working Girls' Club Life," *American Federationist* 1 (May 1894): 68–69.

37. Mary White Ovington, "Working Girls' Clubs," 1900, Ovington Collection, Archives of Labor History and Urban Affairs, Wayne State University.

38. Dodge, "Working Girls' Societies," p. 225.

39. Kriegel, "Daughter of Privilege," p. 43.

40. Grace H. Dodge, *A Bundle of Letters to Busy Girls on Practical Matters* (New York: Arno Press, 1974 [1887]), p. 224.

41. *The Revolution*, October 1, 1868, p. 197. This attitude seems to have prevailed among wage-earning women until around 1910–12, when the National American Woman Suffrage Association made special attempts to recruit wage earners and trade unionists as speakers. For the switch in attitudes see Rose Schneiderman, with Lucy Goldthwaite, *All for One* (New York: Paul Erickson, 1967), p. 12, and Leonora O'Reilly to John Hanrahan, April 19, 1911, file 4, box 5, O'Reilly Collection.

42. "National Labor Congress," *The Revolution*, October 1, 1868, p. 204.

43. "Workingwoman's Association," *The Revolution*, October 1, 1868, p. 197.

44. *The Revolution*, August 26, 1869, p. 120. Ellen Carol DuBois, *Feminism and Suffrage: The Emergence of an Independent Women's Movement in America, 1848–1869* (Ithaca, N.Y.: Cornell University Press, 1978), Ch. 5.

45. *The Revolution*, September 9, 1869, p. 154.

46. "Working Women's Association," *The Revolution*, October 21, 1869, p. 251. See also *The Revolution* of January 21, 1869, p. 39, which reports and denies the accusation that the Working Women's Association "is at

this moment unfortunately controlled by a handful of strong-minded women, who use it to back up their demands for female suffrage, for Negro equality, and so on."

47. New York *Times*, February 14, 1869, p. 7; the *World* estimated the number at 300,000 (December 1, 1863, p. 4).

48. Lillie Devereux Blake, testimony of September 18, 1883, in U.S. Education and Labor Committee, *Report Upon the Relations Between Capital and Labor*, 2:597.

49. *Daily Evening Voice*, January 7, 1865, p. 2.

50. *The Revolution*, May 13, 1869, p. 296.

51. *Workingman's Advocate*, May 8, 1869, p. 1.

52. Virginia Penny, *Think and Act: A Series of Articles Pertaining to Men and Women, Work and Wages* (Philadelphia: Claxton, Remsen and Haffelfinger, 1869), p. 29. Penny also proposed (p. 28) that a tax be levied on "such work as women might do but that is monopolized by men."

53. *Daily Evening Voice*, December 17, 1864, p. 4; see also Birmingham *Labor Advocate*, March 2, 1901, p. 1; Catharine Beecher and Harriet Beecher Stowe, *The American Woman's Home, or Principles of Domestic Science—Being a Guide to the Formation and Maintenance of Educational, Healthful, Beautiful and Christian Homes* (New York: Arno Press, 1971 [1869]), p. 13.

54. "Marry the Women," Birmingham *Labor Advocate*, May 25, 1901, p. 1. The *Labor Advocate*—the AFL voice in the South—was particularly adamant about getting women out of the work force. See "Work Is for Men," March 21, 1901, p. 1., which acclaims an employer who refused to hire women even though he could have saved $2,500 yearly by doing so. See also "Labor and Industry," September 22, 1900, p. 3. Theodore Roosevelt, in a prefatory letter to Mrs. John Van Vorst and Marie Van Vorst, *The Woman Who Toils* (New York: Doubleday Page, 1903), p. viii, declared that "if the men of the nation are not anxious . . . to be fathers of families, and if the women do not recognize that the greatest thing for any woman is to be a good wife and mother, why, that nation has cause to be alarmed about its future."

55. *Daily Evening Voice*, April 7, 1865.

56. Penny, *Think and Act*, p. 95. Penny's argument rested first on a surplus of female labor and then on limited numbers of jobs: "A surplus of labor always produces depreciation of wages. Wages should depend on ability and application. The competition of women's labor with boys' in the non-domestic departments, is one cause of their low wages. Thousands of women never marry, that must and do earn a living, but work for less wages than men, even doing as hard work, and doing it as well. When more employments are opened to women, they will be able to command higher wages; for if one occupation does not pay, they can enter another." See also Penny's *How Women Can Make Money: Married or Single* (New York: Arno Press, 1971 [1870]).

57. Elizabeth Beardsley Butler, *Saleswomen in Mercantile Stores, Baltimore*

1909 (New York, Russell Sage, 1912), pp. 144, 121. Mary Van Kleeck, *Artificial Flower Makers* (New York: Survey Associates, 1913), pp. 28–29.

58. U.S. Commissioner of Labor, *Working Women in Large Cities*, p. 16.

59. Horace G. Wadlin, "Compensation in Certain Occupations of Graduates of Colleges for Women," from Massachusetts Bureau of the Statistics of Labor, *Twenty-fifth Annual Report, 1894* (Boston: Wright and Potter, 1895), p. 40. "One reason for the low salaries paid in private schools is that there are plenty of young women who will teach merely to obtain pocket money" (p. 29).

60. Van Vorst and Van Vorst, *Woman Who Toils*, pp. 83, 33; see also p. 78. Another version of this kind of opinion came from Annie Marion Mac-Lean, *Wage-Earning Women* (New York: Macmillan, 1910), p. 22, who condemned married women who worked for luxury: "the combined income of husband and wife makes possible a manner of living far ahead of the ordinary laborer. Many . . . spend a considerable amount on amusement, own pianos, fine clothes, and in one case, an automobile."

61. Helen Campbell, *Prisoners of Poverty: Women Wage-Workers, Their Trades and Their Lives* (New York: Garrett Press, 1970 [1883]), p. 73.

62. Carroll D. Wright, *The Working Girls of Boston* (New York: Arno Press, 1969), reprinted from the *Fifteenth Annual Report, 1884* of the Massachusetts Bureau of the Statistics of Labor, p. 120.

63. U.S. Commissioner of Labor, *Working Women in Large Cities*, pp. 22, 24, 18, 17, 14; Mary Coynington, *Relations Between Occupation and Criminality of Women*, Vol. 15 of *Report on Condition of Woman and Child Wage-Earners in the United States*, Senate Doc. 645, 61st Cong., 2d sess. (Washington, D.C.: Government Printing Office, 1911) (hereafter referred to as *Report*), p. 9.

64. Ibid., p. 21.

65. Massey, *Bonnet Brigades*, p. 9. Massey quotes McClelland as saying, "There is such an obvious impropriety in the mixing of the sexes within the walls of a public office that I am determined to arrest the practice."

66. Testimony of William Pollner, in U.S. Education and Labor Committee, *Report Upon the Relations Between Capital and Labor*, 1:597. Alan Dawley, *Class and Community: The Industrial Revolution in Lynn* (Cambridge, Mass.: Harvard University Press, 1976), p. 115, cites the Rev. Joseph Cook, who toured Lynn shoe factories in 1871, to the effect that young girls "grew coarse in appearance, lost the natural 'freshness of complexion'—no longer showed a 'lustreful flash of the eye.'" His report, which included a comment that the incidence of venereal disease had risen alarmingly, drew the ire of female factory employees, who apparently responded that he was "unjust and unchristian." See also Linda Gordon, *Woman's Body, Woman's Right: A Social History of Birth Control in America* (New York: Grossman, 1976), Ch. 8, which suggests some of the fears of working-class sexuality.

67. *Wage Earning Women in Stores and Factories*, Vol. 5 of *Report* (1911), pp. 10, 54.

68. Ibid., pp. 75–76; U.S. Commissioner of Labor, *Working Women in Large Cities*, pp. 21, 14–15.
69. *Final Report and Testimony of the U.S. Commission on Industrial Relations*, 22 vol., Senate Doc. No. 21, 64th Cong., 1st sess. (1916), 3:2343.
70. *The Glass Industry*, Vol. 3 of *Report* (1911), p. 180.
71. Coynington, *Relations Between Occupations and Criminality of Women*, pp. 29, 34. But a cautious approach to these figures is suggested by a comment from one warden: "What's the use of asking these women what their occupation is? . . . They won't tell the truth about it, anyway, so I just put it down as housework. Maybe some of them do something else, but then others don't do anything at all, so it probably averages up all right" (p. 14).
72. *Juvenile Delinquency in Its Relation to Employment*, Vol. 8 of *Report* (1911), pp. 94, 95.
73. Coynington, *Relations Between Occupations and Criminality*, p. 54.
74. Testimony of Lillie Devereux Blake in U.S. Education and Labor Committee, *Report Upon the Relations Between Capital and Labor*, 4:599. The *Revolution* articles can be found in the issues of January 14, 1869; October 8, 1868; October 29, 1868; August 19, 1869.
75. Campbell, *Prisoners of Poverty*, p. 71.
76. Union News Items, January 1913, 3:7, file 5, box 1, WEIU Collection, Schlesinger Library, Radcliffe College.
77. Letter from R.S.P., A Working Girl, New York *Sun*, November 17, 1863, p. 1.
78. J. A. Philip, "The Factory Girl," *Workingman's Advocate*, April 19, 1873, p. 1.
79. *Cry for Justice*, November 29, 1902, p. 15.
80. Ruth Rosen and Sue Davidson, eds., *The Maimie Papers* (Old Westbury, N.Y.: Feminist Press, 1977), p. 12.
81. O'Hare, "Whose Is the Shame?" *Fair Play*, November 17, 1903, pp. 26–27.
82. Penny, *Think and Act*, p. 64. "You touch dirt and it will stick to you," was the way an ironworker described what happened to women in the factories. New York State Factory Investigation Commission, *Second Report to the State Legislature* (1913), p. 939.
83. "Truth About Women in Industry," *North American Review* 178 (May 1904), reprinted in Edna D. Bullock, ed., *Selected Articles on the Employment of Women* (Minneapolis: H. W. Wilson, 1911) p. 107.
84. "Work Is for Men," *Labor Advocate*, March 2, 1901, p. 1.
85. Young Women's Christian Association, *First Report of the Commission on Household Employment* (Los Angeles, May 5–11, 1915), pp. 18, 22. See also pp. 11 and 12; and Lucy Maynard Salmon, *Domestic Service* (New York: Macmillan, 1911), p. 137, and David M. Katzman, *Seven Days a Week: Women and Domestic Service in Industrializing America* (New York: Oxford, 1978).
86. Azel Ames, Jr., *Sex in Industry: A Plea for the Working Girl* (Boston: James R. Osgood, 1875), pp. 26–27. Ames argued that menstrual and

uterine disorders induced by certain kinds of work resulted in insanity
and accounted for the large numbers of working-class women patients in
Massachusetts mental hospitals.

87. Bullock, *Selected Articles on the Employment of Women*, p. 1.
88. Penny, *Think and Act*, pp. 57–58.
89. *Causes of Death Among Women and Child Cotton Mill Operatives*, Vol.
    14 of *Report* (1911), pp. 18, 31. The data were based on studies of Fall
    River, Pawtucket, and Manchester, N. H. See also Alice Hamilton, *Ex-
    ploring the Dangerous Trades* (Boston: Little, Brown, 1943), and Maude
    Swartz, Typescript of address to Fourth New York Women's Trade Un-
    ion League Conference (1926), in New York Women's Trade Union
    League papers, New York Public Library, p. 5.
90. Ames, *Sex in Industry*, p. 24, quoting Dr. Edward Jarvis in the *Fifth
    Report of the Massachusetts Board of Health*.
91. Mrs. Arthur Gray, "Marriage—Woman's Destiny," February 21, 1903,
    p. 11.
92. Catherine Markham, "The Accident of Marriage," February 7, 1903,
    pp. 10–11. See also the editorial "Should a Married Woman Work?"
    February 14, 1903, p. 6.
93. Lydia Kingmiller Commander, "The Bachelor Girl," *Fair Play*, January
    24, 1903, pp. 29–30.

5. Women's Choices in an Expanding Labor Market

1. U.S. Bureau of the Census, *Historical Statistics of the U.S.: Colonial
   Times to 1970*, 2 vols. (1975), 1: 49. The following table charts live births
   of each 1,000 women aged 15–44 years old. Up to 1920, these data are
   available only for white women.

Year	White	Negro & other
1800	278.0	
1810	274.0	
1820	260.0	
1830	240.0	
1840	222.0	
1850	194.0	
1860	184.0	
1870	167.0	
1880	155.0	
1890	137.0	
1900	130.0	
1910	123.8	
1920	117.2	140.8
1930	87.1	105.9
1940	77.1	102.4
1950	102.3	137.3
1960	113.2	153.6
1970	84.1	113.0

For marriage figures, see Conrad Taeuber and Irene Taeuber, *The
Changing Population of the U.S.* (New York: John Wiley, 1958), pp. 148,

261. Wilson H. Grabill, Clyde V. Kiser, and Pascal K. Whelpton, *The Fertility of American Women* (New York: John Wiley, 1958), pp. 12–13, comment on the regional exceptions within these data. For example, the birth rate in New England between 1891–95 and 1921–25 climbed nearly 10 percent for native-born women, while the rate for foreign-born women dropped 26 percent. This reflects the low fertility rate of New England as a whole in the period before 1890.

2. Grabill, Kiser, and Whelpton, *Fertility of American Women*, p. 14; Taeuber and Taeuber, *Changing Population of the U.S.*, p. 250; Robert Wells, "Demographic Change and the Life Cycle of American Families," in Theodore Raab and Robert I. Rutberg, eds., *The Family in History* (New York: Harper & Row, 1971), p. 88.

3. Grabill, Kiser, and Whelpton, *Fertility of American Women*, p. 380; *Historical Statistics of the U.S.*, 1:42. By 1950 only 11 percent of the population lived in households of five or more, and less than 5 percent lived in households of seven or more. Wells, "Demographic Changes and the Life Cycle of American Families," pp. 88, 91.

4. Massachusetts Bureau of Labor, *The Relative Cost of Home-Cooked and Purchased Food*, Bulletin 19 (August 1901), p. 98.

5. U.S. Department of Agriculture, *Domestic Needs of Farm Women*, Report 104, March 18, 1915 (1915), pp. 22–23. See Joan Jensen, "Cloth, Butter and Boarders: Women's Household Production for the Market," *Review of Political Economics* 12 (Summer 1980): 17–19.

6. Janet Hooks, *Women's Occupations Through Seven Decades*, Women's Bureau Bulletin 218 (Washington, D.C.: Government Printing Office, 1947), p. 145. This figure compares with one worker for every 679 people in 1870.

7. Siegfried Giedion, *Mechanization Takes Command: A Contribution to Anonymous History* (New York: Norton, 1969 [1948]), pp. 560 ff. For a study of the impact of technology on women of different classes, see Susan J. Kleinberg, "Technology's Stepdaughters: the Impact of Industrialization on Working Class Women, Pittsburgh, 1865–1890" (Ph.D. diss., University of Pittsburgh, 1973).

8. Hooks, *Women's Occupations Through Seven Decades*, p. 96.

9. In 1870 there was one service worker for every 8.4 families. By 1920 the figure was one for every 18 families. Ibid., p. 139. The other side of this coin is of course what happens to the notion of service where domestic workers correctly perceive their tasks as increasingly onerous and abandon them for new jobs in laundries, stores, factories, and offices as they become available. This process helps to create America's perpetual servant crises, and forces affluent women to consider a transition in the notion of service from sleep-in to daily help.

10. The work of Carroll Smith-Rosenberg is important in illuminating the problems of middle-class women in the nineteenth century. See, for example, "Hysterical Women: Sex Roles and Role Conflict in Nineteenth Century America," *Social Research* 39 (Winter 1972): 652–78. Good perspectives on the forces driving the late-nineteenth-century

middle-class woman can be obtained from any of a number of autobiographies and biographies, including Vida Scudder, *On Journey* (New York: Dutton, 1937); Mary Kingsbury Simkhovitch, *Neighborhood: My Story of Greenwich House* (New York: Norton, 1938), Josephine Goldmark, *Impatient Crusader: Florence Kelley's Life Story* (Urbana: University of Illinois Press, 1953); Allen F. Davis, *American Heroine: The Life and Legend of Jane Addams* (New York: Oxford University Press, 1973).

11. This figure began to change after 1900. Yet, according to Roberta Wien, "Women's Colleges and Domesticity, 1875–1918," *Harvard Education Quarterly* 14 (Spring 1974): 37, 38, even when the classes up to 1908 are included, only 45 percent of Bryn Mawr graduates and 57 percent of Wellesley graduates married.

12. Sheila Rothman, *Woman's Proper Place: A History of Changing Ideals and Practices, 1870 to the Present* (New York: Basic Books, 1978), pp. 65–66.

13. Allen F. Davis, *Spearheads for Reform: The Social Settlements and the Progressive Movement, 1890–1914* (New York: Oxford University Press, 1967), describes the work of some of these people. The results of their efforts are found in such books as Helen Campbell, *Prisoners of Poverty: Women Wage Workers, Their Trades and Their Lives* (New York: Garret Press, 1970 [1887]); Elizabeth Butler, *Women and the Trades: Pittsburgh, 1907–1908* (New York: Charities Publication Committee, 1909); and Elizabeth Butler, *Saleswomen in Mercantile Stores: Baltimore, 1909* (New York: Russell Sage, 1912).

14. Mary Roth Walsh, *Doctors Wanted: No Women Need Apply. Sexual Barriers in the Medical Profession, 1835–1975* (New Haven: Yale University Press, 1977), Ch. 6, and especially pp. 191, 193, argues that the women's medical colleges had "virtually disappeared" by 1903.

15. The Bureau was headed by Frances Cummings, then by Emilie Hutchinson.

16. Joseph Hill, *Women in Gainful Occupations, 1870–1920*, Census Monograph 9 (Washington, D.C.: Government Printing Office, 1929), p. 56. See Dee Garrison, *Apostles of Culture: The Public Librarian and American Society, 1876–1920* (New York: Free Press, 1979), Ch. 11, for the role of female librarians in the professions.

17. See Susan Cayleff, "The Eradication of Female Midwifery" (M.A. diss., Sarah Lawrence College, 1978). For data on the number of professional workers see Hooks, *Women's Occupations Through Seven Decades*, pp. 65–66.

18. Barbara Ehrenreich and Deirdre English, *For Her Own Good: 150 Years of the Experts' Advice to Women* (Garden City, N.Y.: Doubleday Anchor, 1978), pp. 145–47; Giedion, *Mechanization Takes Command*, pp. 519–520.

19. Heidi Hartmann, "Capitalism and Women's Work in the Home: 1900–1930" (Ph.D. diss., Yale University, 1974).

20. The shift occurred largely at the expense of Negro and immigrant

women, as the following table indicates. The table is derived from data in Hill, *Women in Gainful Occupations*, pp. 85, 94, 102, 110; and U.S. Census Bureau, *Eleventh Census of Population* (1890), p. clx, and *Fourteenth Census of Population* (1920), p. 15 (Orientals and Indians excluded).

Comparison of Wage-Earning Women in Different Groups with Their Proportion in Population as a Whole, 1890–1920

	Native-born of Native-born Parents	Native-born of Foreign Parents	Foreign-born	Negro
	Percentages of Total Number of Women Engaged in Gainful Occupations			
1890	35.3	20.9	20.4	23.4
1900	36.7	22.6	17.4	23.2
1910	38.3	22.0	16.1	23.9
1920	43.8	24.9	13.4	17.6
	Percentage of Total Population			
1890	55.03	-18.37	14.4	12.2
1900	53.9	20.6	13.4	11.6
1910	53.8	20.5	14.5	10.7
1920	55.3	21.4	13.0	9.9

21. Isaac A. Hourwich, *Immigration and Labor: The Economic Aspects of European Immigration to the United States* (New York: B. W. Huebsch, 1922), p. 232.

22. Susan J. Kleinberg, "Technology and Women's Work: The Lives of Working Class Women in Pittsburgh, 1870–1900," *Labor History* 17 (Winter 1976): 61.

23. Donald Cole, *Immigrant City: Lawrence, Massachusetts, 1845–1921* (Chapel Hill: University of North Carolina Preess, 1963), p. 118.

24. Margaret Byington, *Homestead: The Households of a Mill Town* (Pittsburgh: University of Pittsburgh Press, 1974 [1910]), Ch. 10, and especially pp. 152 and 154.

25. Anthony F. C. Wallace, *Rockdale: The Growth of an American Village in the Early Industrial Revolution* (New York: Alfred Knopf, 1978), Ch. 2. Wallace notes that in this small Pennsylvania town wives could and did work in the mill, but it was normally much more lucrative for them to work at home by taking in boarders. Single people needed places to live, and three or more boarders could provide as much income as an entire family could earn at the mill. A family unit, whether headed by a male or a female, could not maintain itself comfortably without the combined mill earnings of a few members and the additional income provided by boarders.

26. Cole, *Immigrant City*, p. 103, estimates that 36 percent of female employees in the textile mills were married. *The Cotton Textile Industry*, Vol 1 of *Report on Condition of Women and Child Wage-Earners in the United States*, Senate Doc. 645, 61st Cong., 2d sess. (Washington, D.C.:

Government Printing Office, 1910) (hereafter cited as *Report*), p. 129, gives a nationwide estimate of 27.9 percent married, with figures ranging up to 35.3 percent for English-born women. See also *Family Budgets of Typical Cotton Mill Workers*, Vol. 26 of *Report*, (1911), p. 22; Wallace, *Rockdale*, pp. 65–69.

27. *The Silk Industry*, Vol. 4 of *Report* (1910) pp. 20–21. The report assessed the extent to which mill owners relied on the female relatives of under-paid male workers. "If the local industries are those employing mostly male labor, such as collieries, tanneries, breweries . . . etc., there will be considerable unemployed female labor in the families of these male workers which can often be secured at a fair price" (pp. 23–24).

28. *Family Budgets of Typical Cotton Mill Workers*, pp. 21, 153, 176.

29. Stanley Lebergott, *Manpower in Economic Growth: The American Record Since 1800* (New York: McGraw-Hill, 1964), p. 154; Hill, *Women in Gainful Occupations*, pp. 75–76. In 1920, 49.6 percent of unmarried women were counted as in the paid labor force.

30. Mary Van Kleeck, *Women in the Bookbinding Trade* (New York: Survey Associates, 1913), pp. 87, 91; *Wage Earning Women in Stores and Factories*, Vol. 5 of *Report* (1911), p. 10.

31. Claudia Goldin, "Female Labor Force Participation: The Origin of Black and White Differences, 1870–1880," *Journal of Economic History* 37 (March 1977): 95–96, 106; and see also Elizabeth Pleck, "A Mother's Wages: Income Earning Among Married Italians and Black Women, 1896–1911," in Michael Gordon, ed., *The American Family in Social Historical Perspective*, 2d ed. (New York: St. Martin's, 1978), p. 496, for a comparative table of income earning among wives in Polish, Irish, Italian, German, black and Russian Jewish families.

32. Marie Hall Ets, *Rosa: The Life of an Italian Immigrant* (Minneapolis: University of Minnesota, 1970), passim.

33. *Report of the Industrial Commission on the Relations and Conditions of Capital and Labor Employed in Manufactures and General Business*, 16 vols. (1901), 15: 326.

34. Ets, *Rosa*, pp. 160, 174.

35. Alice M. O'Connor, "A Study of the Immigration Problem in Lawrence, Massachusetts," c. 1915, typescript in the Merrimack Valley Textile Museum, p. 49.

36. *Report on the Strike of Textile Workers in Lawrence, Massachusetts, in 1912*. Senate Doc. 870, 62d Cong., 2d sess. (1912), pp. 24–25; Cole, *Immigrant City*, p. 108.

37. Byington, *Homestead*, p. 152; Virginia Yans-McLaughlin, *Family and Community: Italian Immigrants in Buffalo, 1880–1930* (Ithaca, N.Y.: Cornell University Press, 1977), p. 200; Thomas Kessner, *The Golden Door: Italian and Jewish Immigrant Mobility in New York City, 1880–1915* (New York: Oxford University Press, 1977), pp. 99–102.

38. *The Cotton Textile Industry*, p. 545; Byington. *Homestead*, pp. 108, 201.

39. Isaac Metzker, ed., *A Bintel Brief* (New York: Ballantine Books, 1971), pp. 65–66.

40. Byington, *Homestead*, Ch. 10 and especially pp. 152 and 154; *The Cotton Textile Industry*, p. 545.

41. Daniel J. Walkowitz, *Worker City, Company Town: Iron and Cotton Worker Protest in Troy and Cohoes, New York, 1855–84* (Urbana: University of Illinois Press, 1978), p. 62.

42. Tamara Hareven and Randolph Langenbach, *Amoskeag: Life and Work in an American Factory City* (New York: Pantheon, 1978), p. 157.

43. Tamara Hareven, "Family Time and Industrial Time: Family and Work in a Planned Corporation," in Tamara Hareven, ed., *Family and Kin in Urban Communities* (New York: New Viewpoints, 1977), pp. 187–207; and Louise C. Odencrantz, *Italian Women in Industry: A Study of Conditions in New York City* (New York: Russell Sage, 1919), p. 283.

44. For example, see *Wage Earning Women in Stores and Factories*, p. 18, which comments, "It is doubted if anything in the whole report is more significant than the large percentage of the women wage earners living at home who were turning into the family fund all their earnings. . . ." Odencrantz, *Italian Women in Industry*, p. 21.

45. Anzia Yezierska, *Bread Givers* (New York: Braziller, 1975 [1925]), p. 248.

46. Agnes Smedley, *Daughter of Earth* (Old Westbury, N.Y.: Feminist Press, 1973 [1928]), pp. 71, 78.

47. Ella Wolff interview, Amerikaner Yiddishe Geschichte Bel-pe, pp. 2, 3, YIVO Archives, New York City.

48. Dania L. Siergiej, "Early Polish Immigrants to Lawrence, Massachusetts: European Background and Statistical Profile" (M.A. diss., Tufts University, June 1977), p. 103. See also Barbara Klaczynska, "Working Women in Philadelphia, 1900–1930" (Ph.D. diss., Temple University, 1975).

49. Virginia Penny, *Think and Act: A Series of Articles Pertaining to Men and Women, Work and Wages* (Philadelphia: Claxton, Remsen and Haffelfinger, 1869), p. 51; pamphlets, Women's Educational and Industrial Union Collection, Schlesinger Library.

50. Anzia Yezierska, *Arrogant Beggar* (New York: Grosset & Dunlap, 1927), p. 61; Rose Cohen, *Out of the Shadow* (New York: George H. Dosan, 1918), pp. 159–59. For more reactions of servants in this period, see David M. Katzman, *Seven Days a Week: Women and Domestic Service in Industrial America* (New York: Oxford University Press, 1978), Ch. 1. Hasia Diner, "New Homes, New Lives, New Women: Irish Immigrants to America" (unpublished ms., Bunting Institute, Radcliffe College), argues that first-generation Irish women chose domestic service for its relatively good pay.

51. Frances Kellor, "The Immigrant Woman," p. 402, article from an unknown journal found in file 152, box 7, Women's Educational and Industrial Union Collection; Hill, *Women in Gainful Occupations*, pp. 101, 106. Among female servants 27.6 percent were foreign-born, as compared with 16 percent of workers as a whole.

52. Mary Van Kleeck, *Artificial Flower Makers* (New York: Survey Associaates, 1913), p. 38.

53. Mary Kenney O'Sullivan, "Autobiography," in O'Sullivan Papers, Schlesinger Library, p. 28.

54. Quoted in Daniel Walkowitz, "Working Class Women in the Gilded Age: Factory, Community and Family Life Among Cohoes, N.Y., Cotton Workers," *Journal of Social History*, Summer 1972, p. 476.

55. Yezierska, *Arrogant Beggar*, p. 63.

56. Clipping from the *Utica Daily Press*, March 29, 1899, in file 85, box 8, O'Reilly Collection, Schlesinger Library.

57. *Wage Earning Women in Stores and Factories*, pp. 134–35.

58. "Statements of Factory Girls on the 9-hour Day," file 38, box 3, Consumers' League of Connecticut Collection, Schlesinger Library, Radcliffe College.

59. Mary Barnett Gilson, *What's Past Is Prologue: Reflections on My Industrial Experience* (New York: Harper and Brothers, 1940), p. 77. Gilson (p. 66) cites as an example of a consciousness of rise in social status that accompanied transfer from factory to office a young woman promoted to forewoman who came to ask for advice about books: "When I was in school I spoke English that was something lovely, but since I've been mixing with the nationalities I've lost it something awful and now that I'm a supervisor I must set an example so the girls will look up to me."

60. Agnes Nestor, *Woman's Labor Leader* (Rockford, Ill.: Bellevue Books, 1954), p. 35.

61. *Wage Earning Women in Stores and Factories*, p. 199.

62. *The Glass Industry*, Vol. 3 of *Report* (1910), p. 300. Another job that exposed women to the constant danger of burns and flying glass but where women worked in an enclosure with no men present was considered fit for women.

63. These quotes are from the Young Women's Christian Association's *First Report of the Commission on Household Employment* (Los Angeles, May 5–11, 1915), pp. 19. 20, 29.

64. *Wage Earning Women in Stores and Factories*, p. 193.

65. Butler, *Saleswomen in Mercantile Stores*, p. 151; Schneiderman, *All for One*, p. 43. By the 1920s the balance had shifted in favor of office work. Frances K. Donovan wrote *The Saleslady* (Chicago: University of Chicago, 1929) to encourage girls to consider department store as opposed to office jobs. The former paid well and offered opportunities to advance, but the latter carried more status and a chance to marry the boss.

66. Odencrantz, *Italian Women in Industry*, pp. 39, 40.

67. Butler, *Saleswomen in Mercantile Stores*, p. 26.

68. U.S. Commissioner of Labor, *Fourth Annual Report, 1888, Working Women in Large Cities* (1889), p. 25.

69. Van Kleeck, *Artificial Flower Makers*, pp. 28–29, 30, 32, 33, 67–68. For work patterns among Italian immigrant women see Virginia Yans McLaughlin, "A Flexible Tradition: South Italian Immigrants Confront a

New York Experience," *Journal of Social History* 7 (Summer 1974): 429–45.

70. Siergiej, "Early Polish Immigrants to Lawrence," p. 103. See also Vera Shlakman, *Economic History of a Factory Town: A Study of Chicopee, Massachusetts, Smith College Studies in History* 20, nos. 1–4 (October 1934–July 1935), p. 181, who reports that by 1875, foreign-born immigrants had disrupted the homogeneity of a family Yankee mill town.

71. Butler, *Women and the Trades*, p. 26.

72. Gilson. *What's Past Is Prologue*, p. 66

73. U.S. Commissioner of Labor, *Working Women in Large Cities*, pp. 19, 26, 20. Penny, *Think and Act*, p. 53, offers the following generalization: "the intellect, education, and intelligence of women engaged in each employment probably vary as much as among men in the same or similar occupations. . . . But an estimate of the proportionate differences would require a careful investigation. For instance, the majority of store girls have more refinement and intelligence than factory girls. An exception should be made of those formerly at Lowell. Those engaged in teaching are superior to both. Among seamstresses there is a greater diversity, descending from the reduced but delicate, refined and cultivated woman, who has lost property and relations, to the most ignorant and stupid specimens of humanity."

74. Helen Campbell, *Prisoners of Poverty: Women Wage-Workers, Their Trades and Their Lives* (New York: Garrett Press, 1970 [1887]), p. 173; Horace G. Wadlin, *Compensation in Certain Occupations of Graduates of Colleges for Women*, from the 25th Annual Report of the Massachusetts Bureau of Statistics of Labor for 1894 (Boston: Wright and Potter, 1895), p. 47; U.S. Education and Labor Committee, *Report Upon the Relations Between Capital and Labor*, 4 vols. (1885), 3: 36; Virginia Penny, *How Women Can Make Money: Married or Single* (New York: Arno Press, 1971 [1870]), pp. 210, 146, and see also p. 217.

75. Butler, *Saleswomen in Mercantile Stores*, pp. 144, 121. Of a total of forty-five Slavic girls in thirty-four shops, thirty-five worked as unprestigious alteration hands.

76. Penny, *How Women Can Make Money*, p. 146; *The Glass Industry*, p 418; U.S. Education and Labor Committee, *Report Upon the Relations Between Capital and Labor*, 3: 36, reproduced the following exchange between Gilbert Whitman, agent of the Amory Manufacturing Company in Manchester, N.H., and committee interrogators.

Q: What nationalities are weavers?
A: One-third are Canadians—the rest are English, English-Americans; Irish, Irish-American; Scotch, Scotch-American; German, German-American.
Q: Have you any of the original American girls?
A: Very few. They go into the cloth room.
Q: Why?
A: Because it is clean, light work.
Q: They prefer it?

A: Yes.
Q: It is a sort of aristocratic employment is it?
A: Yes.
Q: Then our American girls are on top, are they?
A: Yes.

77. U.S. Commissioner of Labor, *Working Women in Large Cities*, p. 25; Testimony of T. P. Rixey, November 14, 1900, *Final Report and Testimony of the U.S. Commission on Industrial Relations*, 22 vols.. Senate Doc. 21, 64th Cong., 1st sess. (1916), 14: 74.

78. Broadus Mitchell, *The Rise of the Cotton Mills in the South* (Baltimore: Johns Hopkins University Press, 1921), p. 221; *The Silk Industry*, p. 21; *The Cotton Textile Industry*, p. 118.

79. Hill, *Women in Gainful Occupations*, pp. 36, 45, 60; Hooks, *Women's Occupations Through Seven Decades*, pp. 140, 66.

6. *Technology, Efficiency, and Resistance*

1. Lucille Foster McMillin, *Women in the Federal Service* (Washington, D.C.: U.S. Civil Service Commission, 1941), pp. 5–9. General Francis Spinner, Treasurer of the United States in 1862, is commonly given credit for bringing women into federal government employment. McMillin argues that the Patent Office employed women in 1854 and the Post Office hired women as postmistresses in the eighteenth century. It is unclear whether those employed in the Patent Office merely picked up their work to do at home. *Gleason's Pictorial* (July 17, 1852), p. 41, illustrates men and women working together in the U.S. Mint, in Philadelphia. The quote comes from Elizabeth Massey, *Bonnet Brigades* (New York: Alfred Knopf, 1966), p. 9.

2. "Women and Their Wages," *Workingman's Advocate*, September 8, 1866, p. 4.

3. *Report of the Industrial Commission on the Relations and Conditions of Capital and Labor Employed in Manufactures and General Business*, Vol. 14 (Westport, Conn.: Greenwood Press, 1970) [1901]) (hereafter cited as *Report of the Industrial Commission*), p. 649.

4. *The Glass Industry*, Vol. 3 of the *Report on Condition of Woman and Child Wage-Earners in the United States*. Senate Doc. 645. 61st Cong., 2d sess. (Washington, D.C.: Government Printing Office, 1970) (hereafter cited as *Report*), p. 286. As a result of these changes, the number of women in the glass industry though always relatively small, increased fivefold between 1850 and 1900, compared to a rate of increase of less than two and a half times for men in the same period. After 1905 the use of both women and boys decreased (p. 283).

5. Quoted in Charlotte Erickson, *American Industry and the European Immigrant* (Cambridge, Mass.: Harvard University Press, 1957), p. 132; Robert Ozanne, *A Century of Labor-Management Relations at McCormick and International Harvester* (Madison: University of Wisconsin Press, 1967), p. 20, offers an example of rapid technological turnover that did not benefit women directly. In that instance, skilled molders were

replaced by machinery that could be operated by unskilled males, with the result that the union run by craftsmen was eliminated.

6. *The Silk Industry*, Vol. 4 of Report (1911), pp. 35–36, cites one Paterson, N.J., plant which in 1875 had 72.5 percent males and 27.5 percent females. By 1905 it had reversed the ratio to 23 percent males and 77 percent females. Edith Abbott, *Women in Industry: A Study in American Economic History* (New York: Arno Press, 1969 [1910]), p. 108. quoting the 1905 census of manufactures. In the South, for example, in 1880, 46.5 percent of the workers in cotton textiles were women. By 1905, only 31.6 percent were women. Cf. *The Textile Industry*, Vol. 1 of *Report* (1910), pp. 28–29.

7. Janet Hooks, *Women's Occupations Through Seven Decades*, Women's Bureau Bulletin 218 (Washington, D.C.: Government Printing Office, 1947), p. 125; Abbott, *Women in Industry*, pp. 148–85. See also Blanche Hazard, *The Organization of the Boot and Shoe Industry in Massachusetts before 1875*, Vol. 23 of *Harvard Economic Studies* (Cambridge: Harvard University Press, 1921), p. 140.

8. Frederick Winslow Taylor, *The Principles of Scientific Management* (New York: Norton, 1967 [1911]), p. 36.

9. David Montgomery, *Workers' Control in America: Studies in the History of Work, Technology and Labor Struggles* (Cambridge: Cambridge University Press, 1979), and Harry Braverman, *Labor and Monopoly Capital: The Degradation of Work in the Twentieth Century* (New York: Monhtly Review Press, 1974).

10. For examples see the comments of organizer Sarah Conboy and United Textile Workers president John Golden, as cited in the *American Federationist*, August 1911, pp. 603–4. For a relatively positive view, see Sue Ainslie Clark and Edith Wyatt, *Making Both Ends Meet: The Income and Outlay of New York Working Girls* (New York: Macmillan, 1911), Ch. 7.

11. Mary Van Kleeck, *Women in the Bookbinding Trade* (New York: Survey Associates, 1913), p. 82. See also Susan Porter Benson, "The Clerking Sisterhood: Saleswomen in American Department Stores, 1890–1960" (Paper presented at the 1976 American Historical Association Convention), pp. 12–13. Montgomery, *Workers' Control in America*, pp. 38, 39, suggests, however, that women, because they were young, were less likely to restrict output than men, so the evidence is clearly not all in on this point.

12. Mary Barnett Gilson, *What's Past Is Prologue: Reflections on My Industrial Experience* (New York: Harper and Brothers, 1940), pp. 186, 122.

13. Anna Lalor Burdick, "Woman's Place in Industry," *Independent Woman*, March 1920. There were problems with promoting women, however as Gilson pointed out (p. 76) in recalling a young Bohemian woman whom she wanted to promote to forewoman to instruct others. The woman refused the promotion despite an offer of higher pay. "Finally she told me she went to the same church as a lot of the other workers, that she went to the same dances and parties, and that it would be

embarrassing for her to be 'over them.' I reminded her that our foremen and forewomen did not exercise authority, but that they substituted
responsibility for authority. I said all of us were performing some function or other and hers would be instruction just as mine was employment.
She hesitated as though she might yield for a moment, and then said,
'How would I feel if I had to correct my boy friend's sister's work?' "

14. Maurine Weiner Greenwald, "The Transformation of Work and Workers' Consciousness in the Telephone Industry, 1880–1925" (Paper presented at the 1976 American Historical Association Convention), pp.
2, 4. Operators were 99 percent female by 1917.

15. George Manson, *Work for Women* (New York: G. P. Putnam's Sons,
1883), p. 10. Hooks, *Women's Occupations Through Seven Decades*, p.
75.

16. Chairman Pitzer of the National Association of Corporate Schools, Fifth
Annual Convention, *Addresses, Reports, Bibliographies and Discussions*
(1917), p. 105.

17. Quoted in Margery Davies, "A Woman's Place Is at the Typewriter," in
Richard Edwards et al., eds., *Labor Market Segmentation* (Lexington,
Mass.: D. C. Heath, 1975), p. 290.

18. Braverman, *Labor and Monopoly Capital*, p. 305.

19. *Final Report and Testimony of the U.S. Commission on Industrial Relations*, 22 vols., Senate Doc. 21, 64th Cong., 1st sess. (1916) (hereafter
cited as *Commission on Industrial Relations*) 4: 3152.

20. Milton J. Nadworny, *Scientific Management and the Unions, 1900–1932:
A Historical Analysis* (Cambridge, Mass.: Harvard University Press.
1955), pp. 99–101, 118. Protocolism lasted until 1917, when the agreements were rejected by the Dress and Waist Manufacturers' Association.
See Hyman Berman, "Era of the Protocol: A Chapter in the History of
the I.L.G.W.U., 1910–1916" (Ph.D. diss., Columbia University, 1956).

21. David Montgomery, "The New Unionism and the Transformation of
Workers' Consciousness in America," *Journal of Social History* 7 (Summer 1974): 509–29

22. Selig Perlman, *A History of Trade Unionism in the U.S.* (New York:
Macmillan, 1923), p. 166. For illustrations of AFL policies, see James
Weinstein, *The Corporate Ideal in the Liberal State, 1900–1918* (Boston:
Beacon Press, 1968), especially Chs. 1 and 2; and Stanley Aronowitz,
False Promises (New York: McGraw-Hill, 1973), Ch. 3.

23. The proportion of foreign-born and native-born daughters of foreign-born
women declined slightly in this period, and women continued to shift
from manual sectors to low-level clerical sectors of the work force. See
U.S. Census Bureau, *Fourteenth Census of Population* (1920), 3: 15. Such
occupations as taking in boarders, home work, and working in family
businesses were not counted by census takers. Women who worked on
their husbands' farms were counted in 1910. Including these legitimate
forms of labor would create drastic upward revisions in the proportion
of working women, but we have no way of knowing by how much. The

figures include black women, more than 40 percent of whom worked for wages, compared to about 20 percent of white women. About 32 percent of married black women worked, compared to less than 6 percent of married white women. Black wage-earning women were far more heavily concentrated in agricultural and domestic-service jobs than their white counterparts. Figures are from Joseph Hill, *Women in Gainful Occupations, 1870–1920*, Census Monograph 9 (Washington, D.C.: Government Printing Office, 1929), Chs. 5 and 9; and Hooks, *Women's Occupations Through Seven Decades*, pp. 37, 39.

24. John Andrews and W. D. P. Bliss, *A History of Women in Trade Unions*, Vol. 10 of *Report on Condition of Woman and Child Wage-Earners in the United States*, Senate Doc. 645, 61st Cong., 2d sess. (Washington, D.C.: Government Printing Office, 1911; reprint ed., New York: Arno Press, 1974), p. 151.

25. John Safford, "The Good That Trade Unions Do," Part 1, *American Federationist* 9 (July 1902): 353, 358; "Talks on Labor," *American Federationist* 12 (November 1905): 846; William Gilthorpe, "Advancement," *American Federationist* 17 (October 1910): 847; John Safford, "The Good That Trade Unions Do," Part 2, *American Federationist* 9 (August 1902): 423; Edward O'Donnell, "Women as Breadwinners: The Error of the Age," *American Federationist* 4 (October 1897): 186. The article continued: "The wholesale employment of women in the various handicrafts must gradually unsex them as it most assuredly is demoralizing them, or stripping them of that modest demeanor that lends a charm to to their kind, while it numerically strengthens the multitudinous army of loafers, paupers, tramps and policemen." Testimony of Edward Parker to New York State Factory Investigating Commission, *Second Report to the Legislature* (1913), 4: 1811. "Some women could not boil water without burning it, and to become the wife of a man they should have a training at home and learn housework."

26. Eva McDonald Valesh, "Women and Labor," *American Federationist* 3 (February 1896): 222; W. T. Provert of the Brooklyn, N.Y., Moulders' Union offered the following testimony to the New York State Factory Investigating Commission (*Second Report to the Legislature*, 3: 934–35):

> . . . when the first women were put in foundries, and the foundrymen were told at that time when they put them in there what the attitude of the men molders were, and they told us that they only wanted these girls to make these little bits of cores, they are not going to hurt you, they are not going to take the place of the men, but will eliminate the boys, and we agreed to that, to let the girls come in and make these small type of cores.
> Today those girls are using these monstrous rammers, and making cores of great size . . . and there are very few men there now.

27. Samuel Gompers, "Should the Wife Help Support the Family?" *American Federationist* 13 (January 1906): 36. See also Stuart Reid, "The Joy of Labor? Plutocracy's Hypocritical Sermonizing Exposed—A Satire," *American Federationist* 11 (November 1904): 977–78.

28. Birmingham *Labor Advocate*, October 10, 1903, p. 1.

29. Editorial *American Federationist* 11 (July 1904): 584.

30. "Mainly Progressive," *American Federationist* 3 (March 1896): 16. "What Our Organizers Are Doing," *American Federationist* 10 (April 1903): 370; "Trade Union History," *American Federationist* 9 (November 1902): 871.

31. Gompers, "Should the Wife Help Support the Family?" p. 36. See also Louis Vigoreux, "Social Results of the Labor Movement in America," *American Federationist* 6 (April 1899): 25. Resistance to organizing women remained unchanged at least until the mid-1920s. In 1918 two women members of the Federation offered a resolution to the national convention urging the addition of two women to the all-male executive board. It was quietly suppressed. See Mildred Rankin to Mrs. Raymond Robins, March 30, 1919, The Margaret Dreier Robins Papers, University of Florida Libraries.

32. On the Chicago Ladies' Federal Labor Union, see Meredith Tax, *The Rising of the Women: Feminist Solidarity and Class Conflict, 1880–1917* (New York: Monthly Review Press, 1980), Ch. 3.

33. "Women's Labor Resolution," *American Federationist* 5 (January 1899): 220; "Talks on Labor," *American Federationist* 10 (June 1903): 447; Massachusetts Women's Trade Union League, *History of Trade Unionism Among Women in Boston* (Boston: WTUL, n.d.), p. 13; Elizabeth Baker, *Technology and Women's Work* (New York: Columbia University Press, 1964), p. 33.

34. Gompers, "Should the Wife Help Support the Family?" p. 36.

35. Alice Woodridge, "Women's Labor," *American Federationist* 1 (April 1894): 66–67; Valesh, "Women and Labor," p. 222; and Massachusetts WTUL, *History of Trade Unionism*, p. 32.

36. "WTUL Action on Policies," pp. 3, 8, box 4, accession no. 55A556, Record Group 86 Women's Bureau Collection, National Archives (hereafter cited as WB/NA); *Proceedings* of the AFL convention, 1923. See also Massachusetts WTUL, *History of Trade Unionism*, p. 32.

37. Blankenhorn manuscript notes, Ch. 4, p. 17, file 24, box 1, Ann Craton Blankenhorn Collection, Archives of Labor History and Urban Affairs, Wayne State University. Such examples of family unity are not unusual in the mine/mill towns of western Pennsylvania and the Appalachian Mountains. Women helped to picket during strikes, provided essential support services, and sometimes spearheaded attacks against mine management.

38. Pauline Newman, undated interview, Amerikaner Yiddishe Geschichte Bel-pe, p. 21, YIVO Archives, New York City. Gladys Boone, *The Women's Trade Union League in Great Britain and the U.S.A.* (New York: Columbia University Press, 1942), p. 166, recounts a similar incident as having taken place in 1918. I suspect that it might be the same one and that her date is incorrect. Andrews and Bliss, *History of Women in Trade Unions*, p. 149, note that women practically disappeared from this union between 1905 and 1910—a period in which master bakers were rapidly being eliminated by machinery.

39. Mildred Rankin to Mrs. Raymond Robins, March 30, 19 Collection.
40. Boone, *The Women's Trade Union League*, p. 167; Alice Henry, *in the Labor Movement* (New York: Doran, 1923), p. 102.
41. Interview with Vail Ballou Press, "Effects of Legislation: Night Schedule, New York," Interviews for Bulletin no. 13, Accession 51A101, WB/NA.
42. See, for example, Mildred Rankin to Mrs. Raymond Robins, March 3 1919, Robins Collection; and M. E. Jackson, "The Colored Woman in Industry," *Crisis* 17 (November 1918): 14; New York Women's Trade Union League, *Report of Proceedings*, Fourth Annual Conference of Trade Union Women, October 9–10, 1926, p. 14.
43. "Undated interviews, unions" (for Bulletin 65), WB/NA.
44. Testimony of Hilda Svenson, *Commission on Industrial Relations*, 3: 2307. The testimony was taken in June 1914. For more examples of union discrimination see Massachusetts WTUL, *History of Trade Unionism*, p. 13; Andrews and Bliss, *History of Women in Trade Unions*, pp. 156, 157; Alice Henry, *The Trade Union Woman* (New York: Burt Franklin, 1973), p. 150.
45. Maurine Weiner Greenwald, *Women, War and Work: The Impact of World War I on Women Workers in the United States* (Westport, Conn.: Greenwood Press, 1980) pp. 167–169. Greenwald points out that only in Kansas City did unionized workers accept women without protest.
46. Emma Steghagen to Mary Anderson, January 15, 1919, "WTUL Action on Policies," Box 4, accession no. 55A556, WB/NA.
47. Interviews with Tony Salerno, Amalgamated Clothing Workers' Union and Hat and Cap Makers' Local 7, Boston, "Individual interviews, Unions," accession no. 51A101, WB/NA. Massachusetts WTUL, *History of Trade Unionism*, p. 11.
48. Lizzie Swank Holmes, "Women Workers of Chicago," *American Federationist* 12 (August 1905): 507–10; Eva McDonald Valesh, "Women in Welfare Work," *American Federationist* 15 (April 1908): 282–84; "Mainly Progressive," *American Federationist* 3 (March 1896): 16.
49. Interview with Faige Shapiro, August 6, 1964, Amerikaner Yiddishe Geschichte Bel-pe, p. 25.
50. *Justice*, April 19, 1919, p. 2.
51. Blankenhorn manuscript notes, Ch. 13, p. 4, file 25, box 1, Blankenhorn Collection.
52. Blankenhorn manuscript notes, Ch. 2, p. 12, file 23, box 1, Blankenhorn Collection. For another example, see Netti Chandler, "Virginia Home Visits," Bulletin 10, accession no. 51A101, WB/NA.
53. Interview with Faige Shapiro, pp. 2, 7.
54. Quoted in Andrews and Bliss, *History of Women in Trade Unions*, p. 173. And see *American Federationist* 6 (November 1899): 228.
55. New York WTUL, *Report of the Proceedings*, p. 18.
56. Vera Shlakman, *Economic History of a Factory Town: A Study of Chicopee, Massachusetts, Smith College Studies in History* 20, nos. 1–4 (Octo-

4–July 1935), p. 216; Andrews and Bliss, *History of Women in Unions*, pp. 166, 168; Massachusetts WTUL, *History of Trade nism*, pp. 22–23.

mmission on Industrial Relations, 4: 2347, 2356.

lvia Shulman, testimony, Commission on Industrial Relations, 3: 2285, 292; Hilda Svenson, testimony, 3: 2307, 2311, 2317; Elizabeth Dutcher, testimony, 3: 2392. Dutcher testified that seventy-five employees of Macy's were discharged in 1907 after they attended a union ball. Exceptions sometimes occurred in small western towns where workers would not patronize nonunion stores.

59. Rose Schneiderman with Lucy Goldthwaite, *All for One* (New York: Paul Erickson, 1967), p. 59; Shapiro interview with Faige, p. 9. See also Lillian Mallach to David Dubinsky, December 18, 1964, YIVO Archives; and "Minutes of the Waistmakers' Conference," January 10, 1911, ILGWU, Ladies' Waist and Dressmakers' Union file, box A95. Rose Schneiderman Collection, Tamiment Library, New York University.

60. Elizabeth Maloney testimony, *Commission on Industrial Relations*, 3: 2346–47; see also M. E. Jackson, "Colored Woman in Industry," pp. 12–17.

61. Agnes Nestor testimony, *Commission on Industrial Relations*, 4: 3389; Elizabeth Dutcher testimony, *Commission on Industrial Relations*, 3: 2405.

62. Elizabeth Maloney testimony, *Commission on Industrial Relations*, 4: 3245; Agnes Nestor testimony, 4: 3382. Leon Stein, *The Triangle Fire* (Philadelphia: J. B. Lippincott, 1952).

63. Blankenhorn manuscript notes, Ch. 4, p. 17, file 24, box 1, Blankenhorn Collection.

64. *Report of the Industrial Commission*, p. 697. This population was of German and Irish descent, with some Americans. Ira Dimock, the president, continued: "If there should be a black sheep among our girls, they would themselves make it too hot and she would have to get out."

65. Benjamin Gitlow testimony, *Commission on Industrial Relations*, 3: 2217.

66. Mrs. Moskovitz, "Lecture for Bureau of Vocational Information," November 23, 1915, file 10, box 1, Bureau of Vocational Information Collection, Schlesinger Library, Radcliffe College (hereafter cited as BVI Collection). *The Cotton Textile Industry*, Vol. 1 of *Report* (1910), p. 127.

67. *Commission on Industrial Relations*, "Department Stores," 3: 2338.

68. Gilson, *What's Past Is Prologue*, pp. 134, 138–39.

69. New York State Factory Investigating Commission, *Second Report to the Legislature*, 3: 936, 1810.

70. The best source on the WTUL is Nancy Schrom Dye, *As Equals and as Sisters: Feminism, Unionism and the Women's Trade Union League of New York* (Columbia, Mo.: University of Missouri Press, 1980). See also Tax, *Rising of the Women*, Ch. 5.

71. Virginia Penny, *Think and Act: A Series of Articles Pertaining to Men*

and Women, Work and Wages (Philadelphia: Claxton, Remsen and Haffelfinger, 1869), p. 53; Caroline Dall, *Woman's Right to Labor, or Low Wages and Hard Work* (Boston: Walker, Wise, 1860), p. 151 ff; Annie Marion MacLean, *Wage-Earning Women* (New York: Macmillan, 1910), p. 175.

72. Agnes Smedley, *Daughter of Earth* (Old Westbury, N.Y.: Feminist Press, 1973 [1928]), p. 4.

73. *Report of the Special Commission on the Hours of Labor and the Condition and Prospects of the Industrial Classes* (Boston: Wright and Potter, 1866), pp. 13. 14.

74. *The Revolution,* January 14, 1869, p. 27.

75. U.S. Education and Labor Committee, *Report Upon the Relation Between Capital and Labor,* 4 vols. (1885), 2: 608. See also Horace G. Wadlin, "Compensation in Certain Occupations of Graduates of Colleges for Women," from the Massachusetts Bureau of the Statistics of Labor, *Twenty-fifth Annual Report, 1894* (Boston: Wright and Potter, 1895), p. 35. U.S. Labor Bureau, "Vocational Guidance," in *Twenty-fifth Annual Report of the Commissioner of Labor, 1910* (1910), p. 4141.

76. Whitelaw Reid to Anna Dickinson, quoted in Massey, *Bonnet Brigade,* p. 348.

77. U.S. Education and Labor Committee, *Report upon the Relations Between Capital and Labor,* 2: p. 606.

78. L. S. W. Perkins to Leonora O'Reilly, June 26, 1898, Leonora O'Reilly Collection, Schlesinger Library, Radcliffe College.

79. Clipping from the Springfield (Mass.) *Republican,* January 13, 1909, file 96, O'Reilly Collection.

80. C. A. Prosser, *Progress in Vocational Education,* reprint of the Report of the Commissioner of Education (Washington, D.C.: Government Printing Office, 1912) p. 240.

81. "Industrial Opportunity for Women in Somerville, 1910–1911," p. 68, typescript in file 60, Women's Educational and Industrial Union Collection, Schlesinger Library

82. Federal Board for Vocational Education, *Retail Selling,* Bulletin 22 of Commercial Education Series 1 (1919), p. 11. Leonora O'Reilly commented in an unpublished manuscript that sewing would provide access to self-expression, not simply a skill. "Has Sewing a Right to Be Termed Manual Training," file 87, box 8, O'Reilly Collection.

83. Quoted in Lois Garvey, "The Movement for Vocational Education, 1900–1917" (M.A. diss., Sarah Lawrence College, 1976), p. 14.

84. National Education Association, "Industries in the Secondary Schools," *Journal of Proceedings and Addresses of the Forty-eighth Annual Meeting,* July 2–8, 1910, pp. 761–762.

85. "Vocational Training for Women in Industry," file 79, box 5, BVI Collection.

86. Mary Woolman, "Trade Schools and Culture," *Educational Review* 37 (February 1909): 184.

87. Quoted in Garvey, "Movement for Vocational Education," p. 35.
88. The lesson is from Violet Pike, "New World Lessons for Old World People," *Life and Labor*, February 1912, pp. 48–49. Eleanor Gilbert, "Filing Is No Longer Something Anybody Can Do, But a Real Job for a Trained Worker," *Evening Sun*, January 26, 1916, clipping found in file 74, box 5, BVI Collection.
89. Cassie L. Paine, "The Origin and Growth of the Movement to Train Teachers of Salesmanship," *Manual Training and Vocational Education*, November–December 1915, p. 164. See also "Industrial Opportunities for Women in Somerville," p. 68; U.S. Labor Bureau, "Vocational Guidance," p. 447.
90. Gilson, *What's Past Is Prologue*, pp. 46–47.
91. "Report of the Committee on the Place of Industry in Public Education," *Journal of Proceedings and Addresses*, quoted in Marvin Lazerson and W. Norton Grubb, *American Education and Vocationalism: A Documentary History, 1870–1910* (New York: Teachers' College Press, 1974), p. 115.
92. U.S. Labor Bureau, "Vocational Guidance," p. 443.
93. This material comes from Prince, "Training for Saleswomen," pamphlet published by the Women's Educational and Industrial Union, Boston, February 1908, pp. 1 and 2, and Paine, "The Origin and Growth of the Movement to Train Teachers of Salesmanship," pp. 162, 164–65.
94. Federal Board for Vocational Education, *Retail Selling*, pp. 11, 5–6, 19–20.
95. "Report of the Committee on Vocational Training for Women in Industry," file 79, BVI Collection.
96. Mary Allinson, *Industrial Experience of Trade School Girls in Massachusetts*, Vol. 9 of *Studies in Economic Relations of Women* (Boston: Women's Educational and Industrial Union, 1917), pp. 235–36. Helen Sumner, *A History of Women in Industry in the United States*, Vol. 9 of *Report on Condition of Woman and Child Wage-Earners in the United States*, Senate Doc. 645, 61st Cong., 2d sess. (Washington, D.C.: Government Printing Office 1910; reprint ed., New York: Arno Press, 1979), p. 31.
97. State Education Department of New Mexico, "Course of Study in Industrial Education Including Domestic Science Manual Training, and Agriculture for the Schools of New Mexico" (February 1913), pp. 4, 11, 12, 16, 17; Prosser, *Progress in Vocational Education*, pp. 282, 284.
98. *Industrial Opportunities and Training for Girls*, Women's Bureau Bulletin 13 (1921), pp. 18–19.
99. Resolutions passed by the National American Women's Suffrage Association, March 28, 1919, box 4, Accession no. 55-A-556, WB/NA. February 14, 1920, file 27, National Women's Trade Union League Papers, Library of Congress.
100. "Industrial Opportunities and Training for Girls," p. 23.
101. Box 5, file 79, BVI Collection.

7. Protective Labor Legislation

1. Elizabeth Faulkner Baker, *Protective Labor Legislation with Special Reference to Women in the State of New York, Columbia University Studies in History, Economics and Public Law,* Vol. 116, no. 2 (New York: AMS Press, 1969 [1925]), p. 36.
2. Charles Persons, Mabel Parton, and Mabelle Moses, *Labor Laws and Their Enforcement, with Special Reference to Massachusetts* (New York: Longmans Green, 1911), pp. 14, 10–12; see the discussion of this issue in Elizabeth Brandeis, "Labor Legislation," in John R. Commons, *A History of American Labor* (New York: Macmillan, 1936), 3: 97–98.
3. Judith A. Baer, *The Chains of Protection: The Judicial Response to Women's Labor Legislation* (Westport, Conn.: Greenwood Press, 1978), pp. 17 and 31. The eight states were New Hampshire, Maine, Pennsylvania, Ohio, New Jersey, California, Rhode Island, and Connecticut. Constance McLaughlin Green, *Holyoke, Massachusetts: A Case History of the Industrial Revolution in America* (New Haven: Yale University Press, 1939), p. 46, points out that workingmen who sought the ten-hour day in 1850–52 excluded women from their agitation and goals.
4. Sarah Bagley, "The Ten Hour System and Its Advocates (Continued)," *Voice of Industry,* February 6, 1846, p. 3; "Legislative Report on the Ten Hour Petitions," *Voice of Industry,* April 17, 1846, p. 2.
5. "Reduction of Working Hours," *Daily Evening Voice,* January 4, 1867, p. 2.
6. Quoted in Norman Ware. *The Labor Movement in the United States, 1860–1890: A Study in Democracy* (New York: Vintage, 1964 [1929]), p. 300.
7. Baker, *Protective Labor Legislation,* p. 59. Sarah Scovill Whittlesey, *Massachusetts Labor Legislation: An Historical and Critical Study* (Philadelphia: American Academy of Political and Social Science, 1901), pp. 80–87.
8. Baker, *Protective Labor Legislation,* p. 27.
9. Cited ibid., p. 42.
10. Brandeis, "Labor Legislation," p. 462.
11. See Box A2, National Consumers' League Papers, Library of Congress; Baker, *Protective Labor Legislation,* p. 58.
12. Lillie Devereux Blake, testimony, U.S. Education and Labor Committee, *Report Upon the Relations Between Capital and Labor,* 4 vols. (1885), 2: 604.
13. Quoted in Baker, *Protective Labor Legislation,* pp. 61, 62.
14. Quoted ibid., p. 63.
15. Louis D. Brandeis and Josephine Goldmark, *Women in Industry: Decision of the U.S. Supreme Court in Curt Muller vs. State of Oregon Upholding the Constitutionality of the Oregon Ten Hour Law for Women and Brief for the State of Oregon* (New York: National Consumers' League, 1908), pp. 18, 20, 23, 29, 30, 35, 37, 38, 40, 44, Apx. 6

and 7. Contrast this statement with the following declaration in *Lochner v. State of New York* just two years earlier: "Limiting the hours in which grown and intelligent men may labor to earn their living, are mere meddlesome interferences with the right of the individual." Quoted in Baker, *Protective Labor Legislation*, p. 42.

16. E. Brandeis, "Labor Legislation," p. 495. Twelve of these passed laws between 1911 and 1913. By 1917, thirty-two states regulated women's hours.

17. "Summary of Labor Laws and Rulings of Industrial Commissions Regarding the Employment of Women in Factories," Industrial Relations file, Women, box B-10, Florence J. Harriman Collection, Library of Congress; *The Eight Hour Day in Federal and State Legislation*, Women's Bureau Bulletin 5 (1919), pp. 11–14. Josephine Goldmark, *Fatigue and Efficiency: A Study in Industry* (New York: Survey Associates, 1913), pp. 298–301; Mrs. Clarence (Jane Norman) Smith testimony, March 15, 1924, p. 937, box 15, Accession no 51A101, Record Group 86, Women's Bureau Collection, National Archives (hereafter cited as WB/NA).

18. See, for example, testimony of Eloesser Heyneman Co., of San Francisco, Cal., "Effects of Legislation: Clothing, California," box 13, WB/NA. See also the accusation of the New York *World* against New York State's cannery owners, "Their Master's Voice," April 9, 1924, p. 12.

19. The WTUL made this argument specifically in its pamphlet "Why Labor Laws for Women?" January 1923, p. 4.

20. Sophonisba Breckenridge, "Legislative Control of Women's Work," *Journal of Political Economy* 14 (February 1906): 107, 108–9.

21. March 27, 1925; February 28, 1925; February 7, 1925, Box 3, Consumers' League of Connecticut Papers, Schlesinger Library, Radcliffe College.

22. Interview with Mrs. Sue Trainum, worker at Whitlock Branch Tobacco Co., Richmond, Va., November 15, 1919, in "Virginia Home Visits" (interviews for Bulletin 10), box 40, Accession no 51A101, WB/NA.

23. Thomas Autotops, "Long Hour Day Schedules, Indiana" (interviews for Bulletin 12), Accession no 51A101, WB/NA. See also *Some Effects of Legislation Limiting Hours of Work for Women*, Women's Bureau Bulletin 15 (1921), p. 10.

24. Interviews with Louis Strauss and Eloesser Heyneman Co., "Effect of Legislation: Clothing, California" (interviews for Women's Bureau Bulletin No. 13), Accession no. 51A101 WB/NA; American Can Co., "Long Hour Day Schedules" (interviews for Bulletin 12), WB/NA.

25. "Nine-Hour Day Schedules," box 7, Consumers' League of Connecticut Papers. Some exceptions were young unmarried women who did not have to do housework. See March 7, 1927, for quotes.

26. *Ritchie* v. *Wayman*, Illinois Supreme Court decision, 1910. Rheta Childe Dorr, *What Eight Million Women Want* (Boston: Small, Maynard, 1910), p. 162; Baer, *Chains of Protection*, pp. 77—79.

27. "Interviews: Union, Upholsterers" (for Bulletin 16), Accession no 51A101, WB/NA; "Rhode Island Home Visits" (interviews for Bulletin 21), box 41, Accession no. 51A101 WB/NA.

28. *Night Work Laws in the United States,* Women's Bureau Bulletin 7 1919), pp. 2–4; See also Testimonies, box 15, pp. 937–38, Accession no 51A101, WB/NA, and Commons, *History of American Labor,* pp. 479–481.

29. "Long Hour Day Schedules, Indiana" (interviews for Bulletin 12), Accession no 51A101, WB/NA. The intensity with which local custom protested the use of women at night is reflected in the impassioned speech of Thomas O'Donnell, secretary of the Fall River Mule Spinners' Association, *Report of the Industrial Commission on the Relations and Conditions of Capital and Labor Employed in Manufactures and General Business,* Vol. 14 (Westport, Conn.: Greenwood Press, 1970 [1901]) (hereafter cited as *Report of the Industrial Commission*), p. 570: "We are opposed to night work on principle. We think that the proper time for people to be employed in our mills is in the day time. . . . Of course we know that other states work at night. Our manufacturers refer to this, and there is no law preventing a man from doing it; but we think that our women and minors ought to be taken care of, and that when they get to 6 o'clock at night it is late enough for any woman or child to be found in a cotton mill, without doing work at night. "

30. Agnes de Lima, "Night Working Women in Textile Mills in Passaic, N.J.," National Consumers' League and Consumers' League of New Jersey, December 1922, passim; "Long Hour Day Schedules, Massachusetts" (interviews for Bulletin 12), WB/NA; "Effects of Legislation, Night Work Schedule, New York and Indiana" (interviews for Bulletin 13), Accession no 51A101 WB/NA. An interesting sidelight occurred in Terre Haute. Ind., where a glass company that had employed fifteen women (out of ninety-eight employees) on two shifts from 6:00 A.M. to 10:00 P.M. fired them in favor of family men because of "disciplinary problems." When the problems persisted, the company "gradually mixed white and colored" and discipline improved.

31. "Report on Investigation of 164 Night Workers in Connecticut," pp. 1, 5, typescript in file 41, box 3, Consumers' League of Connecticut Papers. The investigation was conducted in December 1917 and January February, and August 1918. Of the 164 workers interviewed, 110 were married with husbands at work, and only 30 were single and self-supporting with no dependents. One overseer reported that he would not hire a young unmarried woman "because it is too hard for her." See also "Report on Investigation of Night Workers in Danielson Mill," April 28, 1918, in Night Work Schedule file (interviews for Bulletin 13), Accession no 51A101, WB/NA, which refers to the "social disadvantages" of night work. "Virginia Home Visits, 1919" (interviews for Bulletin 10), box 40, Accession no. 51A101, WB/NA; and testimony of Mrs. Ella Sherwin, in Testimonies, p. 1047, WB/NA. For more recent confirmation, see Dale Newman, "Work and Community Life in a Southern Town," *Labor History* 19 (Spring 1978): 309n.

32. "Report on Investigation of 164 Night Workers," pp. 10, 12, 14.

33. Nine Hour Day Testimony, Consumers' League of Connecticut Papers.

34. Barbara May Klaczynska, "Working Women in Philadelphia, 1900–1930" (Ph.D. diss., Temple University, 1975), p. 119. The bookbinding industry was said to be among the worst offenders in employing women overtime and at night. See Mary Van Kleeck, *Women in the Bookbinding Trade* (New York: Survey Associates, 1913), p. 1. "Home Visits, Rhode Island" interviews for Bulletin 21, 1922), box 41, WB/NA; "Home Visits, Virginia" (interviews for Bulletin 10, 1919), box 40, Accession no. 51A101, WB/NA.

35. Benjamin Squires, "Women Street Railway Employees," *Monthly Review of the Bureau of Labor Statistics* 6 (May 1918): 18; see also Maurine Weiner Greenwald, *Women, War, and Work: The Impact of World War I on Women Workers in the United States,* (Westport, Conn.: Greenwood Press, 1980), Ch. 4.

36. Mrs. Clarence (Jane Norman) Smith in Testimonies, pp. 986, 988, 1029, box 15, WB/NA. *Women Street Car Conductors and Ticket Agents,* Women's Bureau Bulletin 11 (1921), p. 14.

37. Testimonies, WB/NA, p. 1039. See also p. 1037.

38. "U.S. Supreme Court Upholds N.Y. State Law Forbidding Employment of Women in Restaurants Between 1 and 6 a.m. in appeal by J. Radice of Buffalo," New York *Times,* March 11, 1924, p. 1.

39. January 30, 1927, p. 14.

40. *Some Effects of Legislation Limiting Hours for Women,* Women's Bureau Bulletin 15 (1921), p. 16.

41. Ibid., pp. 17–18.

42. Commission on Industrial Relation file, box 10, Florence J. Harriman Collection.

43. D. Douglas, "American Minimum Wage Laws at Work," National Consumers' League pamphlet (1920), p. 5; Judith Babbitts, "Mary W. Dewson and the Entry of Women into the Democratic Party in the 1930s," (M.A. diss., Sarah Lawrence College, 1976).

44. Massachusetts Minimum Wage Commission, "Recommendations for August 1, 1918," pp. 2–3.

45. Douglas, "American Minimum Wage Laws at Work," pp. 8, 20.

46. Ibid., p. 6; Ethel Smith to George Gordon Battle, December 19, 1921, in Legislation file, box 22, National Women's Trade Union League Papers, Library of Congress. Italics in original.

47. Douglas, "American Minimum Wage Laws at Work," p. 9; "Labor the World Over," *Justice,* January 20, 1922, p. 9; Alexander Trachtenberg, "Minimum Wages for Women Workers," *Justice,* February 3, 1921, p. 4; Rose Schneiderman, with Lucy Goldthwaite, *All for One* (New York: Paul Erickson, 1967), p. 255. Schneiderman, in "Attitude of Organized Labor," February 3, 1921, p. 4, notes that organized labor "never warmed up to" minimum-wage laws though it was at the time defending women workers wherever their minimum rates were being cut. But the Birmingham *Labor Advocate* did attack the Supreme Court for its decision invalidating minimum wages in 1923 (April 21, 1923). See also Mrs. Wille-

brandt, memo of April 20, 1923, in Minimum Wage Conference file box C-1, National Consumers' League Papers, Library of Congress.

48. Quoted in Emilie Josephine Hutchinson, *Women's Wages: A Study of the Wages of Industrial Women and Measures Suggested to Increase Them* New York: Columbia University Press, 1919), p. 8.

49. *Adkins* v. *Children's Hospital,* quoted in Baker, *Protective Labor Legislation,* pp. 91, 92.

50. Agnes Nestor, "The Experiences of a Pioneer Woman Unionist," *American Federationist* 38 (August 1929): 929.

51. "Uniform Hours of Labor," Massachusetts Bureau of the Statistics of Labor *Twelfth Annual Report, 1881* (Boston: Rand Abbey and Co., 1882), p. 139.

52. "Rhode Island House Votes 48 Hour Week," New York *Times,* March 16, 1922, p. 19.

53. *Report on Strike of Textile Workers in Lawrence, Massachusetts, in 1912,* Senate Doc. 870, 62d Cong., 2d sess. (1912), p. 40; testimony of Miss F. O. Johnson, typescript of Labor Committee Hearings, March 2, 1923, pp. 10–11, Consumers' League of Connecticut Papers; "Assembly Defeats Smith's Labor Bill," New York *Times,* April 8, 1924, p. 9.

54. *Report of the Industrial Commission,* p. 61

55. Commission on Industrial Relations file, box 10, Harriman Collection.

56. "Rhode Island House Votes 48 Hour Week," New York *Times,* March 16, 1922, p. 19; John Miller, "Long Hour Day Schedules, California" (interviews for Bulletin 12), WB/NA; Harrisburg *Public Ledger,* March 20, 1929.

57. Miller, "Long Hour Day Schedules, California"; Mahan Paper Box, "Long Hour Day Schedules, Indiana" (interviews for Bulletin 12), Accession no 51A101, WB/NA.

58. Apex Chocolate Company, Groton and Knight Leather Products, in "Long Hour Day Schedules, Massachusetts" (interviews for Bulletin 12), WB/NA. "Long Hour Day Schedules, Indiana" (interviews for Bulletin 12), WB/NA. See also Horace G. Wadlin, "Compensation in Certain Occupations of Graduates of Colleges for Women," from *25th Annual Report, 1894* Massachusetts Bureau of the Statistics of Labor (Boston: Wright and Potter, 1895), p. 37, and the comments in "Effects of Legislation on Night Work, Illinois" (interviews for Bulletin 13), WB/NA.

59. Goldmark, *Fatigue and Efficiency,* Ch. 3; "Uniform Hours of Labor," pp. 139–41. Hoosier Kitchen Cabinets, "Long Hour Day Schedules, Indiana" (interviews for Bulletin 12), WB/NA. New Jersey factory managers claimed that the shorter day attracted "more efficient girls" to work and significantly reduced labor turnover. See *Some Effects of Legislation Limiting Hours for Women,* Women's Bureau Bulletin 15, p. 10. Harrisburg *Record,* March 21, 1929.

60. *Report of the Industrial Commission,* p. lx.

61. Whittlesey, *Massachusetts Labor Legislation,* p. 27.

62. "Long Hour Day Schedules, Indiana" (interviews for Bulletin 12),

WB/NA. In Iowa, which had no restrictions on women's hours, the Women's Bureau reported in 1922 that only 2.8 percent of women worked more than sixty hours a week compared with 7.4 percent of men. *Iowa Women in Industry*, Women's Bureau Bulletin 19 (1922), p. 19.

63. Page and Shaw, "Long Hour Day Schedules, Massachusetts" (interviews for Bulletin 12), WB/NA. *Some Effects of Legislation Limiting the Hours of Women*, p. 10. Investigations of the potential effects of New York State's 1927 law reducing hours from fifty-four to forty-eight hours per week discovered that two-thirds of the workers in one industry notorious for its poor conditions already worked less than fifty hours per week. *Hours and Earnings of Women Employed in Power Laundries in New York State*, Special Bulletin 153, Bureau of Women in Industry, New York State Department of Labor, August 1927. "Long Hour Day Schedules, California."

64. John Commons and John Andrews, *Principles of Labor Legislation*, 4th rev. ed. (New York: A. M. Kelley, 1967), pp. 69, 30.

65. Quoted from the *Cigar Makers' Journal*, September 15, 1879, in John Andrews and W. D. P. Bliss, *A History of Women in Trade Unions*, Vol. 10 of *Report on Condition of Woman and Child Wage-Earners in the United States*, Senate Doc. 645, 61st Cong., 2d sess. (Washington, D.C.: Government Printing Office, 1911; reprint ed., New York: Arno Press, 1974), p. 94.

66. U.S. Education and Labor Committee, *Report Upon the Relations Between Capital and Labor*, 1: 453. See Andrews and Bliss, *History of Women in the Trade Unions*, p. 155, for Samuel Gompers's fears of female competition as expressed in 1887.

67. Sir Lyon Playfair, "Children and Female Labor," *American Federationist*, April 1900, p. 103. See also Martha Moore Avery, "Boston Kitchen Help Organize," *American Federationist*, April 1903, pp. 259, 260.

68. Ira Howerth, "The Kingdom of God and Modern Industry," *American Federationist* 14 (August 1907): 544.

69. Birmingham *Labor Advocate*, February 10, 1900, p. 1.

70. Testimonies, p. 939, WB/NA.

71. Baker, *Protective Labor Legislation*, pp. 266–67.

72. New York State Factory Investigating Commission. *Report of the Commission* (1913), pp. 261–62. James L. O'Donnell, "Take Mary With You!" *Equal Rights*, April 1923, pp. 1–4. Baker, *Protective Labor Legislation*, pp. 261–64. In other states exclusion was not so successful. Ohio and Pennsylvania passed laws, New Jersey and Massachusetts failed to do so.

73. "Individual Interviews, Massachusetts," April 12, 1920, box 40, WB/NA. Her preference rested on the union's ability to ask for wage raises to compensate for the reduction in hours.

74. "Individual Interviews, Massachusetts, New Jersey," ibid. See especially interviews with A. J. Muste; with Mr. Sims, secretary of the Weavers' Union; and with a meeting of Amalgamated workers at Princeton Worsted Mills. These are undated but must have occurred in early 1921. Liberal

elected officials like New York's Al Smith agreed with this reasoning. Men, he argued, could take care of themselves through organizations. Since women could not, the state had to step in. "Assembly Defeats Smith's Labor Bill," New York *Times*, April 8, 1924, p. 9.

75. Fannia Cohn to Dr. Marion Phillips, September 13, 1927, Fannia Cohn Papers (Box 4), Rare Books and Manuscripts Division, The New York Public Library, Astor, Lenox and Tilden Foundations.

76. Ada Wolff in Testimonies, p. 1091, box 15, WB/NA. This is in sharp contrast to the comments of Agnes Nestor quoted above.

77. National Consumer League Executive Committee minutes, November 21, 1918, and November 15, 1916, box A2, National Consumers' League Papers; Katherine Sullivan to Florence J. Harriman, April 22, 1914, box 10, Harriman Collection.

78. "Why Women Seek Six Special Laws," undated clipping from file 310, box 25, Bureau of Vocational Information Collection; "Why Labor Laws for Women?" NWTUL pamphlet, January 1923.

79. Testimonies, pp. 935, 941, box 15, WB/NA.

80. Crystal Eastman, "Equality or Protection," *Equal Rights*, March 15, 1924, in Blanche Wiesen Cook, ed., *Crystal Eastman on Women and Revolution* (New York: Oxford University Press, 1978), p. 159.

81. Lillian Wald to Florence Harriman, April 15, 1914; Florence Harriman to Lillian Wald, April 27, 1914; Lillian Wald and Florence Kelley to Florence Harriman, April 27, 1914, box 10, Harriman Collection.

82. Mary Van Kleeck, "The Task of Working Women in the International Congress" (Address at First International Congress of Working Women, Washington, D.C., October 28, 1919).

83. Maude Younger to Ethel Smith, October 8, 1921, Legislation: Equal Rights file, box 22, National Women's Trade Union League Papers, Library of Congress (hereafter NWTUL Papers).

84. Ethel Smith to Maude Younger, October 11, 1921, ibid.

85. Albert Leavitt to Mildred Gordon, November 28, 1921, ibid.

86. Crystal Eastman, "Equality or Protection," *Time and Tide*, January 18, 1924, in Cook, *Crystal Eastman on Women and Revolution*, pp. 113–14.

87. "Call on Miss Paul to Drop Campaign," New York *World*, February 27, 1922, p. 2.

88. Felix Frankfurter to Ethel Smith, September 8, 1921, Legislation: Equal Rights file, box 22, NWTUL Papers.

89. "Minutes of the Board of Directors Meeting," December 3, 1921, box A2, National Consumers' League Papers; see January 9, 1922, minutes for full-scale debate and denunciation. See also Mary Dawson to Miss M. C. Wells, January 1, 1922, file 24, box 3, Consumers' League of Connecticut Papers.

90. Proposition No. 56, International Typographical Union, Colorado Springs, Colo., September 13–18, 1926, Mary Van Kleeck Papers, Sophia Smith Collection.

91. "Working Women Want Equality Not Blanket Laws," *Justice*, March 17, 1922, p. 3.

92. Max Danish, "Topics of the Week," *Justice*, January 20, 1922, p. 2.

93. Women's International League for Peace and Freedom, *Report of the Fourth Congress* (Washington, D.C.: May 1–7, 1924), p. 170. "Interviews: Unions," box 16 WB/NA.

94. "Memoranda as to Women's Bureau," Women's Bureau file, box 27, NWTUL Papers; and Executive Committee minutes, February 10, 1921, box A2, National Consumers' League Papers.

95. Mary Anderson, "Should There Be Labor Laws for Women? Yes," *Good Housekeeping*, September 1925, pp. 53 ff.

96. Mary Anderson to Mary Van Kleeck, January 1, 1926; Mary Van Kleeck to Mary Anderson, January 27, 1926; Van Kleeck Collection.

97. Minutes of Technical Committee meeting, March 31, 1926, in "Effects of Legislation" file, box 14, WB/NA. See also Mary Winslow memo in Mary Van Kleeck file, July 20, 1926; and "The Real Issue: A Fact Finding Investigation of Women's Party Propaganda," in *Life and Labor Bulletin*, June 1926.

98. See "History of Labor Legislation for Women in Three States," Women's Bureau Bulletin 66–I (1927); and Mary Anderson to Mary Van Kleeck, April 17, 1926; Mary Van Kleeck to Mary Anderson, May 23, 1927; Mary Van Kleeck to Henry Goddard, April 24, 1928; all in Box 63, Women's Bureau Correspondence Van Kleeck Papers.

99. Anderson, "Should There Be Labor Laws for Women?" p. 4.

100. Henry R. Seager, "Plan for Health Insurance Act," *American Labor Legislation Review*, 6 (March 1916), p. 25; Mary Anderson to Mary Van Kleeck, December 5, 1924, Box 63, Women's Bureau Correspondence Van Kleeck Papers.

101. "Industrial Standards for Women," *American Federationist* 32 (July 1925): 21.

102. Alice Henry, *Women and the Labor Movement* (New York: George H. Doran, 1923), p. 108.

103. Typescript of "Complete Equality Between Man and Woman," from the December 1917 issue of the *Ladies' Garment Worker*, box 7, Fannia Cohn Papers.

8. Ambition and Its Antidote in a New Generation of Female Workers

1. Mary Dewson Blankenhorn, "Do Working Women Want It?" *Survey* 58 (February 15, 1927): 631.

2. Robert S. Lynd and Helen Merrell Lynd, *Middletown: A Study in American Culture* (New York: Harcourt, Brace and World, 1956 [1929]), part 2.

3. See Gwendolyn Salisbury Hughes, *Mothers in Industry: Wage-Earning Mothers in Philadelphia* (New York: New Republic, 1925), p. 23.

4. Bessie M. Seely, "Opportunities for Women in Trust Work," *Bulletin of the American Institute of Banking*, October 1928, p. 422.

5. *The New Position of Women in American Industry*, Women's Bureau Bulletin 12 (1920), pp. 25, 30, 31.

6. *The Negro Woman in Industry*, Women's Bureau Bulletin 20 (1922), pp. 5–6; M. E. Jackson, "The Colored Woman in Industry," *Crisis* 17 (November 1918): 12, suggests that the war opened huge possibilities for black women.

7. Janet Hooks, *Women's Occupations Through Seven Decades*, Women's Bureau Bulletin 218 (Washington, D.C.: Government Printing Office, 1947), pp. 96, 98–99, 102, 109, 123, 126, 130–33; *The New Position of Women in Industry*, Women's Bureau Bulletin 12 (1920), p. 89.

8. Joseph A. Hill, *Women in Gainful Occupations, 1870–1920*, Census Monograph 9 (Washington, D.C.: Government Printing Office, 1929), pp. 36, 40, 41, 44.

9. Anna Howard Shaw to the War Labor Board, December 1919. Correspondence file, box 4, Accession no 55–A–556, Record group 86, Women's Bureau Collection, National Archives (hereafter cited as WB/NA).

10. "Emancipation of Women in Industry," *Christian Science Monitor*, June 27, 1919, p. 5.

11. Laverne Morris, "Working It Out for 56 Years," *Ms.* 6 (February 1978): 45.

12. Mary Gilson, *What's Past Is Prologue: Reflections on My Industrial Experience* (New York: Harper and Brothers, 1940), p. 168.

13. C. V. McCord, "Systems and Services: New York School for Filing," *Bulletin of the Bureau of Vocational Information*, December 14, 1916; Kathryn Marshall to Emma Hirth, July 28, 1925, file 428, box 37, Bureau of Vocational Information Collection, Schlesinger Library, Radcliffe College (hereafter cited as BVI Collection).

14. Edward Woods, "Selling Life Insurance: A Vocation for Girls," *The Scholastic*, February 9, 1924, p. 9. See also Ida White Parker, "Women in the Insurance Fields," *The Businesswoman*, January 1923, pp. 17–18; Eugenia Wallace, "Filing, a Stepping Stone," *The Spotlight*, February 1918, p. 4; clipping from the New York *Times*, dated February 29, 1923, in file 63, box 4, BVI Collection.

15. Mrs. Crocker, "Women in Civil Service," March 28, 1916, in file 23, box 1, BVI Collection; Elizabeth G. Cook, "Finance," April 11, 1916, file 21, box 1, BVI Collection; interview with Miss Izora Scott, April 10, 1919, in file 80, box 5, BVI Collection.

16. Unidentified clipping, July 1922, file 98, box 6 BVI Collection.

17. Robert S. Lynd and Helen Merrell Lynd, *Middletown*, p. 163. And see "Virginia Home Visits" (interviews for Bulletin 10), box 40, Accession no 51A101, WB/NA.

18. Interviews with Florie Atkinson, January 17, 1922; Willie Briggs, January 14, 1922; and Mrs. Ingram, November 28, 1921, all in "South Carolina Home Visits," box 43, WB/NA.

19. See interviews of February 11, 1919, and February 27, 1919, in "Phila-

delphia Candy Study Home Visits," box 40; November 28, 1921, "South Carolina Home Visits," box 43, WB/NA.

20. Rhoda Elizabeth McCulloch, *The War and the Woman Point of View* (New York: Associated Press, 1920), p. 11.

21. Maud Swartz at the Fourth Annual Conference of Trade Union Women. See "Report of Proceedings," October 9 and 10, 1926, typescript in New York Women's Trade Union League Papers, New York Public Library; Rhoda Elizabeth McCulloch, lecture notes, Sophia Smith Archives, Smith College.

22. McCulloch lecture notes, Smith Archive.

23. Hooks, *Women's Occupations Through Seven Decades*, p. 39.

24. Ida Pataglin to the Editor, *Advance*, October 29, 1926, p. 8.

25. Birmingham *Labor Advocate*, March 11, 1922, p. 2.

26. "Married Women Here Fight for Right to Earn," Baltimore *Sun*, January 10, 1926, part 2, sec. 2, p. 6.

27. Typescript in possession of Louise Levitas Henriksen, p. 4. Quoted by permission.

28. "Demand for Women in Office Work Now Exceeding Supply," New York *Times*, October 19, 1924, p. 9.

29. Interview with P. H. Mayo, November 5, 1919, "Virginia Survey,", file 2, box 40, group 86, WB/NA.

30. (Chautauqua, N.Y.: Chautauqua Press, 1921), pp. 9, 12, 15.

31. Ibid., pp. 73, 74, 65, 186.

32. "Banking and Business Training for Women," The *Bankers Magazine* (August 1917), p. 30; Noil Chemical, New York City, "Effects of Legislation: Night Work Schedule, New York" (interviews for Bulletin 13), WB/NA.

33. New York State Factory Investigating Commission, *Second Report of the Legislature* (1913), p. 936.

34. Elizabeth Cook, "Finance"; and see Gephardt, in same file.

35. J. L. Ziman to Beatrice Harrow, May 27, 1921, file 84, box 6, BVI Collection. The writer was the manager of the National Shorthand Reporting Company. And see Bureau of Vocational Information to James Lomax, May 29, 1923, file 84, box 6, BVI Collection. See also BVI to Julia Loughlin, June 2, 1921 ibid.

36. "Make Listening Their Specialty," unidentified clippings *c.* 1925, from file 430, box 37, BVI Collection.

37. *Newark Star Eagle*, January 13, 1925, clipping in file 93, box 6, BVI Collection.

38. Opinions of Miss Amy Rowland, editorial secretary, file 433, box 37; BVI Questionnaire of Margaret McMillan, Alabama Home Building and Loan Association, file 353, box 29, BVI Collection.

39. Questionnaires in file 353, 354, box 29, BVI Collection.

40. Genieve Gildersleeve, "The Private Secretary—To Be or Not to Be?" *Bulletin of the National Committee of the Bureau of Occupations* 1 (October 1920): 3. Margery Davies, "Woman's Place Is at the Typewriter:

The Feminization of the Clerical Labor Force," in Richard Edwards et al., *Labor Market Segmentation* (Lexington, Mass.: D. S. Heath, 1975), pp. 274–96.

41. Typescript notes on "Secretarial Responsibilities," p. 4, file 433, box 37, BVI Collection.

42. Responses to questionnaires sent to directors of "Welfare Departments in Industry" *c.* March/April 1918, file 177, box 14, BVI Collection.

43. Ella V. Price, of the Narrow Fabric Company, Reading, Pa., April 12, 1918, file 179, box 14, BVI Collection.

44. Interview with Mrs. Wilson, of Wilson Home Renting, October 10, 1919, file 81, box 5, BVI Collection.

45. "Training Women for a New Occupation," *School Life,* 1922, clipping in file 63, box 4, BVI Collection. "For example," the article said, "the withdrawal of an account gives indication of possible distress in a household. In such a case, the home service director may investigate the circumstances, and after she can suggest methods of retrenchment that will enable the family to continue saving."

46. Gildersleeve, "The Private Secretary," p. 3.

47. Lecture, March 7, 1916, file 20, box 1, BVI Collection. Such opinions seem to have been general. The BVI concluded a "Survey of Employment Opportunities for Women in Advertising" in 1919 (file 62, box 4) with the comment, "Many men still stop short of sending women out to secure accounts and it has required the proof of especial capacity on the part of the individual woman to have gained their present standing."

48. File 63, box 4, BVI Collection.

49. Clipping from unidentified paper, dated March 20, 1923, in file 23, box 1, BVI Collection, about Mrs. E. M. Abernethy of Lexington, Oklahoma.

50. Unidentified clipping dated March 9, 1925, in file 69, box 4, BVI Collection.

51. New York *Herald,* July 3, 1925, p. 3.

52. John B. Watson, "The Weakness of Women," *The Nation* 125 (July 6, 1927): 11.

53. Mildred Dunham to Mary Van Kleeck, December 13, 1929, in Mary Van Kleeck Collection, unsorted. In 1978 the New York *Times* interviewed one of the daughters of a female physician who had practiced in the 1920s. The daughter, aged seventy, said that her mother had discouraged her and her sisters from becoming professionals "because she thought it would be too hard!" See "Notes on People," New York *Times,* January 13, 1978, p. D-13.

54. *American Banker,* October 17, 1928, clipping in file 63, box 4, BVI Collection. Her feeling was confirmed by the fact that the Association of Bank Women founded in New York City in 1921 had only 188 members in 117 cities by 1929. See *U.S. Investor,* September 6, 1924, p. 16; Hooks, *Women's Occupations Through Seven Decades,* p. 159.

55. New York State Department of Labor, "Hours and Earnings of Women Employed in Power Laundries in New York State," Special Bulletin 153

(August 1927), p. 13. There were 18,200 laundry workers in power laundries in New York State in 1925 and 385,000 home laundresses nationwide.

56. Consumers' League of New York, *Behind the Scenes in Hotels*, pamphlet (February 1922), pp. 18, 22, 14.

57. Bertha Shippen interview in "Virginia Home Visits" (interviews for Bulletin 10), box 40, WB/NA. See also interviews with Minnie Slaughter, Vicola and Estelle Gibson, and Bessie Campbell.

58. Typescript replying to request of WEIU for information on conditions for women executives in candy factories, March 19, 1920, file 75, box 5, BVI Collection.

59. Interview with Anna Beaumont, "Rhode Island Home Visits" (interview of Bulletin 21), WB/NA.

60. Typescript replying to request of WEIU on candy factories.

61. Mary E. Jackson, "The Colored Woman in Industry," *Crisis* 17 (November 1918): 12–17; Elizabeth Ross Haynes, "Two Million Negro Women at Work," *The Southern Workman* 51 (February 1922): 64–72; Hill, *Women in Gainful Occupations*, p. 109.

62. Elizabeth Ross Haynes, "Two Million Women at Work," in Gerda Lerner, *Black Women in White America* (New York: Pantheon, 1972), p. 257; Jackson, "Colored Woman in Industry," p. 14.

63. Birmingham *Labor Advocate*, November 11, 1922; Jackson, "Colored Woman in Industry," p. 16. Interviews with P. Lorillard and Co., and Siedenberg and Co., November 1919, "Virginia Surveys," file 2, box 40, group 86, WB/NA.

64. Indianapolis Vocational Information Service, *Opportunities for Women in the Telephone Service* (Bloomington, Ind.: Indiana University, 1923). The company also offered a "silence room" and a cafeteria that provided food at cost.

65. Interview with Frances Poore, "Rhode Island Home Visits" (interviews for Bulletin 21), box 41, WB/NA.

66. "Virginia Home Visits" (interviews for Bulletin 10), box 40, WB/NA.

67. Matilda Robbins, "From the Notebook of a Labor Organizer," p. 4, typescript, in Matilda Robbins Collection, Archives of Labor and Urban Affairs, Wayne State University. Clipping from Frances Perkins, Supervising Commissioner, New York State Bureau of Women in Industry, file 310, box 25, BVI Collection.

68. Responses nos. 142, 155, 90, 5, file 73, box 5, BVI Collection.

69. Mrs. Lower, "Employment Agency Schedule," file 428, box 37, BVI Collection.

70. Questionnaire of workers in service, "Educational and Employment Departments," May 1918, file 178, box 14, BVI Collection.

71. Gilson, *What's Past Is Prologue*, p. 210.

72. Interview with Mary Newman, "Rhode Island Home Visits" (interviews for Bulletin 21), box 41, WB/NA.

73. "Southern Mill Hands," in *Vineyard Shore Magazine*, 1930–31, p. 7, in

file 33, box 4, Hilda W. Smith Collection, Schlesinger Library, Radcliffe College.

74. Alice Kessler-Harris, "The Autobiography of Ann Washington Craton," *Signs* 1 (Summer 1976): 1028, 1030.

75. "A Dialogue," file 23, box 3, Hilda W. Smith Collection.

76. Report on Viscose Rayon Co., Roanoke, Va., file 10, box 12, Katherine Ellickson Collection, Archives of Labor and Urban Affairs, Wayne State University.

77. "The Barnard Summer School," pamphlet in file 17, box 2, Hilda W. Smith Collection. The school had forty-seven students at its start.

78. Letter from Constance Ortmayer, in excerpts from student letters, March 5, 1927, file 31, box 4, Hilda W. Smith Collection.

79. Thelma Brown, "Thoughts," from the Bryn Mawr *Daisy*, file 23, box 3, Hilda W. Smith Collection. The opposite set of feelings also existed. For example, the poem "Release" by Emily Warrick, a typescript dated 1933–34, in file 31, box 4, Hilda W. Smith Collection:

> To bathe my body when the need arises;
> To don fresh raiment whenever it pleases;
> To lose the swollen things that were my feet;
> To watch my hands grow shapely again;
> Brywn Mawr, thou restorer of bruised and tired bodies,
> None know how pleased I am.

80. Joyce Floyd, "Why I Believe Workers' Education Necessary to the Industrial Girl," file 23, box 3, Hilda W. Smith Collection.

81. Robbins, "From the Notebook of a Labor Organizer," p. 14. And see Grace Lumpkin, *To Make My Bread* (New York: Macaulay Company, 1932), a fictional account of the transition made by one rural family to the mills.

82. Mary Heaton Vorse, *Strike* (New York: Horace Liveright, 1930), p. 56.

83. Ella Mae Wiggins, "The Mill Mother's Lament," In Evelyn Alloy, ed., *Working Women's Music* (Somerville, Mass.: New England Free Press, 1976), p. 30.

84. "Amalgamated Women Demand Attention and What They May Get," *Advance*, September 3, 1926, p. 1.

85. *Advance*, October 29, 1926, p. 11; October 8, 1926, p. 6.

9. Some Benefits of Labor Segregation in a Decade of Depression

1. Anonymous, "Man at the Fireside," *Harper's* 68 (May 1933): 757–58; Lorine Pruette, ed., *Women Workers Through the Depression: A Study of White Collar Employment Made by the American Women's Association* (New York. Macmillan, 1934), pp. 21, 22, and Ch. 5 argues that the psychic readjustment was even greater for single women than for the married.

2. In 1931, two million women out of a labor force of ten million could find no jobs. Between April 1930 and January 1931, the women's unemployment rate doubled. "Employment Conditions and Unemployment Relief: Unemployment Among Women in the Early Years of the Depression," *Monthly Labor Review* 38 (April 1934): 792, n. 7.

3. James Bossard, "Depression and Pre-Depression Marriage Rates: A Philadelphia Study," *American Sociological Review* 2 (October 1937: 693–95. Among Jews in Philadelphia, the rate jumped from 35.5 marriages per thousand marriageable men to 45.4. In contrast, the Irish rate fell from 30.9 to 26.3. The rate for native-born sons of native-born parents fell from 31.7 to 28.2.

4. Dorothy Dunbar Bromley, "Birth Control and the Depression," *Harper's* 69 (October 1934): 563, 564.

5. Paul Douglas, "Some Recent Social Changes and Their Effect Upon Family Life," *Journal of Home Economics* 25 (May 1933): 368, 369.

6. William Haber, "The Effects of Insecurity on Family Life," *Annals of the American Academy of Political and Social Science* 196 (March 1938): 25.

7. Joanna C. Colcord, "Remedial Agencies Dealing with the American Family," *Annals of the American Academy of Political and Social Science,* 160 (March 1932): 125 ff; Joseph K. Folsom, "The Changing Role of the Family," *Annals of the American Academy of Political and Social Science* 212 (November 1940): 70–71.

8. Ruth Shonle Cavan and Katherine Howland Rouck, *The Family and the Depression: A Study of One Hundred Chicago Families* (Chicago: University of Chicago Press, 1938), pp. 7–8.

9. William Ogburn, "The Changing Family," *Family,* July 1938), p. 143; Folsom, "Changing Role of the Family," p. 64; and see the discussion of family theory in Christopher Lasch, *Haven in a Heartless World* (New York: Basic Books, 1977), Chs. 2 and 3; Douglas, "Some Recent Social Changes," p. 368.

10. Frank L. Hopkins, "Should Wives Work?" *American Mercury* 39 (December 1936): 411.

11. Claire Howe, "Return of the Lady," *New Outlook* 164 (October 1934): 34–38; and Jane Allen, "You May Have My Job: A Feminist Discovers Her Home," *Forum* 87 (April 1932): 228–31.

12. Winifred Bolin, "The Economics of Middle Income Family Life: Working Women During the Great Depression," *Journal of American History* 65 (June 1978): 60–74, argues that this shift had as much to do with shifting values as with economic necessity. While this may be true, Bolin's evidence is not convincing. She defines "middle income" as over $1,000 a year and argues that 40 percent of married wage-earning women had husbands who earned more than that. But $1,000 a year—though it does represent a median income figure—does *not* represent an adequate wage for urban families. Relief checks during the depression commonly averaged between $20 and $25 per week. Since the husbands of 60 percent of wage-earning women earned less than this minimal wage, and 64 percent

of all families brought in less than $1,500 a year, the data suggest that need preceded a value shift. One must also ask to what extent the family standard of living depended on women's earnings (rather than those of children): under that rubric, some additional families might not have "absolute need"—a term not defined by Bolin, and whose meaning surely varied from family to family. But this number must have varied with children's capacity to start their own families. Mary Anderson, asked in 1939 whether married women should work, began her response by saying, "So long as two thirds of the families in the United States have incomes of less than $1,500 a year, there is a very good economic reason why married women should work." Interview, "Should Married Women Work?" *Current History and Forum* 41 (September 1939): 16.

13. Norman Cousins, "Will Women Lose Their Jobs?" *Current History and Forum* 41 (September 1939): 14. See Hadley Cantrill, ed., *Public Opinion, 1935–46* (Princeton: Princeton University Press, 1951), p. 1044, which reports the results of a national American Institute of Public Opinion poll indicating that 82 percent of Americans and 75 percent of women thought women should not work if their husbands could support them. In another poll, 82.3 percent of those asked felt married women should not work outside the home but a third relented in cases of financial need.

14. Marion Elderton, "Unemployment Consequences on the Home," *Annals of the American Academy of Social and Political Science* 154 (March 1931): 62; Allen, "You May Have My Job," pp. 228–31; see also Poppy Cannon, "Pin Money Slaves," *The Forum* 84 (August 1930): 98–103; Claire Howe, "Return of the Lady," pp. 34–38.

15. Douglas, "Some Recent Social Changes," p. 368.

16. Anonymous, Man at the Fireside," p. 750.

17. Allen, "You May Have My Job," p. 229.

18. "What Do the Women of America Think About Careers?" *Ladies' Home Journal* 56 (November 1939): 12.

19. Sarah Comstock, "Marriage or Career?" *Good Housekeeping* 94 (June 1932): 32–33, 159–62.

20. Joseph K. Folsom, "The Changing Role of the Family," p. 69; Bernard J. Stern, "The Family and Cultural Change," *American Sociological Review* 4 (April 1939): 206 and 207.

21. Anna Garlin Spencer, "Should Married Women Work Outside the Home?" *Eugenics* 4 (1931): 25.

22. Mary Ross, "What Ten Million Women Want," *Parents* 6 (August 1931): 15–16.

23. Cousins, "Will Women Lose Their Jobs?" p. 14.

24. "A Timely Quiz," typescript attached to a letter from Mary Robinson to Elizabeth Christman, September 19, 1939, in WTUL files, Women's Bureau Collection, National Archives (hereafter WB/NA).

25. Quoted in Cousins, "Will Women Lose Their Jobs?" p. 17.

26. *Women in Industry: A Series of Papers to Aid Study Groups*, Women's Bureau Bulletin 91 (1931), p. 17; and Harriet Byrne, *The Age Factor as*

It Relates to Women's Business and the Professions, Women's Bureau Bulletin 117) Washington, D.C.: Government Printing Office, 1934), p. 11. In 1930 the Bureau indicated that of 10,700,000 gainfully occupied females, 3,000,000 were married. These constituted 29 percent of all gainfully occupied women. The divorced and widowed made up 17 percent of all gainfully occupied women. The rest were single. Looking at women as a whole, one of every ten married women worked for wages; three of every ten widowed and divorced women worked for wages; and five of every ten single women worked for wages.

27. National Women's Trade Union League, news release, December 21, 1931, in WTUL file, box 4, WB/NA.
28. Marguerite Thibert, "The Economic Depression and the Employment of Women: II," *International Labor Review* 27 (May 1933): 621. Pruette, *Women Workers Through the Depression*, p. 156.
29. Sample headlines included: "BAN ON MARRIED WOMEN AS CITY HALL EMPLOYEES BEING CONSIDERED HERE," Springfield (Illinois) *Republican*, November 1920, p. 1; "MOVE TO OUST WIVES FROM JOBS SCORED," New York *Times*, December 24, 1930, p. 3. For a more complete discussion of attempts to remove married women from jobs, see Lois Scharf, *To Work and to Wed: Female Employment, Feminism, and the Great Depression* (Westport, Conn.: Greenwood Press, 1980), Ch. 3.
30. National Women's Trade Union League news release, December 21, 1931.
31. Edna McKnight, "Jobs—For Men Only?" *Outlook and Independent* 159 (September 2, 1931): 12. McKnight notes the tendency of such women to raise emyployers' expectations of a worker's output.
32. Ibid., pp. 13, 18. McKnight quotes Eleanor Roosevelt, then wife of the governor, who on being told that department stores favored girls from good families, responded by saying that it was "wicked in a crisis like this for such girls to hold positions that less fortunate girls could fill." Such girls, Eleanor Roosevelt thought, ought to have vocational counseling that would put them into what she called "the right type of things."
33. Ibid., p. 18.
34. Typescript attached to letter from Mary Robinson to Elizabeth Christman, September 19, 1939, WTUL files, WB/NA.
35. Thibert, "Economic Depression and the Employment of Women: II," p. 621.
36. Pruette, *Women Workers Through the Depression*, p. 155
37. Mary Elizabeth Pidgeon, *Differences in the Earnings of Women and Men*, Women's Bureau Bulletin 152 (Washington D.C.: Government Printing Office, 1938), pp. 47, 3, says that from 1914 to 1935 the ratio of women's wages to those of men never went above 60.2 percent or below 56.6 percent. In the second World War, the ratio widened to 55 percent. For levels by industry, see Mary Elizabeth Pidgeon, *Women in the Economy of the United States of America: A Summary Report*, Women's Bureau Bulletin 155 (Washington, D.C.: Government Printing Office, 1937), pp. 56–57, 72–74.

38. John B. Parrish, "Changes in the Nation's Labor Supply," *American Economic Review* 29 (June 1939): 328–30; U.S. Census Bureau, Sixteenth Census of Population (1940) III: 7. Bolin, "Economics of Middle Income Family Life," p. 72, points out quite correctly that these four million women still made up only 15 percent or one out of every six or seven married women, though the figure should be contrasted with the 1930 figure of one in every ten.

39. Mary Elizabeth Pidgeon, *Employment Fluctuations and Unemployment of Women: Certain Indications from Various Sources, 1928–31*, Women's Bureau Bulletin 113 (Washington D.C.: Government Printing Office, 1933), pp. 4, 6; "Employment Conditions and Unemployment Relief," *Monthly Labor Review*, 38 (April 1934): 791, indicates that in 1930, two million of ten million were unemployed.

40. Pidgeon, *Employment Fluctuations and Unemployment of Women*, pp. 4, 11.

41. Pidgeon, *Women in the Economy of the United States*, p. 87; *Trends in the Employment of Women, 1928–36*, Women's Bureau Bulletin 159 (1938), p. 4.

42. Parrish, "Changes in the Nation's Labor Supply," p. 332. Parrish's findings are confirmed by John D. Biggers, *Final Report on Total and Partial Unemployment*, Vol. 4 of *The Enumerative Check Census* (Washington, D.C.: Government Printing Office, 1938).

43. John Parrish, "Women in the Nation's Labor Market," *Quarterly Journal of Economics* 54 (May 1940): 528; see Julia Kirk Blackwelder, "Women in the Work Force: Atlanta, New Orleans and San Antonio, 1930–1940," *Journal of Urban History* 4 (May 1978: 331–58, for a discussion of the effects of segregation in southern cities. Broadus Mitchell, *Depression Decade: From New Era Through New Deal, 1929–41* (New York: Harper Torchbooks, 1947), p. 201, adds, "During the depression the share of service industries in the national income, as compared with commodity producing industries, continued to increase. This was mainly because the prices of services did not fall as much as the prices of commodities."

44. *The Effects on Women of Changing Conditions in the Cigar and Cigarette Industries*, Women's Bureau Bulletin 100 (1932), pp. 22–23.

45. Sumner H. Slichter, *Union Policies and Industrial Management* (Washington, D.C.: Brookings Institution, 1941), pp. 206, 225–26. See also Resolution 118 in the American Federation of Labor, "Report of Executive Council," in *Report of Proceedings to the Annual Convention*, n.p., 1934.

46. Mitchell, *Depression Decade*, pp. 268, 272; Leo Wolman, *Ebb and Flow in Trade Unionism* (New York: National Bureau of Economic Research, 1936), pp. 138–39.

47. Mary Anderson, "Report" (delivered at the Annual Meeting of the International Association of Governmental Labor Officials, September 27, 1934, mimeographed), p. 7.

48. *Justice* 15 (August 15, 1933): 5, and November 1, 1933, p. 15.

49. Anderson, "Report," p. 7.
50. Pidgeon, *Women in the Economy of the United States*, p. 94.
51. Helena Hill Weed, "The New Deal That Women Want," *Current History* 36 (November 1934): 183.
52. Pidgeon, *Women in the Economy of the United States*, p. 50.
53. Ibid., pp. 94, 95.
54. In the South, codes written without distinctions as to age virtually eliminated child labor.
55. "Women Workers and the N.R.A.," *Christian Century* 51 (January 10, 1934: 43; New York *Times*, July 9, 1933, clipping in box A97, Rose Schneiderman Collection, Tamiment Library, New York University.
56. Pidgeon, *Women in the Economy of the United States*, pp. 95, 96.
57. Ibid., pp. 91, 92. Declines in male-employing industries were much smaller, averaging 16 percent.
58. Elizabeth Christman to Mrs. Maurice Lieber, February 7, 1935, box 20, National Women's Trade Union League Papers, Library of Congress (hereafter NWTUL Papers).
59. Amy Hewes, "Women Wage Earners and the N.R.A.," *American Federationist* 42 (February 1935): 159, 160, 163.
60. Slichter, *Union Policies*, pp. 217–222.
61. Janet Hooks, *Women's Occupations Through Seven Decades*, Women's Bureau Bulletin 218 (Washington, D.C.: Government Printing Office, 1947), p. 102.
62. Ethel Best, *Hours, Earning and Employment in Cotton Mills*, Women's Bureau Bulletin 111 (Washington, D.C.: Government Printing Office, 1933), pp. 1, 27.
63. Hooks, *Women's Occupations Through Seven Decades*, p. 106. Women's share in 1940 was 43.4 percent; A. R. Burns, *The Decline of Competition* (New York: McGraw-Hill, 1936), p. 470.
64. See *Justice* for 1931–32, and especially 13 (June 1931): 14, and 13 (May 1931): 3.
65. Hooks, *Women's Occupations Through Seven Decades*, p. 115.
66. Pidgeon, *Women in the Economy of the United States*, pp. 98–99. The Cloth Hat and Capemakers also returned to piecework in these years. See Slichter, *Union Policies*, pp. 286, 300, 313.
67. *AFL Weekly News Service*, April 21, 1934, in Schneiderman Collection.
68. *Local No. 2 Edition*, UAW-CIO. November 15, 1939, Women Employment vertical file, Archives of Labor History and Urban Affairs, Wayne State University.
69. Pidgeon, *Women in the Economy of the United States*, pp. 67–68.
70. Anderson, "Report," p. 8.
71. George Stigler, *Domestic Servants in the U.S., 1900–1940*. Occasional paper 24 (New York: National Bureau of Economic Research, 1946), pp. 41, 42; Marie Correll, *Standards of Placement Agencies for Household Employees*, Women's Bureau Bulletin 112 (Washington, D.C.: Government Printing Office, 1934), p. 46. The Women's Bureau thought the lowest-paid home servant got $5.79 a week plus board in 1937; see

Pidgeon, *Women in the Economy of the United States*, p. 148. See also Alice Hanson and Paul Douglas, "The Wages of Domestic Labor in Chicago, 1890–1929," *Journal of the American Statistical Association* 25 (March 1930): 47–50, for a survey of wages before the depression.

72. Ella Baker and Marvel Cooke, "The Bronx Slave Market," *The Crisis* 42 (November 1935): 330–32. The first CIO chapter to domestic servants appears to have been issued in September of 1942. See Caroline Ware, "Labor and Democracy in the Home," typescript in file 43, Hilda W. Smith Collection, Schlesinger Library, Radcliffe College.

10. "Making History Working for Victory"

1. William Chafe, *The American Woman: Her Changing Social, Economic and Political Roles, 1920–1970* (New York: Oxford University Press, 1972), p. 195; Sheila Tobias and Lisa Anderson, "What Really Happened to Rosie the Riveter?" *Ms.* Modular Publication 9, 1974. See also Paddy Quick, "Rosie the Riveter: Myths and Realities," *Radical America* 9 July–August 1975): 115–32; Chester Gregory, *Women in Defense Work During World War II* (New York: Exposition Press, 1974); and Janice Trey, "Women in the War Economy—World War II," *Review of Radical Political Economy* 4 (July 1972): 42–57.

2. Theresa Wolfson, "Aprons and Overalls in War," *Annals of the Academy of Political and Social Science* 229 (September 1943): 47.

3. Susan B. Anthony II, *Out of the Kitchen—Into the War: Woman's Winning Role in the Nation's Drama* (New York: Stephen Daye, 1943), pp. 41, 42.

4. Florence Kerr, "The Administration of War Public Services," internal memo, October 15, 1943, Florence Kerr file, box 229, Federal Works Administration, National Archives (hereafter cited as FWA/NA). Wolfson, "Aprons and Overalls in War," p. 47, suggests that 84 percent of adult men were employed in April 1942.

5. Anthony, *Out of the Kitchen*, p. 4; Laura Nelson Baker, *Wanted: Women in War Industry* (New York: E. P. Dutton, 1943), p. 9; "Women Workers in Power Laundries," p. 9, typescript for Women's Bureau bulletin 215, Women's Bureau Collection, National Archives (hereafter WB/NA). Child Care file, box 228, FWA/NA; *Fortune* 27 (February 1943): 99.

6. Mary Elizabeth Pidgeon, "Women Workers and Recent Economic Change," *Monthly Labor Review*, December 1947), p. 667.

7. For a discussion of these issues see Clarence D. Long, *The Labor Force in Wartime America*, Occasional Paper 14 (New York: National Bureau of Economic Research, 1944), pp. 10–31.

8. "Women Workers in 1947," p. 2., typescript in file 36, Frieda Segelke Miller Collection, Schlesinger Library, Radcliffe College.

9. Pidgeon, "Women Workers and Recent Economic Change," p. 668.

10. These figures are calculated from tables in National Manpower Council, *Womanpower: A Statement by the National Manpower Council* (New York: Columbia University Press, 1957) p. 112. They are higher than

these in Valerie Kincaide Oppenheimer, *The Female Labor Force in the United States: Demographic and Economic Factors Governing Its Growth and Changing Composition,* Population Monograph Series 5 (Berkeley: University of California Press, 1970), p. 3; Oppenheimer estimates the gain at 14.2 percent. Gladys Palmer, "Women in the Post-War Labor Market," *Forum* 104 (October 1945): 133. The data are confirmed by Secretary of Labor Frances Perkins, who warned in 1945 that only three to four million women, out of nineteen million women then earning wages, "took jobs only because of the war." The rest, she noted, would continue to work out of economic necessity. "Labor Safeguards after War Sought," New York *Times,* February 13, 1945, p. 26.

11. Child Care file, box 229, FWA/NA.

12. Pidgeon, "Women Workers and Recent Economic Change," p. 667.

13. Oppenheimer, *Female Labor Force,* pp. 8, 16, 17, calculates participation rates as follows:

Age-cohort	1940	1950	Percentage Change in Women Working
25–34	33.3	31.8	−4.5
35–44	27.2	35.0	+28.7
45–54	22.5	32.9	+46.2
55–64	16.8	23.4	+39.3

See also Frieda Miller, "Women in the Labor Force," *Annals of the American Academy of Political and Social Science* 217 (May 1947): 38.

14. *Michigan Chronicle,* November 7, 1942, and February 28, 1942, clippings in Women Employment vertical file, Archives of Labor History and Urban Affairs, Wayne State University.

15. See the *Michigan Chronicle* for September 12, 1943, January 16, 1943, November 14, 1942, November 14, 1942 for examples. See also Nell Giles, *Punch in Susie: A Woman's War Factory Diary* (New York: Harper and Brothers, 1943), p. 140, for an example of an employer giving in to pressure to hire black women.

16. *Handbook of Facts on Women Workers,* Women's Bureau Bulletin 242, 1952), pp. 24–25. Forty-six percent of black women were in the labor force, compared with 32 percent of all women.

17. Susan M. Hartmann, "Women's Organizations During World War II: The Interaction of Class, Race and Feminism" (paper given at the Organization of American Historians meeting, New York, April 1978).

18. "Postwar Labor Turnover among Women Factory Workers," *Monthly Labor Review* 64 (March 1947): 411–16.

19. *Women Workers after V-J Day in One Community: Bridgeport, Connecticut, Women's Bureau Bulletin* 216 (1947), p. 30; *Handbook of Facts on Women Workers,* p. 3.

20. *Womanpower Committees During World War II,* Woman's Bureau Bulletin 244 (1953), pp. 141, 45, 40.

21. Mrs. F. Kerr to Bess Wilson, April 17, 1943, in Biographic Sketch of Mrs.

Kerr file, box 229, FWA–NA; Josephine Von Miklos, *I Took a War Job* (New York: Simon and Schuster, 1943), p. 178.

22. Giles, *Punch In Susie*, p. 20. See also Report 10, April 1943, in unmarked file, box 1, accession no. 55A45, WB/NA, which records attempts by employers to get women to wear safety clothing and the union's agreement to try to get women to comply.

23. Typescript on "Seniority," December 8–9, 1944, Women's Bureau file, box 27 (War Policy), War Policy Collection, UAW, Archives of Labor History and Urban Affairs, Wayne State University. (Hereafter cited as WPC.)

24. Dorothy S. Brody, "Equal Pay for Women Workers," *Annals of the American Academy of Political and Social Science* 217 (May 1947): 53; National Association of Manufacturers testimony in *Report of Special Subcommittee on Education and Labor on HR 1584*, 81st Cong., 2d sess. (1949), p. 4.

25. Brody, "Equal Pay for Women Workers," p. 53.

26. Ibid., p. 54. The five states with equal pay laws were New York, Massachusetts, Michigan, Illinois, and Rhode Island; Dorothy S. Brody, "Equal Pay—What Are the Facts?" in *Report of the National Conference on Equal Pay, March 31 and April 1, 1952*, Women's Bureau Bulletin 243 (1952), pp. 14–15. This figure excludes domestic workers' salaries. Including them brings the figures for women's earnings down to 59 percent of male earnings in 1939. By 1950, these differentials were even greater. Women then earned only 53 percent of men's earnings—only 45 percent if domestic-service wages are included.

27. Report 7, January 1943, p. 9, in box 1, accession no. 55A45, WB/NA.

28. Elizabeth Christman, Report 4, typecript of October 8–16, 1942, "Trip to Dayton, Ohio," p. 6, in box 1, accession no. 55A45, WB/NA.

29. Wolfson, "Aprons and Overalls in War," pp. 54, 46. Women, inexperienced at industrial jobs, responded variously to the stint. Informal sources disagree. Giles, *Punch In Susie*, p. 46, seems to deny that it existed at all, asserting that women pushed each other to produce. Von Miklos, *I Took a War Job*, pp. 33, 46, in contrast, depicts women who worked deliberately slowly so as not to outproduce each other. One woman objected that women tired themselves out, setting a pace that forced older men out of jobs, after which the women had to stay home and rest for two months.

30. Gladys Dickason, "Women in Labor Unions," *Annals of the American Academy of Political and Social Sciences* 251 (May 1947): 71.

31. James Green, "Fighting on Two Fronts: Working Class Militancy in the 1940's," *Radical America*, July–August 1975, p. 27; Wolfson, "Aprons and Overalls in War," p. 50.

32. April 22, 1944, War Policy: Women's Bureau file, box 27, WPC. Sometimes these activities had mixed motives, as for example when the UAW sponsored a three-day trip for women members to Fort Knox "to promote a better understanding among our women members and the men and women in the U.S. Army." See "Fort Knox Trip," War Policy: Women's

Bureau file, box 27, WPC. In a mimeographed report entitled "What the Girls Say about the Trip" the following comments appeared. From Hazel Wright of Local 645, North American Aviation, Dallas: "Girls, let's stop and analyze ourselves: Ae we doing all we can?" And from Cherie Anastasie Kaptur of Local 12, Champion Spark Plug Co., Toledo, Ohio: "The question put most to me was: 'How about strikes?' Needless to say, I assured the soldiers we were sincere in our 'No Strike' pledge."

33. May 1, 1944, Women's Bureau report, War Policy: Women's Bureau file, box 27, WPC.

34. See Convention Resolutions, Women's Bureau Report, May 1, 1944, and Mildred Jeffrey memo, April 12, 1944, in War Policy: Women's Bureau file, box 27, WPC.

35. "Conference Resolutions: Seniority," in War Policy: Women's Bureau file, box 27, WPC.

36. "The Margin Now is Womanpower," *Fortune* 27 (February 1943): 224.

37. Lois Meek Stolz, "Living History Interviews," in James L. Hymes, Jr., ed., *Care of the Children of Working Mothers* (Carmel, Calif.: Hacienda Press, 1978), p. 53.

38. "Policy of War Manpower Commission on Woman Workers," *Monthly Labor Review* 56 (April 1943): 669.

39. Florence Kerr, typescript, in Child Care and War Nursery Releases file, box 228, FWA/NA.

40. "War Production Board, Office of Labor Production," October 30, 1943, typescript in Child Care and War Nursery Releases file, box 228, FWA/NA.

41. *Womanpower Committees During World War II*, Women's Bureau Bulletin 244 (1953), p. 45.

42. Raymond Clancy, "War Nursery Schools," *The Wage Earner*, May 14, 1943, p.

43. Child Care and War Nursery Releases file, box 228, FWA/NA; Anthony, *Out of the Kitchen*, p. 7.

44. Clipping from the *Journal of Commerce*, July 6, 1943, in Child Care file, box 229, FWA/NA.

45. Chicago *Times*, August 18, 1943, p. 1.

46. War Production Board: Office of Labor Production, October 30, 1943, typescript in Child Care and War Nursery Releases file, box 228, WPC.

47. Bureau of Budget, "Memorandum for President," August 12, 1943, in Child Care file, box 228, FWA/NA; Allen B. MacMurphy to Mr. Taylor, August 17, 1945, Child Care Correspondence file, box 230, FWA/NA.

68. See the discussion of this issue in Howard Dratch, "The Politics of Child Care in the 1940's," *Science and Society* 38 (Summer 1974): 167–204; and Chafe, *American Woman*, pp. 166–70.

49. Typescript of radio interview with Florence Kerr, released April 17, 1943, in Biographic Sketch of Mrs. Kerr file, box 229, FWA/NA. The interviewer was not satisfied with this answer. She went on to ask Kerr, "But are you fully convinced that mothers of young children actually are

needed in industry, or are these women merely tempted by the wages offered?"

50. Office of Information, "Digest of Press Comment," mimeographed, dated November 2, 1943, Child Care and War Nursery Releases file, box 228, FWA/NA.
51. Quoted from Charles P. Taft, director of Community War Services of the Federal Security Agency, typescript released by Office of War Information, Day Care Nurseries file, box 3, WPC.
52. "Suggestions for Philosophy and Content of Child Care Service Portrayed," typescript in Child Care and War Nursery Releases file, box 228, FWA/NA.
53. *Womanpower Committees During World War II*, pp. 10–11.
54. Lucy Greenbaum, "Wall Street: Man's World," *New York Times Magazine*, May 13, 1945, p. 16.
55. Frieda S. Miller, "What's Become of Rosie the Riveter," *New York Times Magazine*, May 5, 1946, p. 21.
56. "The Fortune Survey: Women in America, Part I," *Fortune* 34 (August 1946): 8.
57. Lucy Greenbaum, "The Women Who 'Need' to Work," *New York Times Magazine*, April 29, 1945, p. 16.
58. Agnes Meyer, "Women Aren't Men," *Atlantic Monthly* 186 (August 1950): 33.
59. Ferdinand Lundberg and Marynia F. Farnham, M.D., *Modern Woman: The Lost Sex* (New York: Harper and Brothers, 1947), p. 370. This book is the classic diatribe against women who chose to leave their homes.
60. Margaret Barnard Pickel, "How Come No Jobs for Women?" *New York Times Magazine*, January 27, 1946, p. 46.
61. "Labor Safeguards after War Sought," *New York Times*, February 13, 1945, p. 26.
62. Miller, "What's Become of Rosie the Riveter," p. 48. "Opportunities for Women in the Post-War Cleaning Services," typescript in Bulletin 215 file, box 1, WB/NA.
63. Maurice Tobin, "Equal Pay—Present Policy or Future Direction?" in *Report of the National Conference on Equal Pay, March 31 and April 1, 1952*, Women's Bureau Bulletin 243 (1952), p. 7. For other aspects of the campaign see Caryl Reeve Grantham, "Why Equal Pay Now," *Independent Woman* 24 (November 1943): 319–31; Frieda S. Miller, "Equal Pay—Its Importance to the Nation," *Independent Woman* 25 (November 1946): 325–26; and Lois Black Hunter, "Equal Pay at Work," *Independent Woman* 27 (February 1948): 37 38.
64. Edith Efron, "A Woman Worker Defends Her Kind," *New York Times Magazine*, March 31, 1946, p. 43.
65. Greenbaum, "Women Who 'Need' to Work," p. 16.
66. Ruth Young and Catherine Filene Strouse, "The Woman Worker Speaks," *Independent Woman* 24 (October 1945): 275.
67. "The Fortune Survey," p. 8.

11. The Radical Consequences of Incremental Change

1. National Manpower Council, *Womanpower: A Statement by the National Manpower Council* (New York: Columbia University Press, 1957), p. 3.
2. Roland Renne, "Shortage Occupations: New Occupations for Women," at womanpower conference, March 10–11, 1955, reprinted in Women's Bureau Bulletin 257 (1955), pp. 72–76.
3. U.S. Department of Labor, Wage and Labor Standards Administration, *Background Facts on Women Workers in the United States* (1968), p. 14; Howard Huyghe, "Families and the Rise of Working Women—An Overview," *Monthly Labor Review*, May 1976, p. 13. Among professional women, the proportion taking full-time jobs in 1975 was higher. In less-skilled jobs, and those related to home or child care, it tended to be lower.
4. Robert Perrin, "Tough Days for Rosie," Detroit *Free Press*, August 30, 1953, p. 1.
5. George Gallup and Evan Hill, "The American Woman," *Saturday Evening Post* 233 (December 22, 1962): 15–32.
6. Margaret S. Carroll, "The Working Wife and Her Family's Economic Position," *Monthly Labor Review* 85 (April 1962): 69; Huyghe, "Families and the Rise of Working Women," p. 15; Stanley Lebergott, *Manpower in Economic Growth: The American Record Since 1800* (New York: McGraw-Hill, 1964), p. 66, estimates that extra income in families increased the proportion of debt. See also Herman P. Miller, "A Profile of the Blue Collar American," in Sar A. Levitan, ed., *Blue Collar Workers: A Symposium on Middle America* (New York: McGraw-Hill, 1971), pp. 47–75.
7. Myra Strober and Charles B. Weinberg, "Working Wives and Major Family Expenditures," *Journal of Consumer Research* 4 (December 1977): 146.
8. U.S. Department of Labor, Bureau of Labor Statistics, *Perspectives on Working Women* (June 1980), pp. 3, 4.
9. U.S. Department of Labor, *1975 Handbook on Women Workers*, Women's Bureau Bulletin 297 (1975), pp. 91–92; and see Mary Stevenson, "Women's Wages and Job Segregation," *Politics and Society*, Fall 1973, pp. 83–96.
10. For example, see interoffice memo from Laura Gibbs and Miriam Keeler to Mrs. Leopold, Mrs. Helmes, Mrs. Behrens, December 17, 1956, in Statistics on Women Workers file, box 1051, Women's Bureau Collection, National Archives (hereafter cited at WB/NA); Frieda S. Miller, "The Employment Outlook for Women" (notes for a speech to the New York State Business and Professional Women's Board meeting, Utica, N.Y., September 26, 1953), file 77, Frieda Miller Papers, Schlesinger Library, Radcliffe College.
11. See Elsie Wolfe, memo, March–August, 1951, and interview with Mrs.

Louise Kiskeddon, August 1, 1951, both in box 2, group 26, WB/NA. What Wolfe saw in Seattle was duplicated in Detroit, where the Detroit *News* reported (March 3, 1953, p. 1) that "because of the critical manpower shortage . . . two GMC plants have begun hiring women for factory jobs held heretofore only by men."

12. Frieda Miller, "The National Economic Scene as It Concerns Women," typescript of speech, Boise, Idaho, August 28, 1950, p. 9, in file 99, and "Older Women Workers," statement to New York State Joint Legislative Committee, December 14, 1950, p. 10, file 54, Miller Papers. See also "Will Women Face Job Draft in U.S.?" clipping from St. Louis *Post-Dispatch*, October 16, 1960, in file 1, Miller Papers; and *Employment of Women in an Emergency Period*, Women's Bureau Bulletin 241 (1952), passim.

13. U.S. Department of Labor Release, February 28, 1955, introducing the 1955 Conference on Effective Use of Womanpower, box 1050, WB/NA; in her remarks Leopold said in part, "In these days when individual contributions can count so heavily for the national good, there is no room for the old cliches that women ought to go home and let the men do it; that women's place is in the home—and nowhere else."

14. Dr. Irving I. Siegel, in *The Effective Use of Womanpower: Report of the Conference, March 10 and 11, 1955*, Women's Bureau Bulletin 257 (Washington, D.C.: Government Printing Office, 1955), p. 70.

15. J. Ellis to Alice K. Leopold, interoffice memo, August 27, 1955, in Adult Education file, box 1052, and Alice K. Leopold to Orreille Murphy, September 9, 1954, in Committee on New Teachers for the Nation's Classrooms file, box 1052, WB/NA; Miller's dittoed statement, February 18, 1948, in file 51, Miller Papers; summary of editorial in Washington *Post*, September 20, 1951; typescript of Miller's testimony to House Ways and Means Committee, April 16, 1949, file 6, Miller Papers; Alice K. Leopold to Will Turnbladh, February 6, 1956, and Alice K. Leopold to Pearl W. Berlin, April 14, 1954, both in Juvenile Delinquency file, box 1052, WB/NA; Ellen Winston to Alice Leopold, Reply to Questionnaires file, box 1050, WB/NA.

16. *The AFL-CIO and Women Workers*, pamphlet, December 1956, box 1052, WB/NA, issued by AFL-CIO, esp. p. 7; George D. Riley to James Roosevelt, February 1, 1957, and George D. Riley to Edith Nourse Rogers, February 1, 1957, file 9, box 92, in Katherine Ellickson Collection, Archives of Labor and Urban Affairs, Wayne State University. Robert D. Moran, "Reducing Discrimination: Role of the Equal Pay Act," *Monthly Labor Review*, June 1970, pp. 30–34.

17. "The Employment Outlook for Women," typescript of talk to New York State Business and Professional Women's Board meeting, Utica N.Y., September 26, 1953, file 77, Miller Papers; "Minutes of Meeting of Committee on New Teachers for the Nation's Classrooms," August 6, 1954, Committee file, box 1052, WB/NA.

18. For a list of organizations opposing the ERA in the mid-fifties, see a

letter to "Dear Senator" signed by thirteen organizations, box B-14, National Consumers' League Papers, Library of Congress. Mary Anderson remained an opponent to the end; see Anderson to Ellickson, February 7, 1955, file 7, box 92, and memo from Helen Louise Mackay, December 1954, file 3, box 92, Ellickson Collection, and Mary Anderson letter to Senators, January 13, 1950, file 4, box 92, Ellickson Collection. See also excerpts from the proceedings of the Sixteenth Constitutional Convention, CIO, Resolution 37 on women workers, Ellickson Collection. Dr. Alice Hamilton, who had opposed an ERA since 1923, withdrew her opposition in 1953; Hamilton to Miss Magee, May 15, 1953, file 5, box 92, Ellickson Collection.

19. U.S. Department of Labor Releases, February 28, 1955, March 6, 1955, 1955 Conference file, box 1050, WB/NA.
20. Alice A. Morrison to Miss Winifred Helmes, October 7, 1954, in March Conference: Working Papers file, box 1050, WB/NA.
21. Renne, "Shortage Occupations," p. 5.
22. Bob Senser, "U.S. Agency Launches Crusade to Lure Wives from Home," WORK, April 1955, p. 1.
23. Mrs. W. B. McPherson to the NLRB, January 7, 1954, special file, box 1052; the letter was forwarded to the Women's Bureau. Memo from Henry Huettner to Homer Kroy, October 25, 1955, and October 26, 1955, all in Complaints: Special file, box 1052, WB/NA.
24. Melva J. Ginyard to Mrs. Alice K Leopold, February 6, 1956; Hilda G. Johnson to Alice K. Leopold, February 9, 1956; AKL to four women in identical letters, March 6, 1956; all in U.S. Post Office, Baltimore, file, box 1052, WB/NA.
25. This series of letters begins on July 12, 1955, and ends March 1956, Anne Jowski vs. Navy Department file, box 1052, WB/NA.
26. Gertrude Bruck and Judy Rosenthal to Women's Bureau, June 1, 1954 in Requests for Aid in Unemployment Problems file, box 1052, WB/NA. This was a Communist union, which might explain the Women's Bureau's refusal to reply.
27. Ruth F. Moore of Festus, Missouri, to "Dear Ike," July 25, 1954. Eisenhower referred the letter to the Women's Bureau. In Discrimination file box 1052, WB/NA.
28. "Three Women Sue Ford, UAW for $3,000,000," Detroit *Free Press*, September 29, 1953, p. 1.
29. H. A. Porker to Kenneth Thornbury, November 16, 1954, in Oil Workers vs. Gulf Oil Co. file, box 1052, WB/NA.
30. Hester Staff of Pleasant Ridge, Michigan, to Women's Bureau, August 17, 1954, Discrimination file, box 1052, WB/NA.
31. Ruth Moore to "Dear Ike."
32. Cathryn Crowley to AKL, May 8, 1956, and reply June 1, 1956, in Discrimination file, box 1052, WB/NA.
33. "Women's International Day" (typescript, n.d., *c.* 1946), p. 4, file 181, Miller Papers.

34. The quote is from the typescript of a speech in Bridgeport, Connecticut, November 22, 1953, in file 81, Miller Papers; see also notes from speeches, December 13, 1951, file 56, and typescript of a speech to National Conference of Social Work on Effects of Mobilization on Family Life, May 16, 1951, pp. 12–13, in file 58, both in Miller Papers.

35. Kluckhohn, speech at Conference on Effective Use of Womanpower, March 10–11, 1955, box 1050, WB/NA.

36. By 1975 the figure was past 44 percent and in 1980 it surpassed 50 percent of all wives. Huyghe, "Families and the Rise of Working Women," p. 13, and U.S. Department of Labor, Bureau of Labor Statistics, "Employment in Perspective: Working Women," Report 643, p. 3.

37. "Statement by the President on the Establishment of the President's Commission on the Status of Women," mimeo, December 14, 1961, in file 5, box 90, Ellickson Collection.

38. Arthur Goldberg to Eleanor Roosevelt, June 15, 1962, in file 35, box 92, Ellickson Collection.

39. Nadine Brown, "Take Heart Girls: Battle for Pay Equality Is About To Be Joined," Detroit *Courier*, October 17, 1963, p. 5; Betty Friedan, *The Feminine Mystique* (New York: Dell, 1963), p. 278.

40. Phyllis Wallace, "Impact of Equal Opportunity Laws," in Juanita Kreps, *Women and the American Economy: A Look to the 1980's* (Englewood Cliffs, N.J.: Prentice-Hall, 1976), pp. 126–27. This order essentially added the word "sex" to the 1965 order (No. 11246) that provided affirmative action on the basis of race, color, religion, or national origin. It was extended by Executive Order 11478 to cover federal government employees in 1969. The provision for goals and timetables was not added until 1971.

41. Quoted in Steven Roberts, "The Family Fascinates a Host of Students," New York *Times*, April 23, 1978, p. 20, section 4.

42. Sue Mittenthal, "After Baby, Whither the Career?" New York *Times*, February 14, 1979, p. C-1.

43. Georgia Dullea, "Changes in Society Traced to Rise of Working Women," New York *Times*, November 29, 1977, p. 28.

44. Jaquie Davison, *H.O.W. Newsletter*, May–June 1973, p. 3; Louise Farr, "Peddling the Pedestal," *New Times* 5 (October 17, 1975): 49–52.

45. Quoted in "Conservatives Join on Social Concerns: Groups Building a Loose Coalition to Support their Moral Values," New York *Times*, July 30, 1980, p. B-6.

46. For illustrations of the attitudes and behavior described here, see Christopher Lasch, *Haven in a Heartless World* (New York: Basic Books, 1977) passim; Frances Beale, "Double Jeopardy: To Be Black and Female," in Toni Cade, ed., *The Black Woman: An Anthology* (New York: Signet, 1970), pp. 90–100; Pauli Murray, "The Liberation of Black Women," in Marylou Thompson, ed., *Voices of the New Feminism* (Boston: Beacon, 1970), pp. 87–102; Morris Stone, "A Backlash in the Workplace," New York *Times*, June 11, 1978, p. F-3; Georgia Dullea, "Sexual Harassment at Work: A Sensitive and Confusing Issue," ibid.,

October 24, 1980, p. A-20; William Serrin, "New Trends Among the Work Force Cloud Validity of Unemployment Rate," ibid., May 9, 1981, p. 9.

47. "Review of Current Trends in Business and Finance," *Wall Street Journal*, February 2, 1976, p. 1.

48. December 28, 1980, p. 1.

Epilogue

1. Tamar Lewin, "Women Losing Ground to Men in Widening Income Difference," *New York Times*, September 15, 1997, A1.

2. U. S. Census Bureau, *Population Profile of the United States* (Washington, D.C.: GPO, 1999), 21ff; Lawrence Mishel, Jared Bernstein and John Schmitt, *The State of Working America: 2000/2001* (Washington, D.C.: Economic Policy Institute, 2001), 94.

3. U. S. Census Bureau, CPS, 1998, p. 21; Eric Schmidt, "Children Just not in the Family Photo," *International Herald Tribune*, May 16, 2001, 3.

4. Cynthia B. Costello, Shari Miles and Ann J. Stone, *The American Woman, 1999-2000* (New York, W.W. Norton, 1998), 297.

5. *See also,* "The Force of the Future," *Working Mother*, May 1969, 168.

6. Mishel et al, *The State of Working America*, 96-7.

7. Arlie Hochschild, *The Time Bind: When Work Becomes Home and Home Becomes Work* (New York: Metropolitan Books, 1997); Pepper Schwartz, "Me Stressed? No, Blessed," *New York Times*, November 17, 1994, C1, 12.

8. Arlie Hochschild with Anne Machung, *The Second Shift: Working Parents and the Revolution at Home* (New York, Viking Books, 1989), 12.

9. Margaret K. Nelson and Joan Smith, *Working Hard and Making Do: Surviving in Small Town America* (Berkeley, University of California Press, 1999), 151.

10. Julia Heath and W. David Bourne, "Husbands and Housework: Parity or Parody," *Social Science Quarterly*, 76 (March, 1995), 195-202; Carin Rubinstein, "Superdad needs a Reality Check," *New York Times*, April 16, 1998, A23.

11. James Schembari, "Derring-Do of the Stay-at-Home Dad," *New York Times*, November 26, 2000, section 3, 10; "The Daddy Trap," *Business Week*, September 21, 1998, 56-66.

12. U.S. General Accounting Office, *1998 Greenbook: Background Material for the U.S. Senate and House of Representatives* (Washington, D.C.: GPO, 1998), section 9, p. 4.

13. Felice N. Schwartz, "Management, Women, and the New Facts of Life," *Harvard Business Review,* (January/February, 1989), 76-76; "'Mommy Career Track' Sets Off a Furor," *New York Times*, March 8, 1989, A18; Elizabeth Ehrlich, "The Mommy Track," *Business Week*, March 20, 1989, 126-133; and "Letters to the Editor," April 17, 1989, p. 5.

14. "Peter T. Kilborn, "More Women Take Low-Wage Jobs Just so Their

Families Can Get By," *New York Times*, March 13, 1994, 24; Heidi
Hartmann, Katherine Allen and Christine Owens, *Equal Pay for Working
Families: National and Stat Data on the Pay Gap and its Costs* (Washington,
D.C.: Institute for Women's Policy Research, 1999); Mishel et al., *The
State of Working America*, 94-6.

15. Nelson and Smith, *Working Hard and Making Do*, 124.
16. The best summary of this legislation is Mimi Abramovitz, *Under Attack,
Fighting Back: Women and Welfare in the United States* (N.Y.: Monthly Review
Press, 1996), ch.2.
17. Jennifer Preston, "Welfare Rules Intensify Need for Day Care," *New York
Times*, November 11, 1986, B1; Rachel L. Swarns, "Mothers Poised for
Workfare Face Acute Lack of Day Care," *New York Times*, April 14, 1998,
A1, B8.
18. Alan Finder, "Evidence is Scant that Workfare Leads to Full-Time Jobs,"
New York Times, April 12, 1998, A1.
19. "Wisconsin Creates Sweeping New Approach to Expanding and
Improving Child Care," *Child Care ActioNews*, 18 (September/October
2001): 1, 4.
20. Michael M. Weinstein, "When Work is Not Enough," *New York Times*,
August 26, 1999, C1, 6; Alan Finder, "Some Private Efforts See Success in
Job Hunt for Those on Welfare," *New York Times*, June 16, 1998, A1.
21. Glenn Collins, "Wooing Workers in the 90's: New Role for Family
Benefits," *New York Times*, July 20, 1988, A1, 14; Pam Belluck, "A Bit of
Burping is Allowed If it Keeps Parents on the Job," *New York Times*,
December 4, 2000, A1, 22.
22. Barbara Ehrenreich, *Nickeled and Dimed: On (Not) Getting By in America*
(New York: Metropolitan Books, 2001).
23. Lewin, "Women Losing Ground to Men," A12; Elizabeth Becker, "Study
Finds a Growing Gap Between Managerial Salaries for Men and Women,"
New York Times, January 24, 2002, A22.
24. In 1990, only 4 of the 506 chief executives of the Fortune 500 companies
were female; 12 percent of top corporate officers were women—a steadily
rising number, and a sea change from a mere two decades earlier when
there were none. "Executive Women at the Top: Still a Very Lonely
Club," *New York Times*, November 17, 1999, G1.
25. The proportion of women holding part time and contingent jobs was
about double the proportion of men. See Mishel, *The State of Working
America*, ch 3.
26. A good summary of the data on occupational segregation, can be found
in Diane Herz and Barbara Wootton, "Women in the Workforce: an
Overview," in Cynthia Costello and Barbara Kivimae Krimgold, eds., *The
American Woman: 1996-97: Women and Work* (New York: W.W. Norton,
1996), 44-78; Data about the entrepreneurial world is sparse: while early
breakthroughs seem to have occurred, these seem less secure in 2000
than they did in the 1980s. See Lois Therrien, "What do Women Want?
A Company They Can Call Their Own" *Business Week*, December 22,

1986, 60-62.

27. Robert Pear, "Reagan Aides Map Repeal of Rules on Bias in Hiring," *New York Times*, August 15, 1985, A1.

28. *Johnson v. Transportation Agency*, 480 U.S. 616 (1987).

29. Peter T. Kilborn, "A Company Recasts Itself to Erase Bias on the Job," *New York Times*, October 4, 1990, A1; Kurt Eichenwald, "The Two Faces of Texaco," *New York Times*, November 10, 1996, Section 3, 1.

30. *United Steelworkers of America v. Weber*, 443 U.S. 193 (1979).

31. Vicki Schultz, "Sex is the Least of It," *The Nation*, May 25, 1998, 12.

32. Cho, "Uneasy Path for Diversity Effort," Section 3, p. 6.

33. *Meritor Savings Bank v. Vinson*, 477 U.S. 57 (1986); *See also* Catherine MacKinnon, *Sexual Harassment of Working Women* (New Haven: Yale, 1979); Clara Bingham and Laura Leedy Gansler, *Class Action: The Story of Lois Jenson and the Landmark Case that changed Sexual Harassment Law* (New York: Doubleday, 2002).

34. Margaret Carlson, "Does Father Know Best," *Time*, March 20, 1995; Melody Petersen, "The Short End of Long Hours," *New York Times*, July 18, 1998, B1.

Index

Abel, Mary Hinman, 118
Abolitionism, 41–42, 63, 77, 114
Abortion, 315, 317
Adams, Elizabeth Kemper, 231
Addams, Jane, 165
Advance (periodical), 248
Affirmative action, 315
AFL, *see* American Federation of Labor
AFL-CIO, 305
Agriculture, U.S. Department of, 111
Agriculture, women in, 11, 188, 224
Alabama, labor legislation in, 188
Alcott, Louisa May, 49, 54, 58, 72
Amalgamated Association of Street
Railway and Electrical Employees,
158, 194
Amalgamated Clothing Workers of
America, 151, 229, 241, 242, 248, 267
Amalgamated Textile Workers' Union of
America, 205
American Association of Labor Legisla-
tion, 213
American Association of University
Women, 286
American Banker (periodical), 236
American Federation of Labor (AFL), 86,
99, 152–57, 202–4, 245, 260, 261, 265,
268, 305; WTUL and, 165, 166; *see also*
AFL-CIO
American Federationist (journal),
154–56
American Medical Association, 117
American Revolution, 4, 20, 21
American Weekly, 9
American Woolen Company, 166, 199
Ames, Azel, 106–7
Anderson, Lisa, 273
Anderson, Mary, 171, 206–10, 212, 213,
263, 288, 296, 305
Andover, Massachusetts, 27
Andrews, John, 69–70, 153
Anthony, Susan B., 79, 82, 95–97
Antislavery societies, 41–42, 77

Appalachians, garment industry in, 241–
242
Appleton, Ann, 32, 34, 35, 38, 52–53, 67
Appleton, Sarah, 34, 35, 38
Apprenticeship, 3, 7, 11, 16, 22–23;
colonial women and, 13–14
Arizona, labor legislation in, 188
Armstrong, James, 164
Army, U.S., 297
Artisans, attitudes toward new mills of,
31
Association for the Advancement of
Family Life, 253
Association of Business and Professional
Women, 227
Atlantic Monthly, 296–97
Automatic Gold Chain Company, 240
Averill, Clementine, 61

Babson, Roger, 213
Bagley, Sarah, 61, 182
Baker, Elizabeth Faulkner, 180, 185
Baltimore, 139; immigrants in, 121
Baltimore, Lord, 11
Baltimore Sun, 230
Banking, 219, 227, 231–32, 235, 236
Banner of the Constitution (periodical),
27
Barnard College, 257–58; Summer School,
244
Beach, Moses, 91
Beecher, Catharine, 112, 117
Beechey, Veronica, 321–22
Bennett, Richard, 32, 45
Bennett, Sabrina, 31–32, 35, 67
Bennett family, 32, 34–35, 45, 67
Beverly, Massachusetts, 18, 23
Bigelow loom, 68
Birthrate, U.S., 110, 252
Black women, 108, 118, 219, 224, 237–38,
270, 301, 311–13, 317, 321; birth rate
and, 110; choices of, as wage workers,

CPSIA information can be obtained at www.ICGtesting.com
Printed in the USA
BVOW02s1017041215

429240BV00001B/1/P

9 780195 157093